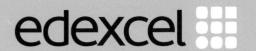

Edexcel GCE in
Applied ICT

AS Single Award

23

Trevor Heathcote   Steve Farrell

Edexcel
190 High Holborn
London WC1V 7BH

ISBN 1 903133 80 7

Designed by HL Studios Ltd, Oxford
Picture Research by Sally Cole
Index by Indexing Specialists (UK) Ltd

Printed and bound by Scotprint

The publisher's policy is to use paper manufactured from sustainable forests.

Contents

Introduction

There are very few people in the UK today that do not have contact with ICT and computers as users or practitioners. Most of us are 'users' in that we 'use' computers to achieve an end, to provide us with information, to instruct us or maybe to entertain us. Less common are those people for whom the computer is an end in itself: technicians and programmers, or maybe network, website and database designers. These people are known as 'practitioners'. The *Edexcel GCE in Applied ICT* contains both 'user' and 'practitioner' units; if you were to study the double award you would study both kinds of units. The single award is made up entirely of 'user' type units and it is the practical use of ICT applications which is fundamental to this qualification.

The first three units, the subject of this book, are compulsory units for all of the single and double award Applied GCE qualifications. They are all user-focused units which act as the basis for further study as either a user or practitioner, as well as forming a significant qualification (the AS level) in their own right. For example, a typical pattern of study for an A-level student is to take four subjects at AS level and choose three of those to take on to A2. Because ICT is used in almost every area of working life, the practical structure of the single AS award could take on a significant importance as the 'fourth' AS. It gives you a firm grounding in practical ICT, which you would take with you into the 'real' world even if you do not necessarily continue on to A2.

Interactive Student CD-ROM

The CD-ROM which accompanies this book provides direct access to files for activities and assessment practice, multimedia presentations and skills demonstrations, all launched straight from the ActiveBook pages.

An 💿 icon in the book indicates that a file is available on the CD to accompany that section. It can be accessed from the corresponding page in the ActiveBook.

Unit 1 – The Information Age

This unit looks at the extent to which the internet has become a source of essential online services. It examines the ways in which information technologies have changed our society. Advances in hardware and software have given us access to information sources that we would hardly have dreamed of even 20 years ago; the ability to manipulate and transfer this information at enormous speeds has changed the way we run almost every aspect of our lives. The unit also studies how these advances have accentuated the difference between the 'haves' and the 'have-nots' in our society – the so-called 'digital divide' – and the disadvantages faced by those without access to these modern technologies.

In keeping with the ideal of a practical qualification, the unit requires you to develop significant ICT skills, especially multimedia skills for the production of the e-book used to assess the unit. It will also require you to use the internet productively, and to assess the quality of the information you gain from it with respect to accuracy and usefulness.

Unit 2 – The Digital Economy

Advances in technology have also changed the way we do business. Payment by cash and cheque, although not yet obsolete, is becoming less common; even a plastic credit card is really mainly a confirmation of identity these days. The modern economy is run almost entirely by technology; a huge number of financial transactions take place every second, some involving mind-blowing amounts of money being wired around the globe in all sorts of currencies.

In this unit you will study the new economy with reference to a transactional website. You will look at how these transfers work and what processes take place behind the scenes to support this method of commerce, commonly called 'e-commerce'.

Once again, the emphasis in this unit is on 'doing', so you will study an existing transactional website. You will need to develop good analytical skills and the ability to describe processes diagrammatically. As most e-commerce 'back office' processes are based on databases, you will need to be able to interrogate a substantial database and find useful information in it. The unit will help you to become aware of the security issues associated with e-commerce: today's bank robbers use a modem rather than a pickaxe, and need to be skilled programmers rather than lock-pickers. You will look at these threats and the corresponding methods of protection used. The unit also provides you with plenty of exercises to help get to grips with the techniques required.

Unit 3 – The Knowledge Worker

If, in our careers, most of us are going to be 'users' rather than 'practitioners', the majority of 'users' will at some point probably use ICT for analysing data and presenting the resulting information. In our careers, many of us will be put in a position where we will have to make decisions about which of many options to take. This unit is about making decisions based on an analysis of some relevant data, and presenting these decisions to a specified audience.

The ICT skills you will need are wide ranging. In business, many of the decisions you will be making will be based on a model of some kind, and the likelihood is that this will be a spreadsheet model. You will need to be able to create, modify and use spreadsheet models as well as develop skills in presentation and reporting software. You will also have to develop an awareness of audience and knowledge of what will help you influence them. The unit will therefore provide you with a number of analysis techniques and some guidance on presentation. Most importantly, there will be problem-solving exercises that you can use to practise these skills.

Assessment

The assessment for all three units will require the use of a computer:
- Unit 1 requires that you design, produce and evaluate an e-book
- Unit 2 requires you to present your findings in the form of an eportfolio
- The assessment for Unit 3 is a practical examination.

This book contains significant guidance for all of these assessment processes and example material for each form of assessment.

The *Edexcel GCE in Applied ICT* is an exciting new qualification and the authors wish you the best of luck in your studies.

Trevor Heathcote
Steve Farrell

Unit 1

The Information Age

    Here you will produce an e-book and evaluate it

Online services

The PC and the internet have fuelled a silent revolution in the way many of us live today. Although still not fully mature, the online services offered on the world wide web have already transformed the way in which people communicate, get, share and store information, spend and save, learn, work and play. In this chapter you will explore these changes in as practical a way as possible so that you can make an informed assessment of the scope and limitations of the internet and online services offered today.

The first online service we will examine is communications. This encompasses blogs, email, chat and various forms of messaging and conferencing. Communication services underlie much of what can be achieved using the internet and are thus crucial as practical tools and sources of information. First we will examine blogs: both because they are an important new online phenomenon and because you will use your own blog as a dynamic record of the different online services you use and your evaluation of them.

A world of blogs

Have a look at some of these websites:

Web standards

Web designers' blog

Travel blog

Directory of wonderful things

Art blog

Gadgets blog

South East Asia Earthquake and Tsunami blog

Blogs

Blogs (or web logs) are a specialised form of website created for the purpose of keeping an online journal. Early on they replaced the personal home pages that many individuals kept to amuse and inform friends and family, or other individuals with similar interests. In order to keep blogs up to date and interesting, in a way that personal home pages rarely were, systems have evolved to facilitate easy posting of material. This usually involves a blog editor interfaced to a database system that:
- manages the posts
- manages links to other articles and websites
- archives old material
- allows for comments to be made on posts
- allows the mechanics of HTML to be managed transparently

so that the 'journalist' simply has to concentrate on the content.

Blogs are now an extremely important in a much wider context. For example, group blogs have grown up to provide a central focus for discussing or promoting events, ideas and concepts.

To gain the most out of your learning in this area, you will create your own blog to:
- act as a log of your activities and investigations
- record as many instances as you can of your use of online services in your daily life
- record web links to the sites and web pages you find interesting and relevant in your explorations of online services and life in the Information Age
- use it to complete the activities in this and the next chapter.

Content management systems

Many websites, especially blogs, but also e-commerce, catalogues and a few encyclopaedias, such as Wikipedia, are interfaced to, and driven by, database management systems. You simply enter content into a web form, without having to worry about how it is constructed, so that you can concentrate on the content. There are usually user-friendly facilities (such as buttons and drop downs) for styling the content, which are also managed by the database system. The content management system will construct web pages from the content and the style information provided. This means you do not have to understand HTML or even how to use a web editor; you just have to know how to enter data.

Your blog will then provide a rich resource when you complete your assessment for this unit.

There are numerous blog-creation packages you can use to create your own blog and it does not matter which you use. One of the most popular, free and easy to use web-logging packages is Blogger by Google. It works very well in the browsers specified by Edexcel for this course. In this chapter we will show you how to create and maintain your own blog using the Blogger service.

ACTIVITY 1 Create your own blog ◀

Watch the demonstration of how to create your own blog. Now enter http://www.blogger.com in your browser address bar and locate the blogger site as shown in Figure 1.1.1.

Work through the process of creating an account (Fig. 1.1.2), and naming your blog (Fig. 1.1.3). To do this you will have to:

The history of blogs

- Web logs probably started around 1997.
- Peter Merholz is often credited with coining the term 'blog' around 1998–9.
- Free blog editors, such as Blogger, started in 1999.
- Blogs may now be the most important non-commercial phenomenon on the web.
- There are now over five million blogs in existence and there are more added every day.
- Look at this website for further perspectives.

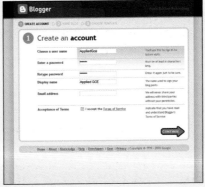

Figure 1.1.1 Creating your own blog

Figure 1.1.2 Creating your own account

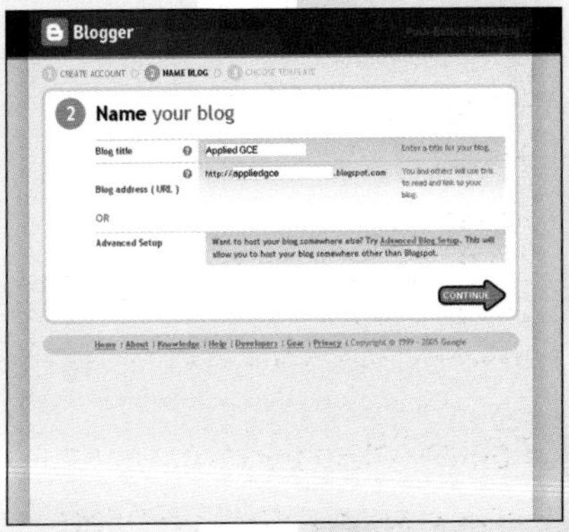

Figure 1.1.3 Naming your blog

- Decide on the user name you will use for your blog. This will almost certainly be your name. Decide whether you wish to use your full name, your email name, nickname etc.
- Decide on a password for your blog. This should be at least six characters long if you want it to be even reasonably secure, and contain letters and numbers (as all your passwords should). You will be responsible for all items posted on your blog so ensure it is secure and that no unauthorised people can gain access to it.
- Decide on a display name for the blog. This is the name that others will see on your blog. It can be the same as your user name or different if you prefer. It will be slightly more secure if you choose a different name.
- Decide on the email address that you will use as your registered address. This is essential as Google will test that this is you. (If you do not have an email address yet then you should obtain one immediately as you will need to use email to do many of the practical parts of this course.)
- Decide on the URL for you and others to access the blog at the host blogspot.com. In general this will be the same as your blog title, but if you want to have a specific, different address then this is fine, and may indeed be necessary if you choose a common title.
- Store all this information in a secure place.

Continued on next page

Figure 1.1.4 Choosing your template

There is a wide range of templates you can use to lay out your blog (Fig. 1.1.4). These are created using cascading style sheets (CSS, see Chapter 1.6) and so are fully customisable and can be changed at a later date independently of the blog posts. Therefore you are not committing yourself to a single style for your blog site.

Once you have chosen the template you will see the message 'Your blog has been created' (Fig. 1.1.5) and you can start posting to your blog or possibly customise the blog more (Fig. 1.1.6).

Any time you want to find out exactly how to do something simply visit Blogger help (Fig. 1.1.7).

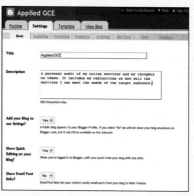

Figure 1.1.5 You are done!

Figure 1.1.6 You can personalise your blog

Figure 1.1.7 Help advises on how to do almost anything in your blog

ACTIVITY 2 Post to your blog ◀

Before you make your first post, watch the demonstration of how to do this. Now log in to Blogger with your name and password. Choose your blog from the 'Blogs' panel (Fig.1.1.8).

You will be presented with a tabbed sheet that allows you to add or edit posts, change your settings, change your template or view your blog (Fig. 1.1.9). Choose the Posting tab. Add your post title 'Online services'. Then write a short paragraph about this being your personal audit of all your communications, research, investigations etc. about online services and the Information Age. You could also add a list of the online services from the Unit 1 Specification.

Now choose 'Publish Post'. Then view your blog (Fig. 1.1.10).

Figure 1.1.8 Logging dashboard

Figure 1.1.9 Making posts

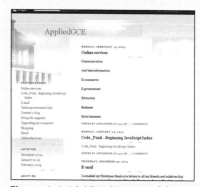

Figure 1.1.10 Viewing your blog

Activity 3 Maintain your blog ◀

You should now post regularly to your blog, preferably at least once a day. The blog should record all the online services you have used, and when you chose some other method rather than an online service. You should comment on why you used an online method, or if not, why not.

Email

Email (electronic mail) was an early online technology (1971). Its use has grown exponentially as the internet has developed. Using email is quite simple. Essentially a message is sent to an individual post box on a mail server where it waits until an email client (see margin) picks it up. To use email it is necessary to have a connection to an email server (which manages the distribution and storage of the mails) and to have an email client. A client is a program such as Outlook Express on a computer connected to the internet, or a browser-based client such as the email services provided online by websites like Hotmail or Yahoo. Email can now also be used on a mobile phone connected using GPRS, WAP or even SMS. It can even be used via a digital TV or games station connection to the internet.

An email system (see the demonstration) essentially allows you to:

- see a list of messages in your mailbox, showing the sender's name, the subject of the message, and the date and time it was sent
- select individual messages to view
- compose messages with a subject heading and textual content, and send them to any other email address
- add attachments to mails and save attachments from mails (binary files of almost any type).

The message is usually composed in an editing window or frame within the mail client. This used to be entirely text-based but can now also be HTML-based. Naturally in modern computers this message can be cut and pasted from another application.

Messages are usually sent using an SMTP server (simple mail transfer protocol-port 25) and received using a POP3 (post office protocol-port 110) or an IMAP (internet mail access protocol-port 143) server.

The advantages of email result from its simplicity. It is very easy to use; it is fast; it provides a permanent record of communications (unlike the phone); it is an informal medium but capable of formality. With attachments, it is capable of delivering almost any message and file type to almost any recipient or group of recipients, provided they are connected to the internet.

As usual though, these advantages also point to some of the disadvantages. It is so easy to use it is often misused. At a simple level people send inappropriate messages. People spoof others' addresses. Viruses, worms and Trojans can be attached very easily. Spam mail can block up mailboxes and whole areas of the internet itself.

Mail clients and mail servers

An email client is a program run by a user to send and receive email. It retrieves all email for its user from the mail server to which it is connected. It sends all mail from its user to the same mail server, for distribution to other users of email on other servers. The server therefore manages the communication of mail between internet domains (such as hotmail.com and yahoo.com).

For example, mail addressed to abc@pearson.com (i.e. generically speaking, user@domain) will be sent to the pearson.com server by other mail servers. When it arrives, the email client for 'abc' will manage it from there, picking up the mail when 'abc' connects to the server. Similarly, when 'abc' wishes to send mail it will all be passed to 'pearson.com', which will pass it on in turn to the appropriate servers.

Spoofing and spamming   It is relatively easy to write a program that will give a fake address in the 'From' field of an email, thus leading the receiver to believe the email is from a trusted source. Email viruses do this routinely. Many individuals have found it funny to send an email as though from the President of the USA. This is spoofing. Spamming is using email to conduct a junk mail campaign. It is so easy to do that unregulated it can flood people's inboxes.

Virus   A harmful piece of code that attaches itself to programs or files. A virus is capable of replicating itself once it is opened. For example, when a new program is opened it can be a further cue for the virus to replicate itself, allowing it to spread rather like a biological virus.

Worm   A particular species of virus that is capable of replicating itself in great volumes once installed without any further files being opened. Furthermore, because they are capable of 'burrowing' into a system without human assistance, some worms can allow their creators to take control of computer systems remotely.

Trojan   Another virus in the form of a piece of code, named after the Trojan horse. It is usually dressed up as an attractive attachment or download but may harbour an unwelcome payload. Once installed on a user's machine it can do damage to a user's system and possibly take control of the user's machine.

ACTIVITY 4 Exchange documents by email   ◀

In a small group, allocate a person to view each of these sites about email and how it works. Write a one-page summary including a diagram using your favourite word processing package.

Email this document to the other people in your group as an attachment. (Look at the demonstration to see how to do this.) Comment on each other's documents and reply to the rest of the group.

Add the one-page summaries and the diagrams to your blog. (Ensure the diagrams are in JPEG or GIF format. See Chapter 1.7 for an explanation of file formats.)

IRC   IRC is a totally open internet service that allows you to exchange simple text messages with anyone who is connected to the internet using IRC, either directly using an IRC client such as mIRC, or via web-based clients; for example, Central Chat which is a free IRC-based chat service that is used worldwide and was started by a young teenager.

Chat and instant messaging

Chat covers a range of scenarios across a range of different networks including:
- internet relay chat (IRC) – an open protocol not controlled by any one provider
- web-based chat offered by ISPs (e.g. BT or Freeserve) or portals such as Yahoo or MSN
- website-based chat offered by anyone with a site – often used to solve problems on a specific topic, whether professional or leisure
- online role-play environments
- chat rooms using SMS on mobile phones.

Instant messaging (IM) also allows you to interact with other users in real time. It is usually more private than chat rooms, allowing a group of people to converse in real time without being snooped on by anyone they don't specifically allow into the conversation. The simplest IM services allow just two participants. More advanced services allow multiple users, and the exchange of images, files and other forms of electronic media. One such popular service is *MSN Messenger*.

Chat and IM, unlike email, require that all participants be online at the same time. Everyone can participate in real time, as though in a real meeting. Chat is very popular among young people for social purposes, perhaps because of its instant nature, its relative anonymity and the simplicity of the messages sent. Even shy people can feel part of a conversation, seeing everything that is being said and contributing at their own pace.

At the moment chat is less developed as a working tool, or even a serious social tool, but some successful attempts have been made to use it in education. For example, the LETTOL (LEarn To Teach Online) course run by Sheffield College has learning sessions where students chat with each other and their tutor about set topics, then keep transcripts of the session in their portfolio.

The advantages also results in its downside. Lurkers on open chat lines may not be shy, but dangerous. Anonymity may allow paedophiles to ingratiate themselves into situations where they can do harm; full profiles may allow them to target individuals. Similarly, the short time it takes to type a message does not encourage long reflection, and so group work may not always be truly communicative, especially as you cannot see each other's body language.

A number of large providers, most notably Microsoft, closed down their free chat rooms in 2004 citing the dangers, especially for children; although some competitors have suggested that the reasons were in part economic. At the same time IM services have continued to grow. (You can read more about this on the Sky News website.)

Chat-room profiles Many chat rooms will allow people to register their details and store them in a profile which other users of the chat room can view. These may contain a user or nickname, a full name, a location, an age, hobbies, favourite food, music, events and possibly even a photo.

Protecting yourself online
Look at these sites:
- Tips from the main internet players on keeping safe online
- Childnet site on the dangers of chat
- Another Childnet site with advice and links on safe internet use
- Safety Guidelines for Children Online issued by the West Midlands Police
- Internet Watch Foundation

ACTIVITY 5 Conduct an online discussion ◀

Use IM (e.g. *MSN Messenger*, *Yahoo* etc.) or *NetMeeting* to have a discussion with a small group of fellow students about your conclusions from Activity 4. Compile a joint list of:
- the purposes of email
- how well it meets these purposes
- the benefits and drawbacks of using email.

Write up the activity in your blog.

ACTIVITY 6 Share your blog address using email ◀

For this next activity you should obtain the email addresses of three other students who are completing this unit. Send them all the same email with the following message:

The following is the address of my blog: http://-------.blogspot.com
Please review this and send me comments.
Please send me the address of your blog.

Figure 1.1.11 Adding links with 'Blog This'

ACTIVITY 7 Add web links to your blog ◀

You can add links to your blog by adding the HTML tags for a link to your post. The simplest way is to add 'Blog This!' to your browser toolbar or links bar. Then just click on this button whenever you visit a good page.

Visit Blogger to find help on 'Blog This!' Follow the instructions to use either the Google toolbar from Internet Explorer or to drag the 'Blog This!' link to the link bar of your browser.

Posting a link

Open your browser and search for 'Direct Gov'. When you have found the UK Government's Directgov website click on 'Blog This' (Fig. 1.1.12).

The link dialogue will ask you for a title for the post and show you the HTML that will be added for the link (Fig. 1.1.13). Click 'Publish' when you are satisfied.

Figure 1.1.12 Use 'Blog This!' to add a link

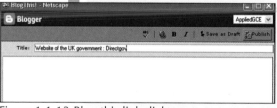

Figure 1.1.13 Blog this link dialogue

Figure 1.1.14 Your posted link

Viewing the blog

Visit the URL for your blog and you will see the results of your posting (Fig. 1.1.14).

Short message service

One of the more unexpected killer applications of the digital age has been the short message service (SMS) or text messaging. Devised originally to utilise the slack times in mobile phone transmissions to send short bursts of textual data, it has become the communication medium of choice for many people. To keep the messages short but allow as much meaning as possible, an SMS language has evolved based on abbreviations and informal phonics.

ACTIVITY 8 Create an SMS haiku message ◀

Form a small group. Using SMS language, create a message that is a Japanese haiku poem. That is, a five syllable line, followed by a seven syllable line and then a five syllable line (17 in total). Don't worry about getting it absolutely correct in SMS, but it should be as close as possible. If you need further guidance, look at this website on writing haiku poems.

Now send your poems to each other. Reply to each other with a translation of the poem into normal grammatical English. Reply in the following three ways:

1 using SMS on your phone
2 using a chat service
3 using email.

The whole group should then compare the purpose and functionality of each type of communication service and record their reflections in their individual web log.

The following is an example of a forlorn love poem from a young man who has let his girl down but desperately wants to make amends.

I rly 1 2 c u – an SMS haiku, 2004
b4icu
br8 me if u 1 2
jus c me l8r

Bulletin boards, conferences, communities and newsgroups

Bulletin board systems (BBSs) have been around since 1978. (You can look at this website to read about the history of BBSs.) The BBS was originally a replica of a physical board which allowed small notices, adverts and other messages to be posted. As BBSs evolved they became more versatile, and allowed downloading and sometimes uploading of images and files. They became useful for companies wanting to offer a place for FAQs, for software updates and advertisements. The world wide web took away the need for the simpler forms of bulletin boards.

There are still many instances of specialist and general-purpose discussion forums based on the structure of the more developed BBSs. These include remotely-hosted forum systems such as EZBoard, Sparklit ActiveBoard or Yahoo groups, which can be used to act as an online community for discussing topics of common interest. These are used by individuals and organisations to host discussions on topics that are either of very general interest with open subscription or to host private discussions for an invited set of individuals. The people involved in these discussions are known as a 'community'.

Newsgroups

See this website for a detailed look at newsgroups.
Review this animation of how Usenet newsgroups work.

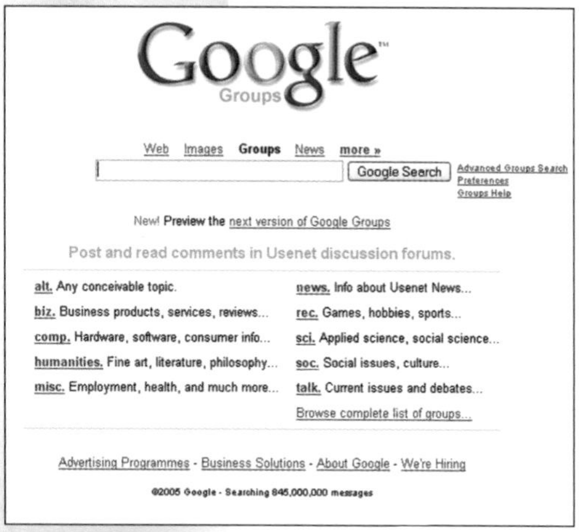

Figure 1.1.15 Using Google to access newsgroups

If you need to host a specialist forum, it is reasonably simple to host it on your server using free or commercial software. The Open University has a private forum system to allow students to see and discuss course content, and in the case of some online courses to upload completed assignments. The BBC has a very open message board system that allows you to comment on programmes and issues of the day.

Newsgroups, like BBSs, are an old part of the internet, preceding the world wide web, but are still used by many people. They are, in effect, a very public forum that allows people to read and post messages organised into a hierarchy of subjects. They can be read using specialist newsreader programs, but now they are generally used with a standard browser (see Fig. 1.1.15).

The name of a newsgroup consists of two or more parts, separated by decimal points; a little like the Dewey decimal-number classification system used by libraries. The parts organise hierarchies of newsgroups. The traditional top-level hierarchies are shown in Figure 1.1.15. The 'alt' hierarchy is a catch all and contains masses of sub topics. For example, 'alt.internet.bbs' is in the internet part of the 'alt' hierarchy, and it contains messages on bulletin board systems. A number of providers, including Google, are currently looking at ways to make groups more accessible to a non-technical audience.

ACTIVITY 9 Use Usenet newsgroups ◀

Use Google Groups' advanced search to find a discussion on the 'digital divide' posted in the last six months. Reflect on how useful you find these discussions. State at least one limitation and one benefit of using Usenet for finding specific information and conclude by stating to what extent it fulfils its main purpose.

Add your reflections to your blog. Include the full address of the Usenet groups you viewed.

CASE STUDY Modern communications and the SE Asia tsunamis ◀

The SE Asian tsunami in 2004 proved to be a very telling demonstration of modern communications and maybe even of the digital divide. The US monitoring station in Honolulu registered the quake and sent email warnings out, but did not have contacts in the less developed parts of Asia to inform them about the impending disaster.

Figure 1.1.16 Devastation caused by the SE Asian Tsunami on Boxing Day 2004

Continued on next page

When the tsunami struck, almost all fixed-line local communications systems failed or were overwhelmed. Nevertheless, people with mobile phones were often still able to send text messages saying they were OK. A Swedish boy of two, who had been found sitting alone on a road near Khao Lok in Thailand, was rescued by his aunt after she recognised his face on a webpage set up by the Phuket International Hospital. Sky TV set up a ticker on its TV channel to relay messages sent by text and email by survivors of the disaster. The BBC news website received 30 000 emails related to the disaster the day after it happened.

Specialist blogs were set up immediately in the aftermath of the disaster to help focus relief efforts and give news (source: Patrick Barkham, 'Frantic search switches to cyberspace as old methods fail', *The Guardian*, 29 December 2004, p.3). BBC News carried a story of survivors sending emails from an internet café in Thailand to reassure people at home. Catriona Davies reported that "hundreds of anxious families logged on to internet bulletin boards yesterday to try to find backpackers missing in South-East Asia" (source: *The Daily Telegraph*, 30 December 2004). The Lonely Planet online Thorn Tree travel forum was used to post hundreds of such messages. The BBC put up a number of message (bulletin) boards to which emails could be sent asking for information on missing people.

Task

Consider how this tragic incident gives examples of:
- presenting information in different ways
- sharing information quickly
- greater interaction between individuals and organisations
- virtual communities, where people are brought together via the internet.

Why were modern communication services used rather than older ones? How effective were each of the services given their purpose?
Write up your answers in your web log.

Real-time information

One of the great changes made by the internet is the possibility of having really up-to-date information available on demand. There are a growing number of such services. Some of these are provided as part of a public service remit, but a growing area is for sites that provide information on the web, and so reduce the demand for providing such information over the phone or face to face. The costs savings can fund the website.

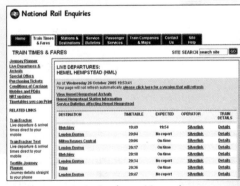

Figure 1.1.17 Arrivals at Hemel Hempstead station

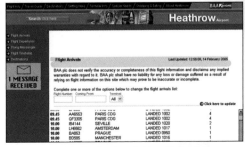

Figure 1.1.18 Arrivals at Heathrow

Activity 10 Plan a journey

Plan a journey from your home town to Tottenham Court Road in London, commencing one hour from when you start the exercise. Contrast the journey by car and by rail.

Write up the results in your blog. Include full details of the journey including dates, times, costs and sources used. State how useful you found the sources in finding real-time information for your journey.

Some useful links

National Rail Company

Stations departure information

Transport for London site real time information

AA Route Planner

AA Live Traffic News

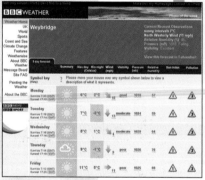

Figure 1.1.19 Weather for Weybridge

Activity 11 Weather in your area

Look up the weather forecast for your local area for the next five days using the BBC weather site or the Met office site.

Write your results in your blog and then every day compare the results against the reality. At the end of the week comment on the information given by the services. Consider also whether you might have had better information if you had been prepared to pay for it, using for example the Met Office's weather service.

E-commerce

▶ Online stores

Online services for business are very varied. The main vehicle for e-commerce is the world wide web. Sellers set up web stores, which are specialised websites with payment processing interfaces. (This process is discussed in detail in Chapter 2.3.) The storefront is usually a set of web pages with pictures and descriptions of the goods available, all linked to a database and probably a search facility. The shopper chooses an item by transferring it to a virtual shopping basket or shopping trolley. When all items have been chosen the consumer goes to a separate set of pages which manage payment and delivery. Watch the online shopping demonstration to see these processes in action. (See Unit 2 for a full explanation of the whole process.)

ACTIVITY 12 Visit eBay ◀

Visit eBay. Then write a short document in your blog on what are its major purposes, who is the target audience, how the auction process works, how well it fulfils these purposes, and what are the benefits and limitations of the service. Explain why it is so successful as a shopping model.

▶ Online banking

Online banking services are a logical extension of the automated branch systems that banks brought in from the 1970s to the 1990s. They use computerised systems to allow customers to access and manage their own accounts using an internet connection, rather than having a bank clerk do it. The only extra major technology that was required to make this happen was internet access with encrypted security technology. It is clearly vital that only the customer and authorised bank staff have access to the customer's account; and that the customer does not accidentally gain access to anyone else's account. In the early days of online banking both of these criteria failed in some cases, but the use of ever more secure methods has now ensured a fairly safe online banking experience for most people.

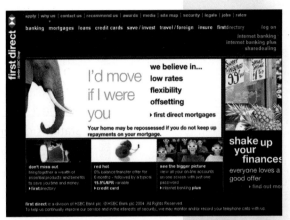

Figure 1.1.20 First Direct Online Banking home page

Furthermore, banks can offer extra services to their customers such as finding their balance, making a payment at any time of the day or night, or even text message (SMS) banking. The use of IT has also opened up services such as offset mortgages, credit cards linked to accounts so that payments can be made immediately, and account sweeping so that funds can be transferred automatically between accounts to ensure that the lowest possible fees are paid.

Clearly the driving force for the online stores and banks is that overheads can be reduced dramatically when fewer assistants are required and even further if retail premises or high-street branches are not required.

ACTIVITY 13 Investigate online banking ◀

Investigate the websites of at least two online banks.

Summarise in a short presentation the purposes of online banking, its target audiences, how it fulfils these purposes, and the major advantages. Consider how online banking might be improved in the future.

Gone phishing

Phishing is a serious scam to hit online shoppers and especially online bankers. In the case of banking, customers are usually sent an email message supposedly from their own bank, asking them to visit the bank's site to update their details. If they take the bait, the site they are directed to is a fake site built to look exactly the same as the real one. When they enter their username and password, their identity is stolen. This can then be used to buy (or, more accurately, steal) things. Phishing has occurred with eBay and the online banks, but no part of the internet is totally immune from such scams.

SMS banking

First Direct, a telephone and internet bank, offers a service that notifies users by SMS of transactions on their accounts over a size specified by the user. This gives users up-to-date information on their account and alerts them to unexpected transactions.

In February 2005 First Direct had 1.2 million customers; 800 000 of these used online services and 430 000 used SMS banking (source: Circular from Chief Executive sent to customers, Feb 2005).

Education

Online education is a big business, but a very disparate one. There are many different education services available, from the National Grid for Learning, to one off simulations or learning objects designed to help students understand a single topic.

ACTIVITY 14 Explore learning objects and simulations ◀

Visit the Science Museum's Making the Modern World learning modules site which is designed to help A-level and vocational students. Find your way from 'Stories Timeline' to 'Personal computers and information networks' and follow this through to the stories on PCs, the internet, the dot com gold rush etc.

Blog the site. Evaluate the site against its purpose. What lessons does it teach us about online education?

ACTIVITY 15 Use a simulation ◀

Visit NetFrog, which is an online simulation of the dissection of a frog, and blog the site.

Evaluate it against its purpose of practising before dissecting, or using the site instead of actually dissecting a frog. What general lessons does it teach you about online simulations in education?

ACTIVITY 16 Macromedia virtual classroom ◀

Visit Macromedia's website, which gives you the opportunity to listen to e-learning recorded seminars or even join a virtual classroom if the timing is right.

Visit one of the sessions (e.g. 'Making the most of virtual classrooms') and watch the presentation.

Evaluate this exciting technology as an example of learning about e-learning. What can it offer that traditional learning cannot? What are the disadvantages?

ACTIVITY 17 Use a learning object ◀

Use the simple demonstration Flash viewlet 'Formatting using the toolbar and format menu'. These types of Flash and Quicktime movies are marketed by a number of companies to the educational market as 'learning objects'. Teachers or students package a number of them to create a unique learning package.

Evaluate this as a way of helping you learn.

For a much larger and more developed view of these types of Flash learning objects visit Macromedia's website. At Lynda.com watch the 'Welcome' and the 'What's a blog really?' videos.

ACTIVITY 18 Research online education ◀

You are an experienced consumer of education. Find five different types of online education on the internet. Rank them in order of how best you would learn via each, and give a short explanation of why this is so.

Prepare a short presentation to share your results. Write up an overall evaluation of the best sources in your blog.

E-government

The UK Government has set itself ambitious targets for developing online services. The Prime Minister, Tony Blair, stated the responsibilities of the government as "Ensuring that IT supports the business transformation of Government itself so that we can provide better, more efficient, public services." (source: e-Government Unit). A Cabinet Office report stated that the vast majority of government services will be available online by the end of 2005. Current take up of these services in 2004 was:

- 1.1 million tax returns were filed electronically.
- 65 per cent of people applying for university entry used Electronic Application Services (EAS).
- 67 per cent of business incorporations were processed online.
- 79 per cent of vehicle registrations were now electronic.
- 40 per cent of bookings for the driving test were online.
- More than 1300 land registration applications were filed online per day.
- 28 per cent of the auditing community visited government websites.
- 6 per cent of the population dealt with various branches of government via websites (making payments, booking etc.).
- NHS direct received 600 000 visits a month.

Automated assessment One of the boom areas of online education is automated testing. Particularly popular are the adaptive tests used by large computer organisations such as Microsoft, Cisco, Novell etc. to assess whether a student has achieved sufficient competence to receive his or her certification.

These types of test are now used in UK education to assess some of the practical elements of key skills. In addition, all new teachers now have to pass automated online skills tests in numeracy, English and IT in order to gain Qualified Teacher Status.

Figure 1.1.21 Some of the UK Government services available online

ACTIVITY 19 Investigate government services online ◀

Research the local and national governmental services that can be undertaken online in the UK. Use the Directgov website as a starting point.

Make a table categorising the services under the following headings: information services, online reporting and advice, online booking, online payments. Rank the services in order of usefulness to a consumer, considering the benefits a consumer would get from the service.

According to a Cabinet office report in 2004, the UK Government hopes to have saved £1.3 thousand million within three years by migrating its services online and to have saved consumers £1 thousand million. How is this possible?

Download services

When media are in digital form it is quite feasible to deliver them using the internet itself, with no need to travel to a shop or if you order online to wait for the goods to be delivered by carrier to a real address. Anything that is digital can be immediately transferred across the internet. The other requirement is that the receiver can understand the format that is used by the sender. The convergence of most media towards standard digital formats means that it is now possible for users to download a massive variety of items from the internet.

▶ Software

The preferred method for delivering software upgrades, driver updates and virus definition updates is now via the internet. A number of programs have automated the download process so that it is transparent or semi-transparent to the user. Virus definitions can be downloaded and installed automatically to computers in the background without the user having to intervene. Windows updates, program patches and firewall updates can be set up to work in a similar way, though often they have a dialogue box for the user to confirm that they want the update. New drivers and program upgrades for virtually all programs can be downloaded from the internet.

The benefits of this are clear:
* Updates can be applied immediately as required and even sometimes automatically.
* Updates can often be free as the cost of providing them is so low.
* User satisfaction should be higher as updates can correct problems immediately, or even prevent them from happening in the first place.

In theory all software could be delivered in this manner, not just upgrades. There are two major reasons why this is not always done at the moment.

1 The size of a lot of software. A 50 Mbyte file takes several minutes to download even with a fast broadband connection.
2 Even with smaller applications the user will often want a physical copy of the software and manuals. Although many software houses now provide their manuals in PDF, this is not the entire solution. One of the problems with delivering everything electronically is what happens if the system fails and the software has to be reinstalled. With free, relatively small upgrades this is not a great problem. With large proprietary software it is a bigger issue. Nevertheless most computer online stores now offer a large amount of software for download.

▶ Music and video

One of the massive success stories of the internet has been music download services based, originally, on the MP3 format (a standard format for storing music in a compressed form with only a minimal loss of quality). One reason this arose was that a number of peer-to-peer (P2P) file-sharing services provided a mechanism for people to share their music and thus effectively acquire expensive music at little or no cost.

Figure 1.1.22 An iPod

Legal action from the music industry has now reduced this activity, and legitimate download services have taken off in a big way. Apple had sold over 500 million tracks for download on its iTunes service by July 2005. Apple uses a higher quality MPEG-4 advanced audio coding (AAC) format which still offers very good compression, but has a quality that rivals CDs. Sony uses its own ATRAC format for better compression and good quality. All of these formats can be easily converted to MP3 if desired, though the rival formats do lead to obvious drawbacks over transferability.

Video has started to follow the same path as audio. There are numerous dubious sites from which it is possible to download films and videos in breach of copyright and with the drawbacks of variable quality, the possibility of viruses etc. The film and video industries are now beginning to supply legal downloadable content. One of the difficulties with video is that the files are very large in comparison with audio tracks. Even in compressed MPEG-4 form, quality video can use up many gigabytes per hour, which makes it less viable with current broadband speeds.

Videos are made available online using streaming technology. This allows you to start watching a video when enough data has been transferred to fill a buffer. You have to wait initially for the buffer to be filled, but you then watch the film from the data in the buffer while the buffer is being refilled in the background. Clearly the effectiveness of this depends on how quickly the buffer can be filled. If it is too slow the buffer has to be massive and the wait for it to start will be very long. With fast broadband speeds 'video on demand' is now possible, and is available in some parts of the UK. With this service, it is possible to order any film from a menu and download it to watch whenever you want, for a small fee.

▶ Books

Many books have been created or transferred into electronic form, either in PDF, HTML, MS Reader or other proprietary format. These can also be downloaded, but easily, because of their small size (see Chapter 1.5).

ACTIVITY 20 Investigate downloading goods and services ◀

In a small group create a list of the different types of items that you and your families have downloaded from the internet.

Create a list of reasons of why you did this rather than buying the physical goods. Consider the extent to which the downloading service fulfilled its purpose. Compile a list of problems you have with any aspect of downloading and consuming online files.

Write these reflections in your blog.

Entertainment

▶ Radio

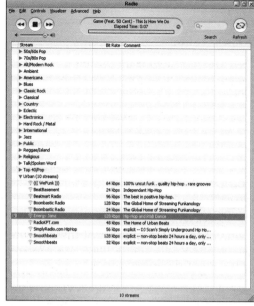

Figure 1.1.23 Internet radio using iTunes

The internet also enables new forms of entertainment services. Digital internet radio is possible using the same form of streaming technology used in downloading video, but it is rather simpler and more mature as a medium as the bandwidth demands are not so great. The benefits of internet radio are enormous. The choice of stations is staggering. You are not limited to any geographical area: it is quite possible to listen to a station at very high quality from the mid-west of the USA or Nile FM from Cairo. It is possible to find the exact type of radio you want to hear.

The drawbacks are similar to those of finding any information on the internet. The choice is potentially so wide it can be difficult to decide what it is best. Some output is clearly mediocre. Services such as iTunes (Fig. 1.1.23), the BBC and Windows Media filter stations and provide a wide choice of more reliable stations, but at the expense of the fantastic range that is otherwise available. Streaming technology makes it possible to have the radio on continuously while working on other applications on the computer, but intensive internet use can cause the buffer to empty and reception to be interrupted.

▶ Games

The internet has also made true multi-player gaming possible. Multi-user dungeon (MUD) games were played 20 years before the world wide web even existed. It is now possible to play strategy, adventure and card games against real players. New multi-player games are now graphics based and more of these will come online as higher speed connections and faster computers make it possible to race cars, have fights, and play football against other players using PCs, or even games stations such as the Playstation or Xbox.

Activity 21 Online entertainment ◀

List all the online entertainment technologies you have used in the last three months.

Consider the purpose of the technology, who it is targeted at, to what extent it is enhanced by being online, what are the current limitations and, overall, to what extent it fulfils its potential. Write this up in your blog.

Archiving

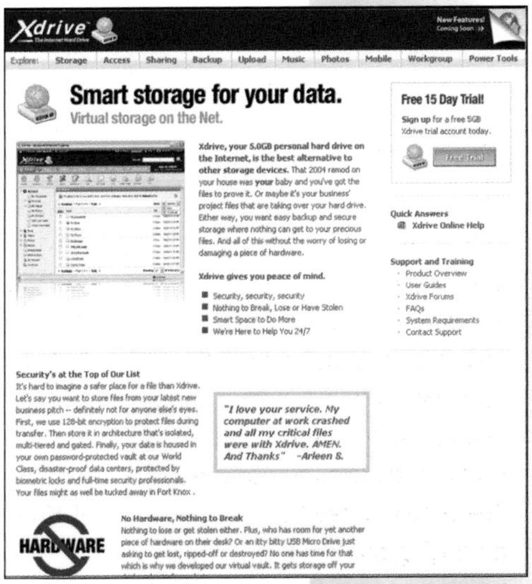

Another common service on the modern internet is archiving computer data. The world wide web itself is hosted on large file systems, and storage is relatively cheap. In older networks, back-up and archiving was an entirely local service. While mission-critical data will almost certainly be archived privately, a good deal of data, especially for home users, can be securely archived on remote file systems on the internet. For a long time there were many free providers of such storage, but as with many services on the internet, most providers now attempt to charge for general archiving services; although specific file types such as photos, blogs, community posts etc. can often be stored for free, or as part of a larger package.

One of the more popular of these secure online storage service providers is Xdrive which allows you to store any type of file on its servers for a small monthly fee. Apple offer a similar facility to .Mac members called iDrive. This allows Macintosh users to back up their systems on an internet drive at Apple, again for a small monthly fee. There is also a public folder on the drives (a common facility of these services) in which users can publish their files if they wish. These are often used to share photos, music or messages. This drive is mounted on the desktop in the same way as a normal drive and files can easily be dragged and dropped between drives (albeit with a little delay with a slow connection).

Figure 1.1.24 Xdrive online storage

Business

Most of the services described and analysed in this chapter can help us in our business lives. One major impact of the technologies on business services has been to allow a much more flexible approach. With the availability of digital technology and the internet, work can be done in many more places and at different times. It is possible to do business using an internet connection on a train or plane. Email can be used almost anywhere. Bulletin boards offer an excellent means of broadcasting messages to all staff. Real-time audio and video conferencing allow people to conduct meetings over large distances without time-consuming and expensive travel.

Conclusion ▶ ▶ ▶

The internet and the services available on it are still maturing. Although there are still limitations, the scope of what is being offered is vast. Over the course of this chapter you will have investigated a number of online services and gained a good idea of how well they meet their purposes.

You should have accumulated your results and thoughts into individual and group blogs that will form the basis of the first part of the assessment for this unit. You will have to evaluate five of these online services in depth and provide evaluative comments on the others, using your practical experience, your research and your reflections. You must also now draw this together to consider the current scope and limitations of the internet.

Life in the Information Age

Figure 1.2.1 You don't have to be at your desk to work

ICT is transforming the way people live in virtually every area of their lives. At home we are able to use a vast array of digital services and equipment to keep us entertained and informed. We use it to help us find jobs and in most modern workplaces we are surrounded by ICT intended to make us more productive. ICT has a large impact on how, when and where we work. It is a central part of the compulsory school curriculum and is used extensively in the push to revolutionise lifelong learning. We use it to keep in touch from anywhere, at anytime. We bank and shop using ICT. We are watched, monitored, and sometimes controlled and governed by ICT. This can all bring enormous benefits, but also has a large potential downside.

In Chapter 1.1 you explored the online services available and gained a picture of the scope and limitations of the internet. In this chapter you will take this further by exploring the positive and negative impacts the information revolution has had on your personal, social and working life.

Working styles

The range of ICT technologies available has enabled a large shift in the working styles of the majority of the working population. The way people work and where they work has changed. There has been a shift in the life/work balance that has been made possible by ICT. ICT should not necessarily be seen as the cause of this shift – which is in large part to do with economics and politics – but rather as the enabling technology.

The descriptions for many jobs have changed dramatically requiring that most roles involve the use of some computer skills. Management accountants used to working with calculators and pencils, now use spreadsheet packages constantly. Most office staff are expected to know how to use basic word processing and email applications on a PC, as can be seen in the video. Shop assistants use computerised till systems (EPOS), payment systems (EFTPOS) and stock control systems. Car mechanics use computerised analysis equipment to diagnose many of the faults they are presented with. Teachers are expected to be able to use PCs, networks, interactive whiteboards and a wide range of software. Illustrators and graphic artists now do much of their work using specialised graphic packages.

Additionally, people use ICT to be more self-reliant and more productive at work, which also reduces the need for employees. Many managers can now word-process their own reports and create their own presentations, whereas a generation ago a secretary would have done this; this is discussed further in the video. Sales assistants can often look at a database to see whether an item is in stock without having to ask a stores clerk to check.

The area of largest change is probably the way people communicate at work. Using ever more sophisticated digital switchboards and mobile phones, it is possible to contact most people whenever required and wherever they are. Email is routinely used in many organisations, even to communicate between people sitting next to each other. Computer conferencing allows discussions

EPOS Electronic point of sale. A computerised till connected to a price look up database, and possibly to the live stock database.

EFTPOS Electronic funds transfer at point of sale. A system that allows debit cards to be used to pay for goods. The funds are transferred automatically by the machine at the till from the buyer's bank account to the seller's.

about a project to take place over weeks or months, even when organisations have to collaborate over different time zones. Video conferencing allows people to have an interactive meeting in real time in which they can see each other, regardless of how far apart they are. Most journalists no longer use shorthand and a snatched phone call to file an urgent report, but instead a laptop computer and a modem that connects them to their office as required. The editor in this video describes how ICT is employed at the *Financial Times*.

In many ways the use of ICT gives more freedom and self-reliance to some staff. In other situations it allows much more control of workers. Being able to use a mobile phone and laptop on the train allows an engineer to get away early to avoid the Friday night rush, but means that he or she can be contacted about a problem even when out for a quiet meal on a Thursday night. Many transport-based organisations, such as parcel carriers, use route-planning software to map out the exact route the drivers must take to maximise efficiency and estimate their journey times. They use satellite-tracking systems to ensure they follow the route and monitor how long they take. Mobile phones help the drivers if there is a problem, but also mean that the office can contact them more simply when desired.

ACTIVITY 1 Tool man ◀

John is a sales representative selling tools to garden centres and DIY stores. He travels over 1 000 miles a week to see new and existing clients. For the past 20 years he has carried round a large diary, an address book, a large road atlas and numerous A-Zs, as well as numerous small coins for phones. He prides himself on his punctuality, but even so he is occasionally late as he struggles to find a new client or is delayed by traffic. He always takes along a calculator, and a bulky sales catalogue with the latest price lists and order forms. He is usually on the road four days a week, six hours a day and spends two further hours every day completing his administration. He spends every Friday in the office ensuring all his administration and sales are handled properly. He has always said he quite likes the time spent in his car between appointments, as it is his time when he can listen to CDs undisturbed.

Figure 1.2.2 A satellite navigation system

State how John could use the following ICT to change and hopefully improve his working style: PDA, GPS, laptop, software, mobile phone, the internet. What possible disadvantages are there for him in employing a lot of ICT? Take a look at this video of another sales manager who uses a lot of ICT.

One of the more pervasive changes to many people's lives brought about through the use of ICT has been the move to a more flexible style of working. There are a number of aspects to this:
- The times at which they work are more flexible.
- The places at which people work are now more flexible.
- The contracts they work under are more flexible.

(Source: Flexibility.)

ICT allows employers to monitor and control more flexible work patterns, and communication and networking technology enables people to work in different ways and in different places.

Many large, and some smaller organisations, have implemented some form of flexible working scheme which allows workers to have more choice over where and when they work. In simple cases, ICT enables the logging of working hours within flexible time slots. In more sophisticated schemes staff can be employed as teleworkers, i.e. they work extensively from home or from a local telecentre using telecommunication links back to the main office.

CASE STUDY Flexible working at BT ◀

Read the report Teleworking at BT and this summary.

Task

- How many BT workers are identified as homeworkers?
- What other companies are identified in the projects?
- What different types of teleworking are identified?
- What differences does the report note in working hours when teleworking?
- What percentage of workers travel significantly less than commuting office staff?
- What are the key benefits for BT?
- What are the key benefits identified by BT employees?
- What negative impacts of teleworking are noted in the report?
- What are the key economic benefits?

Work and the family today

According to a report published by the National Family and Parenting Institute:

- Almost almost two-thirds of working families contain a parent who works outside the traditional Monday to Friday, nine to five work pattern.
- Around half of all employees make use of at least one flexible working arrangement. The most common of these is part-time working, accounting for 27 per cent of all employees.
- 11 per cent of women and 8 per cent of men worked flexitime hours.
- 7 per cent of women and 1 per cent of men work term-time only.

One of the major impacts of ICT on working styles has been to shift the work/life balance. ICT has made working life more productive and more efficient, and allowed individuals to take on more responsibility. It has enabled individuals to do and achieve more. It allows us to communicate more effectively in ever more places at ever more times, and thus to have much wider teams to work in with more opportunity for social contact.

However there is a potential downside to this. As fewer people are employed in a particular area and more responsibility is devolved to an individual, working hours can be much longer. Unison, a union for service-sector employees, in a report on work life balance estimates that the number of people working more than 60 hours a week has increased from 12.5 per cent to 16.5 per cent from 2002 to 2004. Work may involve less teamwork and less opportunity to socialise. It can seem beneficial that work can be done at home or on the train, but less so when it takes over home life and you cannot get away from it even when travelling. Of course the 24 hour a day, all-year service we enjoy as consumers means that others are having to work during these times.

CASE STUDY Ambulance services

UK ambulance services have experienced a revolution in working styles as a result of technology. ICT has been used extensively in command and control centres to make the service more efficient and responsive. New secure digital communications systems have replaced crackly broadcast systems. Satellite tracking of resources (such as ambulances, helicopters, paramedic cars and bikes) and geographical information systems allow the optimal resource to be deployed at all times by centre staff. Technology is used to analyse patterns of usage to roster (call in) the exact number of staff required. It uses geographical analysis to decide where it is best to position ambulances and other resources so that they can be deployed to nearby locations very quickly. Ambulances are placed at points that are closest in travel time to places of peak demand and are tracked at all times to show where they are.

Figure 1.2.3 The location of an ambulance is tracked at all times

The Staffordshire ambulance service says of the impact of new technology:

"The adopting of this modern approach has resulted in remarkable results in the Trust performance in recorded response times. This has given the Trust the lead position in national ambulance tables for the last seven years. It has also seen dramatic improvements in the cardiac survival figures." (Source: Staffordshire Ambulance Service.)

The introduction of this system in London in the 1990s, however, was extremely problematic, not least because of the working practices that were brought about by the introduction of these measures.

Task

Research the impact on the working styles of ambulance workers in your area, and of the London Ambulance Service, after the introduction of new technologies.

Why have some workers objected to being sited in their 'resources' in the most efficient place rather than being sited in the ambulance station? What other drawbacks have there been with the introduction of these ICT systems? What have been the benefits of these systems?

Further sources

Report on London Ambulance Service problems
Case studies on implementing vehicle tracking technology solutions

CNC Computer numerical control is a method of controlling industrial machinery; the most common application being turning machines such as lathes. The machines are programmed to perform a task rather than being set up manually, which makes them potentially easier to use, faster and more accurate.

Employment opportunities

The types of jobs people do, the way they do them and where they do them have changed dramatically, largely, though not exclusively, as a result of ICT. There are three vital, but related, aspects to this: automation, globalisation and flexibility.

Particularly hard hit have been the careers of people with specific skills that are capable of being directly or indirectly automated. In the manufacturing sector, some factories have been replaced, either in the UK or overseas, by factories employing CNC, automated machines and robotics. In the service sectors in the 1960s and 1970s colleges were teeming with people training for careers in banking, insurance, and shorthand and typing skills. Now these make up a tiny proportion of the college population.

Banks very early on realised the advantages of automation. Before the start of the 1970s, they jointly established an automated clearing system for cheques and other payment systems (BACS). In 1970 it processed approximately 70 million cheques and 30 million direct debits. “Currently BACS processes over four thousand million financial transactions a year and handles over 60 million payments on a peak day, including Direct Debits, Direct Credits, Standing Orders and other inter-bank payments.” (Source: The McCue Interview: BACS’ IT chief Nick Masterson-Jones, 14 September 2004.) BACS meant that a lot of back-office work could be automated and numerous administrative jobs in banks could be replaced by computers. Skilled and well-trained bank staff who performed all the clerical tasks associated with collecting, counting, transferring and checking cheques paid to and from other banks could be replaced by computing power plus less skilled staff, who could be trained in days rather than years. Many bank tellers (counter assistants) have been replaced by ATMs (automated teller machines). Branches have been closed as a result of automation and centralisation with the loss of the knowledgeable and independent bank manager.

Shorthand and touch-typing represent the other, decentralised, end of the spectrum. Most small, and all large, businesses used to employ one or more people in this role. They would take notes, type up memos, letters, reports and invoices, and do any other small volume jobs that required better presentation than a handwritten note. The advent of office software such as word processing, spreadsheets, databases and presentation software has meant that many administrative and managerial staff can do the work themselves faster than if they involved another person. The demand for shorthand typists has therefore diminished enormously. There is still an active and strong demand for good secretaries, but more at the personal-assistant rather than typist end of the market.

Activity 2 Analysing the ‘good old days’

Client: ....

Accounting period: .... Prepared by: .... Date: ....

Subject: .... Reviewed by: .... Date: ....

Date	Description	Amount	Postage	Food	Stationery	Sundries	
Jun 3	Stamps	18.50	18.50				
Jun 3	Vegetables	9.50		9.50			
Jun 4	Envelopes	7.20			7.20		
Jun 5	Pens	5.55			5.55		
Jun 5	Sausages	8.22		8.22			

Figure 1.2.4 A typical accounting worksheet

In the 1970s the expenses for a small business were entered onto analysis paper (see Fig. 1.2.4). A date, description and amount were entered in the first three columns and then the figure was double-entered into an analysis column on the right. Individual expenses (e.g. postage, food, sundries and stationery) could then be analysed simply by adding the columns. An automatic check was made on the accuracy of the addition as the individual columns had to sum to the same as the amount column on the left.

Continued on next page

Around the same time one large multinational organisation with an HQ in London might employ over 100 managers in the finance area to set, manage and control the budgets for the European area. The managers used techniques similar to the small business. They entered budget figures onto A3 analysis sheets, which were typed up as required by their secretaries. These were then used as the basis for analysing what would happen given different sales performances, different commission rates, different interest rates etc. These were well-paid, well-qualified and skilled accountants who were able to work quickly and efficiently to analyse potential changes using the latest calculators and replicate them quickly with only a tiny proportion of mistakes across all columns, and down all rows.

The speed at which they worked necessitated continual retyping so the secretaries were also kept very busy. When sheets were returned they had to be proofed, but as the managers were skilled and the secretaries well trained and highly efficient for the most part there were only a few occasions when the sheets had to be retyped. A dramatic change occurred in the early half of the 1980s to this organisation when microcomputer software became widely available.

Tasks

- Name two different office applications that could be used by the small business to improve upon the paper-based systems employed in the 1970s.
- Describe two advantages of each over the paper-based system and one advantage of each over the other.
- How were secretaries' and typists' employment prospects affected by the advent of these office packages?
- What new job opportunities were opened up by the advent of office applications?

Call centres in India

Call centre staff in India operate hotlines for many Western banks, credit card and computer and technology companies. Staff in the call centres often adopt a western name, swot up on western customs and geography, and take voice coaching lessons in an effort to sound as Western as possible to visitors to the centre. There have been some problems (Dell is one company that dropped a call centre in Bangalore because of language and cultural problems), but overall they have been a great success. One Delhi-based company has been so successful it is now able to hire about 10% of its workforce from Europe (although these often stay short term as part of a travelling experience).

(Sources: ZDnet and BBC News.)

At the same time as many jobs have disappeared as a result of ICT and related economic factors, many new jobs have been created. The most obvious area is that of IT itself. There was a vast growth in IT jobs up to the end of the last millennium, and in internet and e-commerce jobs during the boom of the late 1990s. The bursting of the e-commerce bubble (see Chapter 2.2) and the damp squib of the millennium bug have led to a shakeout in the industry, but it is still a very important new industry.

One of the most successful instances of the globalisation phenomenon has been the call centre. Modern telecommunications equipment not only allows individuals to work successfully from home, but also allows centres that handle calls to be placed in the most economically and socially advantageous position. People phoning their local bank branch, insurance broker, or computer helpdesk on a free or local access telephone number these days may be phoning Scotland, Ireland or even India without realising.

Figure 1.2.5 Call centres like this didn't used to exist

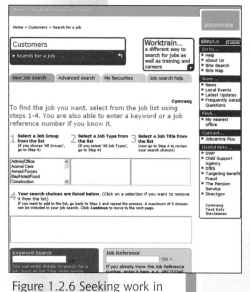

Figure 1.2.6 Seeking work in the Information Age

Communication

Communications has been a key focus of change in the Information Age. The way most businesses and young people communicate in the 21st century has changed enormously from the way their parents and grandparents communicated in the middle of the 20th century. Email, chat, SMS and digital voice and mobile videophones have rapidly become the way to communicate. In 2004, according to the BBC, there were more than 40 million mobile phones in the UK and over 30 000 base stations. People can now work anywhere, play anywhere and keep in touch from anywhere. We communicate much more, more quickly and more globally.

DISCUSSION Digital communication versus voice conversation

Does communicating with SMS in text language have any social downside compared to having a proper voice conversation?

Are there any social downsides to firing off a quick email rather than having a short conversation?

Email has been one of the internet's killer applications. In 2001 it was estimated that 12 thousand million messages were sent daily, and that by 2003 there were 31 thousand million sent every day. Estimates of usage at the start of 2005 are close to 72 thousand million messages a day. The reasons for this are to do with the massive benefits email can bring to individuals and businesses. One of the major benefits of email is the relatively low cost to the user of sending messages. A consistent theme of the developing internet, however, is that providers are trying to find ways of charging for services that have traditionally been free and email may not always be quite as free as it is at this moment. One of the major drawbacks is spam, or junk mail. Most estimates suggest that between 30 per cent and 40 per cent of all email sent is junk.

ACTIVITY 3 When do you use email?

Evaluate your personal, social and work (school/college) uses of email:

- For what purposes do you use email?
- How and where do you use email?
- What are the major benefits for you in using email?
- What problems or disadvantages do you have in using email?
- When does email make you more productive and when less productive?
- Does email fulfil its intended purposes?

This site about email may be useful in your thinking.

Activity 4 When do you use mobile phones? ◀

Evaluate your personal, social and work (school/college) related uses of mobile phones:

- For what purposes do you use your mobile phone?
- How and where do you use your mobile phone?
- What are the major benefits for you in using your mobile phone?
- What problems or disadvantages do you have in using your mobile phone?
- Does your mobile phone fulfil its intended purposes?

Activity 5 Evaluate your communications ◀

Evaluate your personal, social and work (school/college) related uses of the other communication services analysed in Chapter 1.1.

Activity 6 Business communications ◀

Research the best practice in modern business communications and create a short presentation on the topic covering main uses, benefits and drawbacks.

Education

The impact of ICT in education has been variable, but is destined to grow a great deal over the coming decade as many programmes progress to fruition or maturity. It has long been recognised that education is now a lifelong activity. Traditionally people went to school and college from the age of 4 to 18 and then perhaps went on to higher education. Having finished this education, a person was expected to embark on a career that would last for a working life. This is now rarely the case. People can expect at least a couple of careers in their lifetime. Even within the same career, the demands change so much because of new technologies and ways of working that people inevitably need to keep learning. This presents an enormous challenge to society and individuals.

There are many people who believe that education should take advantage of new technologies to deliver better lessons, and at a time and a place suited to the consumer of the education. The dream is to have the best lecturers give their best lectures on video, which can be watched by students all over the country at a time and place of their choosing; for software to monitor and control totally individualised learning plans for all students; for really high quality resources to be available to all teachers to aid them in preparing the best possible lessons. This is 'wired up' education. The UK has gone a long way towards having the infrastructure in place to deliver this. All schools and colleges have some connection to the internet and the world wide web, and most have high-speed connections. The Grid, which is the backbone of the dream, is a reality. Not all students yet have personal, grid-based email addresses; but many have access to a virtual learning environment (VLE) which has potential for delivering some of the benefits of wired up education. There is no common experience as yet in very high quality educational experiences, but there is a clear trend to more and better use of ICT in the curriculum.

One of the more interesting parts of the debate about the future of education concerns the student as a consumer of education. In theory, the student will be able to pick and mix 'learning objects' or online blocks of learning to create a curriculum suited to their exact needs. Although more relevant to adult lifelong learners than school-age students, the model can be extended to that of the teacher having control over a variety of learning resources that are mixed and matched to create the perfect individualised learning plan. Typical resources of this sort are short online videos, short exercises, reading materials, quizzes and tests, access to specialised forums etc. as discussed in Chapter 1.1.

One of the great benefits of the internet is easy access to unlimited libraries of information. Teachers in primary schools can ask their students "Where is Timbuktu?" and be confident that some will be able to find out from the internet. A student doing a project on the Globe Theatre in London will find access to drawings, history, photographs and much more. Someone wanting to learn JavaScript has numerous courses immediately available. It is possible to discover material on almost any subject from your desktop.

There are drawbacks to the internet as a source of information however:

- Some students copy large chunks from the world wide web without quoting the source of their information. This opens them up to charges of plagiarism, which is one of the greatest academic sins. The universities see this as such a large problem that they have invested a great deal in devising programs that spot such copying.
- As it is so easy to publish on the internet, almost anyone literally can do it. Therefore it is as easy to publish inaccurate, biased or plain incorrect material on the web as it is to publish properly edited and refereed material. The reasons for doing this may be innocent, humorous or wicked, but either way the material is basically misinformation rather than information.
- Another growing problem is that many information providers are finding means of charging for their information that had previously been free. It is now commonplace to have to join a site, and pay a small fee, to be able to access information that may have been freely available in the past. Newspapers and magazines have started charging for access to many articles. Encyclopaedias often have extra paid-for content. A number of specialist forums, newsletters, intelligence analysts etc. now charge for information. This is a growing trend on the internet that is not likely to slow down, and thus it may become harder to gain access to reliable, free information.

Activity 7 Finding reliable, valid information

Study the hoax sites listed in the margin.

How can we assess that information found on the internet is probably real? What signs should make us distrust a site?

◀

Hoaxes on the internet

Look at these examples of <u>some famous hoax sites</u>.

The impact of ICT on education has other potential downsides that should be considered. There are so many potential educational media that it is difficult to ensure any form of standardised quality of experience for students. It is in many ways a pioneering age, with an enthusiasm for novelty and invention that has many positive aspects. At the same time it is not clear whether the claimed advantages of all the new technologies will be sustained. Already a number of highly-funded initiatives, especially in the field of distance learning, have been dropped or totally reorganised. Even where they prove themselves over the longer term, the cost advantages may not be sufficient to justify the changes that are now under way in the lifelong learning sector. As will be discussed in Chapter 1.4, the impact of ICT is potentially divisive, with better funded schools and training centres being able to afford all the best software and equipment, such as electronic whiteboards, while others cannot.

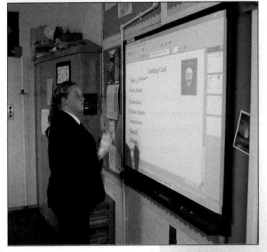

Figure 1.2.7 Some schools can afford the latest equipment

Entertainment and leisure

The impact of the convergence of digital technologies on entertainment and leisure has been enormous, and is still ongoing. Virtually every area of entertainment has been touched by digital technology, both in its production and distribution, and there is still further scope for change. As with other areas, digital technologies enable more personal creativity and choice, even to the point of overload. It is now simple, and relatively inexpensive, to produce creative works such as music, video, sound, radio, magazines, books and art digitally. These entertainment media are usually stored and transmitted digitally at both professional and amateur levels.

It has, for example, become a great deal easier to make and record music. Midi input devices, sequencers and sophisticated sound cards have made it possible to record and mix music successfully on a home computer. Software has made it possible to create sophisticated backing tracks by selecting a key signature and a musical style. Computerised drum machines take the hard work out of providing a solid rhythmic backing. Almost anyone with some patience can put together a convincing recording. Mistakes can be edited out in the same manner as typing mistakes are removed by a word-processing package. At the higher end of music production even out of tune voices can be 'corrected'. The impact of this can be seen in the growth of independent (indie) music. As with the internet itself, this has the effect of:

- providing fantastic variety and allowing new talent to publish
- allowing a great deal of mediocre work to be published
- creating a certain similarity in feel to a great deal of what is published.

DISCUSSION Access to original entertainment ◀

It has never been easier to publish original entertainment.
It has never been harder to see and hear original entertainment.

Consumers have experienced a boom in choice in entertainment as a result of the digital age. Films can be sent to a multitude of locations simultaneously in digital form and thus release dates can be brought forward; and DVD release and broadcast distribution can be brought closer to the original date, thus funding more movies and more choice. As with music, small independent production companies are able to produce TV and radio programmes. Simpler means of distribution allow broadcasting from almost anywhere in the world. All this broadens the choice for the consumer; although there are many people who feel it dilutes the quality. It is certainly true that there is so much new music, so many radio stations, so many TV stations and so many films available that an individual can feel overwhelmed by choice and not be able properly to take advantage of these sources – a phenomenon known as 'information overload'.

One of the more interesting means of dealing with the explosion of choice are services such as Sky+, which allows consumers to record TV onto hard disc. The simplicity and flexibility of the system allows people effectively to build up their own personal channel onto which they can record their favourite programmes, ignoring other possibilities. It is also possible, of course, to skip the advertisements that effectively fund many programmes at the moment. This may have a longer-term impact on the way in which we pay for TV.

Another massive impact of ICT on entertainment echoes that of communication. Entertainment is not restricted to the lounge or the theatre at set times, but is available anywhere and anytime. The iPod and the many MP3 players allow you to transport and listen to the equivalent of whole CD collections at near CD quality anywhere you roam. Portable media players allow you to record TV or DVDs and watch them anywhere. DVD recorders allow you to capture permanently movies and broadcast programmes in high quality and watch them anywhere and anytime a DVD player is available.

DISCUSSION Pirated entertainment ◀

- What is the advantage of paying a supplier such as Apple for a legal music download?
- What is the disadvantage of buying a pirate DVD from a market stall?
- What is the disadvantage of getting a pirate download of the latest Hollywood blockbuster before its UK release?
- What is the disadvantage to you of visiting an illicit music download site?
- Does widespread illicit downloading discourage the funding of new talent?

DISCUSSION Impact of games players

Perhaps one of the largest impacts of ICT on the personal lives of young people has been the explosive growth of home games players or 'play' stations. An article in *New Scientist* (23 October 2004, p.26) stated that $3.8 thousand million of games were sold in 1995, rising to $6 thousand million in 1998 and $7 thousand million by 2003. It estimated that 25 per cent of these games were violent.

- Why are computer games so popular?
- Do computer games make you more violent?
- Do computer games make you more isolated?
- Do networked computer games make you more or less social?

Figure 1.2.8 What is the impact of games players?

Decision making

The most obvious effect of the Information Age is the sheer amount of information and the sheer number of information sources available. As described above for entertainment, people are bombarded with data and choice in a way that they were not in the past. One impact of this is that people can feel stress and a sense of hopelessness as a result of this overload of information and choice, especially where the information is contradictory or inconclusive.

ACTIVITY 8 Making choices

Your grandmother wants a mobile phone. She does not have a price limit as such but wants to spend as little as possible.

Investigate the phones available and suggest one for her. Evaluate very carefully why she should buy the one you suggest. State any assumptions you make very clearly.

ACTIVITY 9 Managing information overload

Many ICT tools have been created to help in dealing with the information explosion. In what ways can the following help in decision-making:

- spreadsheets
- simulation software
- data mining tools
- exception reporting tools?

Banking and shopping

The Information Age has been subtly changing the way we conduct our lives as consumers. It enables consumers to carry out many transactions for themselves, for instance by shopping for most goods and the vast majority of services using the internet. The developed world is rapidly becoming a self-service economy.

Figure 1.2.9 Improvements in ICT make it possible for customers to scan their own purchases at the checkout

▶ Benefits of buying online

- **Lower prices**   Lower overheads (resulting from not having to support expensive storefront real estate and all the associated costs) have allowed web stores to charge less than their high-street equivalents. In the main, however, the early days of very low prices online are gone; although good deals can still be had, especially in areas where there is a good deal of competition, such as travel, books, CDs, DVDs etc.
- **Convenience**   Perhaps the most persuasive argument for online shopping is the convenience factor of researching through hundreds of outlets in a single session at the computer, of shopping when you want and without having to leave home. The goods are even delivered to the home without the fuss of having to queue, pay, stack them in the car, and unload them at home. Grocery stores such as Tesco, Sainsbury, Ocado/Waitrose and Asda clearly rely on this a great deal to fuel the growth of their internet businesses.
- **Choice**   The choice at any individual store is of necessity limited but there is a perception that choice on the web is limitless. Whether this is really the case is still open to question.

▶ Drawbacks of buying online

- **Delivery problems**   The delivery policies of many sites are often arranged for the convenience of the carrier to minimise costs rather than the consumer. It is quite common for delivery to be arranged so that the customer has to stay in all day waiting for the goods to turn up. The successful, large grocery stores arrange much smaller delivery 'windows', typically of between one and two hours. Other successful retailers rely on the package being small enough to use normal mail.
- **Hidden costs**   Another major drawback of web stores is that the prices are often quoted without postage and packing, or with a number of hidden extras that are only apparent immediately before the final payment is made.
- **Returns**   Perhaps one of the major problems for consumers is the difficulty of arranging returns on faulty or unfit goods. Even the better organised companies usually have a returns policy that involves phoning a call centre and obtaining a returns authorisation number (RAN), then having to repeat the waiting in for the carrier that was initially required when the item was delivered.
- **Security**   Some people have bought goods and services online, and never received them, or received them late and damaged. This includes major purchases such as cars where individuals have lost more than £20 000 in a single transaction. Other people have had their method of payment compromised and have had money taken out of their credit card or bank account without their knowledge.

▶ Online banking services

According to Forrester Research 60 million, or one in five, Europeans in the EU banked online in 2003 and that figure will rise to over 130 million by 2007. The rationale for this increase in online banking is the same as for online shopping. It is possible to bank 24 hours a day from the convenience of your own home, without having to queue or wait. Information on the state of your accounts is always available. A survey by Pew Internet and American Life Project, in November 2002 showed the top six reasons for banking online as:

- convenience
- saves time
- better control over finances
- privacy, and not having to talk to anybody
- more information available online than in a branch
- saves money
- more bank services available online.

(Source: eMarketeer.)

There are of course drawbacks with online banking, which are mainly to do with imagined and real security risks. So far most online banks have made these risks relatively low by giving 100 per cent guarantees against internet fraud, but the risks are still present. The other potential disadvantages are in the area of personal service. Internet banking does not allow the same degree of personal and individual assistance that a local branch can offer; although some people believe the banks could offer a great deal more than they do, given the efficiency savings they have made by going online. Although transactions can be specified by a customer 24 hours a day, 7 days a week, the actual transactions are only made during normal banking hours. Banks do not clear cheques and other incoming funds any more quickly either. Further research can be undertaken at Bankrate.com.

Crime and crime prevention

The police service has seen ICT as a major driving force to improve methods and efficiency. Numerous officers have been trained in the use of ICT at all levels in order to ensure the police service takes advantage of the benefits that can be gained from its use. ICT now affects the job of every police offer. Street officers can type up their reports more efficiently using word processing software and templates than when every report had to be laboriously typed. Clear, secure, digital radio systems are used to communicate between mobile officers and a computer-aided-despatch (CAD) room at base. At a national level, huge integrated crime databases are used to record crimes and attempt to find patterns in them; biometric databases are used to store fingerprints, handprints and DNA evidence; and sophisticated network and geographical analysis is used to try to analyse patterns in criminal behaviour. In addition to all of this, evidence gathering has improved through the use of digital video and CCTV as well as more sophisticated computerised forensic analysis.

At one level the benefits are really clear. It is possible for officers to work through their administrative duties much more quickly. The number and sophistication of the tools available to help track down criminals, and hopefully deter them, has increased enormously. Communication systems have greatly improved. Evidence collection, tracking, analysis and availability have improved dramatically. The amount of data available to help the police in their work and monitor how effective they are has grown in proportion to all of this.

On the other hand, many people believe that the police are now too driven by technology. They look back to the days of the 'bobby on the beat'; the local

High Technology Crimes

ICT has had a major impact on crime and crime prevention. The largest and most obvious impact is on the types of crime committed. Bank robbery is as likely to be committed by programmers as by armed robbers; safe cracking is becoming less common than electronic cracking; virus threats, hacking, and internet and email frauds are each a massive problem. The response to this is to have much more IT-aware detection forces. As with many other areas of our lives crime has also become more global and the crime prevention agencies have had in turn to try to respond on a global level.

Figure 1.2.10 Strathclyde Police's vulnerable persons database

PNC Police National Computer.
Genesis Good Practice
Database.
MEND Mobile Equipment
National Database.
SEND Stolen Equipment
National Database.
HOLMES 2 Home Office large
and major enquiry system for
sharing information on major
investigations such as the
'Yorkshire Ripper' or terrorist
investigations.
Assault Database.
National Injuries Database.
Mass Disasters Database.
Forensic Medicine Database.

Satellite tracking of offenders

"Satellite technology will be
used to track 5000 career
criminals who are responsible
for one in every 10 crimes in
Britain". A quote by the then
UK Home Secretary, David
Blunkett. (Source: Sophie
Goodchild and Andrew
Johnson, *The Independent*,
18 July 2004.)

police officer who knew what was happening in the local community. We now
have a mountain of data, but it is not easy to assess the impact all these major
initiatives have had on detecting and reducing crime overall.

Civil rights

One of the more contentious areas in the debate about the impact of ICT is that
of civil rights. The more data there is on people, and the more technology is
used to monitor and control people in order to keep society as a whole safe,
then the more likely it is that people's right to privacy and civil rights as a whole
may be compromised.

In the UK one particularly sensitive area of debate in this arena is that of
compulsory ID cards. One aspect that makes these so controversial is that they
will be linked to a national database that will be capable of storing a good deal
of information about each individual, and of being linked through keys such as
the national insurance number, driver's licence number, NHS number etc. to a
number of other key databases which put together will give access to an
unprecedented amount of information about an individual. The proposed ID
register (or database) is intended to be the foundation of identity management
in the UK in the coming years. The card would have a biometric signature, i.e. a
digital version of a thumbprint, retinal print or some other unique characteristic,
or some combination of these. This would help to prevent fraud, protecting the
owner of the card, but would allow police and other officials to identify an
individual uniquely and then potentially have access to a fantastic amount of
information about that person.

A number of civil rights groups have protested that the scheme is anti-
libertarian. For example, Privacy International described the scheme as "draconian
and dangerous" as it gives so many government agencies such wide-ranging
powers against individuals (source: a UK ID cards blog by Trevor Mendham).

Figure 1.2.11 The website of the NO2ID campaign

ACTIVITY 10 Investigate the pros and cons of ID cards

Using the internet research exactly what is being proposed by the UK
Government and what the objections are.

Write a list of all the ICT that is involved in the UK's proposed card scheme.
State what the purpose of the ID card is meant to be.
Evaluate whether it will meet this purpose.
Enumerate the advantages of such a system and the drawbacks.
Make your personal recommendation as to whether we should have ID cards.

DISCUSSION US Passports and RFID ◄

The US Department of Homeland Security has decided that 1 million US passports will contain radio frequency ID chips in 2005, moving to a universal system from 2006. These RFID tags will allow customs officials to scan passports using special radio receivers. They will not have to approach the travellers directly but can scan them from nearby. The passports will contain biometric and other information. (Source: 'We don't need to see your ID', *New Scientist*, 23 October 2004.)

It will be faster and more convenient for customs but what are the dangers?

DISCUSSION Teen Arrive Alive GPS tracking system ◄

"Teen Arrive Alive is a private company founded specifically to provide support to parents who are concerned about the driving safety of their teenagers. Our goal is to bring the teen problem to the forefront, assist in critical education, and recognize the positive driving behaviors of our nation's teens." (Source: Teen Arrive Alive.)

The company claims that nearly 78 per cent of teenagers in the US are ticketed or crash by the time they are 18. Among other services, the Teen Arrive Alive organisation offers GPS tracking of teenagers to parents who may be worried that their child is late, missing, lost, abducted or not driving very well. Using a cell phone and GPS technology, parents can track their teenager's driving in real time. The route shows up on a digital map showing the speed travelled.

Research the website and discuss the benefits and drawbacks of this use of technology to 'protect' teenagers.

Figure 1.2.12 Tracking individuals through their mobile phone

CASE STUDY Monitoring internet and email use ◄

A large estate agency with multiple branches monitors all network activity by its staff (including each internet access and each email) using content monitoring software.

Website access is strictly controlled and monitored. The amount of time accessing different categories of websites is logged. Each month a report is sent to the line manager of each employee so that any undue time spent on the internet or any part of the web can be immediately seen and discussed with the employee. Sites deemed unsuitable can be blocked and reported immediately by email for immediate action.

Emails are scanned for inappropriate usage. Pornographic and defamatory content is blocked by recognition of particular keywords and reported. Keywords such as 'salary', 'cv', 'job', 'employment' and other details related to the possibility of moving to new employment are also scanned for. Emails containing these words are parked in a special area where the network manager can read them. He decides if they are harmless, and thus sends them on, or whether the employee should be reported.

Task

- Describe the advantages the content monitoring system has for an organisation such as this estate agency.
- Describe the negative impacts it might have for the organisation.
- Describe the advantages it has for employees.
- Analyse the problems this system might have for an employee who only uses the system for business purposes.
- Make recommendations about the use of this system.

DISCUSSION Society and the individual ◀

George Orwell wrote about how technology could be used to control us in his famous vision of a totalitarian future, *1984*, published in 1948 (see comments and E-book at this website).

Review some of the comments on the US's response to homeland security at the following websites:

The Whitehouse
Robert Gladd
Human Rights First

To what extent should we allow society to 'look after' us and as a result, deprive us of individual freedom?

Legislation and ICT

The Information Age has brought with it the need for its own set of laws to regulate, monitor and control the way in which we conduct our personal, social and working lives when using ICT. In the UK these include:

- Health and Safety at Work Act (1974), as amended
- Health and Safety (Display Screen Equipment) Regulations (1992)
- Data Protection Act (1984), as amended
- Copyright, Designs and Patents Act (1988)
- Computer Misuse Act (1990)
- Regulation of Investigatory Powers Act (2000)
- Freedom of Information Act (2005)

ACTIVITY 11 Investigate ICT legislation ◀

In a small group, divide these Acts between you so that each individual has about the same workload. For their Act(s) each person should investigate the Act and create a three-page presentation on it covering:

- the main provisions of the Act as related to ICT
- the main benefits of the Act for individuals and groups in the Information Age
- the main disadvantages of the Act for individuals and groups in the Information Age.

Continued on next page

Each member must send the other members their presentation.

It is essential that each presentation should use at least two sources of information and that each source be noted in full. Care should be taken that the information is UK based and up to date. See Chapter 2.7 for information on the Data Protection Act and Computer Misuse Act.

Conclusion ▶ ▶ ▶

The impact of the Information Age on the way we conduct our personal, social and working lives has been, and continues to be, enormous. There are a number of consistent themes running through this topic however. We are able to do more for ourselves; we are able to have, or are forced to have, more flexibility and choice. We can work, learn or play, be alone or socialise in more places then ever, with more choice than ever, at more times than ever. We have a mass of data to deal with in all areas of our lives. New tools, new industries and new laws have grown up to manage this information explosion. You will have to decide what the balance is in each case between the benefits and the drawbacks that these changes in our lives have brought.

The digital divide

ICT has transformed the way many of us live. It has brought enormous educational, social, cultural and indeed economic benefits to those with access to it. The Information Age has, however, touched us unequally. It will be apparent that in some parts of the world it has had almost no impact for a variety of physical, social, political and economic reasons. In Africa it is estimated that in July 2005 less than 1.8 per cent of the population used the internet in contrast to over 68 per cent in North America (source: Internet World Stats). The United Nations has, as part of its landmark document *The Millennium Declaration*, committed member nations to "ensure that the benefits of new technologies, especially information and communication technologies, are available to all" (source: CNET). In this chapter we will examine the factors creating the divide, and the impact the divide has on individuals and societies. We will investigate the extent of the divide and review critically the many measures being taken to eradicate or reduce it.

Factors creating the divide

Figure 1.3.1 To what extent would these villagers need or want digital technology?

Economic prosperity plays a large role in determining the prevalence of modern technologies in society. A subsistence economy will be more concerned with basic survival than ICT. A prosperous developed economy can both afford to devote energy and resources to fund the research and development needed to create digital technologies, and has the affluent consumers to purchase the technologies created. In the developed world the primary motive for the use of ICT is economic. It is usually seen as more productive to automate a process by using ICT than hire expensive staff. This factor is often reversed in developing nations. Computers are really expensive and labour is cheap. A computer in West Africa might cost six years' salary. Furthermore, even if the computer was affordable, the resulting unemployment might not be.

Economic prosperity also has an underlying effect on a number of factors that increase the divide. A poor economy often has a poor technological infrastructure, which makes it harder to put in place the digital technologies that would improve its situation. People existing at a subsistence level have no motivation to learn the skills necessary to use ICT. Rich nations can bridge physical obstacles, and for example take electricity across mountains and ravines, whereas this may be low priority for poorer nations. Mr Magga, member of the reindeer-herding people of northern Europe, speaking at the World Summit on the Information Society (discussed later) said:

"People are sick, starving, they are fighting day to day to survive. That is the situation in many indigenous communities … It's not a question of whether we use a computer or not, because there are no computers. It is not a question of seeing a television, because there isn't one. Now we are knocking at the door of the information society and the question is, will we get in." (Source: World Summit on the Information Society.)

Economic factors alone do not determine the extent of the digital divide. A very large factor in the take up of ICT in less developed nations is the state of the technological infrastructure. If there is not a stable electricity supply it is not easy to use the digital technologies that are so reliant on it. Africa Renewal, a UN publication, states that in no African country outside Egypt and South Africa does more than 20 per cent of the population have direct access to electricity, and that only 2 per cent of Africa's rural population have access to mains electricity. Even large companies in large cities are regularly subject to black outs. A similar story is revealed when looking at the global statistics for fixed line telephone systems (see Table 1.3.1).

	Population	Main telephone lines		Mobile subscribers		Internet users	
	000s	000s	%	000s	%	000s	%
North Africa	147 495	14 151	9.6	16 455	11.2	4 890	3.3
South Africa	46 365	4 800	10.4	16 860	36.4	3 300	7.1
Sub-Saharan Africa	647 686	6 230	1	18 363	2.8	5 667	0.9
Africa	**841 546**	**25 181**	**3**	**51 678**	**6.1**	**13 857**	**1.6**

Table 1.3.1 ITU statistics on infrastructure (A country by country breakdown of this table can be found at the International Telecommunication Union website)

"Fewer than three people in 10 even has a telephone line, much less access to and interest in the internet. Forecasts suggest that five in 10 people will have telephones by 2012, but other newly developed countries such as Korea and Singapore already have teledensities in excess of 100 percent". (Source: Burkhart, Grey E. and Older, Susan The Information Revolution in the Middle East And North Africa for Rand, page xiv.)

Teledensity Literally the number of telephones as a proportion of the population. It is often used in the development and aid industry as a measure of a country's ICT infrastructure.

The comments in this document are confirmed in the opening remarks made by Yoshio Utsumi, Secretary-General of the International Telecommunication Union at an ITU workshop on 'Building Digital Bridges' held in Korea in September 2004. He stated that while:

"Some economies in the Asia–Pacific region have more mobile phones than citizens, in other parts of the region, fewer than one in every twenty citizens have access to information and communication technologies. In the Republic of Korea, as many as 80 per cent of households have broadband internet access. But across the region as a whole, around three out of every four families have no internet access at all."

 In this video, teenagers in Bombay discuss what ICT they use, how this has developed and how it is different elsewhere in India.

Figure 1.3.2 The use of ICT in India is varied

Sometimes the problem is that there is a lack of a joined up approach to digital development. A ministry will follow one approach, a UK charity will pursue a different option, while a French charity funds a third way. The end result is a lack of sustainable development. This may be a result of the disparate interests of the funding providers, but is also normally heavily tied to the notion of differing digital standards. Even in ICT within the developed world where there are numerous standardising bodies (e.g. IEEE, ITU, ISO, W3C etc.), open standards are hard to embed and maintain against commercial pressures. In the under-served nations this is a chronic problem. Even the electricity supply, which is taken for granted in the West, may not be standard across a developing nation, which may have several different voltages, frequencies and plug types. Telecommunications and computer standards are even less embedded; and this has an impact on interoperability, on transferable skills and on training.

Politico-social factors often co-exist with the technological. The state is often the main or only telecommunications provider, and it is noticeable in many of these ITU case studies that it charges monopoly prices for its services, and will prevent other organisations providing competitive services. Other political factors also have a part to play. Wars in places such as Laos and Cambodia, North and Sub-Saharan Africa and the Middle East have had a negative effect on the technological infrastructure and have adversely affected the economies and motivations of these peoples. The current 'impoverished' state of an economic area may benefit some individual inhabitants. If these individuals have the power as well as the vested interest to keep the situation this way, bringing in new technologies with the potential to transform lives may not be very easy. This can apply equally to a millionaire politician overseeing a whole state, a city warlord, a tribal chief in an isolated community, or a man in a society where his wife has fewer rights than his male child.

Another compelling factor behind the digital divide is geographical, although as always this is related to the other factors. Mountainous countries such as Nepal, desert areas such as North Africa, and rainforest regions such as Central Africa, South America and South East Asia all present special problems for the uptake of digital technologies, on top of the fact that most of these areas are already poor. In these regions even the simplest physical infrastructures such as roads and bridges may be missing for at least some part of the year. There will usually be little in the way of reliable fixed communications systems and the social organisation may also be less centralised.

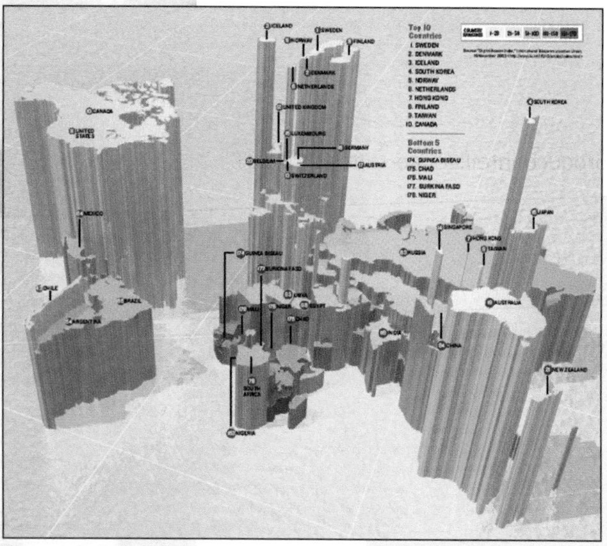

Figure 1.3.3 ITU internet coverage map (Source: IEEE Spectrum online; data originally from Digital Access Index, ITU)

ACTIVITY 1 What leads to being on the wrong side of the divide?

The least digitally-developed countries according to the ITU are Guinea Biseau, Chad, Mali, Burkino Fasso, and Niger.

Using an atlas plus information from the ITU, Spectrum Online the World Bank and CIA Factbook, write down some reasons why they might be on the wrong side of the digital divide.

ACTIVITY 2 Data response ◀

Read the article 'Women and information technology in Sub-Saharan Africa' by
Dr Mayuri Odedra-Straub.
  In the section, *Current status of information technology in Sub-Saharan Africa*:

- Dr Odedra cites a number of infrastructural reasons for the lack of effective ICT. What are these?
- What is identified as the most pressing need for Africa (in terms of ICT)?
- How successful have computer-aid projects been?
- Why have they failed?
- What computer skills are identified as lacking?
- What lack of business skills are identified as a major problem?

Sources on the digital divide

There are numerous statistical sources detailing the differences between the developed and developing nations:

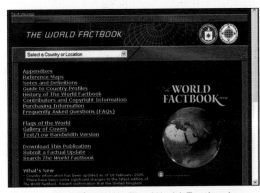

Figure 1.3.4 The CIA's The World Factbook

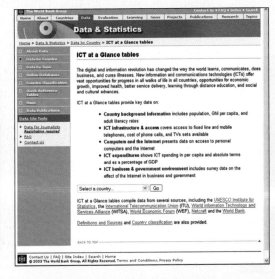

Figure 1.3.5 The World Bank keeps copious statistics on the state of the world's economies

- The CIA World Factbook provides a snapshot of the world as seen by the USA. The communications section gives a good snapshot of the state of the digital economy.
- The World Bank produces world development indicators, including detailed statistics on ICT usage.
- The International Telecommunications Union produces reports on the market penetration of telecommunications, a major indicator of ICT penetration in world economies.
- Global commercial firms such as Nielsen/NetRatings and Rand produce intelligence reports on ICT in world economies.
- Spectrum Online has a very good analysis of the digital divide.

ACTIVITY 3 Investigate the impact of access to telecoms ◀

Using the CIA World Factbook as your main source, compare the telecoms sectors of the Central African Republic, Costa Rica, Singapore, the UK and one other under-served country of your choice. Create a table for your findings with the headings shown:

Continued on next page

Population	Telephones – land lines	Mobile/ cellular	Telephone system	Radio broadcast stations	Country code	Internet hosts	Internet users

Use this to draw some statistical conclusions about the gap between the 'haves' and 'have-nots'. State any assumptions you have made and any reservations you have.

Economic and social impacts of the divide

A question you need to ask is what difference does a global divide in terms of access to ICT make? There are some that argue that it is a fact of economic life that there are some 'haves' and some 'have-nots', and that market forces will dictate the balance between these. On the other hand there are those that feel that the digital divide is a massive problem for the economic, political and social destiny of the whole world, both rich and poor.

Former US President Bill Clinton, at the Progressive Governance for the 21st Century conference held in Florence on 21 November 1999, argued that the internet is the key to wealth in the world. He said that reducing the digital divide is essential in order to promote growth in the world economy and fight poverty; that the digital divide is one of the largest problems facing the developed economies. He told delegates:

Figure 1.3.6 Kofi Annan, seventh Secretary-General of the United Nations

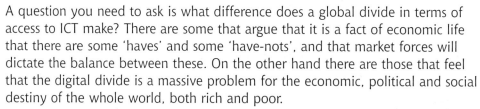

"I think we should shoot for a goal within the developed countries of having internet access as complete as telephone access within a fixed number of years ... It will do as much as anything else to reduce income inequality ..." (Source: <u>BBC News, 21 November 1999</u>.)

Meanwhile, Kofi Annan, Secretary-General of the United Nations, has said:

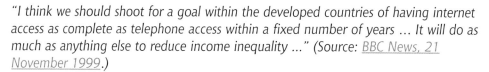

"Information technology ... is a powerful force that can and must be harnessed to our global mission of peace and development. This is a matter of both ethics and economics; over the long term, the new economy can only be productive and sustainable if it spreads worldwide and responds to the needs and demands of all people. I urge everyone in a position to make a difference to add his or her energies to this effort." (Source: '<u>Challenges and Partnerships, A contribution by the Information and Communication Technologies Task Force</u>' to the World Summit on the Information Society.)

The Digital Opportunities Task Force, a global body set up to consider concrete measures to bridge the digital divide, is quoted in the same document from a presentation to the G8 leaders as saying that "Access to knowledge and information is a prerequisite for modern human development".

The United Nations believes the issue is so critical to world development that attempting to eradicate the digital divide is fundamental to many UN programmes. Kofi Annan also said in November 2002 that:

"The new information and communications technologies are among the driving forces of globalization. They are bringing people together, and bringing decision makers unprecedented new tools for development. At the same time, however, the gap between information 'haves' and 'have-nots' is widening, and there is a real danger that the world's poor will be excluded from the emerging knowledge-based global economy."(Source: CNET.)

Dr Odedra, in her article, discussed earlier, says that information is one of the major determinants of economic and social development, and that one of the major reasons for Africa's underdevelopment is the inadequate use of data. However, you should notice she also concludes that merely providing ICT without changing the underlying skills, knowledge and social circumstances of the population may have a negative effect on the situation, rather than improve it. This argument echoes the general argument about aid – that providing short-term relief for obvious gaps merely makes a people dependent rather than allowing them to grow and flourish.

DISCUSSION Reducing the divide ◄

- What advantages are there for the developed world in bridging the global digital divide?
- What advantages are there for the poorest nations?
- Was President Clinton correct in saying that matching internet access levels with telephone levels will do as much as anything to reduce income equality?
- Do charities such as Computer Aid do more good than harm?

How great is the divide and is this changing?

An examination of the world internet usage statistics in Figure 1.3.7 shows clearly the divide in internet usage between North America, Europe and Oceania and the rest of the world, most starkly Africa. George Sciadas, a researcher who helped launch The Global Information Technology Report at the UN-sponsored World Summit on the Information Society in Geneva, in December 2003, said that "the digital divide is massive" and added that the divide "is closing at a hugely slow pace which will take generations." (Source: World Summit on the Information Society.)

Undoubtedly the digital divide is not static. Differences between some countries shrink and others grow over time. The different bases from which countries start also inevitably affect any measurements made. The difficulty in measuring anything absolutely means that it is very hard to make very definite claims about whether the gap is shrinking or widening

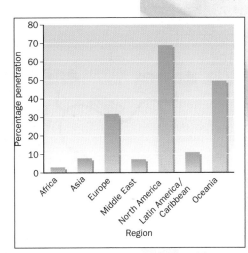

Figure 1.3.7 Internet usage by world region (source: Internet World Stats)

overall. George Sciadas (see earlier), has provided a significant and detailed statistical analysis of the rate and types of change, in which he establishes the extent of the digital divide has moved over time. He suggests that progress has been made everywhere to some extent. Some countries such as Botswana, Argentina, Samoa, Mauritius, Kyrgyzstan, Jordan, Moldova, Malaysia, Croatia and Poland have progressed a great deal. Others such as Djibouti, the Central African Republic, Qatar and Costa Rica have progressed slowly in spite of being at a very low base to start with, and South Africa has progressed slowly from a higher base. (Source: George Sciadas (ed.) _Monitoring the digital divide and beyond_, Orbicom 2003.) Some of the difficulty in assessing changes in the divide is illustrated by the fact that Costa Rica has been praised by Kofi Annan as for its great success with its IT development strategies (source: CNET). This would seem to be contrary to the Sciadas report.

ACTIVITY 4 Investigate changes in access ◀

The ITU has also created an index to measure and monitor access to digital technologies over time.

Pick two case studies from its list of countries and create a short presentation on how these countries' access to digital technologies has changed over time.

Tackling the divide on the ground

ICT is capable of being very empowering. Unlike steel or car manufacturing, for example, ICT can be extremely cost-effective. Targeting investment in basic education and access to ICT can yield disproportionately great returns. Putting a community IT centre or IT kiosk in a central point in a village community, and teaching villagers how to use the facilities can give masses of people access to information and communications through the internet and mobile telephony that can transform lives. Information kiosks, cybercafés and community telecentres are now commonplace in places as diverse as Egypt, Kazakhstan and Peru. In Bolivia, internet centres are used to provide rural workers with up-to-date information on crops, markets, and policies and regulations that might affect them. (Source: Challenges and Partnerships, A contribution by the Information and Communication Technologies Task Force.)

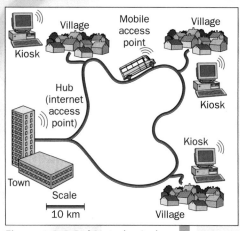

Figure 1.3.8 DakNet physical and wireless network

CASE STUDY DakNet in India and Cambodia ◀

The DakNet solution is an interesting example of the ingenious solutions that are proposed to infrastructure problems, in this case, lack of internet access. With this system, a bus, car, motorcycle or, even in one case, an ox cart is driven round a fixed route once a day, collecting and transmitting wirelessly to villages on a set path (see Figs 1.3.8 and 1.3.9). The vehicle carries a mobile access point – a PC, a wifi-transceiver and a battery-powered UPS. When the vehicle arrives within range of a village information kiosk it transmits and receives data point to point at a bandwidth of up to 11 Mbytes per second, uploading and downloading to and from the internet. Although this is not a real-time (i.e. 'when you

Continued on next page

want') access solution, it allows data to be transmitted in a way that ordinary modems could not achieve because they require a permanent power source and phone line connection.

Thanks to this ingenious system, remote villages now have access to email, messaging, bulletin boards, video and audio broadcasts, information collection, and more. People in remote locations can now access digital solutions to some of their problems, and do so affordably. In India, for example, there is evidence of villagers saving money and time in running aspects of their lives. Meanwhile in Cambodia some school students have been able to access internet services for the first time and as a result feel more connected to the rest of society. (Source: 'DakNet: Rethinking connectivity in developing nations', IEEE Computer Society.)

Figure 1.3.9 DakNet uses locally available transport to carry mobile access points

▶ Broadcasting

Digital broadcasting is a good example both of an empowering technology and of the political barriers that sometimes may stall the elimination of the digital divide. Satellite broadcasting allows geographically remote areas to receive news and information in a manner that was previously unavailable or difficult to achieve. Villagers in rural Asia who had to rely on low-quality terrestrial broadcasts provided on often unreliable equipment now have access to high-quality images and sound and, even more importantly, to a range that was previously unimaginable. This provides educational, entertainment and informative benefits for the populations of otherwise remote places. Simple wireless base stations can make access to previously inaccessible terrain relatively simple and inexpensive. Mountains, jungle, rivers and densely populated cities are all traversed better with wireless technology than with expensive cable.

In some states however, such as some in the Middle East and North Africa, digital TV is regarded as a major problem. Access to Western values and norms is not universally regarded as a good thing, and is even seen as corrupting in some particularly religious areas. At one extreme some countries have banned the reception of Western channels, and at the other, virtually all digital technologies have been banned. In the Muslim world, television stations such as Al Jazeera have grown up to provide an authentic local voice on world affairs. Community radio stations in Africa have been used to provide health warnings, agricultural information, weather disaster warnings and to disseminate vital information about HIV.

▶ Mobile phones

The quality of life in rural Pakistan and Bangladesh has been improved by the use of cellular phones, which allow people to stay in touch in remote locations. Indeed the introduction of mobile phones has been so successful in Pakistan that in April 2004 oneworld.net reported:

"Mobile phone-users in Pakistan will double next year (to more than 7m), outnumbering fixed-line customers for the first time and marking a new era of communications in the poverty-stricken nation"

- Why is wireless technology successful as a solution to the digital divide?
- Which of the problems that cause the digital divide does it overcome?
- Does the growth in available wireless technology have clear social, economic, educational and cultural benefits for the society involved?

▶ Governance

Low-technology, or simple high-technology, solutions are not the only answer to what is a much larger problem, however. A major challenge often comes in the form of the governments of the under-served nations. For example, the state is often the main or only telecommunications provider, charges monopoly prices for its services, and prevents other organisations providing competitive services. There are sometimes high tariffs on importing high technology or other trade barriers, and sometimes a massive amount of red tape or regulation that has to be overcome. In all these cases a government strategy is clearly needed to deal with the problem, often this is in association with the United Nations. Successful strategies of this kind have been adopted in Afghanistan and the United Arab Emirates, among other states. In UAE, the Dubai Internet City has been set up to act as a free-trade zone to encourage ICT investment throughout the Middle East, Asia and Africa, using Dubai as a hub.

CASE STUDY Laos ◀

Figure 1.3.10 Laos, a country at the wrong end of the divide

The yearly income in Laos is equivalent to about $1 900 per capita (2004 estimate). There are no credit-card facilities offered by Laotian banks. Literacy is low at 47 per cent. Therefore it cannot be assumed that access to a largely English-language web will be a high priority for the majority of the population. Indeed, text-based messaging is the most popular ICT application at the moment. Laos language support (Lao has its own alphabet) is available for Windows and Mac users, but there are few manuals or help applications written in the language.

There are thought to be less than 15 000 computers in Laos. The costs of PCs and the internet are too high for the average Laotian. A working, if somewhat obsolete PC, would cost about $200, so computer use is restricted mainly to the wealthy. Just over 1 per cent of the population has a fixed telephone line, perhaps amounting to about 4 per cent of households. The cost of installing a phone line is approximately $40; the monthly line cost plus 100 minutes of calls are around a further $30 per month. Electricity is only available in a few urban areas.

All of these factors, as in so many under-served nations, are a massive obstacle to bridging the digital divide. Only just over one-third of the population are in areas reached by the telephone network. There were about as many mobile phones as fixed lines in Laos in 2002. There has been massive growth in mobiles in recent times, but the mobile signal only reaches urban areas, and so covers about 10 per cent of the population. The main means of access to the Information Age is through internet cafes that were

Continued on next page

originally set up for foreign tourists, but where locals now constitute the main driver of the demand.

The main obstacles to progress in reducing the digital divide in Laos have been identified as:

- the mountainous geography
- the weather with its monsoon rains
- a frustrating lack of coordination among government agencies
- the lack of IT standards to allow integration between systems
- a lack of IT knowledge at policy and skills levels
- a poor power and telecommunications infrastructure
- a poor ISP service
- the high relative costs of ICT
- the lack of Laotian language support, especially for training materials.

Nevertheless, some ingenious solutions are being found. Here are some of them.

Solution 1: Cantennae

Although commercial solutions are subject to theft, vandalism and weather-related failure, low-tech solutions based on DIY 'cantennae' have been very successful as phone base stations, wireless local area networks etc. (see Fig. 1.3.11). Factory manufactured versions of these are available in the UK to boost wireless reception.

Figure 1.3.11 This mobile antenna 'cantennae' is made from a discarded can

Solution 2: Pedal powered wireless computer in Phon Kham

Phon Kham is a poor village in Laos, one of the poorest countries on Earth. All 200 villagers live in bamboo houses and walk dirt roads that are only passable before the monsoon. There is no electricity and no telephone system, and yet they have computers with internet access thanks to some ingenious thinking and pedal power.

A generator, powered by pedalling a bike, charges a battery that runs a small 486-type computer designed to run on only 12 watts. "It has no moving parts, the lid seals up tight, and you can dunk it in water and it will still run." says Lee Felsenstein, the inventor. "The idea is to be rugged, last at least 10 years and run in both the monsoon season and the dry season." Wireless PC cards connect each PC to a hilltop relay station connected to a computer in town, which in turn is connected to the Laos phone system and the internet. The total cost of the network is thought to be about $19 000 and it will cost about $21 per month to run.

The main impacts of the system on the locals are not to do with chat or playing games, but are founded on a solid economic basis. Villagers wanted the system to find information to help them, and in particular the price that commodities were being sold at in Phon Hong, the local market town and in Vientiane, the capital. With this information they can make informed decisions about where and whether to travel, for commercial or any other purposes – a serious decision when talking of distances greater than 30 km through dry and barren terrain in the dry season, and near impassable in the wet season.

Sources

Jhai Foundation
San Francisco Chronicle

The Economist
Max PC

Figure 1.3.12 Jhai Foundation website

Solution 3: The Jhai Foundation PC and communication and internet learning centres

The Jhai Foundation (an American–Lao non-profit organisation whose aim is to help empower the next generation of Laos) has funded a number of community IT projects including internet learning centres in schools. These have rapidly become self-sustaining hubs for community learning. Although based in schools, they teach adults as well as children. The main reason for their success is that members of the community feel they own the centres.

Tasks

Summarize the case study into a short presentation answering the following questions:

- What is the extent of the digital divide in Laos?
- What problems have caused the divide?
- What is the impact of the divide on Laos?
- What solutions have been provided so far?
- What do you think the educational, social, economic and cultural impacts of these solutions are?

You could try to find further information about Laos on the internet to help you with your answers. The background material for this study is derived from the CIA website and from the UN Task Force paper 'Low cost access and connectivity – Local solutions' by Vorasone Dengkayaphichith, pp. 58–74.

ACTIVITY 5 Email in the Solomons ◀

Study the news report on the creation of an internet link for the Solomon Islands on the BBC website alongside the World Bank data on the islands. Try to identify the extent of the digital divide, the problems that caused the divide, the impact of the divide and the solutions provided so far. Propose at least one further initiative that would be useful to the islanders in reducing the digital divide.

Figure 1.3.13 Email stations like this are being introduced in the Solomon Islands

Further sources

Article by Michael J. Field
UNESCO Bangkok

Tackling the divide: political initiatives

There have been numerous political initiatives intended to find ways of reducing the digital divide. The United Nations has organised two summits as part of its global plan. The first of these, The World Summit on the Information Society in December 2003, was considered a mixed success. Delegates did endorse what some have called the first constitution for the Information Age. This amounts to a statement of principles and an action plan intended to ensure that more than half of the world has access to some form of electronic media by 2015. On the other side, however, many people argued that words do not change things, and that it is money and resources that are really needed. Some also argued that debate and policy making on the digital divide were undermined by discussions on political issues.

Figure 1.3.14 Logo from the World Summit

ACTIVITY 6 What did the World Summit achieve? ◀

Study these reports on the World Summit:
The Guardian/Associated Press
BBC News
Daily report from the Summit

- State the main aim of the summit.
- List three positive points that have come out of the summit.
- List three negative points that have come out of the summit.
- Write a short conclusion stating whether you feel it was successful, or not.

Conclusion ▶ ▶ ▶

There a clear digital divide between the developed and developing countries. It has been said by many world leaders that bridging this divide is one of the essential steps towards the abolition of world poverty, and would be the precursor of a great economic age. There is clearly some truth in this proposition but it should be treated with caution. For example, remember that half of the world's population has never even made a telephone call. 70 per cent of the world's poor live in remote, rural areas with almost no telecoms links to the outside world. There have been some innovative technical and political solutions to the problems causing, and caused by, the divide, but we are at the start of a very long process which is as much a socio-economic and political one as a technical one.

The digital divide is not simply a global phenomenon. It also has enormous local relevance in the developed nations as a whole, and in the UK in particular. In many less-developed parts of the world there may even be little or no electricity supply to sustain the infrastructure for ICT. But even in the most affluent areas of the most developed nations, there are still many people who do not have meaningful access to the benefits of digital technologies, even though they have electricity.

Western governments have identified this as a major problem and have set up multiple initiatives to deal with the situation. In the USA as early as 1995, this was identified as a serious issue in the first of a series of surveys by the Department of Commerce entitled 'Falling through the net'. Similarly in the UK, national and local government have identified the problem of a digital divide and put in place many measures to attempt to bridge this. Victor Keegan, in _The Guardian_ (24 April 2003) stated that:

Figure 1.4.1 "We've got a mouse now, but how do we connect it?"

"While only 20 per cent of people in the rich social class AB are webless, 68 of DEs are unconnected – three percentage points higher than last year. We have become too blasé about web access. We moan about email spam, information overload and the quality of data that search engines throw up. We hardly think about the huge advantages it gives us compared with those deprived of it altogether."

Although the problems of the digital divide are different from those of the places, such as Laos, discussed in the previous chapter, they are still fundamental. The digital divide potentially has the same detrimental impact on economic equality, social mobility, and economic growth.

At the same time, you need to be aware of arguments against the notion of the 'digital divide'. For example, in January 2000, Steve Cisler, in an article subtitled 'Subtract the digital divide' in the _San Jose Mercury News_, argued that "The term is simplistic and insulting in framing the debate over computer connectivity." He discusses how the term arose and how it has changed to that of the gulf between the online haves and have-nots, and is used essentially as a shorthand to attract funding for a project rather than being a helpful and meaningful phrase. He quotes Mario Morino of the Morino Institute: "The digital divide is a manifestation of economic and educational gaps that have existed in this country long before the microchip and the internet were invented." Steve Cisler argues that "Digital divide is a term as demeaning as one from a past era, 'They live on the wrong side of the tracks'."

> **Social class** Modern definitions of social class used by market researchers and government statisticians are usually based on occupation. Under this definition classes A, B and C1 are regarded as upper to lower middle class, and C2, D and E as lower middle to working class. See Chapter 3.3 for more discussion of this topic.

ACTIVITY 1 What is the impact of internet access for the homeless?

- Write down five ways in which access to the internet could change the life of a homeless person for the better.

Continued on next page

- Write down the impact that not having access to the internet has on that person.
- Write down five things that are more important to that person than the internet.

Dimensions of the divide

Whatever term you use, a number of studies have shown that there is a clear divide between socio-economic classes when we are talking about access to technology. As seen above, the AB income group enjoy more than twice the internet access as the DE group. More people are online who are in work than unemployed. A Department for Education and Skills report in 2000 showed that 71 per cent of working people have used a computer, but only 32 per cent of those not working have done so; 52 per cent of working people had a computer at home – but for those not working the figure goes down to 23 per cent. (Source: 'End the digital divide', 31 January 2000.)

More owner-occupiers are online than people who rent their homes; only 4 per cent of council tenants are online, whereas 22 per cent of residents in high-income areas are (source: 'ICT access and use: Report on the benchmark survey' by Neil Russell and Nick Drew (Research Surveys of Great Britain), Research brief 252, 2001).

There is also a gulf between the sexes. More men than women and more boys than girls are online. Educational computing is often seen as a male activity. The National Curriculum has ensured that all young people have access to computers but even so numerous studies show boys take the most interest in computers and computing subjects. This is most stark in post-compulsory education where girls are vastly under-represented.

ACTIVITY 2 Who studies computing subjects? ◀

What is the situation where you are studying? How many girls and how many boys study computing subjects post-16?

If there is a significant difference between the two then investigate why this is the case. What impact do you think it has on girls and on society as a whole?

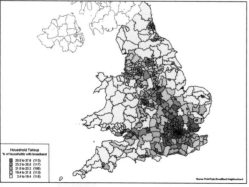

Figure 1.4.2 Broadband take up in England and Wales (source 'Mapping the digital divide', Point Topic, 2005)

There is also a distinct geographical divide. ONS statistics (December 2001) revealed that levels of internet access vary enormously within the UK, the average being 37 per cent for the year ending September 2001. Connectivity in London and the South East was 45 per cent. In Northern Ireland and the North East only 26 per cent of households had internet access. Rural areas were particularly poorly served, often having a poor infrastructure and low access rates. Broadband access is likewise often restricted to places of reasonably dense population.

There has been some progress since this benchmark survey in bridging the divide as is shown in the article 'Mapping the digital divide' in Point Topic's guide to the issues surrounding broadband and the 2005 election. This same article does still reveal great disparities in the availability and take up of broadband between rural and prosperous urban areas (see Fig. 1.4.2).

Then there is the disability divide. Computer use is lower amongst the disabled ('ICT access and use: Report on the benchmark survey' by Neil Russell and Nick Drew (Research Surveys of Great Britain), Research brief 252, 2001). Web designers have often failed disabled people, though there is now a strong movement to providing accessible web sites.

Finally there is a clear age divide. Over 65s now constitute over 20 per cent of the population in the UK, but they are the least likely to have digital TV or connections to the internet.

Some analysts, however, see all of this as irrelevant. In an article in _Business Week Online_, 19 August 2003, entitled 'The digital divide that wasn't' it is argued that while there is a gap, research shows it is reducing, "and that no problem serious enough to earn the scary label 'digital divide' really exists". It argues that there are now more women than men using the internet in the US and that ethnic minorities will soon "match their representation in the broader population, according to Nielsen Net Ratings."

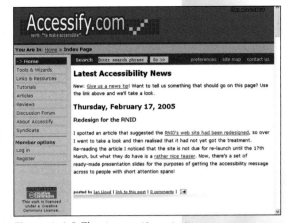

Figure 1.4.3 The Accessify website encourages accessible websites with free tools and services

Causes of the divide

Many causes of the digital divide, and barriers to its reduction, have been identified. In part the digital divide simply mirrors the economic divide within societies. Socio-economic factors clearly have a large impact, as ICT equipment is expensive and rental charges and fees for connection to the internet can be high. It is not surprising then that people on low incomes, or without a job, are disadvantaged, and this may include the unskilled, disabled, the elderly and the young. In addition, as digital providers are commercial organisations, they tend to target the better off with their content and services, making these seem potentially less relevant to disadvantaged groups. More subtly, but no less importantly, socio-economic factors are often disguised as technical issues. In many rural and remote locations there may be very limited access to the faster technologies. It does not make economic sense to private organisations to provide the infrastructure necessary to support these communities with the cable or digital telephone lines that would enable faster and more reliable internet access.

Clearly, a lack of skills is a large contributory factor. People with low ICT skills can find it very hard to use a PC and the internet to access the knowledge and services that might be useful to them. Even more crucially, a lack of basic literacy and perhaps numeracy can be even more of an obstacle. This is also often associated with a lack of confidence. Many groups who have not been trained in ICT are very wary of the technology. Some pensioners, who may even have very good basic skills and a high level of education may feel unskilled in this area and lack the confidence to try it out. There are also social factors contributing to these issues. Some groups may be unwilling to expose any gaps in their skills or lack of confidence in front of a mixed audience.

Accessibility

Some sites are designed with beautiful front pages that require detection of subtle changes in hue in response to mouse movements in order to be able to enter the site. Others display text in a wonderfully complementary colour to the background so that the text does not break up the subtle visual design effect. These and many other techniques render the websites inaccessible to people with poor vision, colour blindness, or having other special physical requirements. There are now strong moral, commercial and legal obligations on web designers to take into account the differing needs of people within society and to make websites accessible to as many people as possible.

There are more mundane barriers to accessing the digital world, too. Where community access is provided there may not be adequate crèche facilities; they may be inaccessible to people with limited mobility, and people without their own transport. Rural and very poor communities, where there are already other barriers to access, may be particularly poorly served in community facilities.

There are many causes of the digital divide. The people in the video clips discuss disadvantages for the elderly and the disabled.

CASE STUDY ICT and pensioners in rural England

Dorothy and Clive live in a very small rural village in the Midlands. They are both in their seventies and until three years ago had not even considered using, let alone owning, a computer. They took a small plunge into digital technology with a mobile phone whose £10 credit lasted for the first year, but which was useful for emergencies, and contacting family when out and about in their caravan.

Clive takes part in many local activities including helping out the Village Hall Committee and at local shoots, and he officiates at a local club. He decided it would be useful to be able to have a computer to do some word processing and keep some records more efficiently. He bought a computer with scanner, printer and modem, and managed with some help to get connected to the internet.

Just after they bought their computer, a local community initiative was set up to teach OAPs basic computing tasks without charge on Wednesday afternoons at the local village hall, using laptops brought in by the itinerant lecturer. Dorothy and Clive both attended the 10-week course every week and learned how to use basic office applications, basic painting programs, use email, browse the net, and take and edit digital photographs.

Figure 1.4.4

Since then their use of digital technologies has grown exponentially. Clive word-processes his own and the committee's letters. He has started researching his family history using genealogy sites on the internet. He has since bought a digital camera and taken numerous pictures, some of which he has also sent by email to relatives. The couple have relatives in Australia and Pakistan and they have been in correspondence with these using email. Dorothy has contacted old friends from school in the 1930s using the Friends Reunited website and enjoyed researching aspects of her younger life on the web. They have found and booked holidays on the internet, and done much more. Until recently the internet supermarkets did not deliver to this rural village, but they have just started a service. The couple now intend to order online which they feel will save a good deal of time and effort especially in the bleaker winter days.

Task

- Do you feel digital technologies have made a genuine impact on the couple's lives?
- Would their lives be poorer if they did not have access to ICT at home?
- The couple were able to afford their own computer. Would access in the community centre three miles away be as useful?

Activity 3 Investigate access to digital technology

Interview an elderly (over 65) member of your own family or a family friend. Ask them what digital technologies they use and what benefits they get from them. Where they have little or no access, ask them what they would like to be able to do and why.

Create a small PDF document about who your interviewee is, where they live, what access they have, what they do with digital technologies and what they would like to do with them. Write a page on what impact technology has had on their life and/or what impact it could have.

As discussed earlier, there are a number of commentators, who suggest that there really is not much of a digital divide in the developed world. They argue that the lack of access in some groups is essentially voluntary. There are sufficient locations where access can now be obtained for low or no cost, within reach of the vast majority of these non-users. But they just do not find access interesting or relevant, so they disconnect themselves voluntarily. This is a powerful argument. Equally though, it can be said that technology's lack of relevance to under-represented groups is a major barrier to the universal take up of digital technologies – and that the divide is real and exists because of providers' attitudes, rather than the potential consumers' attitudes.

For example, content can be seen as irrelevant for a number of reasons. If the content is very wordy then this will disadvantage the less literate. If the content is predominantly targeted at the white middle class it may be totally irrelevant to large sectors of society. In many cases this can be seen to be true, though less so now than a few years ago. The growth of digital TV, and latterly digital radio, has brought a great deal of cultural and language diversity. But this is still not as true for the computing and internet market. If groups are excluded because the content is irrelevant to them, then the content can be seen as an important underlying factor of the digital divide. However, if the lack of relevance is because a group simply has other more appealing activities to do, then this is not an issue of a digital divide.

As with developing countries, some of the barriers to universal access arise because of the processes involved in funding projects. Government, local government, charities, local businesses and other organisations all fund projects directly and indirectly. They are funded in a myriad of different ways with different but overlapping aims. The funding is often time limited and/or insecure. The lack of a joined up approach can mean that true value for money is not always obtained even where the projects' precise aims are met. Literally thousands of millions of pounds has been spent over the six years up to July 2004 in a variety of different education projects in the UK in an attempt to bridge the digital divide. (Source: 'Closing the digital divide', Amy McLellan, *The Independent*, 8 July 2004.) In schools particularly, an enormous amount has been gained with this expenditure on systems and software. The vast majority of students are now exposed to digital technologies at school, but there are those that argue that this has not made the difference that this amount of money should have. Ofsted still reports the use of ICT in enhancing learning as patchy, and dependent more on the skill of individual teachers than on ICT being embedded into the whole school curriculum. The interrelated nature of many of the causes is borne out by the fact that ICT is still, in the postcompulsory sector, predominantly a male activity.

Figure 1.4.5

ACTIVITY 4 Search for the causes of the digital divide

The following list of words all relate to causes of the digital divide. Open the wordsearch in Figure 1.4.5. On a print out of it find and encircle the words.

confidence	cost	facilities	skills
connectivity	culture	location	social
convenience	economic	relevance	

The impact of the digital divide

Digital technologies can be used to help people overcome barriers in a cost-effective and empowering manner, but the digital divide is caused by socio-economic factors and also has many related socio-economic consequences:

- The unemployed can use the internet, kiosk technology and online databases to help find work, but one of the impacts of the divide is that they have less access in general to these technologies than the employed.
- People and businesses in geographically more remote places could benefit from using high-speed telecommunications in place of the face-to-face communications yet these facilities are more accessible to those near the large centres of population. Given their distance from shops, and information sources such as libraries and government, they would have much to gain from access to online shopping and information.
- The elderly and infirm have similar issues. A person with restricted mobility could benefit a great deal from internet access to help with shopping, banking, seeking information and contacting others. Unfortunately one of the impacts of the digital divide is that they are among the groups under-represented in the use of digital technologies.

The digital divide also has a large impact on education and life chances. It is argued that if groups do not have sufficient access to digital technologies in education they will be disadvantaged in the knowledge economy. While home income generally determines the chances of personal computer ownership, it is education that determines the chances of using a work computer. (Source: 'The growing digital divide: Implications for an open research agenda', by Donna

Hoffman and Thomas Novak, Vanderbilt University.) A digital divide in schools can reinforce that due to the socio-economic circumstances of the parents and have a double impact on the life chances of affected children. This is a theme taken up by critics who claim that the introduction of computers in education can deepen rather than bridge the divide. Lawrence Gladieux and Watson Scott Swail from the USA College Board ('Education online increases inequality', BBC News, 19 April 1999) propose that the use of ICT advantages those students who have access to it outside school, and that therefore it magnifies existing racial and economic inequalities.

The impact of the digital divide in the UK could potentially become greater as more businesses and government organisations move to web provision. It is already harder for people in rural villages to access post office and banking services than a generation ago. The number of real physical job centres, libraries, tax offices, banks and other similar outlets is likely to decrease with time. This could exacerbate any existing social disadvantage for the affected groups but also has an affect on all of us; that is the economy as a whole may suffer as a result of disconnected groups being disadvantaged and not being able to contribute to overall wealth.

Bridging the gap: examples of initiatives

There have been and are still numerous initiatives to bridge the gap sponsored by the national government, local government, private industry and charities. In the following section we will look at a number of these to give a flavour of the breadth and range of initiatives in this area in the UK. This list is not intended to be exhaustive, but still indicates the amount that has been done and the extent of investment that has been poured into this area.

▶ UK Online

UK Online is major government project, started in 2001, to give computer access to people in the community and to help them learn new ICT skills. There are now over 6000 UK Online Centres, located in libraries, schools and community centres.

▶ University for Industry (Ufi)

The University for Industry is a partnership between the government and private industry aimed at improving job prospects for individuals and boosting competitiveness for businesses through the use of Learn Direct centres.

Working as a public–private partnership in England, Wales and Northern Ireland, Ufi aims to put individuals in a better position to get jobs, improve their career prospects and boost business competitiveness.

Learn Direct

Learn Direct is aimed at teaching adults how to use ICT, in schools, libraries and colleges.

British Educational Communication and Technology Association (BECTA)

The British Educational Communication and Technology Association was set up to help education professionals, including teachers, make the most of ICT.

Wired up Communities initiative

£10 million funding was provided in the Wired up Communities initiative to connect seven disadvantaged communities to the internet to test what impact this would have on their lives. One of these was Newham in East London where 750 households and one primary school were connected to the internet. The aim of the initiative was to improve educational standards and increase job opportunities for the socially excluded.

Computers within Reach

Computers within Reach was a £15 million initiative aimed at helping learners on benefits by enhancing their employment prospects and learning opportunities through providing access to computers.

Figure 1.4.6 The Get Started campaign helped older people to start using ICT

Get Started campaign

'Get Started' was a six-week campaign up to the end of June 2003 aimed at giving a kick start to access for the elderly, the unemployed, the disabled and other disadvantaged groups, to show them the benefits they could get from accessing IT. (See 'Spanning the digital divide – UK's Get Started campaign', *Computer Weekly*, 17 June 2003.)

Community Access to Lifelong Learning (CALL)

CALL is a massive (£200m) programme to enable schools, libraries and other lifelong learning institutions to become connected to the internet and provide access to all groups within society, with the hope of providing particular benefits to socially excluded people who otherwise have less access to online learning opportunities.

Activity 5 Research initiatives to fund the digital divide ◀

Choose one of the projects described previously. Using the sources given, research in depth:
- What is its purpose?
- How it relates to the digital divide.
- Who are its main target clients?
- What are its strengths and weaknesses?
- What improvements could be made?

Make a presentation of five slides evaluating the project in terms of its potential to reduce the digital divide.

▶ People's Network Project (Hertfordshire)

This is a local initiative designed to give free access to more than 400 computers with internet connection, Microsoft Office software, desktop publishing, photo editing and a variety of information resources in libraries in Hertfordshire. "Even the smallest of our libraries has at least one computer for people to use" said county councillor Iris Tarry, "This offers everyone opportunities to get online, whether they are looking for information, putting together a CV, studying, or using email to keep in touch with friends." (Source: Hertfordshire County Council.)

Activity 6 Research your local community ICT access ◀

Research the provision of ICT in the community within your home town. Identify the disadvantaged groups who could benefit most from having more access to digital technologies and what is the impact of the current digital divide. Evaluate the extent to which disadvantaged groups are served by the initiatives.

Activity 7 Investigate ICT at your library ◀

Visit your local library. Ask what it does to enable the community to have internet access. Ask why and how ICT is used at the library, how convenient it is and what, if any, impact it has made on library life. Assemble the results into a short presentation to show to your class.

▶ BT Internet Rangers

The Internet Rangers is a British Telecom project to help overcome the barriers to using the internet for technically illiterate parents and grandparents – using their children and grandchildren to help and encourage them. (Source: 'Kids key to closing the digital divide' by Graeme Wearden, DNet UK, 26 November 2003.)

Rural broadband cooperative initiative

In January 2004, the Rural Affairs Minister Alun Michael launched the Community Broadband Network at the Access to Broadband Campaign Conference. The aim is to encourage rural communities to help themselves obtain access to broadband technologies, and to provide community websites. There are three strands to this:

- organise the expertise to support local initiatives using the UK Online Direct Support system
- helping with financial and administrative back-office services
- working with the community broadband sector as a pressure group.

CASE STUDY Wi-fi in the UK

A number of local communities are fed up with the private sector's reluctance to allow high-speed access to their communities. They have become active in setting up wireless hot spots to encompass whole sectors of society. A massive number of these have been set up with varying degrees of sophistication, including some solutions that recall those devised for remote developing countries (see Chapter 1.3), and others, such as Preston, involving large investment in city-wide wi-fi. One group has enabled wi-fi for Brighton Beach between the piers. Some of them offer permanent broadband for free and others charge a commercial rate. These community initiatives generally follow a cooperative model, with individuals and businesses setting up wireless nodes to cover as large an area as possible, and only charging what is necessary to keep the service going. This can be seen in the wlan.org.uk website, which displays the following statement on its home page:

Figure 1.4.7 Computing on Brighton Beach

"The technical innovation of licence-exempt wireless LANs (WLANs) releasing high-speed data interconnections from buildings, makes it possible to develop something entirely new in ICT, namely 'Amateur and Community LANs'. These are not for profit, local community owned and managed Social ICT broadband networks. They introduce the welcome prospect of completely profit-free broadband internet access, local non-commercial (internet) radio, television, telephone and video communications delivered via a local small community-owned cooperative, business or club."

ACTIVITY 8 Find out about WLANs

Research the local community WLANs mentioned at wlan.org.uk:

- Where are these projects mainly located?
- Why have they been created?
- What groups do they serve and in what way?
- Have they, and/or will they have, any impact on the digital divide?

Figure 1.4.8 wlan.org.uk is a group creating pressure for community wi-fi

Conclusion ▶ ▶ ▶

In this chapter we have discussed the many causes of the digital divide in the UK, and the social and economic impact that it has on our society. It can be seen that there are an enormous number of projects to help overcome the problems associated with lack of access to digital technologies, many of which are funded directly or indirectly by the government as well as by local organisations and private companies. These initiatives have provided a great deal of practical help in allowing those who are motivated to have access to digital technologies, by trying to remove some of the economic, social and mobility barriers responsible for the perpetuation of the divide. However, a possible criticism of these is that there is little to encourage groups who have little or no motivation to use the internet to access it in the first place. In addition, a number of the more exciting, interventionist projects such as the Wired up Communities project have now finished and the benefits for the population as a whole are not clear.

We have seen in the preceding chapters that the Information Age has empowered people as consumers, developers and distributors. The e-commerce world is a self-service economy with great choice and variety. It is also a world in which it has become easier to produce creative work to a commercial standard. Individuals with a computer and an internet connection can publish material on the web as a blog, an e-zine or a full blown website. Music of commercial production quality can be produced at home on a PC or Macintosh with a few hundred pounds worth of software. A radio station might broadcast from a front room in the Australian bush. It is possible through the internet to distribute material at almost zero cost.

E-books are a manifestation of these trends. They are a means of distributing and selling books with very low overheads. They are also a medium by which individuals with no previous access to book publishing can produce and distribute a quality product over the internet. In addition, as the e-book is a digital product, it is possible to embed multimedia features in the book and potentially make it even more engaging to a much wider audience than a paper book.

In this chapter we will investigate the world of e-books and the range of e-books available in order to consider the form, style and content of the e-book you will submit for your Unit 1 coursework.

CSS

Cascading style sheets involves using a set of style definitions to determine how a particular HTML page is presented. Using different styles with the same HTML means that the same page can be presented appropriately for different audiences. One cascading style sheet can be used to present the page for a modern artistic audience viewing on a large flatscreen monitor, another CSS for a person with poor vision and another for viewing on the small screen of a phone. The flexibility of CSS means that no compromises are necessary – the layout can be exactly as the designer requires – see this website for examples of designing with CSS.

E-books

An e-book is simply an electronic version of a book. There is no one standard definition beyond this. In its simplest form, an e-book is nothing more than an electronic file containing the text of an existing book. In a more complex form, it is a rich multimedia experience based around textual material. One of the more confusing aspects of e-books is that they are available in such a variety of formats, each with its own purpose, features and particular benefits (see Table 1.5.1). Some e-books are intended simply to be just like paper books, but available on a computer or possibly a PDA. For this purpose the ideal is to be able to carry a device the size and weight of a paperback, or less, but containing a whole library of books. Other e-books are intended to do a lot more than a paper book can. For example, a complex e-book can show a film clip to accompany a textual description, or play a music file to accompany a piece of music.

Format	Description	Advantages	Navigation	Platform
Text file	Text only	Very simple to create Very simple to use Searchable	Scroll only	All computers
Word/RTF	A word processed document file, including text, images, colours and links	Familiar package Easy WYSIWYG interface	Hyperlink Scroll ToC	Windows and Macintosh
Adobe Acrobat	A document file created to look like the original paper, including text, images, colours and links	The most popular e-paper format The look of the printed page is preserved but adds navigation	Hyperlinks Scroll ToC Bookmarks	Virtually all computers, pocket PCs and Palms
HTML/XHTML	Web based Rich multimedia multipage sites Hand crafted	Easy to create Easy to embed Anyone with a browser can view	Hyperlinks Scroll ToC Bookmarks	Virtually all computers, pocket PCs and Palms (and phones, cameras etc. if CSS used correctly)
Open e-book (OEB)	Web based XML based XHTML format	Open standard for e-books Based on well known XHTML so anyone with a modern browser can view	Scroll ToC Chapters	Virtually all computers, pocket PCs and Palms
Compiled HTML (e.g. Instant e-book)	Web based HTML compiled into stand alone .exe file	Can be distributed as a single file rather than a directory of files Anyone with IE can view	Hyperlinks Scroll ToC Bookmarks	PCs
Microsoft Reader	An encrypted streaming text format based on XML that assembles output to a screen page at a time	Reads like a book Cleartype technology makes text very viewable Text-to-talk technology allows books to be read to you Allows annotations	Library Scroll ToC Bookmarks	Windows Pocket PC
Palm Reader	An encrypted streaming text format based on XML	Reads like a book	Library Scroll ToC Bookmarks	Palm PDAs Pocket PC

Table 1.5.1 Popular formats for e-books. This is not an comprehensive list of formats, but gives an overview of the types of formats available

Structure and format of e-books

▶ Text e-books

Text document-based e-books are the simplest form of e-book. All that is necessary is to write the text in a text editor, or scan it into text from paper using a text converter. The file format is simple text, and so all the text is inevitably in a linear form in the one document. Although this might seem overly simple, it has been used extensively for computer manuals in the past, prior to Adobe's portable document format (PDF) gaining wide acceptance. A number of e-books are still available in text format. Despite its simplicity, they have the advantage of being very easily searchable, editable and portable to almost any platform.

▶ Word e-books

Word document books are created using simple word-processing software and usually stored in a single word-processed document file that manages the content and layout in a proprietary format within the file. It is also possible to have hyperlinks within the document, which makes it possible to have some multimedia content. However, the files tend to be relatively large, especially when images are embedded. As a result, this format can be useful in environments where everyone shares the same Microsoft Office software and where a number of authors might be required to collaborate simply on a project, but it is not generally used as a finished format.

▶ Adobe PDF e-books

Adobe's portable document format (PDF) books are stored in a single PDF file. This format has been a fantastic success story. Virtually all computer and software manuals are now published and distributed in this format. Websites which allow downloading of reports, newsletters and articles will almost certainly use PDF for such documents. It is also a growing medium for fully fledged e-books. The Adobe reader and the specialised e-book reader are available for free download.

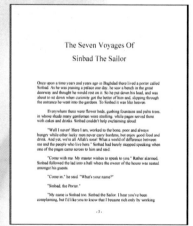

Figure 1.5.1 An example of a PDF e-book that can be downloaded for free

To create the files a specialised writer program such as Adobe Acrobat, or one of a range of similar PDF creators, may be required. Having said this, some operating systems and software (e.g. Mac OSX) now allow direct printing of documents straight into PDF. Usually a file is created using Word, HTML or some other document creation package; then it is 'printed' to PDF.

PDF has a number of features that make it very useful for the presentation of textual material. A PDF file is designed to store the text and layout in a device-independent manner so that the original full-colour print layout for text and graphics is maintained regardless of the platform being used to view the file. Usually the file is also much smaller than the equivalent file in a word-processing package. Look at the demonstration of a PDF-based e-book. Tables of contents, chapters, word searching, dynamic zooming and hyperlinking are all supported. You can even embed multimedia and security features, including encryption, passwords and digital signatures. Used with Adobe Content Server, it is even possible to lend books for a set time and have them automatically deactivate after this time, thus facilitating a lending library of e-books.

The format's main strength is also a drawback. The fidelity of the PDF e-book to the original book means that it is not as flexible as the HTML solution for all situations. For example, you can change small sections of an HTML-based e-book with ease, taking out a single HTML page and/or replacing it with another. Changing a small part of a PDF e-book on the other hand requires that the entire file be re-saved. Where a rich and alterable multimedia experience is required, the PDF may therefore not be a perfect solution.

▶ Reader e-books

Microsoft Reader is another free proprietary product designed to simulate reading a book as closely as possible, and gives the reader access to extra facilities, including full searching, the ability to bookmark pages and make notes, and the facility to have the book read to you. Watch the demonstration to see these features in action. To create a Reader book it is usual to write the original content in word-processing software such as Word, and then use a converter or add-in program to convert it into the required format. The format is a single encrypted file (.lit) containing XML data structuring and the content itself.

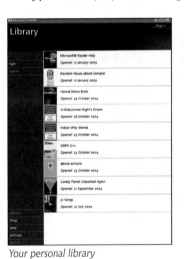
Your personal library

Title page of a book

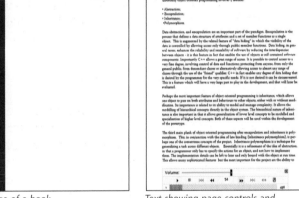
Text showing page controls and speech controls

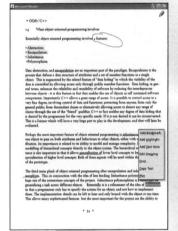
Text showing use of electronic editing tools

Figure 1.5.2 Features within Reader

Opening Microsoft Reader reveals your personal library. Clicking on any of the books within the library takes you to that book. If there is artwork for the book cover this will be shown for a short time and then the book front page will be shown.

This format has been devised to be the computerised equivalent of reading a book, complete with annotations, highlights and so on (see Figure 1.5.2). Microsoft is not the only organisation to offer this type of format. Palm, Mobipocket, and others offer very similar solutions. They work very well on PCs, pocket PCs and personal digital assistants (PDAs). In fact it was hoped at one time that it would be a 'killer application' for PDAs (see Activity 1). Unlike PDF, which is essentially a file format with a small accompanying reader program, these readers are full applications that manage libraries of e-books. This makes them a more heavyweight solution than PDF. They have some advantages, in that at their best they do allow a very good simulation of the total paper-book reading experience, but as with PDF this does also restrict them when you want an e-book to be more than this.

Figure 1.5.3 The contents page of *Unleashing the Killer App*

ACTIVITY 1 Explore an e-book ◀

Investigate the e-book *Unleashing the Killer App* and answer the following questions:
- What is the purpose of this book?
- What format is it in?
- What is its structure?
- What navigation is available?
- What are its strengths and weaknesses?
- Does it fulfil its purpose?

Figure 1.5.4 Shakespeare in quarto

Figure 1.5.5 Many educational e-books now provide a rich multimedia experience

▶ Website e-books

The most important and flexible format of e-book is that created as a website in HTML or XHTML format. Look at the demonstration of a web-based e-book. All the pages are created as web pages and linked together in such a way as to simulate a book experience, usually with a table of contents or chapter list and sequential page navigation. Since websites allow images, sounds, movies and animations to be included and shifted around quite simply to wherever and whenever you want them, this format allows the richest and most flexible multimedia experience (see Fig. 1.5.4). In practice the flexibility of the web format means that there is a rich variety of different e-books available falling within the general category of 'web based'. There are simple text-based websites with page-to-page navigation. There are web books with a collection of scanned images presented with navigation to simulate moving to the next page.

A specialised version of this can be seen in the British Library's Shakespeare in quarto pages (see Fig. 1.5.4). These allow scholars to view a web facsimile of a number of the priceless original editions of Shakespeare.

There are also websites with complex multimedia such as *The Guinness Book of World Records* where the web format allows a richer experience than a paper book could.

As the website is a collection of files, it is more complex to manage and thus some web-based solutions have been created which compile the site into a single .exe file. The disadvantage of this is that it adds another stage to creating the book, and the resulting file might be quite large. As it is an .exe file, it also means that some firewalls will not trust the content when an attempt is made to deliver the file as .exe files are commonly used to hide viruses and Trojan horse programs.

Front cover *Chapters (ToC)* *Text*

Figure 1.5.6 A compiled, instant e-book from eBookMall

▶ Open e-book format

The open e-book format takes a different web-based approach. It simplifies the structure using XML. It puts the content into a single .html file, a document definition in another (.opf) file, and the presentation styles into related CSS files. This format is most useful for books without multimedia content. As with any website structure it is a very flexible format as it can be viewed over the web or downloaded. The CSS-based approach, described in more detail in Chapter 1.6, allows for almost infinite customisation.

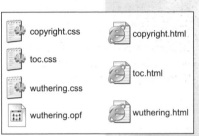

Figure 1.5.7 Open e-book file structure

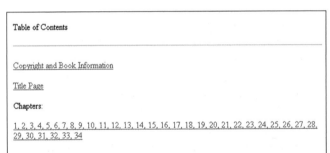

Figure 1.5.8 An example of the open e-book format

ACTIVITY 2 Compare e-book formats ◀

Sample a selection of free e-books in a variety of formats. Download all the different formats you can handle, and compare the books using a table like this:

Book	Format	Ease of use	Best feature	Needs improving

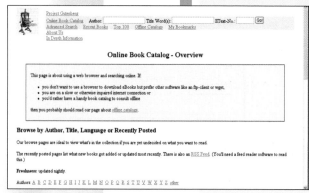

Figure 1.5.9 Project Gutenberg assembles and organises public-domain texts on the web to make them available to all

Activity 3 Find out about Project Gutenberg ◀

Project Gutenberg offers copyright free books for you to download and use completely free of charge. Search for Shakespeare's *Romeo and Juliet*. Look at it using the online viewer or download it.

Add a line about it to your table from Activity 2.

XHTML and CSS

Modern web design is based around the use of XHTML to structure the web page into headings, paragraphs, lists, links, tables etc. and then the use of CSS to style the presentation of these structural elements. Good HTML editors all support this method of development. In the following chapter this method will be used to develop an e-book.

It can be argued that although all the formats discussed have a valuable role to fulfil, overall it is web-based solutions that offer the most flexible solution to e-book creation and viewing. To create a web-based e-book you do not need a specialised plug in, conversion or authoring package. You can use a simple text editor, a free web editor or the web-authoring package you probably already have access to. To view the book, your readers do not need any specialised software, just the browser that comes free with virtually all computers, or as a free download from the internet. Furthermore, a web-based book can be read either by downloading it to your computer or viewing it on the web. The use of style sheets (CSS) ensures accessibility of the e-book for different audiences on a massive range of platforms. In addition to all of this, the web-based solution allows e-books to be more than paper books. You can add animations, music, voice, video and more to enhance the reader's experience where appropriate. However, care must be taken as the flexibility also can lead to messy, poorly designed e-books that lack a coherent sense of identity.

Activity 4 Accessibility ◀

Accessibility is an important issue on the web, as can be seen throughout this book. Bruce Ingraham and Emma Bradburn of the University of Teesside have produced 'A guide to producing readable, accessible onscreen text' which is of particular interest to e-book authors.

Look at these guidelines and list their most important recommendations, particularly their 'Guidelines for the creation of readable, accessible HTML encoded text'.

Range of e-books

The ActiveBook that accompanies this book is also an e-book. Take a tour of its features.

▶ Literature

The largest number and range of e-books available is probably in the field of literature. The most common among these are the classics, mainly when they are out of copyright and are thus usable by anyone without having to pay any royalties. Typical of this category of e-books are those offered by Project

Gutenberg and institutions such as the University of Virginia Library (see Fig. 1.5.10). The latter institution distributes literature in Reader (Microsoft e-book and Palm formats) and e-text format and facilitates searching for keywords and phrases through the e-texts.

From the *University of Virginia Library*

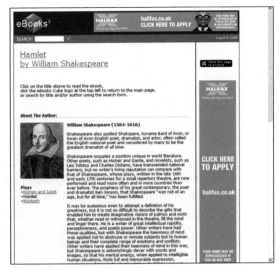

From *eBooks cube*

Figure 1.5.10 *Hamlet* in two different e-book forms

ACTIVITY 5 Compare e-book versions of Hamlet ◀

Compare the web version of Hamlet in the Virginia Library with the same text held at eBooks Cube (see Fig. 1.5.10).

In each case describe the purpose of the book, the format, the structure, the presentation, and the navigation. Evaluate which one best meets its purpose and why.

There is also a flourishing market for modern literature, most of which has to be paid for. The best sellers in the e-book market mirror very closely those of the paper books (see Fig. 1.5.11). There is also a considerable supply of self-published books, vanity books and 'make a mint from ...' type books. Some of these are extremely good books but, like the content of the web in general, the quality is very variable.

2004	Best Selling e-books
1	**The Da Vinci Code** Dan Brown Doubleday $14.95
2	**Angels & Demons** Dan Brown PocketBooks $6.99
3	**Deception Point** Dan Brown PocketBooks $6.99
4	**Digital Fortress** Dan Brown St. Martin's Press $5.99
5	**Darwin's Radio** Greg Bear Del Rey $6.99
6	**Holy Bible, New International Version** International Bible Society Zondervan $14.99
7	**I, Robot** Isaac Asimov Spectra $4.99
8	**Electronic Pocket Oxford English Dictionary & Thesaurus Value Pack** Oxford University Press $19.95
9	**Darwin's Children** Greg Bear Del Rey $6.99
10	**Merriam-Webster's Collegiate® Dictionary** Merriam-Webster $25.95

Figure 1.5.11 Open eBook Forum's e-Book Top 10 for 2004

▶ Reference materials

The next most popular category of e-books available is reference books. This area, more than most, covers a wide range of styles and formats: from simple text streams to complex multimedia. The encyclopaedias produced by the major publishers are now virtually all published on the web, quite often with a subscription service for the more interesting content. The same applies to online dictionaries. The simplest are simple text based lists, but the more interesting, such as the _Oxford English Dictionary_ allow a great variety of search forms and techniques for the word expert. One of the difficulties of e-books for publishers mirrors that of music publishers – how to ensure that they are paid fairly for the content. Large reference works usually charge a subscription for access to the more interesting content, although they attempt to make the content as accessible as possible with low subscription rates for individuals. Libraries, colleges and schools will often have a subscription that allows members of the public to access these works as required.

Activity 6 Compare online encyclopaedias ◀

Search the following encyclopaedias for concepts associated with computers and online services:
- _Hutchinson Encyclopaedia_
- _Britannica Online_
- _Encarta_

Describe the purpose of each, the format, the structure, the presentation, and the navigation. Evaluate which one best meets your purpose and why.

Encarta is an interesting case of how multimedia content can truly enliven and enrich an e-book. The demo pages, which everyone can access without subscription, show how images, sounds and games can combine to immerse the reader in the experience in a way that a paper reference book simply could not.

Open the demo

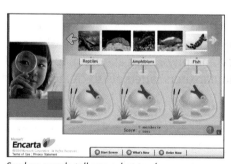
Spoken words tell you what to do

Drag the amphibians, reptiles and fish to their habitat

Figure 1.5.12 _Encarta_ Multimedia Encyclopaedia

▶ Children's books

Another very rich area of e-book content to explore is that of children's books. The largest availability, especially of free or cheap texts, is unsurprisingly 'classic' literature. There are also many examples of young children's reading tutorial type books, simple animated books, as well as the mainstream youth literature in e-book format.

Value of e-books

E-books offer the reader access to almost unlimited libraries from wherever they are. Users can carry their own personal library with them or, with internet access, view books from the web. Unlike 'real' books, electronic books can be searched by keyword, and organised by chapter, page, topic or any other method the author decides would be useful. The user has the ability to control the look and feel of the e-book within parameters set by the author. The font size and colour can be altered to make a book more accessible and the text can even be read aloud. E-books can be faster to produce and amend than conventional books, and thus reference books can be kept up to date more easily. As the costs of storage and distribution are so low, e-books can be substantially cheaper than paper books and often, especially where there are no copyright issues, they are free. In addition to all of this, e-books can be enhanced with multimedia and interactive functionality to make them more exciting and enriching than their paper counterparts.

E-books have been a success, but a qualified one. Many readers have not taken to them as well as e-book pioneers had hoped. Linda Bennett, in her report on 'Promoting the uptake of e-books in FE and HE' quoted comments about drawbacks of the format from users surveyed for the report, including eye strain from reading on screen, pages that are slow to load, not liking page-to-page scrolling, the poor navigation of some books, struggling with keywords (especially for readers with poor spelling), and simple things like missing the physical sensation of holding a book. Even avid readers, with Reader software installed, broadband access and a great deal of experience of ICT, still prefer to read paper books on occasion.

People often want to read books in the bath, on the beach and in bed. These are not ideal places for electronic equipment. Books can be tossed aside and picked up again. There is an immediacy and physicality about a paper-based book that is appealing. Even some manufacturers' attempts to create e-paper will not replace this.

To make an e-book truly valuable, it therefore has to be more than simply a good facsimile of a paper book at the same price. Clearly for major reference works and literature, price is an important factor. If an e-book is substantially cheaper it will be more attractive, but it is not the only factor. When you are creating your e-book for your coursework price will not be an issue at all!

Some sources of e-books

Microsoft Reader books
Penguin books
eBook directory
Questia
eBookMall
Adobe digital editions
Amazon

Home page

Collection of scanned pages

Front cover with arrows to navigate

Scanned page with arrows to page through the book

Figure 1.5.13 *David Copperfield* in scanned web format from the Rosetta Project

ACTIVITY 7 Compare e-book formats for children

Figures 1.5.13 to 16 show a number of different e-book formats used to interest and amuse children. They are all based on the website viewing format.

View these e-books. Consider the structure, format, style, and features of these different offerings and the exact purpose of each book.

Rank the books in the order for how well they meet their purpose and explain your thinking.

List the features you would like to include in an e-book for children and explain why.

HTML format

PDF

Figure 1.5.14 Simple HTML-format and PDF of Oscar Wilde's *The Happy Prince*

Figure 1.5.15 *Treasure Island* by Robert Louis Stevenson in simple HTML text. A simple contents page allows you to navigate through the book

Home page

The words are spoken, and the arrows are used to move backwards and forwards

Figure 1.5.16 Spoken word, learn to read book from We Read

ACTIVITY 8 Which do you prefer? ◀

Many reference books and some fiction books are excellent examples of what makes an e-book valuable. Having completed the previous activities you are an experienced reader of e-books.

List what you liked most about them. List what you liked least about them. What features would you consider to be essential to ensure the benefits outweigh the drawbacks for you?

Conclusion ▶ ▶ ▶

In this chapter we have investigated the world of e-books, their features, formats, and strengths and weaknesses, with the dual aim of preparing you to create your own e-book in a web-based format, and to enable you to evaluate your own work in a balanced way. In the following two chapters we will describe a general method for designing and building web-based e-book sites and give specific help on adding the content, both textual and multimedia, to your e-book.

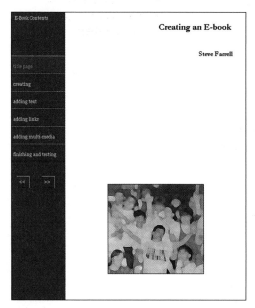

Figure 1.6.1 Creating an e-book. The book will be web based. It will have easy to use chapter headings and page controls. The look is based loosely on the Microsoft Reader interface

In Chapter 1.5 we explored a number of methods that can be used to create e-books and a number of styles that can be adopted to present the final book. Whichever method is used, the process is not complex, but the final product will benefit enormously from an ordered and disciplined approach. In this chapter we will use the website approach to creating an e-book, as required for the coursework. The final website can then stand alone as the e-book itself. It could also be converted at a later date into a distributable .exe file if desired, using an e-book maker.

We will go through all the stages of creating an e-book, starting with the specification, establishing page layouts, navigational design, site design, assembling the required resources, production, testing and finally evaluation. To put this into context:

- we will work through the process for the creation of a simple demonstration e-book, describing how to create a simple one
- at the same time, you will create your own, different, simple e-book using the same process in order to prepare for creating the e-book on the Information Age as required for the coursework.

The web-design methodology we recommend is the efficient and flexible method of cascading style sheets (CSS) to do the styling and HTML (XHTML 1.0) for placing the content. You can, however, use any web creation tools you are comfortable with to follow the tutorial and create the e-book. The main work, as with almost any development project, is in the design rather than the final production. A graphical user interface, a simple text editor and a web browser are all that are actually required and will often be the best tools for creating the website, provided that it has been fully designed.

Purpose and target audience

The first questions we must always ask when starting any web-based project are:
- What is the purpose of this site?
- Who is the target audience?

You will need to structure the site to their needs and use design metaphors that are familiar to them. A pre-teen audience will probably require a book that is very sequential and full of large, bright pictures. Dedicated fiction readers may want an e-book to mimic as closely as possible the paper-based media they are familiar with. A sophisticated A-level audience will be familiar with menu buttons, the more complex non-linear structures of the web, and a mix of text, graphics and other media. A computer 'techie' may even sniff at an e-book that is not full of massive interactivity. You have to decide where to pitch your e-book.

Concept and theme

The audience for the demonstration book we will create in this chapter is students new to Applied A-levels. The purpose is to produce an electronic pocket reference on creating a very simple, HTML-based e-book.

You should follow this process through step by step. The files used to create this e-book are available as ActiveBook items towards the end of this chapter. This will help you in creating a similar e-book of your own, though with the different purpose of explaining the use of the following online services – email, chat, forums, video-conferencing, text and downloading – to an audience made up of 'silver surfers'.

Silver surfer The name given to older people (over 50 usually) who regularly surf the web, based presumably on a whimsical reference to the Marvel Comic's superhero. Clearly the needs of over 50s and those of teenagers will be different. Look at this website about Silver Surfers' Day.

ACTIVITY 1 Plan your e-book

Given your target audience of silver surfers and the purpose for your e-book, choose the attributes you would expect your e-book to have under the following headings. Give a short rationale for each:
- book metaphor (strong, intermediate or weak)
- structure and navigation (simple, intermediate or complex)
- images (big, bold and dominating, or small, informative and contextual)
- text (a little, an intermediate amount, or a lot)
- colours (bright and bold, medium or sober).

Purpose
An electronic pocket reference on creating a very simple, HTML based e-book.

Audience
Applied ICT A-level students.

Content
Brief information on creating a web-based e-book; adding text; adding links; adding multimedia; and finishing it off.

Front page
A cover with the title and author's name, and an abstract graphic representing the author.

Links
To be able to link to any main area of content from any page.

To be able to read through sequentially as if a textbook if desired.

Multimedia
Images as necessary to enhance the content, to be provided later.

Resolution
Must be suitable for viewing at 1024 x 768 pixels; with the maximum flexibility possible.

Browser support
IE 5 and later, Netscape 5 and later, Opera, Mozilla.

Bandwidth constraints
None, though the fastest loading speed possible is desired.

Figure 1.6.2 Example specification for the demonstration e-book

Having specified your audience and purpose, you can now consider how to create a design that will satisfy these. Then a final specification can be drawn up detailing the content such as front page details, text, multimedia, tables, contents, outlines, scripts etc. Other factors to take into account will be the overall size of the site, timescale, and technical details such as the screen resolution(s), the browser technology to be supported and any bandwidth constraints. This may be a very detailed document or a brief table (see Figure 1.6.2).

ACTIVITY 2 Produce your e-book specification ◀

Create a tabular specification for the silver surfers' online services book. Use the example in Figure 1.6.2 as a guide.

Once the specification has been established it is possible to consider a look and feel as well as a general concept for the site that can be worked up into a full design at the next stage.

ACTIVITY 3 Decide the feel of your e-book ◀

Based on the specification, consider some general ideas for how you want your silver surfers' e-book to look:
- What colours might you use?
- How many colours will you use?
- What type of fonts will you use?
- What types of buttons and/or links do you want to use?
- Is there a general metaphor you might use?

In each case explain the rationale behind your decision.

The general concept we will use for the demonstration book for A-level students is an e-book that looks similar to Microsoft Reader books, but is more active. It will allow the reader to jump to major chapters from every page using a button similar to the Reader buttons, and will allow paging to the previous and next page using small '<<' and '>>' buttons similar to those used on most audio/video devices.

Page design

Once the specification has been established and the general concept and theme worked out, you can begin to design the e-book in detail. Establishing the basic look of your page will help you to structure your navigation and guide the storyboards you create later.

It is possible that every page in your book will look totally different from each other, but this is neither very likely, nor generally, very desirable for design or production reasons. If your pages are all original and different from each other, each page will be a new challenge that may work or fail. This is an excessively difficult challenge, and so is best avoided. Also users want consistency to help guide them through what might otherwise be a difficult virtual world. The more consistency there is, and the more obvious the metaphors being employed, the more user-friendly the e-book will be. In addition if you choose a basic structure or grid for your page, then you can create a template page and just change the content and other minor features of each page, rather than having to create each new page from scratch. This is much more efficient than hand-coding each page.

1 Basic book-like page

2 Page with left-hand margin with menus

3 Page with margin and header

4 Two-column page with header

5 Three columns with left-hand-margin menu

6 Top menu and basic page

Figure 1.6.3 Sample page grids

Although there are an infinite number of possible layouts, it is helpful to consider some of the more usual basic page grids which designers use and then enhance these at the storyboard stage. In the sample page grids (see Fig. 1.6.3) the basic book-like grid (grid 1) is often used by e-book designers because it simulates perfectly the paper media. Grid 2 is another common grid, allowing for a left menu and other common information to be held on the left, and the changing text to be held in the main content pane. Grid 3 shows a simple variation on this that is a little more dynamic. Grids 4 to 6 show more variations on these themes: two using two columns for content – with or without a menu column – and another with a top menu bar.

ACTIVITY 4 Choose your e-book grid ◀

Which of the grids in Figure 1.6.3 would be most suitable for your e-book? Choose two grids and give a rationale as to why these two are better than the others, given the specification.

Note: there is no absolute correct answer to this, though you should have clear justifications for your choices.

In order to fit in with the general concept and theme established for our demonstration, the A-level students' book, we will use grid 2, with a large page title on each page to echo grid 3, but with a cleaner, simpler, more book-like interface. This fits in well with the Microsoft Reader style that we are after.

Navigational design

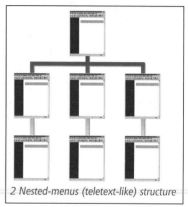

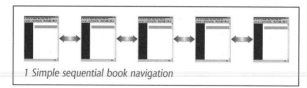

1 Simple sequential book navigation

2 Nested-menus (teletext-like) structure

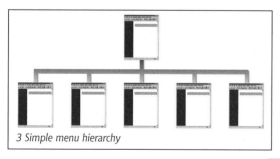

3 Simple menu hierarchy

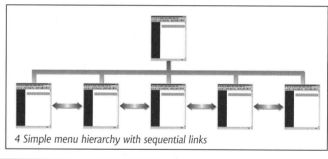

4 Simple menu hierarchy with sequential links

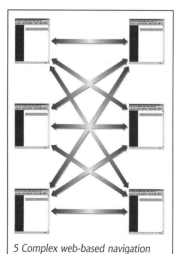

5 Complex web-based navigation

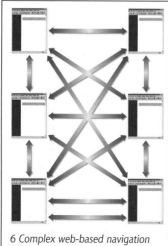

6 Complex web-based navigation with added sequential links

Figure 1.6.4 Typical navigation structures

The navigation or site design is a crucial stage in the process. Figure 1.6.4 shows progressively more complex site navigation for an e-book, with complexity increasing as you go from top to bottom and from left to right. The further down the figure we choose, the more complex the site will be for the user to navigate.

Navigation structure 1 is the simplest form, following the simplest metaphor of a paper-based book – you can 'turn' pages back and forth. Structure 2 shows a teletext-like structure where the user has to follow menus downwards to find exactly the right content. This is less likely to be appropriate for an e-book project but may be suitable for organising a large topic into simple chunks. Structure 3 shows a wide, but shallow, hierarchy, where all content can be reached from a top-level menu. This is suitable for projects where the number of chapters (categories) is not too great.

Structure 5 shows a web- or mesh-based structure where each main page can be accessed from the other ones. This is the most flexible and potentially the most complex structure for the user. Structures 4 and 6 show the addition of extra navigation to allow a linear path through the book if desired. This latter structure is the model for most real websites.

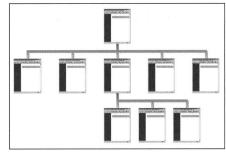

Figure 1.6.5 Web-based structure in hierarchical form

In practice, most websites with a main menu that is repeated on each page will have elements of navigation structure 5, but they are often drawn as though they are structure 3. This is intended to simplify the drawing and to reveal the underlying hierarchical nature of the navigation that the menu gives the user. There is a top-level menu system that can be accessed from anywhere, and other content that can only be accessed from particular pages. In Figure 1.6.5, for example, all pages can access the front cover and the five main chapters (menu pages), but only page 3 can access the three second-level pages. Physically this is a complex web structure, but logically, and to the user, it appears quite simple.

ACTIVITY 5 Determine your navigation structure ◀

Decide on the navigation structure you wish to use for your book and explain briefly the rationale behind your choice.

For our demonstration e-book for at A-level students, the best choice would seem to be exactly the type of structure shown in Figure 1.6.5 with the addition of sequential navigation. There will be a chapter or category menu in the left menu bar, allowing the user to choose any chapter from any page. This means that the structure is a complex web structure. In addition it is possible to traverse the book page by page if the user desires, simulating the normal action of reading a book page by page. If any extra pages are required at a later date to expand the content, they will be accessed from within a chapter (i.e. a lower level). A really crucial task at this stage is to decide on the chapter or category headings. If these are later decided to be incorrect, the whole book will have to be altered at the cost of a great deal of time and potential expense.

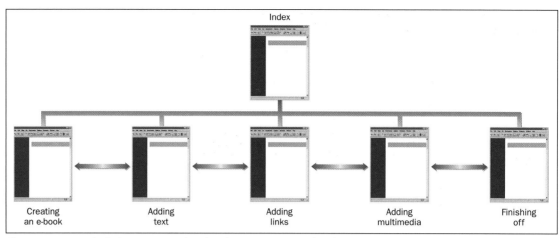

Figure 1.6.6 Logical site structure for the demonstration e-book

In our case, the A-level Specification points to what the main chapters should be:

- a front cover
- creating a web-based e-book
- adding text
- adding links
- adding multimedia
- finishing off.

This allows us to create a logical site structure, as shown in Figure 1.6.6.

Storyboard

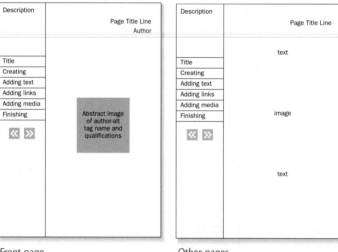

Front page   *Other pages*

Figure 1.6.7 The basic grid for the demonstration e-book

At this stage a storyboard for each page, or for each group of pages, should be constructed. The initial version must specify where the links are and what they link to. It must show the major placements of all text and multimedia content in sufficient detail for the web-page creator to build the page. Clearly this is an expansion of the basic grid chosen earlier in the process, with the addition of the detailed information gained from deciding on the navigation structure. Variations can be added to the basic grid to enhance and add interest, but it will provide a consistent experience for the user and designer. Figure 1.6.7 shows how this will look for the demonstration e-book which has a front page that is slightly different compared to the other, content, pages.

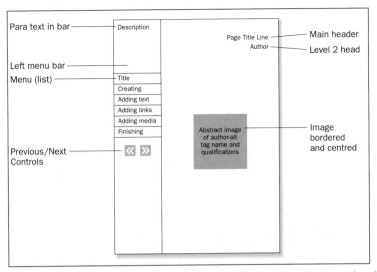

Figure 1.6.8 Detailed annotated storyboard for demonstration e-book

The initial storyboard can now be used as the basis for more detailed design work, such as adding labels for each of the parts, and specifying particular styles to be used. An idea of this can be seen in Figure 1.6.8 where the major styles that will have to be defined are all identified and in part specified.

In this case, because a book metaphor is being used with a high resolution, a portrait view is employed. But it is important to remember that most electronic media are viewed on monitors that are landscape rather than portrait. Some of these monitors may only have resolutions of 800×600 pixels or in extreme cases 640×480. This would mean that users would only see a narrow window onto your design. The storyboard must reflect this. In Figure 1.6.8 the main menu and all the initial content is within the top half of the page.

Final detailed styling

The left menu bar shown on the storyboard is repeated across all the pages in the book so it is perhaps the most crucial aspect of the design. It is often worth designing it in even more detail, with a full colour work-up, to be sure the design works. This will also form the basis for specifying the exact RGB colour values in the style sheets. The final storyboard for the demonstration-site menu-bar design is shown in Figure 1.6.9.

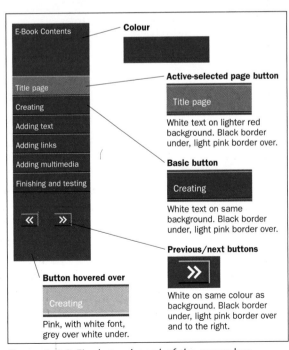

Figure 1.6.9 Final storyboard of the menu-bar design for the demonstration e-book

The design for the eportfolio

There is no absolute requirement to include your final designs in your eportfolio, but in order to gain top marks it is best to do so. You should include at least the storyboards (see Figs 1.6.8 and 1.6.9) and the final navigation structure (see Fig. 1.6.10) for your website. The more detail you show it in, the more simply you will be able to implement your e-book regardless of your method of implementation. Furthermore, it will help convince the assessor of the quality of your performance as it will be clearly based on good working practices.

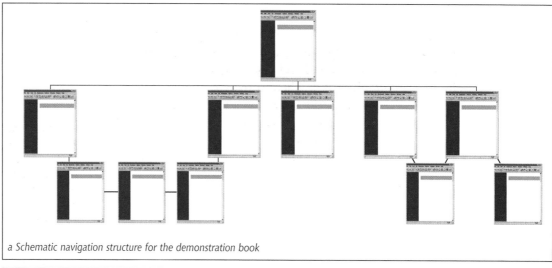

a Schematic navigation structure for the demonstration book

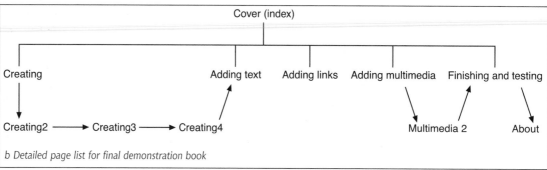

b Detailed page list for final demonstration book

Figure 1.6.10

The design calls for a front cover plus five main chapter headings. Within the first, fourth and fifth chapters there are extra pages. Each page must be able to access the cover and main chapters. It must be also be possible to page backwards and forwards through the book. In total there is a cover plus ten other pages.

Assembling the assets

The next step is to gather together all the existing assets and create any assets that do not already exist. The assets will comprise the text that makes the bulk of the content for the e-book, plus any images, videos, sound files, scripts etc. that have been specified as part of the book. These should be collected into an assets' directory ready for conversion and adaptation, or simply to be copied into the final site when it is created. The final book has to be totally self-contained and therefore any web pages, sounds, videos or images that are required from the internet must be downloaded ready to put into the final e-book folder. In addition, any scans of journals, digital images, recordings of audio and video must be collected ready to be put into the same e-book folder.

ACTIVITY 6 Get organised! ◀

Locate any textual material you need for your silver surfers' project. An internet search will yield a mass of information, and it can be reused later in your final coursework. Find one or two A4 sheets of material on each of the main online services we looked at in Chapter 1.1. Adapt the material as required, ensuring you include the source with the text (see Chapter 1.7). Save the text in a plain text file. Proof read it to ensure it is free from spelling and grammatical errors, and make a note of when you did this, what you found and any errors you corrected.

Find some useful relevant graphics and, where copyright permits (see Chapter 1.7), copy and adapt them for your e-book. Save them in .gif or .jpg format as appropriate (see Chapter 1.7 for more information on file formats). Repeat this process for any sounds, video, scripts, animations or other media.

Copy all of these files into an assets folder ready for final production.

Production decisions

The design can now be used as the basis of the production of the e-book regardless of the production method chosen. As long as the production method generates HTML suitable for fifth-generation browsers, it is acceptable to Edexcel. Thus the final e-book can be created in a package such as Microsoft PowerPoint or Publisher and saved as HTML, it can be handcrafted in a plain-text editor such as Notepad, or it can be created in a specialist web design package such as Microsoft FrontPage or Macromedia Dreamweaver.

Whichever method you choose, the time spent designing the book will be worthwhile. Firstly, the book is likely to work better first time if it has been designed. Secondly, the navigation will have been thought through and it should therefore be effective right from the start. Thirdly, it is likely to have all the necessary elements. Overall it will enable faster development of the book and a better outcome.

The choice of production method is mainly a matter of what resources are available, the skills you already possess and the time available to create the e-book. It is possible to create a *reasonable quality* book very easily using the method of converting from an Office package to HTML format. It would probably take a little longer using a specialist web design package or handcrafted HTML. To create a *top quality* e-book, it is probably simpler and quicker to use a specialist web design package. To create the *very best possible* e-book, taking full account of accessibility issues and cross-browser compatibility issues, then it is almost certainly best to build it using a web design package to create XHTML pages styled by CSS.

In the following section we will develop an e-book using methods from both ends of this spectrum. Firstly we will show how to create an e-book using Microsoft Publisher and then we will show how to create the same book using HTML with CSS by developing it with Macromedia Dreamweaver.

Cascading style sheets (CSS)
These are the ideal method for styling a website. They can be styled independently of the HTML for the site and applied to every web page to give a consistent look and feel to a whole site.

- CSS can be used to style HTML tags such as h1, h2, p etc.
- CSS can be used to style individual objects given an individual ID attribute, such as <div id="menu">.
- CSS can be used to style whole classes of objects using the class attribute, such as <td class="firstColumn">

CSS can be used for styling individual characters or whole areas, for creating attractive and flexible controls (such as menus or dialogues) and for creating whole layouts by styling the positioning and colours of whole blocks of a page.

It is essential to research the type of styling that can be used, using one of the many excellent web tutorials or book references, but once learnt the same style attributes can be applied to virtually all objects and thus it makes a very flexible and powerful tool.

Implementing the demonstration site in Microsoft Publisher

Figure 1.6.11 and the demonstration show a ten-step method to create an e-book using Microsoft Publisher. The more detail it has been designed in the easier it will be.

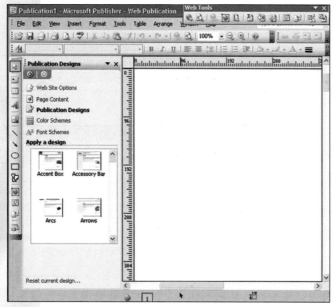

1 Create a new blank web page

2 Set it to work in pixels, to make it easier to work with the required dimensions of 1024 × 768

3 Insert ten pages in addition to the home page as this is what is specified in our final design

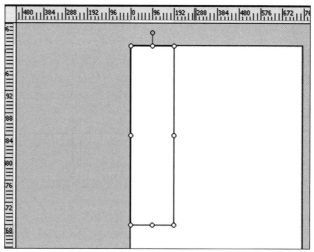

4 Create a menu division 768 pixels high and about 20 per cent of the page width. Then change the background colour of the rectangle

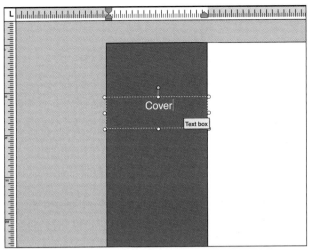

5 Enter the text for the chapter headings, following the main row of the design (see Fig. 1.6.10b), using the style (font family, size, colour etc.) required

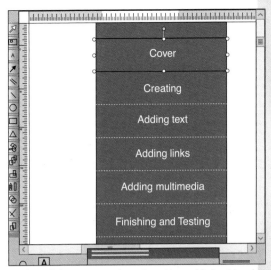

6 When all the menu text items have been added, add a plain rectangle over each text frame and insert a hyperlink for each rectangle

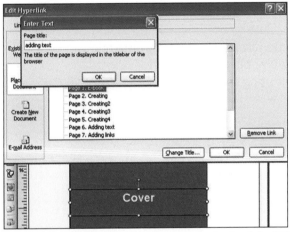

7 When adding the hyperlinks change the page titles for all the HTML pages. Then link the rectangles to each of the chapter headings

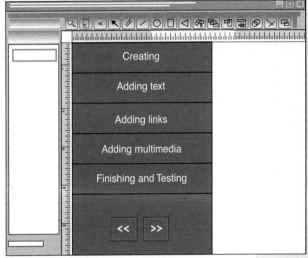

8 Add the page controls in the same way. Then link to them the previous and next page as appropriate. Add any other text etc. at this stage

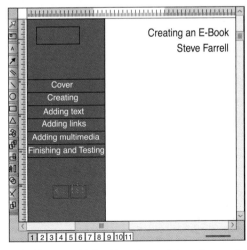

9 At this stage add the title and copy it to each page. It will be placed in exactly the same position on every page and give a sense of unity to the book. Now simply add the content as you would with any publication

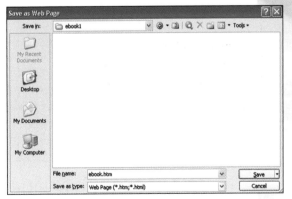

10 Finally save the file as an HTML file. It will be saved as a main page with a subfolder for all the other pages and a folder for all the other pages and elements.

Figure 1.6.11 Ten-step guide to creating an e-book in Publisher 2003

▶ Evaluation of an e-book created in Publisher

When a book has been designed in detail it can be created very simply using Publisher, and the results are impressive for the time taken to produce it. A high quality e-book with all the necessary navigation and multimedia features can be put together very quickly. Many design features can be implemented reasonably well. However, to include features such as fast-acting buttons is difficult. The buttons in this website are clear and work, but they do not respond like proper buttons. In addition the text and other elements added to the Publisher e-book are all in fixed positions and this is difficult to change; whereas it is easy in CSS-based solutions to make text that flows into the available space if the browser window is resized.

The HTML created is very inflexible and verbose. It is extremely difficult to customise the book once complete (although there is a feature within Publisher that allows you to enter HTML directly to customise components that reduces this problem a little). Changes to the styles in the book, especially in the main content areas, are hard to make after the book has been completed. This means that it is a great deal more difficult to build in more than rudimentary accessibility features.

In summary, the e-book is very close to the original design and was created very efficiently. Certainly with some careful planning, this method can be used to gain a top mark in the coursework, but on the negative side it lacks some flexibility and it would be difficult using this method to implement all the desired functionality.

Implementing the demonstration site in Dreamweaver with HTML and CSS

There are demonstrations of each of these stages.

▶ Stage 1: Define a new site

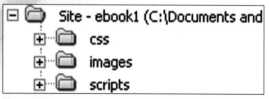

Figure 1.6.12 View in Dreamweaver MX

First create a website to hold your e-book project. All website projects should always be contained in a separate folder. Create a web folder. In this create three new subfolders ('css', 'scripts' and 'images') to hold the CSS files, the images and any scripts required for the project. Open Dreamweaver and define a new site (choose Site Menu' then 'New Site'). Call the site 'ebook1' and set the local folder to the new folder you just created (see Fig. 1.6.12).

▶ Stage 2: Define the CSS

In the HTML plus CSS method we are employing, the HTML will contain the basic structure of the page, along with the content, but virtually all presentation issues will be contained within the CSS. Thus the HTML will specify what the structural elements are (main headings, subheadings, paragraphs, main page divisions etc.), and the CSS will specify how all these elements are to be presented (i.e. the colours, backgrounds, positioning, borders, shading, font style etc.).

Virtually all projects from the simplest to the most complex will have the basic structural elements of:

- a main heading <h1> and a subhead or two <h2> and <h3>; possibly more depending on the hierarchy of headings on each page
- a basic paragraph style <p>
- images <img>
- lists and links (menus)
- perhaps tables and forms.

In addition, a site will define a number of elements depending on which underlying grid is chosen. A two-block grid with menus and content, such as the demonstration book, will have to define a menu and a content block, or division <div>. Depending on how individual the designer wants the page to be, more structural elements may be defined. In our case the storyboard reveals the following main elements:

h1	heading/page title
h2	major subheading
h3	in text subheading
p	main paragraph text
img	images
content	content division (the book's text area)
menu	menu division (the main menu area)
controls	previous/next (or << / >>)controls

At this stage it is possible to work out, from the storyboard, the main CSS necessary to style these elements, although it is possible that some adjustment will be required once the template page is tested. In Dreamweaver open a new page, of type 'basic CSS' (see Fig. 1.6.13a). Save it as 'ebook.css' in the CSS subfolder. Write in a style definition for each HTML element in the web page (h1, h2, h3, p, img etc). Unique elements such as the menu area and the content area will need to be given their own unique ID and styled separately (see Fig. 1.6.13b). Then save and close.

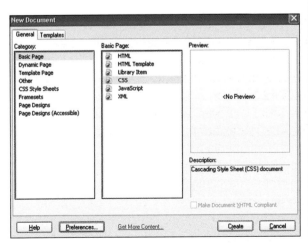

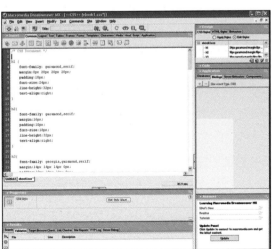

a Create a new CSS page

b The CSS page in Dreamweaver

Figure 1.6.13

Stage 3: Create a template page

Now create a new page of type 'Basic HTML' and save it as 'template.html'.

Add a link in the header to the CSS file, by right clicking in the 'CSS styles' tab of the design window and choosing 'attach style sheet'. Browse to find the CSS (see Fig. 1.6.14).

Figure 1.6.14 Linking to the style sheet

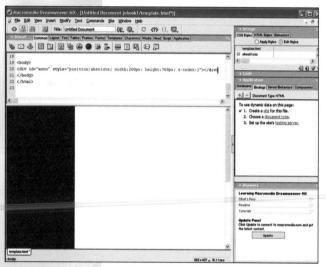

Figure 1.6.15 Creating the menu division

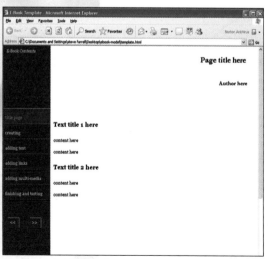

Figure 1.6.16 The demonstration template

Insert a new layer (div). Give it the ID 'menu' so that it connects to the menu style in the CSS sheet (see Fig. 1.6.15). If Dreamweaver gives the tag extra attributes then it is important to delete these (in 'code view') so that it is styled purely by the CSS. Do exactly the same for content.

Write the text 'Page title here' in the content area and style it as heading 1 <h1>; write the text 'Author here' underneath and style it heading 2 <h2>; write the text 'Text title 1 here' underneath and style it heading 3 <h3>; write the text 'Content here' and style it as paragraph <p>; write the text 'Content here' and style it as paragraph <p>; write the text 'Text title 2 here' underneath and style it as heading 3 <h3>; write the text 'Content here' and style it as paragraph <p>; and write the text 'Content here' and style it as paragraph <p> to finish with the page as shown in Figure 1.6.16.

Adding the menu elements

To add the menu items, create a new div inside the menu called 'navcontainer'. We will use this later to style the menu items in a flexible and very fast manner. Now create a simple list of links with each of the chapter headings being a single hyperlink, linked to the appropriate page name as taken from the design (i.e. 'index.html', 'creating.html', 'text.html', 'links.html', 'multimedia.html' and 'finishing.html'). Give the list the ID 'navlist' so that it too can be styled along with the 'navcontainer' at a later stage.

To add the page controls, simply add a new div called 'controls', which is already styled in the CSS. Add the symbols '<<' and '>>' and link these to the next page and the previous page in each case. Give the page the title 'template' and save the page again. Now we are ready to style the links to make them look and work like super-fast buttons.

Styling the links

Many e-books use simple hypertext links for all menus. Others use JavaScript rollover scripts with a set of images for each button. Others will use Flash to create the same effect. The most efficient, and still visually effective, method is to use CSS styles to create the effect of buttons without the bandwidth overhead. This is not very difficult to do but can be time consuming.

The easiest method is to find buttons that have already been created and adapt these to suit your needs. A number of websites, in the spirit of the early non-commercial internet, provide this service. In the main, all they require is that you credit them properly for their intellectual work, which is also the least any proper student should do for any sampled work.

One such source is the site shown in Figure 1.6.17. A designer called Claire Campbell has submitted an idea called vertical buttons. This is not exactly what we want, but it has most of the required elements. All that is needed is to adapt the idea by changing colours and widths to make the buttons match our final detailed storyboard. It is possible to view the HTML and the CSS and then modify it to your exact requirements. If the same names are used as on the Listamatic site then it is also quite simple to slot in different CSS styles from the site to work with the corresponding HTML on your site, and see which works best with your own e-book.

Bandwidth overhead   When a web browser requests a web page from a server (when the address of the page is entered or because there is a hyperlink to it), the page and all its associated components (images, sounds, video, animations etc.) have to be transmitted along the communication media to the browser's computer. Multimedia such as images and sounds enhance the experience of the user, but take up a lot more space and thus take a lot more time to be transmitted. This extra time is known as 'bandwidth overhead'. The best web designers therefore avoid unnecessary use of large images.

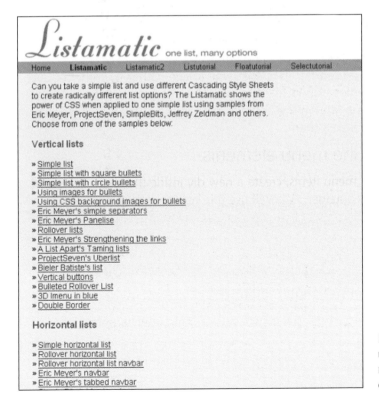

Figure 1.6.17 Listamatic shows how to use CSS to create a huge variety of menus by styling the same HTML with different CSS

Open the CSS file, add the code to style the links, and resave it. Test it in the template page, adapting until the CSS is just right (see Fig. 1.6.18).

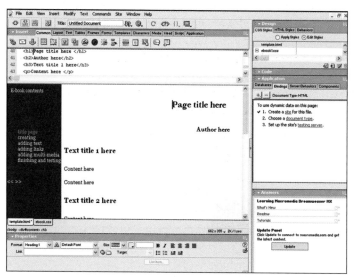

Figure 1.6.18 Template with styled links

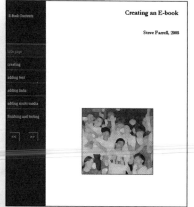

Index.html

Creating.html

Figure 1.6.19 The final output of the demonstration website

▶ Stage 4: Add the pages and the content

Once the template page is ready simply save it as 'index.html', 'creating.html', 'creating1.html' … 'about.html' (11 pages in total). Add the appropriate content to each of the pages in the normal way, as far as possible keeping the styling to only those tags defined in the CSS. In general terms all that is required is to replace the title with the new title for the page, replace the paragraph headings as appropriate, and add the appropriate text and multimedia (see Fig. 1.6.19). In general all images will be inserted into the page, although if they are too large then a thumbnail can be used linked to the large image. Other multimedia, such as movies, flash files, sound files etc. should be put into the book folder and accessed via a link on the appropriate page to allow the viewer to choose when to access them.

ACTIVITY 8 Create your template page ◀

Using your chosen web editor create a template page for your silver surfer website, following one of the methods described.

ACTIVITY 9 Create your pages ◀

Create the HTML pages for your silver surfers' site using your template.

Flexibility of using HTML and CSS

This method of using HTML for the structure and CSS for the presentation is an extremely efficient and flexible method of website creation. The structure of the HTML page is, as stated earlier, defined by the two main divisions, within which there is a menu on the left and content on the right. Any basic two-block design can be created using the same HTML, simply varying the CSS attributes and values. Figure 1.6.20 shows the same HTML still with a left-hand menu, but with green buttons and an individualised logo in the top right corner.

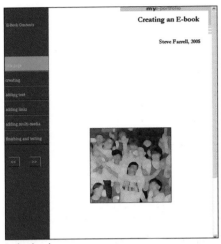
Index.html

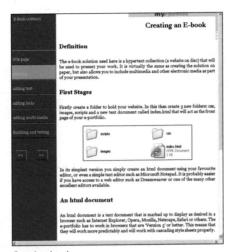
Creating.html

Figure 1.6.20 A green version of the demonstration website

It should be noted that the basic grid 6 (see Fig.1.6.3), although totally different in presentation from grid 2 which we used, is actually also a two-block grid. This means the same HTML will work with this as well, provided the CSS styles the divisions to be below each other; though of course, new menu styles will have to be chosen. But as we used the names given by Listamatic we can simply choose the horizontal menu we feel is best, change any colours or fonts as desired, and re-present the e-book in its new form, as shown in Figure 1.6.21.

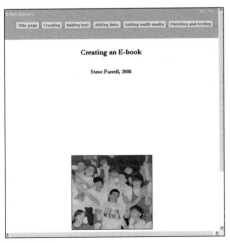
Index.html

Creating.html

Figure 1.6.21 A lilac top-menu version of the website

ACTIVITY 10 Experiment with different versions ◀

The finished demonstration project is available in the ActiveBook in all three styles:

- the initial version
- the green version
- the lilac version.

Run the e-book in the style you like best. Look at the effect the style has on the presentation of the HTML. Examine the different CSS files to see how the different styles have been achieved.

One day all websites will be designed this way

Separating content and presentation is the ideal for most advanced computing and indeed conventional publishing systems. It is a very flexible and powerful technique if used correctly. HTML and CSS together allow the publication of websites in a flexible yet consistent manner. Using this method it is possible to use the same content, but with different style sheets, to publish for audiences with large widescreen TVs, conventional PC screens, PDAs or smart phones, and to produce printed output for different audiences or even voice output from a screen reader for visually impaired surfers. It can be used to help in the automation of website production for content management systems and for the production of one-off web pages.

This method is not totally without problems, however. CSS are specified in global standards that new browsers try to adhere to. Unfortunately there are sometimes misunderstandings, and not all browsers do everything the same way. Current versions of Internet Explorer for the PC have a different way of handling margins than other browsers, including IE for Macintoshes. Until all browsers are totally standardised, work-rounds will have to be used occasionally. You can see an example of this in the negative margins in the CSS file for the lilac e-book. Fortunately these work-rounds are commonly available on the web with detailed explanations.

One day all browsers will be standardised and this method of designing sites will be universally adopted.

Testing

The final stage in any e-book project is to test and evaluate it.
- You should have proofread the content as you developed it, but you must do it again at the end.
- Check that the layout fits to the design, and that it meets the specification. This should be true for every browser mentioned in the original specification. If there are any inconsistencies these should be noted.

- Check that every link works, and that you can indeed follow the links in the manner intended originally.
- Does your e-book work as a rich and complex experience? Does it allow linear progression?

Record all these tests in a standardised manner to prove what has been done and at what stage. It is unlikely that it will all work first time so write down what changes were made, and why, and then retest.

When you are satisfied, ask others to test it to see what you have missed, and again note their comments in a standard form. Note any corrections made and why, and what re-testing is done.

If testing is completed thoroughly this forms the factual basis of the evaluation, which will mainly consider how good the product is against the specification.

ACTIVITY 11 Test your e-book ◀

Test your silver surfers' e-book. Write an evaluation of it using the following headings:
- Fitness for purpose
- Fitness for audience
  Strengths and weaknesses (Ensure you cover content, structure, layout, components, presentation techniques, ease of navigation, consistency and accessibility.)
- Possible improvements
- Conclusions.

Conclusion ▶ ▶ ▶

In this chapter we have created a simple, web-based e-book using HTML and CSS together. This is the technique that will be most powerful when creating your coursework, regardless of whether you use Dreamweaver, Composer, Notepad or any other web editor to make your e-book. If you follow the design process described in this chapter you should end up creating a quality product.

Developing an e-book: Practical skills

Figure 1.7.1 Production of a rich multimedia e-book requires that you assemble a collection of multimedia assets

The coursework for this unit requires you to produce an e-book about life in the Information Age. (This is described in detail in Chapter 1.8.) A large proportion of the time taken in the physical production of your e-book will be spent in locating, adapting, and creating the textual and multimedia assets that will provide the physical content of the book. This chapter will examine the important techniques and issues involved in this aspect of production, starting with efficient search strategies for locating useful information and techniques for storing it. We will then look at adapting and creating your own multimedia components and storing them in the most useful format for use in your e-book. You will be creating many small media items as you progress through the chapter, a number of which will be directly relevant to your coursework. You should create a folder to store all of these in. This will make it much simpler for you to create your e-book and e-portfolio for your coursework.

Searching the internet

One of the most frequent tasks you will perform during this Unit, and others, is searching the internet to find the information you will need for the content of your e-book. Good knowledge workers do this efficiently and skilfully, using all the tools at their disposal. The problem is not so much about finding information, but rather finding the most relevant information amongst a mountain of data, then storing what is found in an efficient and retrievable manner. Then there is the challenge of presenting the information found in a manner that takes account of copyright legislation.

Your main tool for searching will be your browser. In most cases, this will be Internet Explorer v6.0 or later (see Fig. 1.7.2) and thus our explanations and examples will relate mainly to IE6; however, the same principles apply to other browsers.

2005	IE 6	IE 5	O 7	Firefox	Mozilla	NN 4	NN 7
January	65.5%	4.4%	1.9%	19.2%	4.0%	0.3%	1.1%

Figure 1.7.2 Popularity of different browsers, based on people visiting the W3 Schools website

There are three main methods of searching the internet using a browser. First, you can use subject directories, secondly you can use a search engine and finally you can search subject databases. We will look at each in turn.

▶ Subject directories

Subject directories are an extremely efficient, useful and under-rated method of locating information on the web. They are a means of organising topics on the web into categories in a hierarchical manner. Assuming you are looking for some statistics about internet usage you would find a top level category that it might fit in (e.g. 'Computers'), then within that find a sub-topic (e.g. 'Internet') and within that a sub-sub topic ('Internet statistics'). At this level there will probably be a possibility of deeper 'drilling down' and/or a selection of very relevant and useful sites with descriptions of these. Unlike search engines a human editor has selected these sites for their relevance to the topic – so they are more likely to be useful for your project.

One of the great advantages of a directory structure is that the information at each level has been categorised, and so it is often a great deal more productive to browse the sites discovered by a directory search than a free search engine search. The disadvantage is that some topics are hard to categorise precisely and thus harder to drill down to. Information on, for example, the 'digital divide' could be somewhere in 'Computers', 'Internet' or perhaps 'Social economics'. Fortunately it is possible to conduct a search of the directory that will reveal where the topic has been found and links to possible related topics. It is then a simple matter to browse that topic heading.

Activity 1 Use a subject directory

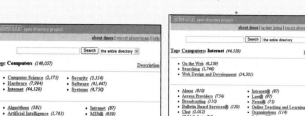

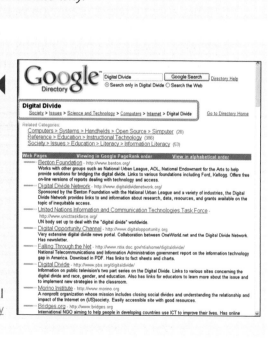

Opening page

Figure 1.7.3 Using Open Directory

Drilling down one level into 'Computers'

At level 2 in 'Internet'

At level 3 in 'Statistics and demographics' you get a detailed list with descriptions

Open Directory Project

The most important subject directories are all based on the Open Directory Project. This is an attempt to deal with the information overload generated by traditional search engines using volunteer human editors to oversee a small section of the overall directory. The project provides the core directory services for all the major engines such as Google, Lycos, Hotbot, AOL, Netscape Search and others. Note that these products present the information in slightly different ways and thus you can choose which to use according to your preference for viewing information.

Use the Open Directory Project or your favourite interface to find internet world statistics for this year for all the major regions of the world, following the process shown in Figure 1.7.3.

Activity 2 Compare subject directories and search engines

Browse through the topics in:

'Computers: Education: Internet: FAQs, help, and tutorials'

to find useful information for your e-book. Decide whether this is more or less useful than a simple search engine search and state why.

Activity 3 Use Google's subject directory

Using Google Directory search for 'digital divide'. Find the category heading and browse this area (see Fig. 1.7.4)

Figure 1.7.4 Finding 'digital divide' in Google subject directory

▶ Search engines

The major alternative method for finding information on the web is to use one of the many search engines available. You will already have had extensive experience of using search engines and will have your own favourite already, but do you make the most of it? In the following section we will look at some simple strategies for finding relevant information more efficiently and refining searches to pinpoint the most relevant information.

How search engines work

Search engines do not actually search the web. They search indexes of databases that relate words (keywords, content etc.) to hyperlinks on the web. The databases are built automatically through the actions of 'spiders' (small software agents that follow the links), which find pages and then pass them on to an indexer program. If a web page has many links to it, it will generally be higher-ranked in the search results. If it has none, the spiders will never find it. It is generally a good idea for developers of a new site to inform the search engines of the site, otherwise it may take a very long time to be indexed. Content stored, for example, on a database rather than on a web server, and delivered as dynamic pages when required, will not appear in most search engines. Other dynamic sites, created by scripting (in PHP, ASP, JavaScript, VBScript etc.) may be very difficult to find or index. Entirely multimedia sites (Flash, Shockwave) are also inherently unfriendly to search engine spiders.

Strategy 1: Use more than one search engine

The first strategy is to use more than one search engine. Search engines have different interfaces with features that are useful in different circumstances. For example, Teoma (an Ask Jeeves website) attempts to order results by subject relevance rather than by number of links to the site (see Fig. 1.7.6). Further, it gives specific suggestions for more refinement. You may find this approach useful. Web Fetch, like other meta search engines, searches the search engines and gives a selection from a variety of sites.

Figure 1.7.6 Some search engines

Teoma

Alternative directories

The Open Directory is the most important project for categorising the web. It is not the only one, however. There is a directory using the Dewey Decimal System of organising knowledge called Dewey Browse and a more eclectic method at About.com (see Fig. 1.7.5).

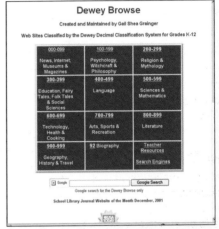

Dewey Browse

About.com

Figure 1.7.5 Alternative directories

Web Fetch

ACTIVITY 4 Compare search engines

Search for 'digital divide' at:

Google	MSN	All the Web
Lycos	Yahoo	Ask Jeeves
Hotbot	Teoma	Web Fetch

Compare the results and the manner in which they are presented.
- How many results does each find? Are 'more' or 'fewer' results better?
- In what manner does each offer choices for refinement?
- Is the results page easy to read?
- Is the results page clogged up with sponsored links?

Strategy 2: Get to know your search engines

The second strategy is to get to know your search engines' features well. If you search for a word or phrase without thinking of how best to optimise the search, the engine will return a long list, which you can then use as a starting point. It is preferable to think of *exactly* what is required, and use a specific search strategy to attempt to pinpoint better what is required and limit the information overload that occurs from too broad a search. Search engines have slightly different methods of specifying more exact searches so it is important that you read your search engines' help pages, and use the advanced search options when available.

Search engine comparison

Most search engines use subsets of a couple of databases (Inktomi and Google being two major ones), and then search these in slightly different ways. For a good explanation of the features of and reviews of the different engines visit the Search Engine Showdown site.

ACTIVITY 5 Refine your search

Strategy	Symbol	Example	Comment
Search for **exact** phrase	" "	"Bulletin board systems"	
Search for one word **and** another	(Default)	Chat "instant messaging"	
Search for one word or phrase, **excluding** another	−	"Digital divide" Africa −"South Africa"	
Search for a word **like** another	~	~spending broadband	
Force use of simple **connective** words	+	~spending +on broadband	
Search for one word **or** another	OR (Note: upper case)	Asda OR Tesco	
Wildcard searching	*	"When * Met Sally"	

Table 1.7.1 Some strategies to refine your search

Open Table 1.7.1 from the ActiveBook. Using Google and another search engine of your choice, try each of the suggested devices; where appropriate contrast with the effect of omitting it. Note your observations in the 'Comments' column. For example, compare results from searching *Bulletin Board Systems* to "*Bulletin Board Systems*".

▶ Subject databases

Another search application that can be tried are subject databases. The contents of these will usually not appear in search engines, as there will often be no static pages to link to, but rather ASP (active server pages) that change according to how you search the database. The more specific the database is to the subject you wish to search, the better, but even the most general databases (such as encyclopaedias) can play a role in this part of your searching.

▶ Saving your searches

There are a number of options for you to save the information you find when searching. You can save whole web pages. This is unlikely to be a good idea as you will soon fill your drive space, and if you do a great deal of searching you will have an un-indexed mass of web pages to search again when you come to write your e-book. At some stage you will paraphrase the main ideas from the sites you find, and take direct quotes where they are very useful and important. You will not usually want to do this, however, until you have found the most useful sites.

To store these sites without clogging up your storage area, the most effective method is to store only the links. You could store them in a word processing file, a text file, an HTML page or similar, but the best and most direct way is to store the hyperlinks in a special folder associated directly with your browser. This method is known by two terms that mean the same thing: 'bookmarks' and 'favorites'. These allow you to link to sites quickly from within the browser itself; you do not have to remember the URL for the site or page and you do not have to search for them every time you want to return to them. In effect, you will be creating your own hierarchical subject directories just like Yahoo, MSN, Google etc. – except that they are customised for you.

The instructions for Activities 6–8 are based on using Internet Explorer; however, other browsers work in a broadly similar way.

Some web databases and directories of databases

CIA World Factbook Digest of useful facts about countries

Encyclopaedia Britannica Some free and paid for content – your library may have a subscription

Complete Planet Directory of databases

Freeality.com Collection of links to popular databases

Wikipedia Free, public domain, database. A fantastic resource for web researchers

Columbia Encyclopedia

Infomine Scholarly resource bank

The Invisible Web Directory Directory to help you search "the invisible web"

ACTIVITY 6 How to add a URL to 'Favorites' ◀

Figure 1.7.7 Adding subject folders

a Give a name to identify the 'favorite'   b Create a folder   c The 'favorite' now appears in its folder

Watch the demonstration of how to add a URL to 'favorites'.

Now locate the Google search engine. When it has loaded click on the 'Favorites' button on the toolbar or select the 'Favorites' menu.

Add an appropriate name to index the site. In this case 'Google' seems the most suitable (see Fig. 1.7.7a).

Before you save it, create a new subject folder by clicking on the 'New Folder' button. Type in 'Searches' as the folder name (see Fig. 1.7.7b) and click 'OK'. This creates a new folder called 'Searches'.

Open the folder and add the Google link by pressing 'OK'.

Add at least ten search engines, subject directories and databases that you might use in your future searches of the web.

a Create folders

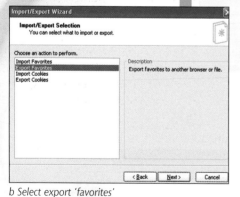

b Create sub-folders

Figure 1.7.8 Organising your subject folders

ACTIVITY 7 How to organise your folders

Before you start a major search activity, create all the folders you might need, for example, 'searches', 'online services', 'impact of ICT' and 'the digital divide'. If you need to create several folders it is easier to use the 'Organize' facility than the 'Add' facility (see Fig. 1.7.8a).

Split your major topics, such as 'searches', into sub-topics such as 'engines', 'directories' and 'databases', in order to organise your search activity better (see Fig. 1.7.8b).

Watch the demonstration of this. You are now prepared for efficient searching.

ACTIVITY 8 How to export and import your bookmarks

Open your browser and select 'File' then 'Import and export ...' (see Fig. 1.7.9a). Follow the steps in the wizard, selecting 'Export favorites' (see Fig. 1.7.9b) and the folders you want to export. Then browse for where you want to put them – for example on the desktop or a floppy disk (see Fig. 1.7.9c).

a Open the import/export wizard

b Select export 'favorites'

c Choose where you want to export the file

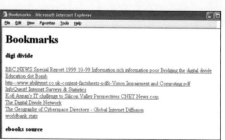

d You can browse the file of 'favorites', but not edit it

Figure 1.7.9 Exporting your bookmarks

The file created is a special browsable, but not editable, XML file of the link (see Fig. 1.7.9d). You can use it to transfer 'favorites' to a different browser or even a different machine. You may find this helpful if, for example, you use a home computer as well as a school or college machine, or if your 'favorites' are deleted regularly by system maintenance.

Creating and storing multimedia

▶ Graphics

Graphics will be an essential part of your e-book. Photos and drawings add impact, interest and variety to a page. As well as being more attractive on the page, an illustration will often make a point a great deal more quickly than text. Your major sources of graphics will be screenshots of your work, photos you have taken and drawings you have made.

You may use graphics created by others, but you must be careful about copyright issues. Fortunately there is a wide variety of public-domain and royalty-free images available for use in educational projects, and you can make use of these to enhance your final product.

When you are attempting the coursework, the area where it is most difficult for you to create your own images on will be the global impact of ICT. However, this is an area in which public-domain databases of photography excel. Many photographers who have been to Laos, Samoa, Bangladesh, Somalia, or other areas you may wish to investigate, have made their work available on a royalty-free basis. Of course, you must take care that you give them proper credit, and ensure that you do not breach any terms they specify regarding the download and use of their images. An example of this rich and varied resource is shown in Figure 1.7.10.

Johannesburg Airport: technical problems at baggage reclaim!

An internet café at Victoria Falls

Figure 1.7.10 Examples of public domain images of Africa from John Walker's 2001 Eclipse Photo Gallery found via jvega.com

ACTIVITY 9 ◀

- Browse the sites in the margin for images of developing countries that would enhance a presentation about the digital divide. Bookmark these images for retrieval later.
- At Pics4Learning browse the images under the categories of 'Objects' and 'Schools' for suitable images to illustrate the 'impact of technology' section. Bookmark these images.
- Read the Image use policy at Wikipedia for what you can and cannot do with its public domain images.

Public domain and royalty-free image links

Wikipedia public domain image resources Fantastic resource which includes large archives of pictures from developing countries

jvega.com public domain images Listing site showing many resources

Pics4Learning Vast range of photos and images

Royalty free clip art

▶ Screenshots

One of the best methods of capturing illustrations about digital communications or the use of ICT is to grab screenshots of the technology in operation. This is a relatively simple process that yields fast and effective results. However, it is important when you do this to ensure that the final dimensions and file format are suitable for the web, otherwise the e-book may not be viewable on other

Save, crop, resize and compress

The crucial processes for saving *any* images in an appropriate format for your e-book are to:

1 Save your original image (so that you can always start again).
2 Crop your original image to the exact part of the image required.
3 Resize it to the desired final size in your graphics package before saving.
4 Compress it to the minimum acceptable quality.

This process will ensure that you have a fast-loading yet rich e-book, whether the eventual format is web-based, Word or PDF.

Screenshots and copyright

As with all material created for your e-book, it is important to respect copyright for screenshot images. If you screenshot your own work as suggested there should not be a problem. If you capture images off the web, however, the graphics and text captured may themselves be subject to copyright, or at least to a fair use policy. You should read the website terms and conditions carefully to ensure you do not inadvertently breach these when taking screenshots.

people's browsers even if it is viewable on your own. It may also take a lot of time to upload to or download from a server.

Using Windows, there are two standard ways to take screenshots:

- You can take a screenshot of the whole desktop area by using the print screen button (usually 'Prt Sc' or 'PrtScr').
- You can take a screenshot of the current window, by holding the 'Alt' key down while pressing the 'Print Screen' key.

In both cases the screen is grabbed to the clipboard and can be pasted into any package. Ideally you will paste it into a graphics package, save it, crop it, resize it and compress it.

ACTIVITY 10 Take a screenshot

Screenshot as taken from the screen (206 kbytes)   Screenshot at low resolution (40 kbytes)

Figure 1.7.11 Effect of altering the resolution of an image

Watch the demonstration of how to take a screenshot.
- Now open Windows Media Player.
- Open the radio tuner.
- Take a screenshot of the current window only (using 'Alt' + 'Prt Sc').
- Paste it into a graphics package.
- 'Save', 'Export' or 'Save for web' the image as a '.jpg'.

Now watch the demonstration of resizing a screenshot.
- Now resize your image in a graphics package to the final size required.
- Resave it with '-resized' added to the filename.
- Resave it with '-lowres' added to the name in the lowest acceptable resolution.
- Compare these two file sizes with the original file size (see also Fig. 1.7.11).

Assuming that an image of 64 kbytes will take approximately 1 second to load on a web page, calculate how long each image will take to load.

▶ Creating your own images with a digital camera

Some of the most effective images for illustrating your book will be photos you take yourself. The simplest and fastest means of achieving this is to use a digital camera. Using a 35mm or APS camera and having the results processed to CD or scanning the final pictures will be just as effective, however, though it will take longer. You may take pictures of people undertaking online processes, the effects of the use of ICT, examples of ICT or scenes connected with the digital divide. It is worth remembering that a page can be enlivened by a consistent background or use of small illustrations.

Take many images and select a few. Take close ups and long shots; plain and abstract shots; still and action shots. Take extreme close ups of objects used by your subjects as these can add interest to a page and make a point quickly.

Screen resolutions and mega pixels

Image size	Typical pixels	Approximate screen picture size at 72 dpi	Typical usage
5 mega pixels	2592 × 1944	36 inches × 27 inches	A4 photo
3.2 mega pixels	2592 × 1728	36 inches × 24 inches	A5 photo
1 mega pixels	1280 × 960	17 inches × 13 inches	Hi-res screens or web pages
VGA	640 × 480	8 inches × 6 inches	Email or web page

Table 1.7.2 Digital camera resolution and pixels per inch

For most web-page pictures it is not necessary to have the best multiple mega-pixel camera. A screen typically outputs its display at 72 dots (or pixels) per inch (known as dpi) – though some screens display a bit more – whereas digital photography prints are usually output at 300 dpi, or more. An image from a 3.2 mega-pixel camera is made up of about 3 200 000 pixels. Clearly, this will not fit a typical modern screen resolution of 1024 × 768 (786 432 pixels) or 1280 × 1024 (1 310 720 pixels). Most of the image will be 'off the page'. So even your 1 mega-pixel phone camera (about 1 000 000 pixels) will take totally acceptable pictures for the web, provided the lens is clean. (See also Table 1.7.2.)

ACTIVITY 11 Take and edit photographs ◀
Take some pictures

Take pictures of a number of objects used in digital entertainment, such as an iPod, a microphone, a Sky+ box, a plasma screen etc. Take a selection of long and close up shots (see Fig. 1.7.12).

Transfer them to your computer and name the photographs appropriately.

iPod   *Microphone*   *Midi keyboard*

Figure 1.7.12 Selection of digital entertainment devices

Original image (8 Mbytes on camera)

Cropped and resized image

Compressed to a few kilobytes

Figure 1.7.13

Edit and save your pictures

Edit one of the photos in a graphics package:
- Crop it to get the exact composition you require (see Fig. 1.7.13).
- Enhance it with the tools available (colour or brightness correction etc.).
- Resize it to 200 pixels wide (about a quarter of a screen).
- Save it as a .jpg image using the maximum compression that yields acceptable quality.
- Test it in a web page.

Graphic formats

There are three main formats (JPEG, GIF and PNG) that are used by virtually all web browsers. Other formats can be understood by some browsers using plug-in software, but will not be viewable in others. These should be avoided in any web-based project. It is not sensible to include BMP, DRW, PSP, DIB or indeed any other graphic format even if they display correctly in your browser. The choice between the three web-friendly formats depends on the type of image you want to store and what you want to do with it.

JPEG files (Joint Photographic Experts Group, .jpg extension)   The JPEG format was devised with photographs in mind. Photographic-type pictures can be rendered accurately at compressions as high as 12:1. It is a 'lossy' format however – that is, information is lost when compressing. The higher the compression (usually shown as a numeric value between 1 and 100) the greater the loss of quality. This is usually seen as unwanted lines, fuzzy areas or peculiar patterns on the image. The trick is to reduce the quality to the minimum acceptable value for the project.

The other reason for choosing the JPEG format is that it is possible to set the image so that it will appear progressively on the screen using a technique called 'interlacing'. This gradually reveals the image coming into focus, thus making the wait for a large web page to load appear shorter.

GIF files (graphic interchange format, .gif extension)   GIF files are stored in a different manner to JPEGs. The compression algorithm compresses by counting blocks of consecutive colours and storing the size and colour. This is extremely efficient at storing simple graphics, line art, bar charts etc. and can achieve compressions of up to 5:1 without any loss of information – it is 'lossless' compression; but it is not very efficient at compressing normal photographs with a more random colour distribution. Furthermore, it is restricted to 8-bit colour (up to 256 colours) and thus is not really suitable for full-colour images, which use millions of colours.

A good reason for choosing GIF pictures is that they can have a colour removed altogether to give a transparent region. This is an extremely useful technique that allows pictures to be floated over backgrounds effectively and easily without having to do any colour matching.

PNG files (portable network graphic, .png extension)   The GIF algorithm was patented by a commercial organisation (CompuServe) and there were fears that they would start charging royalties on what had been a common format. Web experts therefore invented a new, improved version that could be used without any fear of being asked to pay royalties. This was the PNG format. It uses a similar type of compression to GIF. It is available in 8-bit format (PNG-8) – the same as GIF – but also in 24-bit format (PNG-24), giving 16 777 216 possible colours. Nevertheless it is not a particularly common format as the fears concerning GIF royalties never materialised, and most web developers have simply carried on using GIF images.

ACTIVITY 12 Which file format?

Open the activity shown in Figure 1.7.14 in the ActiveBook and match the file format to the pictures.

File Formats

GIF/PNG-8	PNG-24
JPEG	PNG-24
GIF/PNG-8	GIF/PNG-8

Photograph   *Windows clip art*   *Graph*   *Screenshot*   *Faded background image*   *Bullets (over the background)*

Figure 1.7.14

▶ Drawing and editing graphics

Don't be afraid to do some basic drawing. If you are a talented artist this is an excellent opportunity to use your skills. Even if you feel you have no talent there is still a lot you can do. You could copy an image as you did at primary school by breaking it up into a grid, create an abstract image or create some coloured shapes. Use anything to make the e-book more relevant and interesting. You could use simple diagrams and objects for backgrounds, bullets, simple illustrations and as blocks of colour on the page. These can enrich the users' experience if used wisely.

ACTIVITY 13 Create a coloured-shape index logo ◀

Watch the demonstration of how to draw a simple shape. Now in your favourite drawing package draw four circles in any colours you wish, each filling a 50 pixel × 50 pixel canvas (see Fig. 1.7.15).

Save them as GIFs (e.g. bluecircle.gif etc.).

Figure 1.7.15 Circles

ACTIVITY 14 Create a transparent GIF ◀

Load the images created in Activity 13 into a package that allows you to create transparent GIFs. (Note: if your standard graphics package does not allow you to create transparent GIFs easily, you could use Microsoft Publisher 2003 or FrontPage.)

Click on the image. Locate the transparency tool. Click on the colour you want to make transparent (see Fig. 1.7.16). Resave the picture with a new name.

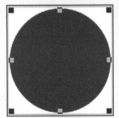 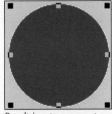

Load the image   *Apply tool to white area*   *Result is a transparent area*

Figure 1.7.16 How to create a transparent GIF

Figure 1.7.17 Indexing by colour

ACTIVITY 15 Add the same image to the top right of every page

In the CSS for the document you can add an image as a background to appear in the same position and in the same manner on every page that has the same CSS (see Fig. 1.7.17).

To do this put the image 'bluecircle.gif' in the CSS folder of the e-book you created in Chapter 1.6. Add the following line to the body tag to put it top right of your document:

background: url(bluecircle.gif) top right no-repeat;

Add it to a div to make it appear at the top right of that part of the page.

ACTIVITY 16 Add transparent GIFs as an indexed menu

Watch the demonstration of how to insert four transparent images into the menu on the left of Figure 1.7.17.

Now do this for yourself. Give them appropriate alt tags so that when you hover over them a helpful tool tip appears, as in Figure 1.7.17.

Link them to the chapters of your e-book. For example:

```
<a href="ch1.html"><img src="bluecircle.gif" alt="Online services"
class="tabimage" ></a>
<a href="ch2.html"><img src="redcircle.gif" alt="Impact of ICT"
class="tabimage" ></a>
<a href="ch3.html"><img src="greencircle.gif" alt="Digital Divide-global"
class="tabimage" ></a>
<a href="ch4.htm"><img src="transbluecircle.gif" alt="Digital Divide-local"
class="tabimage" ></a>
```

Note if you add a class name to the images you can control how they display through the CSS file. Add to the CSS file the class, but start it with a dot (.) as follows:

```
.tabimage{
  width:20px;
  height:20px;
  border:0px;
  margin:0px 10px 0px 0px;
  display:inline;
}
```

These images will now act as a coloured tab index. (Note: You will need to create a separate CSS file for each chapter to have a different circle at the top right, but this is a simple exercise.)

Activity 17 Create a thumbnail

Occasionally you may want to include a large high-resolution image in your e-book. When you do this it may take a long time to load. In these circumstances it may be wise to include a small thumbnail on your page and a link to the whole image. This is a very simple exercise. First watch the demonstration, then:

- Load a large graphic of your choice into your picture editor.
- Resize it to a thumbnail size (e.g. 100 pixels wide).
- Save it under the same name as before with a '_small' suffix; for example, if the main image is 'marlowes.jpg', call the thumbnail 'marlowes_small.jpg' (see Fig. 1.7.18).
- The alt tag should include the file size for the large image.
- Link the thumbnail to the main image.

The HTML that will be generated will look like the following:

```
<a href="marlowes.jpg"><img src="marlowes_small.jpg" alt="Marlowes
Shopping centre (770,048 bytes)" </a>
```

The browser will load and show the large image if requested in its own window.

Thumbnail 'marlowes_small.jpg'

Full size image 'marlowes.jpg'

Figure 1.7.18 Creating a thumbnail image

Figure 1.7.19 The completed thumbnail image of the Marlowes with tooltip

▶ Movies and animations

Full-scale and third-party movies are hard to include and evidence convincingly in your e-book though there are public domain movies which may have some research interest at the Internet Movie Archive. There is some scope, however, for short clips. These may be used to illustrate sequences for any section of the book, but particularly the online-services section where simple actions can be captured by a digital video camera or a digital still camera with movie mode. The main formats for capturing video are MPEG4, AVI and QuickTime. These are often included in modern PC set-ups, but if they are not, helpers or plug-ins may be required to view them.

Figure 1.7.20 You can view a short tutorial about animation at this website

▶ Animations

The best animations on the web are created using technologies such as Flash and Shockwave.

Video formats

MPEG (Moving Picture Experts Group, .mpg extension) This is the generic standard for compressed video on all computers. Many video and still video cameras will output in MPEG-4 format. Digital TV is often transmitted in MPEG 4 format. Virtually all media players can understand it.

QuickTime (.mov extension) This is Apple's format for movies and sound, which has now been standardised and made available across all platforms. It is a very flexible format with a good compromise between quality and speed.

AVI (audio-video interleave, .avi extension) This is Microsoft's original answer to QuickTime. It is viewable on virtually all PCs and is the default output for many digital cameras. It is most useful for showing small movie files in a window on a screen.

Windows Media Video (.wmv extension) Microsoft Windows Media Video format is a very flexible and high-quality format allowing the developer to target the output to the connection and screen size required.

These require separate plug-in files in the browser for the viewer to be able to experience them. However, the Flash plug-in is commonly available and is a standard for the Applied GCE, and so if you are already experienced with this, or can learn it, then you can include Flash animations very effectively in your e-book. If not, the demonstration shows how a simple GIF animations can be a straightforward and effective alternative.

There are many public domain or royalty-free animations available, e.g. Royalty Free Clip Art has a collection. As always it is important to quote the source if you use these. But it is better and often simpler to make them yourself using a drawing tool such as Photoshop, Paint Shop Pro, Serif Draw, Fireworks or MS Gif Animator (a free download).

Figure 1.7.21 Look at this sequence of images which forms an animation of a flying dragon (Source: reduced from the original dragon_anim.gif by Vicky Hoskin, a student at West Herts College 2003.)

Be moderate with moving elements. They can look a little amateur if they are not fully integrated into the look and feel of the site. The same caveat applies to marquees. Ensure if they are used that you use CSS to style them to fit in with the rest of the site and explain in your write up that you have done this.

Figure 1.7.22 Sound capture on a PC

▶ Sounds

Sounds enliven a site, and it is relatively easy to include sound files such as background music or short interviews. There are libraries of public domain sounds available, which you can use as long as you give proper accreditation. These include songs, sound effects, voice etc. Remember that with sounds the words may be copyright and the performance of them may also be separately protected. The best method of including sound files is to make your own (see Fig. 1.7.22). It is relatively easy to create midi music if you have access to a sequencer, with or without an instrument. It is easy to record sound effects and small interviews by connecting a voice recorder (cassette, minidisk, iPod with voice attachment, DAT etc.) to the sound card of your computer or even by recording directly from a microphone to your sound card.

ACTIVITY 18 Record an interview

In pairs brainstorm a number of ideas for interviews for your e-book. Consider people who have experienced a large impact from the use of ICT, people who have taken part in digital-divide projects, people who use online services etc.

Draw up a short list of the points you want to make. Arrange an interview with the person stressing the purpose of the interview, ensuring you obtain permission in writing from the interviewee.

Record the interview and edit it until you have short clips. Record it to your PC in .wav format. If you have MP3 conversion software, compress the file to .mp3 format.

Include the file in your web page, using:

<a href="interview.mp3">interview </a>

Sound file formats

AIFF (audio interchange format, .aif, .aiff extensions)   This was developed by Apple for storage and transfer of sound files.

AAC (advanced audio coding)   AAC is a flexible and very high quality compressed format used as the default on the iPod. It stores music files at similar compressions to MP3 with virtually no quality loss.

ATRAC (adaptive transform acoustic coding for mini disk)   Atrac is Sony's alternative to MP3, and is used on its minidisk and similar media players. It loses some quality, but it is claimed that the loss is outside of the human ear's range.

MIDI (musical instruments digital interface, .mid, .midi extensions)   This is a standard for communication between midi input devices, sequencers (processors) and sound sources (output devices). It does not store digital audio but rather it stores frequency, pitch, rhythm, tone and event information in a time-line format. It is therefore an extremely efficient and flexible format to use for storing music. The exact sound output, however, will depend on the quality of the midi output on the browser's computer.

MP3 (.mp3 extension)   This is the de-facto standard for compressed digital music files. The quality is nearly the same as CD but the files are compressed to about a tenth of the size.

Unix Audio (.au, .snd extensions)   These are the standard audio files for Unix, but are poorly supported outside this community.

Wave (.wav extension)   The standard means of capturing sound on a Windows PC is to use .wav files. These can be compressed, although they are nearly always very large.

Conclusion ▶ ▶ ▶

In this chapter you have learnt how to search the web effectively and store the results of these searches in an efficient and easily retrievable manner. You have learnt how to find, create and use media items in diverse forms, from small graphics to video, animations, sound and music.

However, it is essential to remember to include your media items only where relevant and interesting to your e-book, not for the sake of it. You will inevitably use graphics and it is important that these are created and stored in the correct format. Other media items should only be included where you have a definite purpose for them. They will then enhance and enrich your content and allow you to achieve a very positive evaluation of your e-book.

Tackling the Unit 1 assessment

For the Unit 1 assessment you are required to submit an **eportfolio** containing two major pieces of evidence:

1 An **e-book** about life in the Information Age
2 An **evaluation** of your e-book and your own performance.

The first major piece of evidence is the e-book. This is intended to be an original, small, interactive, multimedia e-book containing your research assembled into a coherent order, along with your reflections on, and evaluations of, this evidence. You will be assessed on:

- the content of your e-book
- the quality of your e-book itself as an item of practical ICT.

The other major piece of evidence is an evaluation of the e-book you have created and of your own performance. We suggest it should contain a "detailed evaluation" of two "key features" of the book and "evaluative comments" on three other features, including some feedback from test users and two realistic suggestions for improving or enhancing its functionality.

Part 1 Produce an e-book

The first piece of evidence is the completed e-book. This involves two equally important steps:

1 an investigation of life in the Information Age
2 the practical creation of a multimedia e-book.

Step 1: Investigation

The assessment is concerned with giving a balanced account of the Information Age at this current moment, in order that anyone reading it in 100 years' time would have a valid perspective on it from the point of view of a participant. You are asked to investigate three specific areas in a number of very specific ways:

a A **description** and **evaluation** of at least **five** different types of **online service**, drawn together to give a picture of the current **scope and limitations of the internet** as a whole.

b A **description** of how ICT is affecting at least **five** different **aspects** of people's lives, **considering the benefits and drawbacks**, drawn together to give a picture of life overall in the Information Age.

c A **description** of at least **three factors** contributing to the **digital divide** and **some of the measures** being taken to bridge the gap, with an **evaluation** of the impact/extent of the digital divide, drawn together to give a picture of the current situation.

(Source: Edexcel Advanced Subsidiary and Advanced GCE in Applied ICT specification)

It is very important that you read these criteria very carefully, and attempt to do exactly what is asked of you.

Statement a

This area asks you to investigate the type of services available in the Information Age. It asks you to describe and evaluate five of these types of online service with the aim of giving a picture of the scope and limitations of the internet.

The five services should be chosen from the nine contained in the WYNTL (What you need to learn) section of the specification:

1 *communication (e.g. email, instant messaging, newsgroups, online conferencing, blogs)*
2 *real-time information (e.g. timetables, news services, traffic reports, weather)*
3 *commerce (e.g. shopping, banking, auctions)*
4 *government (e.g. online tax returns, e-voting, applications for services/grants, revenue collection)*
5 *education (e.g. online learning/training, VLEs)*
6 *business (e.g. videoconferencing, collaborative working, business networks)*
7 *entertainment (e.g. multi-user games, radio players)*
8 *download services (e.g. music, film, upgrades, software)*
9 *archiving (e.g. 'x drives')*

(Source: Edexcel Advanced Subsidiary and Advanced GCE in Applied ICT specification)

Statement b

This asks you to describe and consider the benefits and drawbacks of five different aspects of people's lives, to give a clear and balanced picture of life today (with an Information Age perspective).

These five aspects should be taken from the ten mentioned in the WYNTL section of the specification:

1	*working styles*	6	*decision making*
2	*communication*	7	*employment opportunities*
3	*education*	8	*crime and crime prevention*
4	*entertainment and leisure*	9	*civil rights*
5	*banking and shopping*	10	*legislation*

(Source: Edexcel Advanced Subsidiary and Advanced GCE in Applied ICT specification)

Statement c

This area looks at how different people are affected differently by the Information Age, the so-called 'digital divide'. You have to describe two global aspects and one local aspect of the divide, and analyse the cause and effects of these. You must then describe and evaluate measures taken to bridge the gap.

▶ Conducting research

While doing your research you must bear in mind that you have to use it to create an e-book with a number of multimedia features. This means essentially that, along with any text and navigation links you employ, you should also incorporate links to other sites, original and adapted graphics, and ideally some sound and animation.

Any worthwhile researcher will investigate material from a number of sources. Perhaps your most valuable source will be this text itself and the accompanying electronic material. Chapter 1.1 covers online services, Chapter 1.2 aspects of life in the Information Age, Chapter 1.3 aspects of the global digital divide and Chapter 1.4 the local digital divide. Each of the chapters also gives references to further areas you should research in more detail and, especially, to current websites that you should investigate and make your own notes about. You should:

- use magazines and newspapers to provide good, up-to-date examples, thereby giving life to your descriptions
- make notes from television and radio programmes
- use search engines and other online resources (databases, encyclopaedias etc.), using the advice from Chapter 1.7 to do this in an efficient manner.

You should not restrict yourself only to publicly available resources. Wherever possible you should consider aspects of your own experiences, and your friends' and relatives' experiences. Make use of this to add individuality and depth to your research. You could, for example, consider your own experience of modern methods of communication, a virtual learning environment (VLE), or downloading services and remote storage. You could interview your parents, neighbours and relatives about changes in the way they have worked over the years, or about their experiences of banking and shopping. You could devise a questionnaire about how people feel some aspects of ICT affect their civil rights, or how effective ICT has been in detecting and preventing crime.

Existing images can come from a number of sources including books, magazines, and the internet. As with textual material, it is important to respect copyright. You should choose copyright-free images, images that can be used for free for educational purposes, or you should obtain permission from the copyright owner. Where you are allowed to use others' images, it is also important to credit the original source properly.

Ideally you will generate a good range of original imagery. The two most important sources for this will be the use of screenshots and digital photos. Screenshots can be used, for example, to illustrate a point made about online services, show some aspect of modern life, or demonstrate a measure taken to bridge the digital divide. A photograph can be used to show technology, demonstrate an aspect of life in the Information Age, or highlight a local aspect of the digital divide. Drawings produced in a graphics package may be used to illustrate a point. A chart created in a spreadsheet from a table or a questionnaire you have devised may enable you to make a point very clearly. A combination of these sources will allow you to create an original and relevant multimedia e-book.

Edexcel has not been prescriptive about the types of multimedia to be used as different students will have access to different technologies. However, if possible and relevant, you should try to include some sound, animation and/or video. For example, an interview can be recorded quite simply as an audio or video file, and can make very compelling evidence for your e-book. Turning static images into simple animations can enliven them dramatically and add extra interest (see Chapter 1.7). For example, you could illustrate chat and email by using simple animated drawings or photos.

Edexcel, however, has been quite specific about the range and type of different sources you must use in each part of the e-book to achieve a particular grade. When researching online services, to get the best marks you should use a wide range of internet-based sources including, for example, extracts from websites, subject databases, web journals, online magazines or online newspapers; or quotes from discussion or Usenet groups. When researching the impact of life in the Information Age it is equally important to use a wide range of paper and electronic sources including the web, broadcast news, books, journals, magazines, newspapers, interviews, screenshots etc. It is also very important that you explicity show the range of sources that you have used as well as providing evidence in the form of screenshots, and sound or other media clips.

▶ Plagiarism and sources

All material copied or adapted from other sources must be sourced in full. The exact method for doing this will vary, but ideally you will reference any source within the text itself, including page numbers where appropriate. You should also provide a full, detailed, cross-referenced list of sources or bibliography on a separate page of the e-book.

- If you are quoting from a textbook give the author's name, the book title, the year of publication, the publisher and the ISBN number.
- When quoting from a newspaper or magazine give the author's name, article title, publication name, publication date and page number.
- When quoting from TV or radio sources quote the speaker's name, the programme title, the channel, and the date and time.
- When quoting from the internet quote the author's name where possible, the title of the article or page, and the full URL. It is also helpful to give the date of access to the web page, given that web pages tend not to be static.

Examples:

Jeffrey Zeldman, *Designing with Web Standards 2003*, New Riders, 0 7357 1201 8.

Roger Highfield, 'How havoc is unleashed from the depths', *The Science, The Daily Telegraph*, 27 December 2004.

George Sciadas (ed.), *Monitoring the digital divide and beyond*, Orbicom 2003, http://www.orbicom.uqam.ca/projects/ddi2002/2003_dd_pdf_en.pdf. Accessed 18 August 2005.

Failure to include a full list of sources will definitely reduce your mark. Passing off others' work as your own, or plagiarism, is considered to be cheating and is treated very severely. However, including full references will improve the quality of your work and allow you to achieve better marks. It is important that throughout your investigation you always make good notes of your sources.

▶ Description, analysis and evaluation

The final step in assembling the content for your e-book is to add your own description, analysis and evaluation about the information you have researched.

The specification gives very exact terms for what you have to do. It is important that you understand the difference between these terms and do exactly what is asked in each case.

The following simplified example of a student explaining his use of chat, shows the difference between these terms.

Chat is an example of a communication service on the internet. I use MSN Messenger to communicate with my friends after school most nights. We all log on before tea and discuss what has happened during the day and what we are going to do later in the evening. (description)

It is a two-way real time service meaning that anyone wanting to take part has to be online at the same time, unlike email where you can send a message that can be collected at any time. (simple evaluative statement)

This has the benefit that a number of people can talk to each other and respond immediately to each other like a real chat without having to be in the same place.

It has the drawback that if I cannot go online when my friends do I cannot take part which I could with email. (analysis of benefits and drawbacks)

The major reason my friends and I use chat is to arrange where to meet and/or what to do each night after school. We always go online between 4:30 and 5:00 pm. The main strength of chat is that we can chat as effectively as if we were together even though we are in our own homes, in our own rooms. The weakness is that occasionally someone cannot get on to a computer at the required time and they miss the conversation. The alternatives we could use to meet our purpose would either be email or mobile phone. Email is not instant enough for the purpose and the mobile phone solution is too expensive, and not all of my friends have mobile phones that allow conference calling. Overall chat meets our purpose extremely well, although it could be improved to allow a transcript of the message to be emailed automatically to a missing member. (evaluation)

Although your real descriptions and evaluations are likely to be more detailed than this example, they should follow the same pattern:

- **Descriptions** should state the facts.
- **Analysis** should go further to draw together patterns or generalisations. An analysis of benefits and drawbacks will draw together the benefits and drawbacks in relation to some part of the information.
- **Evaluation** should consider how well the purpose is met overall by considering the intention, the strengths, the weaknesses and possible alternatives and improvements. An 'evaluative statement' is a diluted form of evaluation in a short form, possibly a single sentence, which will contain some statement of possible strengths and/or weaknesses, related quite probably to an alternative or improvement.

For each of the three areas you investigate you should also provide a conclusion that gives your overall view on the area, based on your evaluations.

- To meet Statement **a** you should attempt to "give a clear and balanced picture of the current scope and limitations of the internet as a whole".
- To meet Statement **b**, your conclusion should show that you have attempted to give "a clear and balanced picture of life in the Information Age".
- To meet Statement **c**, it is only necessary to "summarise your overall views regarding the digital divide".

Step 2: Create your e-book

You will be provided with a technical specification for your e-book. The purpose of your e-book is to provide a snapshot of life in the current Information Age to form part of a virtual time capsule on the internet that is programmed to open in 100 years' time. The target audience will be anyone with internet access in 100 years' time. The content is as specified earlier. The specification of the e-book can be tailored further by detailing:

- navigation methods
- amount and type of multimedia required
- target resolution(s)
- browser support required
- bandwidth constraints.

The e-book is intended to be a simple variation of a website, as explained in detail in Chapter 1.6. Edexcel does not specify how you achieve the website, provided it is designed well and implemented to your design. You could use an office package that translates the final documents to html. You could use a simple text editor or a web design package such as Dreamweaver. In the end a great deal will depend on the tools you have available and the time you have to spend on the project. The practical aspects involved in creating the book itself and the content are equally weighted in the final assessment. It is important, therefore, that you take the opportunity to demonstrate your skills in using the tools to create a rich multimedia website rather than a static essay. If you master and use the tools and techniques described and explained in Chapters 1.6 and 1.7, you will be able to demonstrate this very well.

You will be marked according to the following criteria; that the e-book:

- includes the specified content
- demonstrates a sound understanding of multimedia design principles for on-screen publications
- demonstrates astute awareness of audience and purpose
- adheres to relevant legislation and codes of practice
- demonstrates selection and effective use of suitable ready-made multimedia components
- demonstrates creation and effective use of suitable original multimedia components
- demonstrates selection and competent use of appropriate software tools
- demonstrates rigorous use of testing and quality assurance procedures.

The specification also states that to gain full marks you should be astutely aware of your target audience and take proper account of accessibility issues. These are important and related issues. As the target audience is anyone with internet access in 100 years' time, it follows that you must make your website as "usable" (easy to use) and "accessible" (open to everyone) as possible. You must use standard file formats that are accessible to everyone. You should provide a site that is easy to navigate and use. You should create it in a style that is suitable for everyone, not, for example, just for a niche teenage market. You should consider font size and acceptable colour schemes. An important implication of the time capsule being examined in 100 years' time is that the e-book must be self-contained. If it was opened in the next century the chance of links still being valid is negligible. Links to websites or other resources not stored with the e-book will not therefore be assessed.

There are a large number of web sources available for information on creating accessible websites, including:

Making the web accessible   Combining colours theory
Web Accessibility Initiative   Website tips for colour
Website of accessibility guru Jacob Nielsen

The final criteria you will have to meet in this step is the application of rigorous testing and quality assurance procedures. This is evidenced mainly by the e-book being error free, although your evaluation (Part 2) should also contain details of how you know it is error free. In order to ensure that this is the case, it is of course essential that you work through a quality assurance process (see Chapter 1.6), proofread your work thoroughly, and then test it exhaustively.

We suggest you submit your final designs (storyboards, structure chart and other design notes) and any testing you do in separate PDF documents in your portfolio as evidence of your good working practices.

Part 2 Evaluate your e-book

The second part of the evidence in your eportfolio is the evaluation of your e-book and your performance. This is essentially an analysis and evaluation of key features of your e-book along with suggestions for improving the functionality of the book and an evaluation of your own performance.

In order to do this most effectively you should choose the two most important features and explain the purpose of each of these in detail. You could describe your navigation structure, or use of a particular style, or use of images or a particular animation. You should consider how well the purpose is met by considering the strengths and weaknesses of the feature, consider what alternative features could have been used to meet the same purpose, and why your approach was better (assuming it was). Ideally you should have at least two other people test your e-book – specifically these features – and give you detailed feedback on how well they work. You should incorporate this feedback into your evaluation. In order to do this, it is probably best to give your reviewers a feedback sheet on which you ask them to provide very specific feedback related to the purpose of your features. In this way they will know what is expected of them and they can give realistic and relevant feedback.

You should then select a further three key features of your e-book and make a simple evaluative comment about these. Again, the best way of doing this is to consider the purpose of the feature and make a statement about a strength and a weakness of the feature related to this purpose.

Finally, you should consider two realistic improvements you could make to your e-book given more time and/or resources, and describe these in sufficient detail for the assessor to understand how and why they would improve the e-book. You must also follow this process for evaluating how well you feel you have performed in creating the e-book. Use this as an opportunity to describe what you have done well and reflect on what you would like to have completed in more detail.

You can decide on the format in which you present this evaluation, although this must be in one of the standard formats specified by Edexcel. The most obvious format would be portable document format (PDF), as this can be created simply from an office document; then the document can be read in its original form whatever system the assessor is using to view the portfolio.

Unit 2

The Digital Economy

Here you will investigate a transactional website, and create and evaluate your own back-office database. You will submit these as an eportfolio

Information in modern organisations

An organisation can be defined as an entity comprising one or more individuals working towards a specific set of goals. The term 'organisation' implies that they work in an 'organised' or structured manner to achieve these goals. The definition covers not just a whole range of businesses, but also schools, hospitals, charities and government institutions; it embraces sole traders, multi-national businesses and governments. Naturally the information needs of these different organisations and the way they use ICT differs widely. In this chapter we will examine the different categories of organisation within the digital economy and the different ways they use ICT.

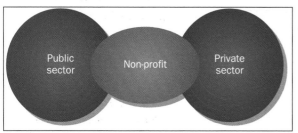

Figure 2.1.1 Economic sectors

Types of organisation and the use of ICT

Organisations can be categorised in a number of ways. One of the most common methods is to differentiate between them by the related factors of 'ownership' and 'objective'. On this basis there are three main types of organisation that can be readily identified:

- commercial organisations
- public organisations
- non-profit or charitable organisations.

Commercial organisations are what we would normally call businesses. They trade in a competitive market with the aim of making profits and growing the business. The smallest of these are single-person businesses (sole traders) such as window cleaners or a stall on your local market; the largest are giant multi-national companies such as the Ford Motor Company, Esso or Coca Cola. Maximising profit will not be the only objective of a business, but it will be the major one. Businesses survive and grow by selling products or services to their customers at a profit.

Public organisations are those that are funded primarily through taxation and are controlled directly or indirectly by the government. These include: direct government bodies such as government departments and the civil service; local government; public educational bodies such as schools, colleges and universities; the health service; the armed forces and the emergency services. The primary objective of these organisations is to provide some form of public service rather than make a profit. State schools are charged with providing education, state hospitals with healing the sick, the armed forces with defending the state and so on. They will still be measured by how well they keep to financial budgets but they will not usually be expected to make a profit from trading.

The distinction regarding profitability is not absolute. There is some crossover in the public sector from time to time. The utility companies (producing and distributing power and water), British Steel, British Airways and the railways were once in the public sector in the UK, but have since been privatised and are now businesses that are expected to make profits. British Telecom used to be public but is now a massive private sector business. The Post Office is still a public sector organisation, but is expected in time to make a profit. The Post Office is owned and is in part funded by taxation, but it also has customers who buy stamps and pay for the many other business services it provides. This is in contrast to the NHS whose services are 'free at the point of delivery'. That is, ill people do not have to pay for their treatment directly.

Non-profit or charitable organisations raise their finance from donations or grant funding and use the funds raised to finance a particular cause or issue, they also provide employment and incomes for the administrators of the organisation. They are regulated by the government commissions to ensure that funds are used properly. They are in many ways privately owned organisations with a form of public service objective. This can be seen clearly in the private education and health-care fields, many of whose organisations are set up as charities.

Charities

The Charity Commission provides a fully searchable database of UK charities and their objects. For example,

- BUPA is a major provider of private health care in the UK. The objects of the BUPA Foundation are given as "to prevent, relieve and cure sickness, ill-health and infirmity of every kind (including physical injuries) and to preserve and safeguard health by conducting and commissioning research".
- Manchester Grammar School is a major independent school in the north of England. The Manchester Grammar School Foundation's objectives are stated as "to advance the education of boys by the provision of a day or day and boarding school or schools in or near the city of Manchester".

ACTIVITY 1 Identify different types of organisations ◀

Create a table with three headings (commercial, public service, non-profit) and put these organisations into the appropriate columns:

- Tesco
- Ministry of Defence
- West Mercia police force
- Hemel Hempstead library
- Amazon.co.uk
- Echoes Under-11 youth football team.
- Boots The Chemist
- Football Association

- BBC
- TVR
- London Ambulance Service
- Patel's Newsagents
- NTL
- Sir John Lawes School
- British Heart Foundation
- Withington Hospital
- Newcastle United FC

Objectives and ICT

The different objectives of the three categories of organisation lead to quite different information needs and different methods of using ICT. Watch the presentation about these.

A large commercial organisation such as Tesco will market goods and services, present information, exchange information, conduct transactions, capture and process customer and stock data, distribute goods, manage customer relations and optimise stock control all using ICT. All aspects of Tesco's business are integrated using ICT, and its business encompasses all aspects of ICT.

The London Ambulance service is not a business and does not have to market itself as such. It does not have to keep records of customers, sales and stock of products. It does, however, rely heavily on ICT for presenting information and exchanging information, just like Tesco. It also uses ICT for public relations, but most critically, within its ambulance fleet-management operation – deploying its many ambulances and staff as efficiently and effectively as possible, in dealing with over 1 million calls a year.

The British Heart Foundation is a non-profit organisation. Having said this, in fighting heart disease, it clearly needs to raise as much money as possible from a range of donors to fund research and education. Once it has raised money, it needs to manage and invest it. It also needs to capture donor information. The BHF uses ICT partly like a commercial organisation, such as Tesco, and partly more like the Ambulance Service.

The primary objective of an organisation does not in itself determine the organisation's information needs. We are still at an early stage of the Information Age and organisations are still working out how ICT can help. The UK Government, in particular, is in the middle of a large change to e-enabled services (as seen in Unit 1).

The emphasis of government interaction with the public is still mainly about presenting and exchanging information. This in itself should not be underestimated, since it can bring significant efficiencies. For example, it is clearly much more economical and efficient to allow consumers to download brochures and information packs from the internet, rather than print copies and send them out. Similarly, it is much more economical to provide answers to frequently asked questions (FAQs) online rather than to provide more staff to answer them either over the telephone or face to face. However, it is increasingly possible to conduct transactions with the public sector over the internet. For example, it is now possible to book driving tests, file tax returns, start companies and file company returns online. The information needs for these different activities are diverse and far-reaching and the public sector is clearly a massive and growing consumer of ICT services.

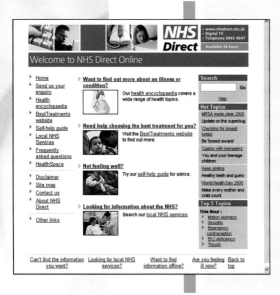

Activity 2 Explore ICT and the health information

Visit the NHS Direct website and the Best Treatments site. List:
- the different forms of information that are presented
- the different methods that can be used to find information
- the different audiences for the information and how the presentation for these audiences varies.

In what ways does this service add to the service from GPs and hospitals? In what ways does this lead to more efficient government?

Figure 2.1.2 NHS Direct – a site set up to offer, where possible, NHS services and information to the general public on the web

Economic scale and ICT

The balance of the different uses of ICT will vary not simply by objective, but also by scale. Mr Smith's small newsagent may require little or no ICT; Echoes youth football club may only use it for informing and amusing members and parents, and the gardens department of a small local council may only use it for payroll purposes. On the other hand, large businesses such as Ford, charities such as the British Heart Foundation and Oxfam, and large government departments such as the Inland Revenue, have ICT at the heart of all their systems and have vast information needs.

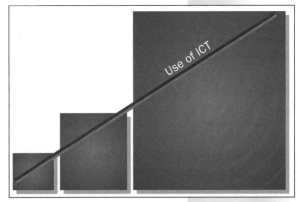

Figure 2.1.3: Economic scale and ICT – the larger the scale of the organisation, the more ICT it will tend to use

ACTIVITY 3 Look for uses of ICT in a charity website

Find at least five of the following uses of ICT that happen through the BHF website:
- capturing and processing data
- presenting and exchanging information
- conducting transactions
- marketing goods and services
- distributing goods
- managing customer relations
- optimising just-in-time purchasing of stock and components.

Take screenshots of the website. Annotate these with arrows indicating each use of ICT that you find.

Figure 2.1.4 British Heart Foundation website

ACTIVITY 4 Look for uses of ICT in a public-sector website

Visit the websites of the British Army and the Metropolitan Police.
   What do you consider the main purpose of each is? Which of the following uses of ICT do they engage in through their websites?
- capturing and processing data
- presenting and exchanging information
- conducting transactions
- marketing goods and services
- distributing goods
- managing customer relations
- optimising just-in-time purchasing of stock and components.

Industrial sectors and ICT

Organisations are often categorised by the industrial sector within which they operate. There are generally agreed to be three sectors within modern economies:

- **Primary** This sector comprises activities relating to natural resources, such as agriculture, forestry and fishing, and extraction industries such as mining, quarrying and oil.
- **Secondary** This sector comprises activities related to manufacturing and production, including the production of energy and goods.
- **Tertiary** This is the service sector, and includes retail, banking and finance, insurance, ICT services and training.

Data logging and analysis, monitoring and control are among the main applications of ICT in the primary sector. In the secondary sector, ICT is also used extensively in design and manufacture, in numerical control and robotics, and in picking and packing. It is used to schedule and optimise production mixes within factories. Manufacturing companies use ICT to automate production and buying processes and control stock levels so that the minimum stock can be kept on site. For example, motor manufacturers such as Ford do not keep huge inventories of parts 'just in case they are needed'. Instead, they have direct automated delivery systems linked to suppliers which trigger requests for additional parts as and when existing ones are used in the production process. This process is called just-in-time (JIT) stock control.

The real boom in ICT use has, however, taken place in the tertiary sectors of the economy. Banking, as seen in Unit 1, is now an ICT-driven industry; insurance and finance are just as ICT dependent. Retail, or the selling of products and services to private customers, is also increasingly ICT dependent, especially with the invention of the virtual online store.

Many organisations cross the boundaries between industry sectors, and make extensive use of IT in all the sectors in which they operate. A primary industry company such as BP will extract oil from the ground, process it and then sell it through its own retail outlets – the service stations. At every stage of the process, IT comes into play in some form or other.

Figure 2.1.5 Vauxhall's website

ACTIVITY 5 Look for uses of ICT in a manufacturing sector website

Visit the Vauxhall website.

List examples of at least five of the following uses of ICT as demonstrated by this website:

- capturing and processing data
- presenting and exchanging information
- conducting transactions
- marketing goods and services
- distributing goods
- managing customer relations
- optimising just-in-time purchasing of stock and components.

Take screenshots of the website. Annotate these with arrows indicating each use of ICT that you find.

Conclusion ▶ ▶ ▶

The rest of this unit will focus on e-commerce and the use of transactional websites. Not all of these websites will be from the retail part of the private sector, because as we have seen, there are transactional websites, and indeed pockets of fully fledged e-commerce, within the public and non-profit sectors too.

We have already seen how much of British industry is vertically integrated; that is where a manufacturer such as Vauxhall will manufacture cars and sell them direct to the public using its own public-facing website. However, the vast majority of websites you will examine and analyse in the remainder of the unit will be those of organisations within the retail part of the private sector. There is a vast array of these with different purposes, diverse products, different payment methods, various fulfilment mechanisms and a variety of data needs. You will study a range of these; and for your coursework you will study a single site in depth.

B2B and B2C

B2B means 'business-to-business', and refers to transactions between two different companies. Many of these are now conducted using extranets – private networks that connect more than one organisation. As we have seen, JIT stockholding as practised by manufacturers such as Ford and retailers such as Tesco similarly rely on these automated links between the databases of the business customer and its many suppliers. These are important uses of ICT, but beyond the requirements of the syllabus.

B2C means 'business-to-consumer', and involves transactions between conventional commercial websites and individual customers. The investigation of these will form the basis of the rest of this unit.

Doing business on the web

Sir Tim Berners Lee spun the world wide web into existence in 1989. In the following 10 years it became a business phenomenon. By 1999 it was said that AOL had 2000 millionaires working for it. This internet portal was valued more highly than General Motors, yet with only a tiny fraction of its sales. An average of nine start-ups a week in the USA, mainly internet based, but all riding on the internet boom, were asking for and getting public investment in their share offerings.

However, following on from some share price falls in early 2000, on Friday 14 April 2000, the bubble burst spectacularly with Wall Street suffering its largest one-day losses in history. The stock market went on to lose around $2 trillion (million million) dollars in value in that one week. Large numbers of transactional websites, some with massive funding, disappeared in the aftermath of the collapse. This event caused vast numbers of investors to lose large amounts of money and shook confidence in the world wide web as a means of doing business. New start-ups barely reached one a week through 2001. There was then as much pessimism about the internet as there was unreasonable optimism before.

However, in the short time since then a more realistic and focused digital economy has emerged. The UK Office for National Statistics, quoting government policy, states

E-commerce is likely to have a huge impact on the way we do business. It has the potential to lead to dramatic growth in trade, increase markets, improve efficiency and effectiveness and transform business processes. In recognition of its significance in the future performance of the economy, the UK Government set itself the target of becoming the best environment in the world to do e-commerce. (Source: Our Competitive Future: Building the Knowledge-Driven Economy, DTI 1998 White Paper, CM4176.)

In this chapter we will look at how and why both private and public organisations do their business successfully on the web. We will:

- examine how the consumer base for online goods and services has grown enormously
- consider how productivity will be the key to a new internet business revolution
- analyse what are the factors that help make a web-based organisation a success.

Growth of the consumer base

The major factor in driving any business is the availability of customers. In spite of the demise of the dot com bubble, there has been a massive growth in the numbers of potential customers connected to the internet. Figure 2.2.1 shows that by the second quarter of 2004 over 50 per cent of all UK households (12.8 million) were able to access the internet from home, compared to less than 14 per cent at the height of the dot com boom in 1999.

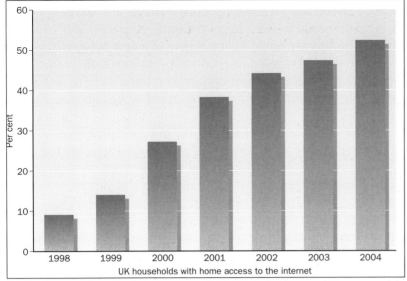

Figure 2.2.1 UK households online (source: <u>National Statistics</u>)

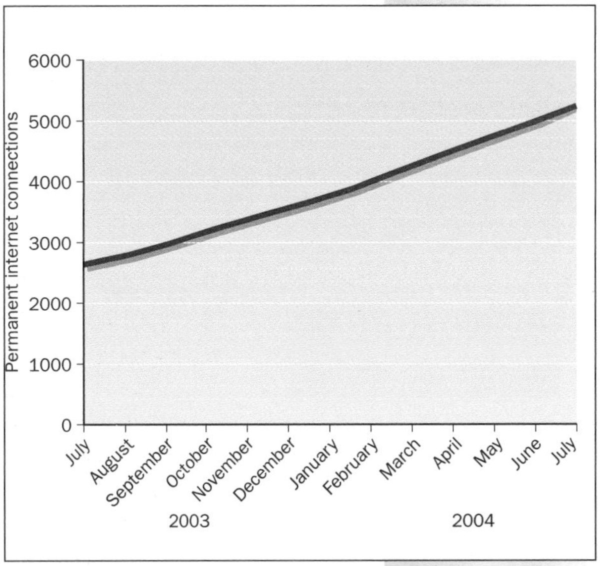

Figure 2.2.2 Index of broadband connections between July 2003 and July 2004 (index at Jan. 2001 = 100) (source: <u>National Statistics</u>)

Perhaps even more crucially, Figure 2.2.2 reveals that although dial up still dominates, broadband technologies (ADSL and cable modem) have grown hugely since the beginning of 2003 and are catching up with dial up. Other statistics show that 'always on' access stood in July 2004 at over a third of the market and is still rising rapidly. Although this in itself does not mean people will use the internet to acquire goods and services, it is a large potential market for organisations that manage to put together the right offer.

ACTIVITY 1 When is there the need for speed? ◀

Which of these services require fast, high quality internet access and why?
- buying the latest CD of your favourite band
- listening to internet radio
- downloading MP3s
- downloading videos
- buying a basket of 100 goods from an online grocer
- creating a travel itinerary for a round the world trip
- subscribing to a news service
- looking up information on the driving test.

The drive for productivity

A legacy of the dot com boom is that a great deal of discussion about the internet concerns how much money can be made or lost by embracing web technologies. However, there is another side that is important, not just to the private sector, but to the public sector as well. How much money can be saved by employing web technologies?

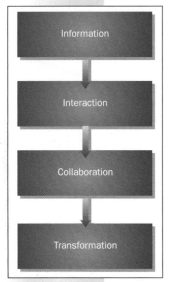

Figure 2.2.3 The four stages of internet productivity

Howard S. Charney, a Senior Vice President for Cisco Systems, in a keynote speech delivered around the world in 2002 to governments, education and industry, suggested that the internet would be the engine of a new business revolution. This revolution would be based on productivity, or increased worker output per hour. His thesis was that in the first 'Information stage' (see Fig. 2.2.3), the world wide web acts as a vast store of information based on billions of websites. It then progresses to the 'Interaction stage', being the hub of e-commerce (buying and selling on the web) and e-services (delivery of customer services on the web). The third phase is the 'Collaboration stage'. Organisations will use "… new technologies that link people together online such as instant messaging, threaded discussions, videoconferencing, web-based meetings and virtual conferences. And it sets the foundation for such exciting applications as digital collaboration in the design of products and services, e-marketplaces, telemedicine and e-learning." Finally the internet will transform our lives, becoming the hub of everything we do – the 'Transformation stage' (source: Cisco).

ACTIVITY 2 Investigate local government online

Look at the website for your local county council.

- Identify the major **information** it supplies and who it supplies it for. Explain at least one benefit for the council and one for the consumer of having this information online, rather than as pamphlets or as information possessed by council officers.
- Identify any opportunities the council gives for **interaction**. For example, does it allow residents or others to pay any bills online? Can you report faults with roads or pavements? Can you complain about dog fouling? Can you vote online?
- Choose one of these opportunities and evaluate the service.

  What is the purpose of the service?
  Who is the target audience?
  What are the major benefits?
  What weaknesses are there?
  What could be done to improve the service?

Figure 2.2.4 Hertfordshire County Council's online services

- Create a proposal for a council service involving online **collaboration**. State what the service would be and who the audience would be. Describe how it works and what benefits the council and the target audience would gain from the service. Describe any potential limitations of the service.

The internet has become firmly established as a major source of information for many people in the developed world. Nevertheless e-commerce and e-service delivery is still a minor player in world markets when compared to traditional bricks and mortar organisations, but it is becoming more pervasive very rapidly. Technology companies and a number of educational bodies use collaboration technologies, although they have yet to gain a firm foothold in the mainstream market. Message boards and hosted forums are a popular means of providing after-sales support.

A number of companies have experimented with live chat as a means of supporting people in buying goods such as computer hardware, providing help with installation of products, hiring cars, and buying products as diverse as sheet music and bicycles. However, there are significant costs involved in maintaining live chat, not least staffing, especially on sites hoping for 24/7 global reach. As a consequence, a large number of organisations have quietly dropped these services.

Activity 3 Find out about live chat

Many organisations have experimented with live chat as a means of giving improved customer service (see Figs 2.2.5 and 2.2.6). Watch the demonstration to see what's involved.

Describe how an ISP could use live chat to help its customers, and the advantages it would gain from using it. Analyse what the main problems with providing live chat are for a web-based organisation.

Figure 2.2.5 Musicroom with live chat

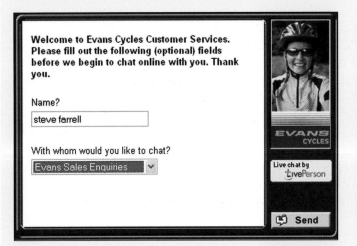

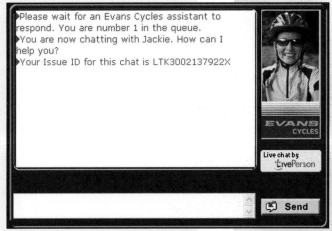

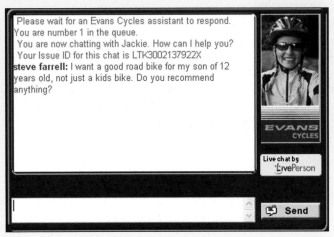

Figure 2.2.6 Example of live chat on the Evans Cycles website

One successful instance of the use of a number of these technologies is Channel 4 TV. The Channel 4 website (see Fig. 2.2.7) has a community section with over 58 000 registered members. It allows viewers to use message boards to discuss programmes and issues arising from them, as well as chat directly with celebrities, directors and stars of shows.

ACTIVITY 4 Investigate commercial benefits of community websites

List all the different communication services available through the Channel 4 Community website.

In what ways can a commercial company such as Channel 4 hope to benefit from running message boards, live chat and other community offerings? How might this translate into a model for other content providers?

Figure 2.2.7 Many TV channels have websites which allow viewers to communicate

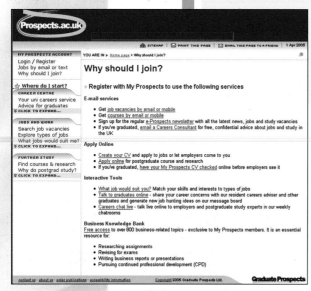

Figure 2.2.8 Prospects website

ACTIVITY 5 Identify website features

View the screenshot of Prospects (see Fig. 2.2.8), which is the official graduate careers website. Identify all the different methods employed to aid graduates in finding careers.

Clicks and mortar

Many of the success stories of the commercial web have been existing organisations that have built a strong internet business based on their traditional business. The reasons for this success are clear:

- Their financing and business practices are clear-cut and established, as they have existing assets and business processes to build on.
- Their logistics are clear-cut and established, as they have existing supplier and distribution channels in place.
- They can gain economies of scale in all aspects of their business and thus can potentially have lower overheads in marketing, purchasing, production, administration and selling.
- They have an existing brand image they can use to promote their new business.
- The risk is lower as they know there is an existing business that already works.

Businesses that build a web presence to complement their existing business can often hope to gain access to a much larger, and potentially worldwide, customer base. A bike shop in Sussex, Glasgow or the Peak District can now aim to sell bikes across the UK and Europe; a clothes designer with a single outlet can sell across the globe; a football club's souvenir store can become a global enterprise. All of these businesses can also offer a 24-hour, seven day a week market presence that would cost a fortune to maintain in a real store.

Activity 6 Examine web development of existing business

Visit Evans Cycles site (see Fig. 2.2.9).

Where is its office situated? Where do they ship to? What other services besides bike sales do they provide now that they have an online presence? How and when can customers contact them?

Figure 2.2.9 Evans Cycles website

Economies of scale

Businesses have a mix of overheads that do not depend in the short term on the level of production and sales. These include property costs, marketing costs, depreciation costs on machinery and vehicles, all administrative staff costs including buyers, clerks, accountants etc. The larger the volume of sales that can be gained from these 'fixed' overheads then the less the average cost of the product or service will be. In addition, the larger an organisation, the more possible it should be to match the scale of the overheads to the scale of the business over the medium term, thereby achieving even greater savings. (In practice this does not always work as larger businesses can become unwieldy.) An e-commerce website contributes to this because it has the advantage that it can help to grow sales without significantly increasing 'fixed' overhead costs. This is what is meant by 'gaining economies of scale'.

The main supermarkets in the UK including Tesco, Asda, Sainsbury's, and Waitrose (in partnership with Ocado) have all used these advantages to a greater or lesser extent in building online businesses.

Tesco has become one of the UK's great internet success stories by using a simple extension of its normal activities. The basic shopping experience for the user is the same as in a real store: the shopper selects his/her goods from a series of virtual shelves ordered in the same way as the store, and puts the goods in a virtual shopping basket. At the end of the transaction the customer checks out and provides the website with credit/debit card payment details.

At the store end the method is equally familiar. A picker walks round the aisles selecting the goods from a picking list generated from the shopping basket of the consumer. The picker selects items from the shelves and puts them in a shopping trolley. These items are scanned and a receipt is generated in a similar way to the in-store experience. The items are packed into a series of small crates and delivered (see Fig. 2.2.10) within a time slot specified by the customer.

Figure 2.2.10 Supermarket van delivering goods ordered from its website

This model of business practice requires some, but not massive, new investment in every shop. It relies on a small refinement of shop processes, and the purchase of perhaps one or two part-refrigerated vans for each store taking on the venture. The main investment was in a centralised website and call centre, both of which can serve all stores. The extra costs involved in having employees pick the goods and deliver them are at least in part offset by a service charge to the customer. Although all the online groceries offer more than this basic service, and have tried hard to make their websites as efficient as possible, the basic processes remain the same. This is in contrast to the US online stores HomeGrocer and Webvan, which disappeared along with many others in the internet shake-up.

CASE STUDY Webvan

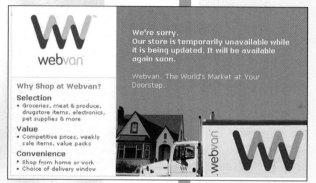

Figure 2.2.11 Webvan closed down (source: Ghost Sites)

Webvan was a product of the internet boom. It raised hundreds of millions of dollars to build dedicated fully-automated warehouses across the USA to sort and despatch groceries. Its business model planned to revolutionise home shopping through technology, using only a virtual store in combination with real-world warehousing and delivery. Initially it managed to build warehouses, hire 2000 employees, and gain very favourable reviews of its service from its customers, but it collapsed within 18 months of its share offer as a result of heavy losses and insufficient sales (see Fig. 2.2.11). At its peak it has been estimated that it only received 1500 orders a day, a level that was totally insufficient to cover its warehousing, packing and delivery costs.

Task

From what you know of Tesco's success, suggest further probable reasons why Webvan failed.

Figure 2.2.12 Shopping online at Tesco

ACTIVITY 7 Consider the pros and cons of online grocery shopping

Order the following list into two columns. One should be headed advantages of online grocery shopping and the other disadvantages of online grocery shopping.

- save petrol
- shop 24 hours a day, every day
- miss out on manager's bargains
- don't have to queue up
- see all the special offers in one place
- don't need a car
- have to stay in awaiting delivery
- have to phone up a call centre when an incorrect item is picked

Continued on next page

- can pick items from previous shopping lists to avoid forgetting essentials
- have to rely on someone else's judgement when substituting items
- have to pay more, especially for small loads
- can't feel the food to check on ripeness
- can compare prices with ease
- can complete a large repeat order very quickly
- don't have to go out in bad weather
- it is harder to return inadequate goods.

ACTIVITY 8 Compare online grocery stores

Compare the websites of the main online grocers in the UK.

What features do they have in common? What is different in each case? Which do you prefer and why?

At the other end of the business spectrum are many small flower sellers from the Island of Guernsey. These retailers have been running flowers-by-post services for many years to the UK and Europe, using specialist advertisements and catalogues. The internet has given them the chance of reaching a wider, potentially global market at relatively small expense, using the same basic business practices as they always had.

Figure 2.2.13 Fresh flowers are delivered all over the world from Guernsey

ACTIVITY 9 Investigate the Guernsey flower business

Find and list several internet flower suppliers based in Guernsey.

Why have they been successful? What is the major difference between these companies and Tesco? What are the similarities between their experience and that of Tesco?

The logistics problem

One great challenge faced by online organisations is logistics. ValueAmerica was forced to close its internet retailing business in August 2000 after suffering immense problems with its warehousing and distribution. The company's demise was detailed in the popular book *Dot.Bomb: My Days and Nights at an Internet Goliath* by J. David Kuo (Little, Brown & Company, 2003, ISBN 0316600059). Items that were sold were often not in stock. Even when stock came in there was inadequate warehouse space and insufficient staffing. When goods went to customers they were often sent too late, were the wrong items, were broken on arrival or had vital parts missing. The goods were often returned but since this was essentially a virtual business, there was no solid system for handling returns.

Figure 2.2.14 Successful web businesses need to consider the physical as well as the virtual dimensions of their organisation

We have seen how the UK supermarkets have used local stores and well-tried business practices to manage their logistics. Even then, problems sometimes occur. Human error is inevitable and sometimes van drivers will drop off an incorrect crate, with the knock-on effect that later deliveries will also be incorrect. This will then result in the customer having to contact a call centre, potentially hanging on for some time in a telephone queue, and then dealing with someone remote from the problem. The store, to maintain its reputation for customer service, often simply allows the customer to keep wrongly delivered items without charge, and so making a loss on the delivery. In the rare cases where poor produce is sent out they will give a total refund without quibble, although the reason that motivated the customer to buy online (e.g. their own lack of mobility) often makes it hard for them to return to the store.

The exact logistical problems faced by organisations depend on the goods or service being supplied. The perfect internet company might therefore be one selling 'items' that can be delivered electronically via its website; and so no warehousing, vans, pickers or drivers would ever be required, the product or service would just pass down the cable or telephone line. This type of business might involve delivering an existing 'item' in a new way, or perhaps the delivery of a completely new type of service, where the customer can gain new benefits and the supplier achieve spectacular successes, as we will see in the next example.

New distribution methods

Figure 2.2.15 iTunes have become extremely popular

CASE STUDY iTunes Music Store

Apple's iTunes Music Store download service is an excellent example of such a success story. Apple has put a massive catalogue of music and audio books online in its music store. Users of Apple's iTunes software can visit the music store and review 30 seconds of almost any work in the catalogue. If they like what they hear, they can download the work with a few clicks of their mouse; a small charge is deducted from their credit card for each song or album downloaded. Watch the demonstration of the store. Some of the customer-orientated features of the site include:

* the customer can gain access to new music instantly from the comfort of their own home
* they can review massive back catalogues of music to find a song they have not heard for a while
* they can buy just the one track they like rather than having to buy a whole album
* they can listen to play lists created by people who like the same kind of music as themselves
* they can buy music in play lists rather than albums if they prefer.

Since the store was launched in the USA it has sold more than one million tunes per week. In the first week of its European launch in June 2004, it sold 800 000 tunes at approximately 79p per tune and has been selling at approximately this level or better ever since.

Continued on next page

The logistics of supply are simple, but extremely well done. The difficult part of the operation has been for Apple to acquire and pay for the rights to the music. This has meant that there are not many indie bands on iTunes, as the independent labels have not been able to agree terms to their satisfaction with Apple. Also, although this form of distribution could be global, it is in fact fragmented, as the rights to the music have to be acquired in each separate market in accordance with the copyright legalities of that particular country.

It is also worth remembering that even with a business of a virtual nature, such as iTunes, it nevertheless still requires a large physical computer infrastructure to support it; that is there are still logistics to consider. In practice, iTunes is a massive database. It is set up on massive fault-tolerant hard disks on very fast servers, with very high-speed internet connections that allow multitudes of simultaneous users. iTunes connects to the hard disk and requests a track. The store then arranges the automated download of the track and attaches a digital rights management code that connects the user to the track bought in order to deter piracy.

The logistics issues were solved through the application of Apple's existing specialist knowledge. As an established hardware and software manufacturer, it already had the expertise for this kind of huge operation. Once the initial investment cost was recovered (in terms of equipment, software and labour), the music store is relatively easy to maintain and update. There are still day-to-day running costs, but the greatest expense for this type of business is almost always in the set-up phase.

The 100 millionth song

Kevin Britten of Hays, Kansas, hit the jackpot when he downloaded the 100 millionth song from iTunes recently. As a reward, Apple gave Britten a 17-inch PowerBook computer, a 40-GB iPod music player and a voucher for 10 000 downloads. Such largesse is not surprising; it was a notable milestone for Apple, which in a very short time frame has claimed a huge percentage of the legal music-download market worldwide. (Source: Erika Morphy. NewsFactor Technology News, 13 July 2004.)

Task

Consider the following factors regarding the fantastic success of legal downloading services such as iTunes:

- access to the service from a computer anywhere
- the ability to buy a track anytime 24 hours a day, seven days a week
- the ability to buy music immediately without waiting
- additional services such as the ability to buy by track or play list; organisation by genre, artist, similar tastes etc.
- reliable and speedy service
- price.

Which do you consider to be the three most important factors, and why? Could these factors be translated to other possible web businesses?

Perhaps an even more perfect web business delivery model would be to be able to charge for viewing the content of the website itself. This model has been taken up extensively by existing and new businesses, and by public service organisations. The main technical requirement is the ability to password-protect pages on the website. It is also necessary to have some method of collecting the money for the content. This may be on a pay-per-article basis, which will require some form of e-commerce facility, or more commonly, on a subscription basis, which can be managed online or offline.

ACTIVITY 10 Investigate making money from online content

- Review *The Economist*, *The Independent*, *The Telegraph* and *The Times* online, to see how existing newspaper and magazine businesses attempt to make money from providing electronic content.
- Review Lifelong Learning UK and Improve, the Sector Skills Council for Food and Drink Manufacturing and Processing, for related but different approaches on how public-sector bodies can gain revenue by providing members-only pages on subscription.
- Review the online versions of the *Oxford English Dictionary*, *Encyclopaedia Britannica* and *Encarta* to see how reference content can be successfully charged for.
- Review Nutrition Matters to see how a business can be set up to sell information to professionals and individuals.
- Review Macromedia to see how a major software company can gain additional revenues by providing online content.

What products and/or services are being sold in each case?

What payment methods do the different sites use?

What do you consider are the factors that make it possible to sell site content?

To what extent do the sites provide free information and why do they do this?

To what extent are these businesses adding to existing businesses?

To what extent are these sales only possible because of the internet?

Successful internet models

Another notable area of success and growth in the UK has been the mobile-phone ring-tone market. Bart Lautenbach, IBM's Head of E-Commerce, has spoken of the rapid take-off of digital media in e-commerce, noting that teenagers are not interested in digital transmission rates or the other concerns of the providers, but rather in getting the latest ring tones or wallpaper. He points out that this is a very profitable and very easy business (source: W. David Gardner, TechWeb, 16 January 2004). Much like iTunes, there is essentially no physical stockholding, distribution or returns. Tunes are created using simple software and uploaded to the website as tones. Money is taken and the customer downloads the ring tone. In practice, downloading ring tones has become so popular that there are now official ring tone charts, including the MTV chart.

Many other apparent success stories have involved companies which deliver small, low-value items via parcel post. Examples of these include booksellers such as Amazon.co.uk and CD/DVD sales organisations such as Amazon, HMV, CD-Wow and many others. The key to success in these cases is to offer a wide choice along with fast delivery, while keeping unit costs as low as possible so that the product can be sold at a price that undercuts ordinary physical stores. It is possible to deliver a CD or DVD from somewhere like Hong Kong using standard first-class post in three days. It is thus possible to locate the distribution centre in a lower wage, higher productivity economy. It is also possible to buy CDs for your warehouse at the cheaper rates prevailing in Hong Kong, thereby undercutting British prices.

There are disadvantages with such a model, however. In the case of music the catalogue, or range of items sold, may not be as extensive as a local shop and will almost certainly not venture far beyond mainstream. Some music companies also attempt to curtail this form of cross-market supply by tailoring the discs sold slightly differently for each market; thus the disc you buy might not be identical to the one in the charts in the UK. Returns can still represent a challenge, and it is often simpler to send a customer a new CD rather than undertake a lengthy returns process.

Books, which are weightier and bulkier than CDs, may cost a lot more than CDs to stock (due to warehouse space) and post, and therefore represent a somewhat larger challenge to the e-tailer. However, the same basic principles apply as with CDs. Economies of scale in warehousing and distribution are gained through having a central warehouse and collaboration with a delivery company. Also, large volumes of sales allow cheaper purchasing and thus lower pricing (though this would also be the case with a traditional high street book chain).

As well as price, such web-based book retailers' major selling point is perhaps convenience and choice. It is possible to buy books 24 hours a day, seven days a week, from an enormous range of books that simply could not be stocked in any physical bookstore. With one central warehouse, such retailers are able to stock more books, but you are also be able to browse stock they do not have, and receive an indication of the likely delivery time as you do so. These websites also have many techniques for tempting you to buy more books from them, such as forums, recommended reads, similar book suggestions, paired book packages and so on.

Delivery is usually by parcel post. Some require signatures on delivery and others do not. The ones that require signatures often suffer because customers are not in, but with standard parcel post and small volume parcels this is rarely a problem – the carrier will redeliver it or allow you to pick it up from a nearby sorting office.

This model translates well into many small niche markets, especially where speedy delivery is not as important, since the specialist buyer is likely to have the patience to wait. The websites that succeed in this area will be the ones with the smartest, automated integrated systems (discussed in the following chapter) so that there will be as little human intervention as possible.

Larger volume and perishable goods represent a significantly bigger challenge to an internet business. In these cases the goods will almost certainly be delivered within a stated time slot, when the customer is expected to be available to receive it. The time slots offered by many suppliers may be as open-ended as between 8 a.m. and 6 p.m., thereby rendering the service impractical for many working people. Better services will provide Saturday morning delivery or delivery to a work address on request. Successful businesses of this kind tend to be of the 'clicks-and-mortar' kind discussed earlier, that have an established delivery network. Nevertheless internet-only companies do exist that offer

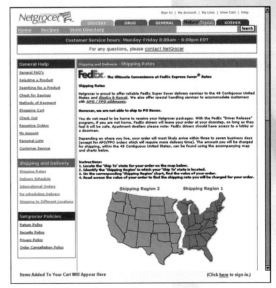

Figure 2.2.16 Netgrocer delivers using a parcel service

this type of service. If you live in the USA, it is even possible to buy groceries online from Netgrocer (see Fig. 2.2.16) and have them delivered by FedEx at your expense, to be left on your doorstep at your risk.

A business model that translates very successfully from high street or out-of-town shopping centre to an online business is the 'showroom plus checkout' business model of Argos and numerous similar stores. In these cases, the customer browses a catalogue or showroom, pays at the checkout and the goods are then collected or delivered from a warehouse. Existing stores are usually run with highly effective computerised systems that completely integrate the sales process and stock control. Translating this to the web is therefore relatively straightforward. Customers can now browse the catalogues online, but with the additional advantages of fast-searching, special web offers, and the real-time stock and sales information available from home that was previously only accessible in store.

Activity 11 Assess businesses for the online viability

Consider the following enterprises:

- selling funerals
- selling sheet music
- selling flower seeds
- selling livestock
- selling custom installed hi-fi equipment
- selling software

- selling market intelligence
- selling bread
- selling specialist herbs and spices
- banking
- booking a driving test
- voting

Create a table with three columns headed 'Viable e-business', 'Challenged e-business' and 'Reasons'. Put each enterprise into the appropriate column and write your reasons in the third column.

Conclusion ▶ ▶ ▶

The internet has grown from its academic and research-based origins to become an extremely important medium for the delivery of products and services for both the private and public sectors. There are a wide variety of ways to make a success of doing business on the world wide web, whether you are:

- an existing bricks-and-mortar business with good business practices that you transfer to the web
- an existing business that invents or perfects a new method of distribution
- a completely new business founded on the web
- a public service that finds ways of delivering improved access to its services while driving the organisation forward and delivering lower costs.

In this chapter we have examined different factors that contribute to the success of different web-based organisations including:

- access to a world-wide customer base
- low set-up and running costs
- extension of an existing product range to include internet-specific goods and services having a 24-hour, seven days a week presence
- the ability to offer faster response times over more varied contact channels
- the ability to deliver integrated solutions with customers having direct access to real-time information from the supplier.

We have also seen that along with the advantages, there are problems that arise as well as complementary advantages and disadvantages for consumers. Successful web businesses do not have a web presence because they merely think they should have one, because they can raise a lot of money to create one, or because they want to 'revolutionise' business, but rather because there is a strong business case for having one. They will match the way they do business to the way their customers want to do business; any 'revolution' will arise naturally from strong customer demand.

Running a transactional website

In the preceding chapter we investigated how the web is used to conduct business, both in the public and private sector. In this chapter we will investigate in detail the processes involved in running a modern transactional website. We will first look at how a site is set up for customers and the processes a customer is taken through on the lead-up to an online purchase. We will then examine the chain of events triggered behind the scenes by an online sale and the different functions of the organisation involved in the fulfilment of the sale. In order to learn how to describe and evaluate these processes as effectively as possible, we will also examine the two major diagrammatic techniques for analysing business processes, using information flow diagrams and flow charts. As a result you will be well equipped to tackle the final coursework for this unit.

Information flow diagrams

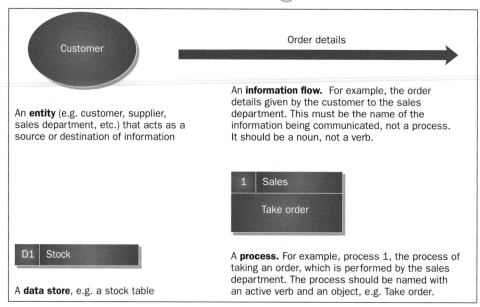

Figure 2.3.1 Information flow symbols

Information or data flow diagrams are used to show the information flows for a system. They can be used to describe complete systems in overview, or at a more detailed level. Since being introduced to model complex systems in the 1970s they have become the most popular means of analysing and designing systems. Their very popularity has meant that there are a wide variety of different methodologies commonly used for this task. They all have the same aim, which is to make complex systems simple to understand by presenting them visually. In practice, it is not important which diagramming technique you use, but rather that you are consistent in your usage.

There are two main versions of the information flow diagram in common use. The first and simplest is based on a document flow diagram. It shows the sources and destinations of all information together with the flows in, through and out of the system. The second more detailed type additionally shows the processes and data stores. Both forms of information flow diagram are useful and should often be used in combination to give a detailed view of a system. The standard symbols used in these diagrams are shown in Figure 2.3.1. Where an even more detailed view of the logic of an individual process within a system is required a flow chart should be employed. These will be described later in the chapter.

Data stores A data store is any place in the system where data is stored. It might be a tray of stock record cards, a rotary file of address cards, a list of customers or a table (or tables) in a database. In the examples we are looking at, a data store will nearly always be a database table or tables.

Simple information flow diagrams

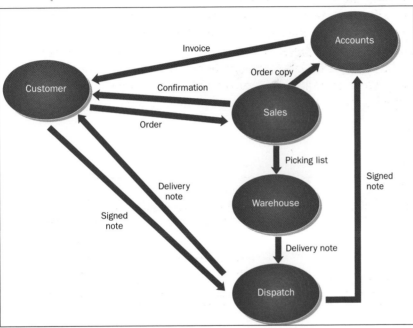

Figure 2.3.2 Simple information flow diagram showing sales order processing

A PC games wholesaler sells games to stores in the local area using the company's website. The sales team receive orders from stores as emails received from the website. If there is stock, they confirm the order to the customer by email and send a copy to accounts. A picking list is created and sent to the warehouse which picks the goods from the store. When the order is complete the warehouse fills in a delivery note and passes it to dispatch who deliver it to the customer. Dispatch returns with a signed copy of the note that is sent to accounts. Accounts match this up with the order number and send an invoice to the customer.

This process is shown diagrammatically in Figure 2.3.2 as in the ActiveBook demonstration. This diagram shows visually all the main flows of information in, out and through the system. If accompanied by a short explanation it reveals very clearly what is happening within the system.

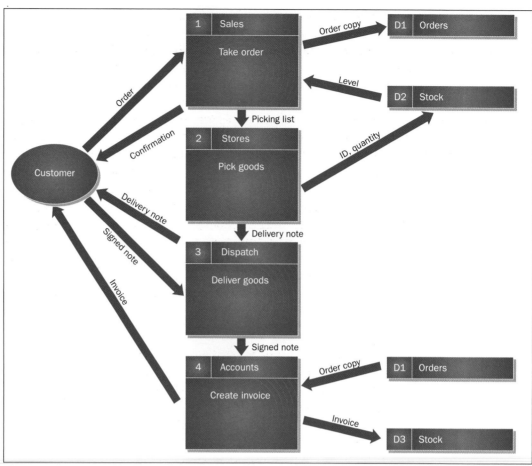

Figure 2.3.3 Detailed information flow diagram for sales order processing system

The more complex view of the system, demonstrated by a more detailed data flow diagram, adds to the understanding of how the system works. In this diagram (Fig. 2.3.3) the emphasis is on the processes. The processes receive input data from external entities, data stores and data that is the output of other processes. These data are transformed to form output information. In fact, all the information in the simpler diagram is incorporated into the more detailed diagram and thus in theory the simpler diagram is redundant. Since the aim of any system diagram is to aid understanding of the system, it is usually best to retain both forms of diagram as they show different views of the same system.

Activity 1 Describe a process in words

Describe in textual form the system drawn in Figure 2.3.3. Write it as a series of processes, starting as follows:

1 The sales department receive an order from a customer. They check the stock level and create an order. They store a copy of the order in the orders file, which accounts will reference later when creating invoices. They send a confirmation of the order to the customer and create a picking list and give it to the stores.

Compare your system description with the initial description used to create the simple information flow diagram.

Information flow diagrams are excellent tools for describing systems. They give a detailed visual representation of a complex set of transactions. However, it should be noted that their power is in simplifying the complex, rather than describing every nuance of the system. For example, in the example earlier, if an item ordered by a customer is out of stock, no confirmation message is sent and the rest of the system is not used. This is simply left implicit in the information flow diagrams. Conditional and repetitive operations can be included but are not detailed as such. These operations would be shown in a separate flow chart that would be drawn for the individual process box within the diagram (see next section). It is also true that no order of processing is strictly implied by the order shown in an information flow diagram, though often the logic is such that only one order is possible. In order to show this extra level of detail (ordering of processes, decisions and repetition of processes) a detailed flow chart is used.

Flow charts

A flow chart is a visual analysis of the detail of the flow of data through an information processing system. They are ideal for showing the logic of a process. They can be used at almost any level of detail, although they are more suited to detailed analyses rather than to overviews, since they reveal the order within processes, repetitive sub-processes and decisions made within processes in a way that an information flow diagram does not.

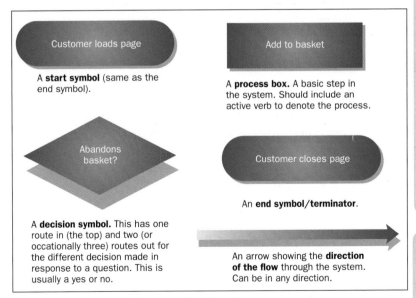

A **start symbol** (same as the end symbol).

A **process box.** A basic step in the system. Should include an active verb to denote the process.

An **end symbol/terminator**.

A **decision symbol.** This has one route in (the top) and two (or occasionally three) routes out for the different decision made in response to a question. This is usually a yes or no.

An arrow showing the **direction of the flow** through the system. Can be in any direction.

Figure 2.3.4 Essential elements of a flow chart

There are a number of other flow chart symbols that can be used to make the diagram richer (see Fig. 2.3.4). It is possible to show that a process is an input/output process, or that the output is a screen display (soft copy) or printed on paper (hard copy), or that

Top tips for better information flow diagrams

- Always give a title to your diagrams.
- Place external entities on the left, processes in the middle and data stores on the right.
- Use singular nouns for the external entities (e.g. 'Customer')
- Avoid crossing flow lines (use bridges/ line hops if absolutely necessary).
- Use active verbs for each process (e.g. 'Take order').
- If there are two possible outputs from a process show them both.
- Always use simple nouns as data names on arrows; never use verbs (e.g. 'Stock number').

Drawing information flow diagrams

The professional way of creating information flow diagrams is to use a Computer Aided Software Engineering (CASE) tool. A CASE tool allows you to create the diagrams, check the logic of the diagrams, and help you build a data dictionary (if required) such as for a database solution. The diagrams in this book are based on the SSADM methodology, which is probably the most popular systems analysis and design methodology in the UK. A SSADM case tool such as Select SSADM could therefore be used.

For the Applied GCE course a CASE tool is not actually necessary. The preferred solution is a 'smart drawing' tool, which will allow smart linking of text and arrows to chart symbols. It is, however, quite possible to create them with any drawing package or by using just the simple drawing tools in your word-processing or spreadsheet applications.

Structured system analysis and design methodology (SSDAM) A set of standards devised primarily for the analysis and design of large-scale government and local government systems. They were developed as open standards to be free to use and have subsequently been adopted by large portions of the UK systems development industry.

data is stored to a serial medium (like tape) or to a direct access medium (like a disc). It is possible to show delays and connections to other systems. This type of detail is occasionally useful but is often simply distracting. The vast majority of the time you will simply require the basic elements. Add in the extra elements only where they are absolutely essential or they add a great deal extra to the analysis. Flow charts may be drawn in colour or black and white. Choice of colour does not affect the logic of the chart. If colour can be used to enhance understanding it should be, but if it distracts from understanding it is best avoided.

Features of flow charts

If properly constructed, a flow chart will allow:

- a detailed analysis of a system, allowing you to consider the logic behind each step and decision
- identification of duplications, omissions and bottlenecks
- very effective and concise documentation of the logic of a system
- a simple visual tool for communicating a system.

On the other hand:

- if the logic is too complex it could be too clumsy and complex
- if the flow chart is too detailed the documentation can be hard to follow.

Top tips for better flow charts

- Always give your flow charts a title.
- Have a consistent line of flow (top to bottom, or left to right).
- Avoid crossing flow lines (use bridges/line hops if absolutely necessary).
- Use active verbs for each process step.
- Use questions for each decision.
- Have at least two possible choices for a decision.

Drawing your flow charts

You can use any drawing tool you wish to create flow charts. For example, it is possible to create adequate charts using word processing or spreadsheet drawing tools. However, specialised flow-chart software has a number of features that make drawing charts a great deal easier. The text and symbols are integrated seamlessly. Arrows stay anchored to their processes. Resizing is easy, line hops are straightforward, and such packages usually also provide extensive and useful tutorials. If you have the opportunity to use such a package, make the most of it.

ACTIVITY 2 Discover additional flow chart elements ◄

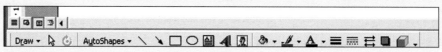

Figure 2.3.5 Word's drawing toolbar

Open Word and its drawing tool (see Fig. 2.3.5), click on 'AutoShapes' and select the 'Flowchart' symbols.

Draw and label, using the tool tip as a guide, the 28 different flow chart symbols on a single page. Save it as 'flow chart.doc'

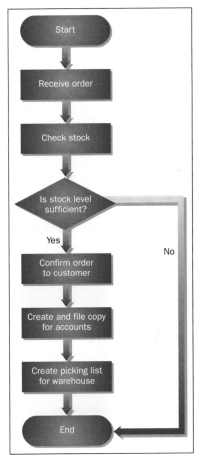

Figure 2.3.6 'Take order' process flow chart with one simple decision

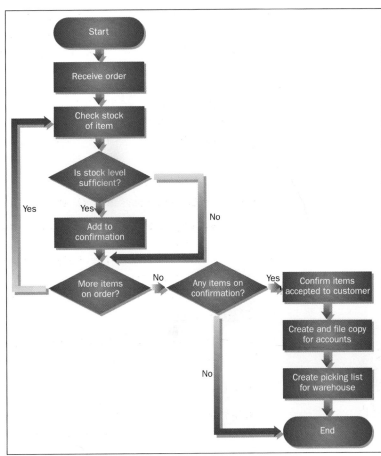

Figure 2.3.7 'Take order' process flow chart showing a repeated sub-process

The detailed flow chart for the 'take order' process reveals clearly that the system is only used in full if the stock level of the item ordered is sufficient for the order, otherwise the order is ignored (see Fig. 2.3.6). This adds to the detailed understanding of the system gained through drawing information flow diagrams. A different, more realistic process is shown in Figure 2.3.7. In this case the sales order can contain many items of information. Each item is stock checked individually. If there is stock of any item it is entered into a confirmation. When each item has been processed, if there are any items that have been confirmed the confirmation is sent to the customer, and an order copy and a picking list are raised, otherwise the order is abandoned.

ACTIVITY 3 Describe 'Create invoice' process ◀

Create a textual description and a flow chart to represent the 'Create invoice' process for the games wholesaler example discussed earlier. You may make any plausible assumption you wish regarding the process, provided it is spelled out in the textual description.

CASE STUDY EVISU

1 Load the website and enter

2 Choose the online store

3 Enter the store. Select jeans category.

7 Checkout (without registering)

8 Add customer details (name and address)

9 Select payment method

Figure 2.3.8 Evisu's website

Evisu is an important jeans designer with celebrity clients. It has an interesting and yet straightforward online store. In this case study you will examine the store part of the website (see Fig. 2.3.8) and attempt to analyse how it works.

Watch the demonstration of the online store. From the users' point of view this is a straightforward sales order process. They enter the store, choose the department they wish to view, browse for items to buy, check the size, add items to the shopping basket and take them to the checkout to pay. At the checkout they give their personal details, select a shipping method, select a payment method, and give the required payment details. If this is authorised they receive confirmation of the order.

Task 1

Assuming that the list below shows the processes the web store goes through up to the point of sale, describe what you feel the inputs and outputs would be to each process:

- display welcome
- display categories
- display individual items
- add to basket
- edit basket
- deal with abandoned basket
- checkout goods

4 *Browse for items required and add to basket*

5 *Add size*

6 *View basket for possible edits/amendments*

10 *Add final payment details*

Details of order confirmed and confirming email sent to customer

11 *Receive confirmation*

Task 2

- List the personal details captured by the web store in a table headed 'Customer'.
- List the transaction details captured (dates, shipping, payment, etc.) in a table headed 'Transaction'.
- List the item details captured in the shopping basket in a table headed 'Transaction-item'.
- Describe how these data stores are related to each other.

Task 3

Draw a flow chart showing the movement between different web pages up to, and including, the checkout.

Processes leading to an online purchase

In this section we will examine all the most important events and processes a web store goes through up to the point of sale by analysing real websites and attempting to relate what is happening on the website to what is happening behind the scenes – in the 'back office'. Not all web stores will present these events and processes in the same order or complete the processes in exactly the same way, but by examining a number of these you will be in a very good position to analyse the web store you choose to investigate for your coursework.

The first set of processes we will examine are:

1 Identify and authenticate
2 Track customers' actions: finding and selecting products
   browse by category   search
   browse by product   other
3 Maintain the shopping basket
   add to basket   remove from basket
   edit basket   abandon basket
4 Checkout
   get and/or confirm customer details
   confirm items in basket
   get and/or confirm shipping details
   get and/or confirm payment details
   get final customer order
5 Authorise payment and confirm order.

Identify and authenticate

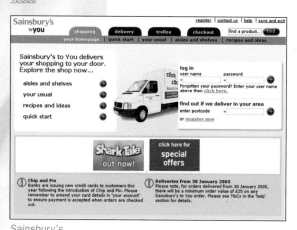

Tesco

Sainsbury's

Figure 2.3.9 Signing in to supermarket sites

There are different methods of dealing with customers in the web-store industry. Some web stores deal with customers exactly as if they are casual customers in a large store. They come in, browse, select their goods, pay at the checkout and leave again. The only identification these stores require is at the checkout when payment is required. At this stage the individual has to be identified to some extent in order that the card payment can be authorised. Usually the store requires a home address (or postcode at least) linked to the credit card, and information from the credit card such as the card number, the expiry date and the special number on the reverse of the card that is there for security reasons alone.

Other stores take a different approach, and require full identification and authentication before the main shopping can take place. The majority of web businesses take a position somewhere between these two and allow the customer to decide whether to identify themselves prior to checkout, and whether to keep their details on the website's server between transactions. Watch the demonstration of the identification and authentication process.

The main grocery websites, Tesco, Sainsbury's, Ocado and Asda, all require that you identify and authenticate yourself prior to starting the shopping process for groceries (see Fig. 2.3.9). The most common method used to identify a customer is his or her email address. An email address is unique, has some element of identity within it, and is usually the primary means of communication between a web business and its customers. Of course, many people know your email address, and thus on its own it does not prove who you are. Authentication is therefore necessary. The most common method of proving who you are is to use a password only you could know. Asda employ a variant on this, using a customer number and PIN (personal identification number), but the principle is exactly the same.

A common part of the authentication procedure for many sites is to use an email address as part of a confirmation process. You register with the site, giving your details that must include your email address. A confirmation is then sent to this email address giving you a link to follow to complete the process. You then follow the link on the email to confirm that it is indeed you. This has two purposes. First, the email address is confirmed by the store and can then be used as a key to the customer record. Secondly, if someone uses your email address deliberately or accidentally you will find out when you receive an email from the store and will have the chance to put it right.

Most web stores also use cookies, described in more detail in the following chapter, to identify the customer as they arrive at the site but before they log into it officially. Cookies allow the site to offer a personalised introduction and even pre-fill the logging-in fields with the customer's name. However, as someone other than the usual user may be on the computer, authentication by password or PIN is still essential.

Sites that employ these techniques usually require that customers register with the site. This involves filling in a series of forms asking for a variety of information. The minimum requirement is a user ID and a password. Some sites ask for full names, address, postcode, phone number, mobile phone number, credit- or debit-card details, and more. Some even ask about hobbies, personal preferences, income and so on. The logging-in process then matches the customer to a record registered in the database, containing these details. For the customer it allows a faster shopping experience, as they do not have to re-enter all their details at the checkout, but just confirm their order. The store-owners also prefer this, as they know with whom they are dealing, can target their marketing more effectively, and the faster checkout means fewer abandoned baskets.

Further authentication procedures

One very common method of authenticating a person is to store and ask for the user's mother's maiden name. This is an easily remembered name for the user, but an obstacle for anyone else attempting to pass themselves off as the user.

Some banks have a series of alternative questions such as memorable place, place of birth, memorable date, first school etc. One of these questions is asked at random when logging in. This makes it even harder for an impostor. Even if the security on the user's computer is compromised, a different question will probably be asked on the next log on.

A further refinement still is to only ask for a few characters from the password (e.g. enter the first, third and last character from your password). This is a very secure method against eavesdroppers.

ACTIVITY 4 Investigate account information

Visit the Amazon website. Choose the 'Your account' button. List the data that is being kept about customers and their orders.

ACTIVITY 5 Set up an account

Visit Tesco's website. View the help pages. Look at 'How to shop at Tesco.com' and 'How do I register?'. Follow the link to the sign-in page.

List all possible events that may occur when registering and signing in. Identify these in Figure 2.3.10. Redraw this figure to match your understanding of Tesco's processes.

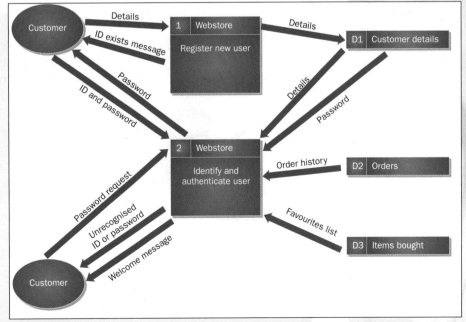

Figure 2.3.10 A generic authentication and identification process

Track customers' actions: finding and selecting products

The first actions the customer undertakes once in the web store are to find products either by browsing or by searching. At this stage the web store tracks what the customer wants to do and presents the customer with lists or details of products as required. Watch the demonstration of this process. Most stores sell a large range of products and, to allow the customer to browse more effectively, divide these into categories.

ACTIVITY 6 Identify sales categories

Draw a hierarchy chart showing the categories and sub-categories used by Comet, the electrical retailer, to organise and sell their products.

ACTIVITY 7 How do supermarkets organise their sales categories?

It is good practice to use a real world metaphor to organise categories in your web store. What metaphor do the supermarket chains use to create the categories they use to organise their products? Can you think of any way this organisation might help them in the post-sales process?

In a small and straightforward store, the action of choosing a category could simply link to another web page, displaying the category or product listing. This is called browsing. In larger or more advanced web stores the click-through that initiates the browse is much more likely to query a database containing either a catalogue of products or an interface to a stock list. This database provides a dynamic web page displaying the results of the query. The added advantage here is that changes to the products in stock do not require any reprogramming of the website, just changes to the database.

The same principle applies to browsing by product rather than category. The page is programmed to display a set of products. When a product is selected the database is queried for more information about that product; a new page, or possibly a pop-up window, is displayed showing this extra information.

Searching for products can use exactly the same technology. The user enters the search term into a search box and the database is queried. A list is returned dynamically with all possible matches. In the Tesco online store a search for 'coffee', for example, will find instant and ground coffee, coffee cakes, coffee biscuits, coffee ice cream and much more. Sainsbury's provides an interesting variant on this (see Fig. 2.3.11) in which the user can jot down the items required in a type of jotter pad. Each item is separated by a comma or is on a new line. The fundamental principle is again exactly the same as with a search box, but now the program has an extra task to perform before it can do the search. It must extract all the key phrases from the text in the jotter pad and present these one at a time as a query to the database engine. The results are then presented on separate pages (i.e. as separate lists).

Boots

Tesco

Next

Penguin

Browse by product or category

Amazon

Tesco

Search

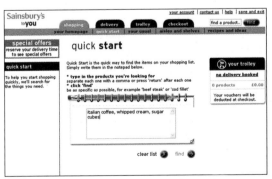

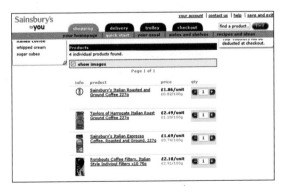

Jotter search on the Sainsbury's site, and its results

Figure 2.3.11 Different methods of finding and selecting goods

ACTIVITY 8 Compare product searches ◀

Visit <u>CD Wow</u> and try to find a CD that is popular at the moment. Then visit <u>HMV's</u> CD department and try to find the same CD.

Compare the actions that a customer can take on both sites, such as: double-clicking on the CD cover photo, clicking an 'Info' button, the range of search and browsing options, and so on.

Which site do you prefer and why?

ACTIVITY 9 Plan a web store ◀

Assume that a CD retailer called MultiMusic stores data about CDs in the following tables:

CD {CDId, title, artist, price, release_date, cover_photo, total_Time, format}
Tracks {trackID, CDId, track_name, composer, artist, time}
Chart {position, CDId}

Draw up storyboards for a simple web store. On each page show how you would present the results of a query from the database, and in response to what event from the customer, e.g. Click on 'Add', Click on 'Info', Double-click on 'Artwork', Enter 'Search' terms.

Maintain the shopping basket

Tesco

Gameplay

Boots   *Next*

Add to basket

Fig. 2.3.12 Continued on next page

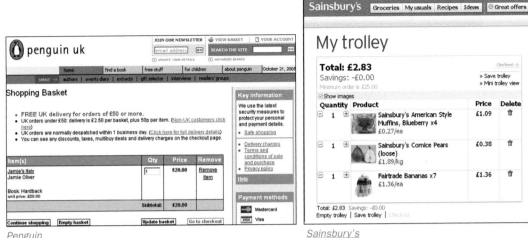

Penguin

Sainsbury's

Edit basket

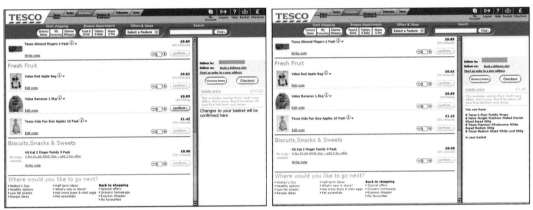

Remove from basket (Tesco)

Figure 2.3.12 Maintaining the virtual shopping basket

One of the crucial tasks that any web store has to perform is the maintenance of its virtual shopping basket. This is an obvious metaphor for a real basket and is one that works well in the virtual environment. The customer can add to a basket, change the quantity in the basket (edit it), remove items from the basket, and either abandon the basket altogether or take the basket to the checkout (see Fig. 2.3.12). Watch the demonstration of this process.

Behind the scenes a virtual shopping basket is usually represented by a list or another database table, which is initially empty. The main operations required to start filling the table are straightforward database operations (see Table 2.3.1). When a customer chooses to add an item to the basket, the stock or catalogue code for the item is added to the basket along with the quantity added (all other information can be retrieved by joining the basket table to the stock or catalogue table). Depending on the type of retailer involved, stock availability may be checked prior to adding the item to the basket, or it may be checked after adding it to the basket, with a message about availability being added to the display. Editing and deleting items from the basket are very straightforward operations. Displaying the basket can take a variety of different forms, depending on the store. Some show the basket, its contents and the total value of the basket continuously on-screen while the customer is still shopping; others use a completely separate web page to display it.

Shopping basket process	Database process
Add an item to the basket	Add an item to the table
Edit an item in the basket	Edit an item in the table
Delete an item from the basket	Delete an item from the table
Show all the items in the basket	Show all the items in the table with the related stock details Calculate and show total price

Table 2.3.1 Shopping basket processes

Not all web stores are equally effective at managing shopping baskets. In some cases, including household names, once the basket has been viewed it is not easy to return to shopping. In other cases, if you leave the shopping environment to check some information on a product, the contents of your basket will be lost when you return.

At the end of the 'maintain basket' process the user may decide to check out the basket or alternatively may simply abandon the basket altogether. DoubleClick, an online marketing company, have estimated that over half of all shopping carts are indeed abandoned before sale (source: iStart). Different stores have different means of dealing with abandoned baskets. The stores that identify users before they add items to a basket often keep a record in their database of the items added to the basket. The shopping basket will therefore be intact next time the user returns to the site. This can be extremely useful if the basket is a very large one (as with grocery shopping) and was abandoned by accident or because the user simply had to leave the online store unexpectedly. It would probably be less important for a one-off purchase such as a new computer game. Sites that do not identify their customers until the final checkout do not store the basket for future use; they simply discard the table in the background that represents the 'live' basket.

ACTIVITY 10 How are out-of-stock items handled? ◀

Why do some retailers allow customers to add items to the shopping basket that are not in stock, whereas others do not?

Investigate how Tesco, Gameplay, Argos and Amazon deal with out-of-stock items.

ACTIVITY 11 Produce a shopping basket maintenance flow chart ◀

Create a flow chart for the maintenance of a virtual shopping basket.

Checkout

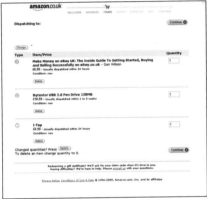

1 Sign in and confirm customer details

2 Confirm address details

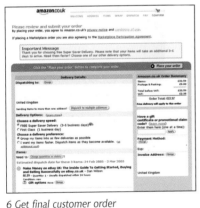

3 Confirm basket details

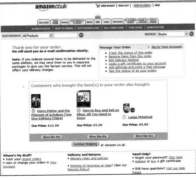

4 Get and/or confirm shipping details

5 Get and/or confirm payment details

6 Get final customer order

7 Order confirmation

8 Confirming e-mail

Figure 2.3.13 Amazon's checkout

The final process in the chain of events leading up to a sale is the checkout.
Watch the demonstration of this process. This process takes the shopping basket
and adds the user details, the shipping details and the payment details to create
the sales order or transaction. As with all parts of the system there are variations
on how different stores manage the checkout procedures. Clearly those that have
identified and authenticated customers at the start of the process do not need to

do any more than confirm details at the end. This is quick and efficient for the customer and store. If, on the other hand, the store has not yet captured any personal information, it must now find out several things (see also Fig. 2.3.13):

- who you are
- whether you are a returning or new customer
- where you want the goods shipped to
- how you wish to pay
- whether the payment can be authorised.

This is the part of the system that creates a legally binding agreement between the store and the customer. Up to this stage the store is simply a website. At this point it becomes a merchant. It is at this stage that an official order is created and payment details are exchanged. The details must then be checked carefully, and communication and storage of these must be totally secure. In order to ensure security of communications with customers, almost all reputable merchants use a technology such as secure sockets layer (SSL) to encrypt the information communicated at the checkout stage.

ACTIVITY 12 Identify the final checkout processes ◀

List the processes Amazon (see Fig. 2.3.13) goes through to capture the final sales information when a basket is checked out at its store.

Authorise payment and confirm order

A specific security challenge arises when an individual buys goods or services on the web using a credit card, as the user and card are not present. Card companies class this as a 'card not present' transaction, which is a less secure transaction than a real transaction in which user and card can be identified and authenticated face to face. A card belonging to a man being used by a 16-year-old girl is easy to spot in a shop, but not so easy on the internet.

On the internet the purchaser may not even have the card in front of them, just the card numbers. The web store therefore needs measures in place to deal with any potential security lapse that could arise. Stores such as the online grocers who require registration and logging-in prior to purchase are relatively safe in this area, not least because the goods are delivered to fixed and known addresses. Another modern trend is for online stores to ask for the postcode to verify the card. This then can also provide another area of identification and authentication. The 16-year-old girl mentioned earlier will be able to give all the card numbers, including the security code on the reverse, by examining the card, but she is less likely to know the address and postcode of the cardholder, and thus a store that uses the postcode to verify and identify will not allow the transaction.

Secure sockets layer (SSL)
This is a protocol for transmitting private information via the internet. SSL uses a private key to encrypt (or encode) data that is communicated over the secure sockets layer connection. Most web-hosting companies offer easy connection to SSL for credit and debit card payments. Many websites then use SSL to obtain confidential user information, such as credit card numbers. It is usual for the URL of web pages that use SSL to start with 'https' rather than 'http'. A padlock is shown in the foot of a web page when secure communication is taking place. This should reassure the user that the transmission of personal information via the internet is safe.

When a payment is received from a customer, the customer name, card number and total amount are transmitted to the issuer (or bank) for authorisation via a payment gateway. The issuer can confirm that the account is still active and that the total amount is within the credit limit. In order to counteract the 'card not present' problem, the issuer also asks for the expiry date and a security code which is written on the back of the card, and, often, the postcode as described before. If all of these are correct, the issuer sends an authorisation number to the merchant that is added to the transaction record and used later by the merchant to claim payment from the card issuer.

ACTIVITY 13 Chart the authorisation system

Create a simple information flow diagram to show this authorisation system:

- The customer submits credit-card information at the checkout.
- The shopping-basket software sends the transaction (card information plus the total amount) to the payment gateway.
- The gateway routes the information to the payment processor.
- The processor contacts the issuer of the customer's credit card.
- The issuer approves or declines the transaction.
- The processor routes the result back to the gateway, which then passes the result back to the shopping basket system.
- The checkout informs the customer that the transaction is authorised or declined.

Post-sale processing

Once the online sale has been made, a further set of processes are undertaken by the store. These processes vary widely depending on the type of business. All web stores, however, have some degree of order fulfilment and stock control to manage. The most efficient web businesses have all of these processes integrated with the website's sales system. Thus a sale might create a picking list for the warehouse, a delivery note for transporting the goods to the customer, and an automatic entry in the sales journal to update the financial records of the sale. When the goods are picked, the stock level is reduced accordingly and the website in turn reflects this change. The most efficient businesses of all, such as Tesco, have their sales systems integrated with their suppliers' systems so that the suppliers know how much stock to re-supply, and when.

Payment processing terms

Customer   The holder of a credit card, a debit card or electronic cheque.

Issuer   A financial institution (usually a bank) that provides the card or cheque for the customer and the account from which payment is eventually made.

Merchant   The e-commerce site.

Acquirer   The financial institution (usually a bank) with whom the web business does their banking.

Payment gateway   Links the e-commerce site to the payment processor. Converts messages between them to the form required by the payment network. E-commerce sites usually subscribe to an organisation running a gateway to do their credit-card processing.

Payment processor/payment network Deals with the banks and card organisations (Visa, Mastercard etc.) to process all payments.

Chip and PIN

The latest method to combat card fraud is the use of chip and PIN cards. Using these, customers enter their card number and their secret personal identification number (PIN), and transmit it using the secure connection to the merchant's site and on to the bank. The PIN provides the authentication for the transaction, which makes using cards simpler and more secure than at present. This has the advantage for the merchant and the banks that the risk of fraudulent use is greatly reduced, although it has the disadvantage for the customer that the responsibility for the secure use of the card falls on them. Currently, the PIN is not used for transactions over the internet

Figure 2.3.14 The Apple iTunes sales process

Order fulfilment: dispatch, delivery and stock control

One of the most problematic areas for websites, as discussed in Chapter 2.2, is that of dispatch and delivery. However, some services provide electronic fulfilment. For example, music downloads, ring tones, some software and research services can fulfil their orders automatically by allowing the customer to download the product directly from their website. This removes many of the problems associated with physical delivery.

ACTIVITY 14 Chart a sales process for downloadable goods

To download a track from iTunes the customer goes through the following processes (see also Fig. 2.3.14):

- The customer clicks on the song they wish to download.
- They sign in to their already-established account to allow the download. Signing in matches the customer to the account details from when the account was registered. Signing in is only required once per session, so multiple tracks can be downloaded using a single sign in.
- The download begins automatically.
- If the download is interrupted it will start again at the next log in.
- Tracks usually cost up to 79p at the time of writing, which is not a great deal of money for a single credit-card transaction. Therefore, it is usual to be charged for tracks downloaded over a period of time, e.g. once a week. The payment is processed and a receipt is sent to the customer by email.

Draw a flow chart to illustrate this process.

Compare this with the processes Amazon goes through to capture final sales information.

Physical goods distribution requires a more complex process involving more parties. It varies depending on whether:

- goods are made to order
- goods are distributed directly from the website company's stock
- goods are bought in from suppliers as soon as the order is made (called 'just-in-time' stock control)
- goods are completely outsourced; i.e. the website company does not have its own physical warehouse, but rather supplies its customers via another company that does.

Distribution also varies based on whether in-house distribution, the post, parcel delivery or specialist delivery services are used to transport the goods. The underlying processes for dispatch and delivery are, however, reasonably similar. The order has to be made up or picked for dispatch. For this process a picking list is required. As the goods are picked the stock records are adjusted accordingly. Once the order is ready for dispatch, payment has to be collected. The goods have to be delivered. For this a delivery or advice note is required. Proof of delivery is often required, which may involve signing a special PDA, a delivery schedule or delivery note. Some websites, such as Amazon or Apple, allow customers to track the status of their order, or view an order history, by entering an order number. Some, such as CD Wow, send email messages notifying the customer of each event.

Case study Online grocer's delivery fulfilment ◀

An online grocer goes through the following stages to fulfil an order:
- An online order is accepted at the website.
- The website creates a picking list from the order and transmits it electronically to the nearest store to the customer.
- On the day of delivery all deliveries are scheduled.
- A delivery schedule is created for each van and the picking lists for the schedule are printed off.
- A picker (who may be the van driver), takes the picking list, collects each item on the list, scanning each one as it is collected, and places it in an appropriate container. Stock is automatically adjusted as each item is scanned.
- If the goods required by the customer cannot be found and substitutions are allowed, a substitution is made.
- A bill is created and printed from the scanned items.
- The customer's credit card is charged with the bill amount.
- A delivery note is printed from the scanned items.
- The van driver loads the batch of containers into the van.
- The driver delivers to the delivery schedule.
- The driver hands over the goods, asks the customer to sign the delivery schedule and hands over a copy of the delivery note as a bill and to allow checking of the goods received.

Tasks

- Create an information flow diagram showing the fulfilment process.
- Create a flow chart for the picking process.

Fulfilment does not always end with a delivery of a single package. If you order books from Amazon some may be in stock, but others may not. You can choose to have them delivered as a complete batch, or bit by bit as they become available. The second option requires a more complex process involving back orders. Similarly, faulty or inappropriate goods are occasionally delivered; some goods never arrive; some arrive damaged from the delivery process itself. A good online store needs a system to deal with all of these possibilities.

ACTIVITY 15 Find out about return handling

Investigate how Amazon, Apple Computers, Tesco and Argos handle returns.

ACTIVITY 16 Chart a stock control system

Complete the information flow diagram for a generic stock control system shown in Figure 2.3.15 by adding the details of the data that is flowing between each point.

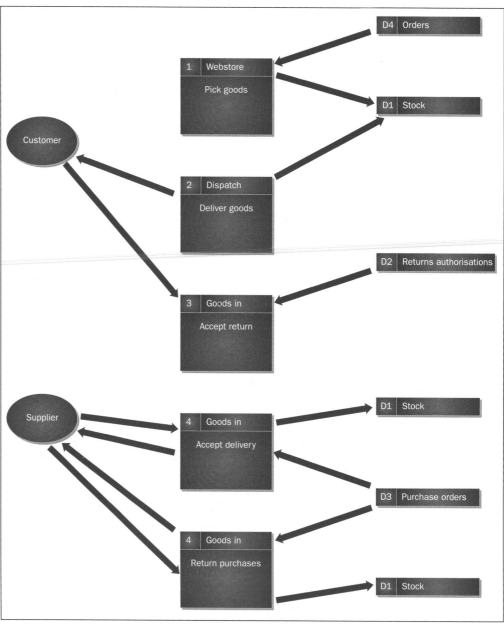

Figure 2.3.15 Generic stock control system

Payment processing

Sites that receive payments using credit cards, which are the majority, do not get paid the instant when the payment is authorised by the issuer (bank). They have to submit a request for payment later. Most wait until the goods have been dispatched, then create the invoice and request payment. The payment process involves the merchant requesting payment from the gateway. To do this the merchant sends details of the transactions along with the authorisations provided by the bank (or issuer) in the authorisation process. The gateway formats this for the payments network. The payments network arranges settlement between the issuer and acquirer. The funds, less fees, are transferred to the merchant's account. A credit-card statement is sent to the customer and the cycle is complete.

ACTIVITY 17 Chart payment processing ◀

Create an information flow diagram showing the flow of information between all the parties when payment is processed.

ACTIVITY 18 Investigate PayPal ◀

Many small merchants use PayPal and similar payment systems to handle their payment processing. They are particularly popular on auction sites such as eBay.

Investigate how the PayPal payment system works by visiting PayPal's website and reading how it works.

Create a short presentation explaining what the supplier has to do to allow payments using PayPal and to manage a PayPal account.

Conclusion ▶ ▶ ▶

In this chapter we have examined the events leading up to an online purchase, what happens at the checkout and the events following the purchase. We have described and analysed the processes a web store goes through at each stage using information flow diagrams and flow charts. We have also examined the parties involved in each transaction and the information flowing between them using the simpler information flow diagrams. You should now be able to understand how an online business works and be able to apply this knowledge to analyse and illustrate how a particular online business functions.

E-customers

In the previous chapters we examined what makes a successful website and analysed the processes at the heart of an online business. In this chapter we will look at online businesses from the complementary point of view – how they deal with their customers. We will examine how an online business sets up its storefront; how it structures and organises its site; what it sells; how it uses marketing and customer service tools; how it uses techniques imported from traditional businesses, as well as others unique to the virtual world.

We will look at how sites make their information accessible to the widest possible audience, the numerous methods used to capture information about their customers, and how they can use this information to personalise the experience on the site. In doing this you will learn to analyse how an online business engages, entices and retains its customers, and you will evaluate the overall customer experience provided by an online organisation.

Comet

Storefront

The storefront, or home page, is in many ways the most important page of the whole website. It must immediately engage the viewer and make them want to stay on the site, browse and buy. It is estimated that a home page can account for as much as 20 per cent of all the traffic to a site and so, for many users, determines their overall customer experience of the site. Most sites therefore tend to use the home page for spelling out all their offers and most attractive deals, displaying as many eye-catching features on this page as possible.

Webmasters in big companies are accustomed to individual departments demanding part of the home page to advertise their own product or service, or announce their success. In some ways this is a good thing, but too much flashiness and the site can become unwieldy. Achieving a good solid message amidst a mass of detail can be difficult. Good websites have to strike a careful balance between supplying detail and achieving a unified, designed look.

Penguin

Next

Figure 2.4.1 Home page showdown

ACTIVITY 1 Compare home pages

Review the home pages in Figure 2.4.1. For each one, looking at just the home page:
- state the purpose of the site
- try to assess how successfully it meets this objective
- describe how the site *appears* to be structured
- list the goods and/or services it offers
- list any techniques you can see that aim to engage, retain and entice customers
- list any usability and accessibility features that are apparent
- evaluate briefly the 'customer experience' it offers
- state which home page best meets the purpose and why.

Structure and organisation

Once visitors have been engaged by the home page the next issue for a site that aims to do business is how easily the customers can move through the site, browsing when appropriate or otherwise locating what they already know they want. The main objective here is to have a site organised for browsing in as natural a manner as possible. The vast majority of stores will tend to organise as they do in physical stores. Supermarkets will organise categories such as salads and fruits, breads and bakery, frozen foods and so on. Shoe and clothes sellers will organise first into categories for men and women, and then with sub-categories. Electrical goods will be categorised by TV, audio, gadget etc.

However, online stores have some advantages and some disadvantages compared to the real experience. A real supermarket maps a route through the store for the customer, putting items in positions where they believe they will maximise sales. They often put fresh food or bakery at the entrance to provide a symbol and smell of freshness to entice the customer. They put goods with high volume sales at the customer's eyeline. They may put child-friendly treats near checkouts. Some electrical retailers put their most attractive plasma screen TV near the entrance to lure you in, and children's games near the exit. Ikea takes you on a journey through made-up rooms and combinations of its goods before you select goods from a functional warehouse at the end.

Websites cannot emulate all of these techniques. They could force customers through a fixed route but hardly ever do so, because it would be too obvious and artificial online. They have to tailor their offers to a slightly different audience, used to the navigational freedom of the web. This does not mean, however, that none of the traditional stores' strategies can be adopted. A good website uses techniques that can be customised to the web audience to attract and retain customers.

The first and most obvious strategy a website must use is to have an extremely easy to follow site structure. It must be possible to navigate quickly to where the customer wants to go. Where browsing is not possible a good search function is an essential alternative. Of course, having a search box does not on its own guarantee a positive customer experience. A good search must find the items being looked for without masses of irrelevant alternatives. If it fails on either of these facets it will eventually not be trusted and used.

ACTIVITY 2 Compare customer accessibility of sites ◀

Look at four different electrical retailing websites, such as <u>Unbeatable</u>, <u>Electricshop</u>, <u>Currys</u> and <u>Comet</u>.

Compare the categories they have used to structure the browsing on their sites. Which do you consider to be the most successful from the point of view of the customer, and why?

ACTIVITY 3 Evaluate search functionalities

Compare the search functionality of online shopping at <u>Tesco</u>, <u>Ocado</u>, <u>Asda</u> and <u>Sainsbury's</u>.

- Which is most successful in finding an individual item?
- Which finds the least erroneous selections?
- Which is the easiest to use?
- State which you prefer and why.

ACTIVITY 4 Investigate structure and navigation

Figure 2.4.2 Structure and navigation at <u>Tesco</u>

- What is the structure of <u>Tesco's</u> online grocery section (see Fig. 2.4.2)?
- Why is it structured like this?
- How much of this echoes the layout of the physical store?
- What does it offer in navigation terms that is not available within a store?
- What does it do to make offers stand out?
- Why does it do it like this?
- Is this more or less successful in your view than their approach in-store?

Figure 2.4.3 Zoom feature in Next's website

A number of retailers will add features to the basic structure to make the shopping experience as full as possible. In a physical store when shopping for clothes it is possible to pick them up and look at them in detail; when shopping for books or CDs it is possible to look at them and see indexes, tables of contents, track lists and so on. A good site will try to provide such options within its structure. The Next site, for example, allows you to click on an image from a selection, then look at a larger image, and then zoom into that image to get a good idea of what the clothes look like (see Fig. 2.4.3).

These features are useful as long as they work quickly and do not interfere with the navigation. Providing this type of feature is not likely to be positive if the customer is forced to wait for large objects to be downloaded. The feature should be provided for commercial reasons rather than technical ones. Online clothing sites in the early days of the e-commerce boom used 3D mannequins of different body shapes to show how the clothes would look from all angles on an individual, but the slow download of these complex images meant that the experience was tedious rather than useful.

ACTIVITY 5 Compare product information ◀

What product information do Tesco, CD Wow and Amazon show?
- What informational features do they use to help the customer have a richer and more informed shopping experience?
- In what ways can a web experience simply not match the real experience of being in a store?

It can be seen that the structure of an online store cannot totally mirror that of a physical store, but it can do some similar things, such as making a big splash on the front page, displaying offers prominently, and structuring the main navigation so that it mirrors the categories customers are accustomed to in a store. In addition, websites can offer extra facilities that make shopping on the internet a different experience. It may be less sensual, but it can be faster and more informative.

Techniques for engaging and enticing e-customers

Figure 2.4.4 Online sales attract customers in a different way to on the high street

Websites use many techniques to engage and entice customers. Many of these have been used in physical stores, mail order catalogues and in advertising campaigns for as long as businesses have existed. The interactivity and the extended possibilities for capturing personal information on the web, however, have opened up further opportunities to make web businesses more successful in dealing with their customers. In this section we will investigate a number of these techniques.

One of the more obvious marketing techniques a retailer can use it is to have a sale or make a special offer. As price is a large factor in a buying decision, a sale can be as successful on the web as it is on the high street (see Fig. 2.4.4). A high-street customer may be casually attracted to a sale in a store while window-shopping in town, but a similar scenario is a great deal less likely on the web. Browsing on the web will tend to be within a store already pre-chosen for visiting by the potential customer.

ACTIVITY 6 Window-shopping on the web

Partner offers (see Fig. 2.4.5), shopping-mall websites and price-comparison sites are all, in part, attempts to give a flavour of window-shopping for offers.

Evaluate these types of online experience with regard to what their purpose appears to be and how successful they are in fulfilling this.

Figure 2.4.5 Partner offers

Spam

Look at these definitions of spam.

Successful online sales tend to be accompanied by an email campaign (see Fig. 2.4.6). Spam email is as likely to antagonise customers as attract them, and in any case will probably be blocked by most modern filters. Good offer emails therefore tend to be a great deal more targeted. From a commercial viewpoint the best offers are those that target individuals from their known buying preferences. These are discussed in more detail later when analysing the capture of personal information. Frequent sources of email addresses are third-party sites selling their sorted mailing lists, and sites' own customer database, or registered user or subscriber database.

A related technique is to send out newsletters to subscribers, detailing the latest offers and products, and giving extra information that might be of interest to the customer. In doing this the online company will usually be trying over time to build a loyal customer base, rather than sell a specific item or set of items, as might be the case in a sale. The real advantage of this technique to the organisation is the low distribution costs of the newsletter. Customers can be given a high quality e-newsletter at an almost negligible cost, which may prompt them to buy immediately, but will in any case remind them of the brand and build brand awareness over time.

Figure 2.4.6 E-mail campaigns are used to alert customers to special offers

Figure 2.4.7 Newsletters build customer loyalty

Most newsletters (see Fig. 2.4.7) require that you register or subscribe, usually at no cost, but therefore rely on you visiting the site in the first place. This process itself is a valuable method of capturing customer information. Sometimes it will only be a customer name and email address, although the information obtained may sometimes be a great deal more extensive.

ACTIVITY 7

Newsletters can be used by almost any sector but they are most useful for companies with a brand to maintain, and for items with a technical and design content that fit well within a magazine format. An ideal market is the new car market, which fulfils these criteria well.

Research car manufacturer websites. Find out which offer e-newsletters.
- What format are these in?
- What interactive features do they use?
- How successful do you believe they are in engaging and enticing customers?

Figure 2.4.8 Surveys are an interactive means of gathering information online

Figure 2.4.9 Competitions are a strong means of capturing users' attention and information about them

Surveys (see Fig. 2.4.8) and competitions (see Fig. 2.4.9) fulfil a similar function to newsletters. They offer fresh interactive content on the site and are another avenue to collect personal information as part of the interactive process.

Figure 2.4.10 Nike ID's website lets you build a custom shoe

Figure 2.4.11 Configure your own Porsche

Some of the most powerful techniques for engaging and enticing customers are to offer novel interactive multimedia experiences. These will usually involve a Java module, or a Flash or Shockwave plug-in. Real estate and holiday village sites often show movies of a property and provide online mortgage calculators. Clothing and footwear sites such as Nike ID (see Fig. 2.4.10) often offer the facility to build an item online, even with a name or other personal identifier on it, and having this custom-built and delivered. Car companies including Audi, BMW and Porsche (see Fig. 2.4.11) allow you to configure your car and see what it will look like and how much the final specification will cost. These are useful and entertaining facilities that go beyond what can be achieved in a face-to-face sales situation.

Customer service

A large part of how pleasant an experience online shopping is concerns overall customer service. This is particularly important online – as there are no face-to-face customer relations, it is harder to build trust. Once a customer feels let down the chance of repeat sales, which are probably the most important part of an online business, diminishes very rapidly. Good customer service encompasses many areas from help in the purchasing process, to an efficient fulfilment process (i.e. delivery), and a straightforward method of dealing with problems and returns if they arise.

ACTIVITY 8 Compare customer help and assistance

Review the Tesco, Dell, Boots and Black & Decker sites shown in Figure 2.4.12.

Analyse the help they provide to surf, search, and buy their products. Which help and assistance features should an e-commerce site provide to give the best all-round customer experience?

Tesco

Dell

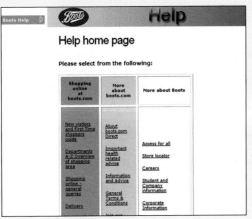

Boots

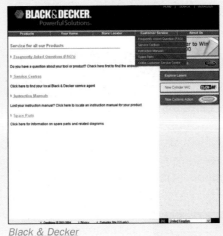

Black & Decker

Figure 2.4.12 Help and assistance

The most cost-effective means of supporting and helping customers is to provide online help in the form of online manuals and reference material, online communities and bulletin boards, answers to frequently asked questions (FAQs), help and support centres, help pages, and interactive tours (see Fig. 2.4.12). This may be sufficient for the vast majority of queries.

Occasionally, however, customers may want or need to contact the organisation. A good website should provide a variety of means of contact including an online form, email, and even traditional methods such as phone, fax and ordinary mail. Some will provide live sales assistance through online chat (see Chapter 2.2) and phone-back facilities. A very customer-focused site may offer free (e.g. 0800) or local-rate (e.g. 0845) phone numbers to contact them at any time of the day. Other sites go to the other extreme and offer only a premium-rate phone number (as a product-support helpline often does), where customers are held for some time before answering, and the company then profits from the large telephone costs incurred by the customer. This is clearly not the best way of building customer loyalty, but nevertheless is not uncommon.

ACTIVITY 9 ◀

For an e-commerce store, which method of communication would you consider it best to provide for each of these customer-centred scenarios, and why?
- Checking stock of an item prior to purchase.
- Finding out the technical specification of a new computer.
- Finding out what the delivery method is and how long it usually takes.
- Informing the organisation that the ordered goods have not arrived.
- Making sure that a wedding suit ordered last week will definitely arrive tomorrow.
- Complaining that a grocery delivery is short by three items.
- Complaining that a new computer does not work.
- Getting some advice as to why a new camera does not work.
- Arranging to cancel an order.

▶ Accessibility

Accessibility is another major issue for commerce stores. It is a moral and legal responsibility not to discriminate against particular sets of users, and it is, in any case, sound business sense to reach the widest possible audience. Some individuals may find it difficult or embarrassing to do business in public; for them it is often much more convenient to conduct as much business as possible online – clearly profitable for the many sites they may visit.

The web is primarily a visual medium and thus people with, for example, partial sight or colour blindness may be put at a disadvantage if they are not considered in site design; navigation by mouse and/or keyboard might be difficult for other users. Good accessible design will attempt to make the experience as rich as possible for the greatest variety of user. Look at the examples in the demonstration.

Figure 2.4.13 Accessibility pages on Stockport Council's website

ACTIVITY 10 Investigate website accessibility ◀

View Stockport Council's website (see Fig. 2.4.13). Navigate to the website help, then to accessibility features. To do this you can use the mouse or the keyboard access key for help which is to press ALT 0 <enter>.

List all the features that the web designers have used in the site to make it accessible and usable for as many of their clients as possible.

ACTIVITY 11 ◀

Visit Next's website and view its accessibility statement. Then visit Marks & Spencer's website and view its accessibility statement.
- List the individuals and groups for whom access is identified as an issue.
- List the measures being taken to make access easier for these individuals and groups.
- Complete a one-page evaluation of these sites in terms of their actual accessibility.

ACTIVITY 12 ◀

Use the AnyBrowser site viewer with the 'check for text-only purity' textbox set to see what sites will look like in a text only viewer.

Choose four of your favourite sites and take screenshots of how they look in a text only viewer. Compare these with screenshots in Internet Explorer and at least one other browser.

Figure 2.4.14 Text only view of Lifelong Learning UK website

XHTML and CSS, and accessibility

A great many accessibility policies centre on having XHTML code that is validated alongside cascading style sheets (CSS) for presentation. The idea of this is that if the structural code is strict XHTML and the presentational aspects of the site are all controlled with CSS, it is possible to use the same code for all version 7 browsers, online TV, PDAs, kiosks, mobile phone browsers, and text-only browsers such as Lynx. They can also be used optimally by screen readers to read the contents of the screen to users with impaired and no vision.

Note, however, that simply using XHTML and CSS, or having an extensive published accessibility policy, does not guarantee accessible site design. Presentational problems may occur especially if XHTML and CSS are used in conjunction with scripting technologies or proprietary code.

Simple examples of how XHTML and CSS aid accessibility

- XHTML requires an alt tag for images as an accessibility tool. User agents (e.g. a screen reader) should read the alt tag when the image cannot be displayed. For example, <img src="dress12.jpg" alt="picture of blue dress" /> should read 'Picture of blue dress' when the image cannot be displayed, such as in a text-only display.
- Using XHTML lists formatted with CSS as buttons and links rather than scripted rollover code (Flash, JavaScript, VBScript etc.) allows easy navigation by people with visual problems, manual problems and small screens.

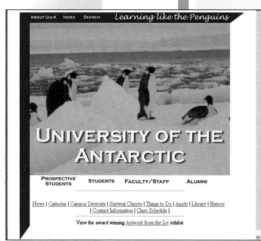

Figure 2.4.15 <u>Web aim demonstration website</u> with deliberate accessibility errors

ACTIVITY 13 Use a screen reader ◀

Visit <u>Web Aim's</u> website to read about the aim of its simulation.

View the <u>simulation</u> (see Fig. 2.4.15) to see what it is like for a visually impaired person to access a website using a screen reader.

ACTIVITY 14 ◀

Visit the <u>Lincolnshire County Council</u> site and navigate to the Access tool: listen to this site being read out loud.

Compare this with the Web Aim simulation in the previous activity. List the strengths and weaknesses of the site vis-à-vis accessibility, and possible improvements that could be made.

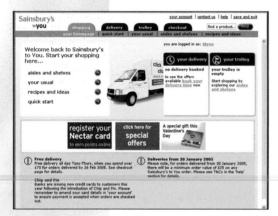

Figure 2.4.16 Registering with <u>Sainsbury's</u> online shopping

Capturing personal information

In order to give the richest possible experience to customers a good online business will attempt to personalise its service. This usually involves creating a customer database and filling it with as much data about customers and their habits as possible. The database might store information on actual sales from the site, on preferences gleaned from surveys, on personal information entered in response to competitions, and possibly information about the links clicked on, the time spent on pages and so on.

By utilising this information creatively a business can really target customers with individualised offers, personalised vouchers and a truly personal service. By using the same information across large numbers of customers it can also: identify pages that are successful in creating sales, find blockages in the site where customers drop out, predict future sales based on what their customer-base prefers, tailor its stockholding to predicted sales and thus reduce wastage.

In this section we will examine how organisations capture personal information, both openly and covertly, and what they do with the information.

The fundamental means of capturing information for most websites, as seen in the previous chapter, is to ask the customer to register (see Fig. 2.4.16). Some sites make it essential to register in order to get any service; others prefer to leave registering as an option so as not to deter anyone from browsing. The amount of information captured at this stage is also variable, with some merely asking for a name and email address and others asking for a great deal more personal information and payment details.

Most good sites will not expect you to register with no benefit to you at all. As has been seen, competitions, surveys, special offers, newsletters and other standard marketing techniques are used to encourage people to give their details to online organisations. Reward schemes are also used widely in both real and virtual shopping environments to give users an incentive to register. Three of the most well-known schemes in the UK are Tesco's Clubcard, the Nectar scheme and the Boots Advantage scheme.

ACTIVITY 15

Boots

Tesco

Nectar

Figure 2.4.17 Compare reward schemes

Visit the rewards scheme sites shown in Figure 2.4.17 and the reward schemes section of the Consumer Deals site.

Create a short report showing for the Nectar, Clubcard and Advantage cards:
- Where points can be collected?
- Approximately how many pounds of shopping are required to get £1's worth of rewards online and in store?
- The range of main rewards on offer.
- An evaluation of the value of the cards to the customer.
- An analysis of the value of the information gained by the store.
- A list of other rewards schemes offered in the UK.

Most rewards schemes are funded by the stores as part of their marketing effort. However, some sites, such as Game (see Fig. 2.4.18) charge for membership.

Once registered in a rewards scheme, a customer presents the card number with payment for goods. This allows the organisation to match all in-store and online purchases to an individual. There is a small potential threat to privacy when a store or group of stores has access to so much information about an individual. Stores therefore usually go to significant lengths to make this minor loss of privacy worthwhile to the consumer: by providing money-back vouchers, individualised money-off vouchers, and targeted emails and newsletters. Individualised

Figure 2.4.18 Game Reward Card

targeting often works very specifically. For example, it is much less likely that vegetarians will receive offers on meat products from a supermarket chain, and much more likely that they will receive a voucher for Quorn or Linda McCartney vegetarian products.

Cookies

Cookies are small files of information and are stored on a user's computers by the web servers on the sites that the users visit. As part of the hypertext transport protocol (HTTP) that is used to manage the web, web servers have the right to store a small amount of information (up to approximately 4 kbytes) on each computer that visits the site. When the user's computer requests a page, the server receives a copy of any cookie that it has stored in the past in the HTTP header. A script on the web page (written in, for example, JavaScript or VbScript) can then access the information in the cookie and use it to make the web page more personal. If a script on a page does set a cookie, the server writes the cookie to the user's computer. It does this by attaching an extra line to the HTTP header that is sent back to the browser as follows:

Set-Cookie: id=1234; path=/; expires Sun, 25-April 2005 14:50:00 GMT

(Note the website (domain) that is being visited is also stored as part of the cookie.)

Cookies have six parameters in total that can be passed to them:
* the **name** of the cookie (e.g. 'id')
* the **value** of the cookie (e.g. '1234')
* the **path** the cookie is valid for (e.g. '/' meaning the whole site)
* the **domain** the cookie is valid for (e.g. www.sainsburystoyou.com)
* the **expiry date** of the cookie – this determines how long the cookie will remain active in your browser (e.g. 'Sun, 25-April 2005 14:50:00 GMT'; though note that this is stored as a long number when you examine the cookie)
* whether it needs a secure connection (e.g. SSL).

Cookies are used by websites to:
* identify a particular user or computer by storing visitor IDs that can be linked automatically to a customer database (as done, for example, on Amazon's website)
* store user preferences such as the style the user wishes to view the site with (View Hertfordshire County Council's website. Increase the text size. When you return it will still be larger.)
* store captured information between web pages. (A large number of non-transactional sites do not store visitor details in a database. In these cases a cookie can be used to store information that the user enters while they remain on the site; e.g. a user name or perhaps the pages visited by the visitor during the session.)
* store captured information between visits (As with the previous item, if there is no database a cookie can be used to store personal or other information ready for a next visit by the user)
* store marketing information (such as how many times you have visited a site).

Look at the demonstration of these uses.

Activity 16 Check your cookies from Internet Explorer

Cookies are fundamental to the way the web works. This can be seen by the state of your cookie folder. Internet Explorer keeps all cookies from each website/server domain in a separate text file in your 'Documents and Settings' folder (see Fig. 2.4.19).

If you have access to your personal 'Documents and Settings' folder view the properties for this folder and see how many cookies you have and how much space they are taking up.

Figure 2.4.19 The cookie folder

A web store primarily uses cookies to store an ID for the user, so that the site can recognise users when they log on again. The ID can then often be matched to the database record of the user where the ID acts as a primary key. (We will look at databases in more detail in Chapter 2.5.) The site can then welcome customers by name and have their order history, preferences and so on set up the moment they access the site (see Fig. 2.4.21). Of course, it is possible that someone else has used the computer and/or account and thus most e-commerce sites will check that it really is the user in question. This can be seen quite simply by examining cookies from online retailers. Both the following examples below show how the cookie is used to store an ID. In the case of Amazon further cookies are also maintained within the cookie file to store session IDs and other information as well. Some internet search engines also use this technology to keep track of what has been searched for and display appropriate advertisements to their users.

Managing your cookies in Netscape

If you use Netscape as your browser it maintains its cookies in a single file called 'cookies.txt'. It also provides a Cookie Manager (see Fig. 2.4.20) that allows you to view and remove cookie information.

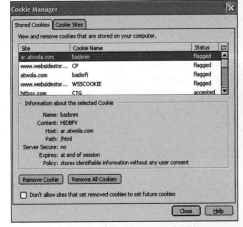

Figure 2.4.20 Cookie Manager in Netscape

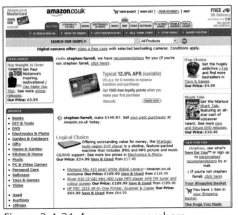

Figure 2.4.21 Amazon remembers

Examples of cookies from cookie folder

You can read cookies by accessing them using Notepad.

Example 1

File: www.sainsburystoyou[1].txt
cookieID
18621742
www.sainsburystoyou.com/

Example 2

File: steve farrell@amazon.co[1].txt
ubid-acbuk
432-2576168-2282217
amazon.co.uk/

Cookies and related technologies

Cookies come in many varieties, including the following:

Session cookie   a cookie that only exists while the website is being accessed.

Persistent cookie   a cookie saved on the hard disk for longer than a single session

Third-party cookie   a cookie placed by an advertiser or other agency, not from the original domain accessed.

Web bug   an invisible image (usually a 1 pixel blank GIF) used to monitor what adverts and web pages a user is viewing.

Some advertising and marketing agencies use cookies in an ingenious way. They make agreements to allow them to place banner ads and other images (see 'web bugs' in the margin) on their clients' websites. When the banner or image is clicked, the server of the advertising agency places a cookie on the computer of the person accessing it. The same cookie is then accessed across the multiple sites on which the banner ads are placed. This enables the agency to track which ads have been displayed and which, if any, have been clicked on, and match this with the user's ID from the cookie. Over time this allows the agency to determine the interests of many users and develop a profile of them. These profiles are stored on a database so that the banners and pop ups that a particular user sees in the future are personalised. The agency can tell which sites are visited most, what pages work best within a site, and can use this information for predicting trends. After analysing over a period what kind of advertising works and what does not, the agency can then sell this information on to its clients.

DISCUSSION Third-party cookies and web bugs ◀

Do third-party cookies and web bugs help users by allowing suppliers to tailor the messages they receive, or are they an intrusion into users' privacy?

Protecting privacy with firewalls

It is relatively easy for a web user to block ordinary cookies, third-party cookies, web bugs and indeed block all private information being sent from their computer, using either the tools built into the browser or a third-party program such as the Zone Alarm firewall (see Fig. 2.4.22). Zone Alarm and other similar programs allow you to customise settings site by site and browser by browser.

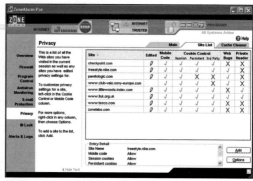

Figure 2.4.22 Using a firewall to protect privacy

Adware, on the other hand, is more intrusive than cookies. It is usually a program that you install on your computer yourself – often without realising – which tracks your online behaviour so that advertisers or market researchers can profile your spending preferences and better predict market trends. If advertisers are open about this and inform the customer clearly what they are doing, adware can be very useful. The customer will often gain some reward for installing the service and will receive tailored offers from participating retailers; the e-industry gains access to direct information on users' online spending trends, thus allowing offers to be better tailored to customers.

However, acceptance of adware is often hidden in the small print of the End User Licence Agreements (EULA) of, for example, free or shareware software, with which most users of the internet will be familiar. When downloading such items you will be asked to confirm that you have read and agreed to the software's terms and conditions. At this point many people simply tick the box and carry on. The EULA may, however, grant the vendor rights to install adware and more on your computer. The most notorious examples of this have come with the file-sharing applications used for downloading 'free' MP3s from the internet. In some cases adware is installed as a suite of programs which both act very aggressively in collecting and reporting information about the user's habits, and also act together to make it really difficult to remove the installed programs permanently from the computer.

Spyware

Spyware often uses the same technologies as adware, but is devious and occasionally even malicious (malware) about what it is doing and how it goes about it. You may end up with a slow and inappropriately customised browser, 'doctored' search results, spam emails, and annoying and sometimes very persistent pop-ups. At worst you will have installed a hidden program which spies on your interactions, sending keystrokes, passwords, credit card details and almost any other information about your computer use from your computer to a controller. The spyware may do this in real time over the internet or it may simply log the information in a file, sending an email when you next connect to the internet.

Spyware tradecraft

Spyware can end up on a user's computer in a variety of ways. Some of these exploit vulnerabilities in browsers and messengers to transfer a program to users' PCs without their permission or knowledge. The most common method, however, is for the user unwittingly to transfer them 'with permission' while transferring another application. There are a number of steps you can take to minimise the risks of spyware. The first and most important is to have an up-to-date virus checker and firewall. It is also useful to have a spyware patroller (such as WinPatrol) that will spot and remove virtually all spyware at source. Good habits are also useful. Sites that are considered 'dodgy' but 'cool' such as free music download sites often transfer spyware to unsuspecting users.

Personalising the experience

Once a person has been identified and matched with personal information then a web business can provide a better experience for the customer. Orders can be processed very quickly without the need to ask for all the customer's delivery and payment details. A number of merchants provide the facility of storing information about special dates such as birthdays and anniversaries in their databases, and send reminders out as these commercially orientated dates

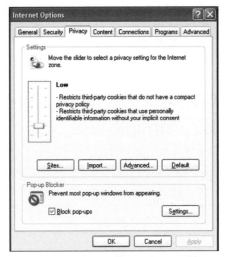

Figure 2.4.23 Controlling privacy with Internet Explorer

Protecting privacy with P3P

A privacy policy says what information a website collects as it interacts with the user. A compact privacy policy is one that conforms to the standards of the Platform for Privacy Preferences (P3P), which is a W3C standard for protecting privacy on the web using policies. A website can write a file stating in detail how it uses personal data (or if it has a compact privacy policy, stating how it uses cookies for personal data). Users state their preferences regarding privacy in their browser settings, and the browser can then decide whether to accept cookies from a site or not. This means in effect that users have the freedom to choose what level of privacy to enforce and what level of personalisation to enjoy.

If you have Internet Explorer 6.0 select 'Tools' then 'Internet Options...'. Select the 'Privacy' tab. Examine the slider options to get a flavour of how policies work to allow the user more control (see Fig. 2.4.23).

World Wide Web Consortium (W3C)

W3C is a body set up to develop standards for the web in order to fulfil its mission which is "To lead the world wide web to its full potential by developing protocols and guidelines that ensure long-term growth for the Web." (Source: W3C.)

approach. This acts as a service to the customer and a marketing opportunity for the organisation (see Fig. 2.4.24). In an almost a perfect model for the use of customer information, order and click histories can be used to make personalised recommendations (see Fig. 2.4.25).

A further service that can be provided to a registered and logged-in customer is in the area of fulfilment. Good websites often enable customers to view the progress of their order online (see Fig. 2.4.26). After sales can also be catered for by providing full order histories and sales analyses (see Fig. 2.4.27).

Figure 2.4.24 Gift reminder services

Figure 2.4.25 Personal recommendations

Figure 2.4.26 Tracking orders

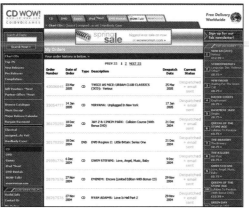

Figure 2.4.27 Analysis of purchase histories and sales information

ACTIVITY 17 Compare previous order information

- What information is stored about customers' past orders by CD Wow and Amazon?
- What will customers use this information for?
- What will the store maintain this information for?

ACTIVITY 18 Find out about retaining customers ◀

Read the article 'Customer loyalty key to e-commerce profitability' by Michael Pastore, ClickZ Network, 30 March 2000.

Summarise the main points from this article which discusses the importance of retaining customers.

ACTIVITY 19 Identify personalised features ◀

Examine the two screenshots in Figure 2.4.28.

List all the personalisation features that Virgin appears to be using. What information are they storing for each user and how are they using this to improve the customer's experience of wine and the online site?

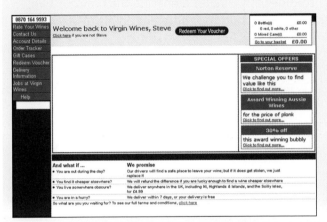
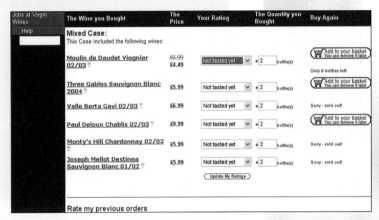

Figure 2.4.28 Virgin Wines

ACTIVITY 20 Compare public and private sector websites ◀

Visit Marks & Spencer's website as an example of a commercial site and Lincolnshire County Council's website as an example of a public sector site. Provide the following information about each:

- the purpose of the site and how successfully it meets its objectives
- how it is structured
- the goods and/or services it offers
- the product information provided
- types of transactions that can be made and how easy it is to do so
- methods used to capture user information (both overt and covert) and authenticate the identity of users
- techniques used to engage, retain and entice users
- its usability and accessibility
- the 'user experience' it offers.

Conclusion ▶ ▶ ▶

In this chapter we have examined how an online business deals with its customers. We have seen how it uses many standard marketing techniques and some specifically adapted to the virtual world to engage, entice and retain customers. The most important of these techniques use information about the customer to build an ongoing virtual relationship and encourage customer loyalty. This information is captured in a variety of ways from the totally open to the covert. It is then used to provide a richer overall experience at every level: from first entrance to the site, through browsing and buying, to after-sales support.

In this chapter you have been given many opportunities to consider what you like and dislike about the way sites do business with customers, and the overall experience an online business or service can offer to them. In order to consider this in the round, you should consider this chapter alongside the previous two, which have both looked at similar issues, but from different points of view.

Designing the back-office database

In the previous chapters you came across a number of processes and concepts that need to be embraced by any organisation running a transactional website. You have looked at the information flow of the information systems needed to undertake these processes. In this chapter we are going to look at one of the most important parts of these systems. Behind every successful information system (and also one or two unsuccessful ones) is a database, these days probably a relational database.

The subject of databases is viewed by ICT users in the same way as mathematics is viewed by the academic world. Many people find it hard to get to grips with while others take to it immediately. Some extremely talented people who are masterful in other areas still avoid databases if they can. The trouble is that although the requirement for many other skills comes and goes, the database seems to have been a constant presence in computing since its inception, and looks likely to be with us for the foreseeable future.

Much of the difficulty with databases is the terminology. ICT professionals tend to cloud every issue with terminology; they have a particular liking for acronyms. Let's be honest, 'ICT' itself is an acronym. The upshot of this is that it often feels as if ICT professionals are talking a foreign language, and the patronising look you may get when you need to ask what something means is hard to take (see Fig. 2.5.1). The good news with databases, however, is that once you master the terminology they become quite easy to use.

What is a database?

The first piece of terminology we have to get to grips with is the term 'database' itself. What is a database? To answer this we need to understand what is meant by data. In ICT terms, data are facts and figures **encoded** in such a way that they can be stored on a computer. An essential concept is that the facts and figures must be of some use, to a person or an organisation.

So data are essentially useful facts and figures held on a computer. What then is a database? A database is simply a lot of these facts and figures stored in one place and structured in such a way that to retrieve this data is pretty easy.

In the early days of computers, this data was held on magnetic tape in the form of what is known as 'flat files'. The easiest way to describe a flat file is as a form of table with rows and columns. As an example consider a payroll file, which is the data an organisation keeps in order to pay its employees. Each month a payroll program is run and the details of each of its employees are input into a program; from these details (e.g. standard hours worked; rate of pay for that individual; overtime rate and overtime worked) the pay due to each

"What's up with Fiona?"
"She's been talking to Simpkins in IT and now she's suffering from OSA."

"What's OSA?"

"Overload of Superfluous Acronyms"

Figure 2.5.1

Encoding A computer stores data internally as a series of 0s and 1s – called binary code – arranged into patterns that mean something to the computer. Data is, however, presented to it in many different forms. The process of converting these forms into the 0s and 1s the computer understands is called **encoding**.

employee for that month is worked out. Using our table analogy, each row in the table represents one employee. Each column represents something about the employee, such as his or her name, address or salary (see Table 2.5.1).

Last name	First name	Address	Date of birth	Annual salary
Aldridge	Steven	12 Ripley Road	16/07/67	£23 025
Anderson	Malcolm	84 Crimble Close	11/02/74	£25 765
Wilson	Mary	9 Teller Way	24/11/78	£32 998

Table 2.5.1 Payroll table

But there are a number of problems associated with holding data in this way. For example, organisations have many functions and many of these functions require data to be held. Certain items of data are required to be held for many different purposes.

For instance, an employee's name may be needed for payroll, assigning company cars, sending newsletters, working out shift rotas and many other things. Each of these functions will require a different flat file; this could cause a number of problems to do with data integrity. For example, imagine if an employee changes his or her name, either by deed poll or as a result of a marriage. This information would have to be updated on every file which contains the name. It would be easy to forget one or two occurrences and therefore not update the relevant files. This means that the data gets out of sync and in places, therefore, is invalid. Similarly, if a new employee is taken on, his or her details have to be added in several different places. If an employee leaves, his or her details have to be deleted from several places. In both of these cases it would be easy to forget one or two places where the data should either be added or removed.

Another problem with duplicating information is simply that of space. In the present day, our abundant storage space for electronic data makes it easy to forget the physical problem of storing the same data in several different places. Quite simply, if an item of data is stored in 50 different places, it takes up 50 times the storage space.

The magnetic tapes originally used for files many years ago could only be accessed serially. That meant that if you wanted information about the 250th employee on the payroll tape, you had to read through the first 249 before arriving at number 250. Naturally, this could make processing the data extremely tedious and time consuming.

With the advent of the magnetic disk (the forerunner to the hard disks, floppy disks and CD/DVD optical disks we use today) came direct addressing – a dramatic change in access method. Now you could go directly to the record sought without looking at all the previous records. Direct addressing made possible the development of the database structure which, with careful design and the use of relationships, allows us to avoid excessive duplication of data and its inherent problems.

Entities and attributes, and other good stuff

In this section we are going to try to get to grips with the dreaded terminology mentioned earlier. It stands to reason that if we are going to save data that will be useful, the data must be about something. For instance, we might be saving data about people, cars, animals, books, in fact, almost anything. The things we are going to save information about are known as **entities** (see Fig. 2.5.2). Using the example of a database that organises sales behind a transactional website, we may have a supplier entity containing information about our suppliers, a customer entity containing details about our customers, and perhaps a product entity containing information about what we sell. An entity, therefore, is a thing about which we want to save data.

Figure 2.5.2 "Somehow Max I don't think it has quite the right ring to it"

An **attribute** is a single item of information to be saved about that entity. For example, regarding our suppliers we may wish to save their names, their addresses and their telephone numbers. The supplier entity would therefore contain a name attribute, an address attribute and a telephone number attribute.

So far it all seems fairly straightforward but this wouldn't be ICT unless things were a little more complex than that: we give completely different names to what are essentially the same things, depending on the context we use them in. The terms 'entities' and 'attributes' are used mainly when we are talking about the database in the abstract, such as when we are designing it. Once you start seriously storing data the terminology changes; to make matters even more complex, the terminology you use depends on the database management system you use.

Data in a relational database is split up into a number of flat files. Each flat file contains data about one particular entity and is known as a **table** or sometimes a **database file**. Inside these tables the attributes are also renamed becoming **fields**.

Just one further definition, at least for the moment. Let's take our supplier entity for instance. In our database we will have a supplier table. This will contain details about more than one supplier. The information in the table for one supplier (one entity occurrence) is known as a **record**.

For the moment, we can leave our terminology and go back to our transactional website.

The transactional website

In Chapter 2.3 we looked at some of the back-office processes which need to be performed behind a transactional website. The most common form of transactional website is, of course, the online store. The online store faces a lot of the same challenges as a normal retail outlet and many of the processes it performs are the same. The requirements of these processes may be slightly different but fundamentally the same things have to happen. As this is a retail process, decisions have to be made about what stock to hold. Stock then has to be ordered from the supplier and sold to the customer. To enable all of these processes to occur, data has to be held and the most efficient way of doing this is on a database. For the processes to work properly the database has to be structured in such a way that the data can be searched and ordered efficiently to provide the information we want quickly. This structure is going to be similar no matter what we are selling, since the basic processes will be the same. So let's look at an example and see how we would go about setting up a suitable structure.

CASE STUDY QwikFeet

Figure 2.5.3

QwikFeet Ltd (see Fig. 2.5.3) is an online retailer of trainers. It was established in 2000 and its revenue has grown steadily each year of its existence. QwikFeet maintains a transactional website. The website can be found through a number of search engines and QwikFeet advertises on many sports and fashion websites. Anybody can access the website and view pages containing pictures and information about the trainers they sell. While they are viewing they can maintain a virtual shopping basket, into which they enter the trainers they are interested in, how many they want, and the sizes required.

To buy, customers must proceed to the checkout. This is a secure area of the website and to access it they must register themselves as a customer. To register as a customer they must fill in an online registration form, providing such details as name, home address and contact number. They must also supply an email address and a password. Customers only have to register once, as the next time they can access the checkout simply by providing their email address and password.

At the checkout the items in their shopping basket are turned into an order and the total price of the order is displayed. The customers then have the opportunity to either 'confirm' or 'cancel' the order. If they confirm it they are asked for further details; for example a delivery address if this is different from their home address. They are also asked to provide credit or debit card names, account numbers and expiry dates. When these details are entered, customers can either 'submit' the order or, again, they are provided with the opportunity to 'cancel'. Once the order is submitted customers can sit back and wait for the trainers to be delivered. However, an awful lot has to happen before this occurs.

A number of things occur simultaneously. A copy of the order is automatically sent to the customer's email address as confirmation that the order has been placed. Another copy is sent (electronically) to the warehouse to be filled and dispatched. The customer's credit-card details and the cost of the order are sent to the customer's own credit-card company along with a request for authorisation.

On receipt of the order, the warehouse staff check whether they have the right trainers in the right sizes in stock. If they have, they are removed from storage and packed in a box. If any items are not in stock they are emergency ordered from the suppliers. While waiting for the emergency order to arrive the partially completed order is put to one side. When the order is complete (all items

Continued on next page

bought by the customer are packed including any emergency orders) the package is sealed and addressed. At this point the status of the order is said to be 'awaiting release'. Release is provided by the accounts department once they have received authorisation from the credit-card company. Upon release the package is sent to goods out where it is picked up and delivered by a parcel delivery service with which QwikFeet has a contract.

At any point in this transaction customers can sign on and look at the status of their order. Customer details are only deleted if a customer requests this; otherwise, customers are free to use their sign-on for as long as they wish. Details of all orders are kept for 5 years. This information is used by the management to decide which lines to sell and by Dean Rabette (the warehouse manager) to decide what stock he will need. In general, Dean orders stock from the supplier. He can only order in batches of 100 pairs of shoes at a time, and in that batch he will always order the same distribution of sizes. Emergency orders tend to cost the company money, so part of Dean's job is to minimise the occurrence of these.

What QwikFeet needs is a database structure to support the processes described. To set up the structure the first thing we need to do is to decide what our entities are.

ACTIVITY 1 Identify database entities ◀

Read the case study carefully and make a list of the database entities required for the complete fulfilment process. Remember an entity is something about which we wish to store data.

The entities needed are listed here:
- customer
- supplier
- order
- credit-card company
- product (trainers)

You might have used different names or you might have a few extras. If you have extras you are not necessarily wrong, entity spotting is not an exact science and what you end up with depends on your point of view. For instance, you may have identified credit card as an entity – it is after all a thing in its own right and we do want to store data about it. On the other hand, you could say it is actually not the credit card we are storing data about, but rather the method of payment for the order. Is credit-card information therefore an **attribute** of a larger order entity? It depends on your point of view.

Database relationships

The modern database is known as a **relational database** because of its ability to maintain relationships between entities – it is these relationships that make it such a powerful data-handling tool. A relationship is simply a connection between two entities. Using our QwikFeet example: a customer creates an order, therefore there is a relationship between customer and order.

In theory there are three types (degrees) of relationship. The most common is the one-to-many relationship (1:M). For example, in our system it is possible for a customer to create many orders, however an order can be created by only one customer, so the relationship between customer and orders is one to many (1:M). Although it is not actually a different degree of relationship, the relationship between orders and customers is described as many-to-one (M:1).

The next degree of relationship we are going to look at is one-to-one (1:1). There are not any obvious one-to-one relationships in our example, so we shall look at the relationship between the entities husband and wife. In most societies a wife has only one husband and a husband has only one wife. The thing about one-to-one relationships is that when they occur you need to question whether both entities are necessary to your database. We could, after all, combine husband and wife to become couple.

The final degree of relationship is the many-to-many relationship (M:M). To illustrate this, let's look at the relationship between the order and the product (trainers). A single order can be for many products, that is, a customer can order more than one pair of trainers in one order. At the same time, a single product can be in many orders, i.e. there is nothing to stop several customers ordering the same type of trainers. Hence, this gives a potential many-to-many relationship between order and product.

Possibly the hardest thing about database relationships is actually ensuring we know when there isn't one. On the face of it, the relationship between customer and product is many to many, since a customer can order many products, and a product can be ordered by many customers. However, the relationship between them is provided through the order entity, so it is not necessary to have a relationship directly between customer and product. In fact, if we were to have one, we could confuse the database management system.

The entity relationship diagram

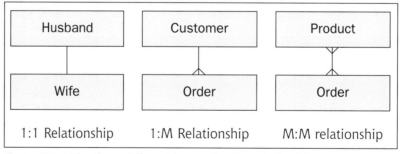

Figure 2.5.4 The three different types of entity relationships

The relationship between the various entities in a database structure can be shown in an entity relationship diagram (ERD). The entities are drawn in boxes and joined together with lines. At the many end of any relationship the line forks off into three lines known as 'crow's feet' (see Fig. 2.5.4).

In Figure 2.5.4 the two relationships from our QwikFeet example appear almost as separate diagrams and consequently the entity order appears twice. In our final ERD each entity will appear only once (Fig. 2.5.5).

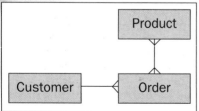

Figure 2.5.5 Entity relationship diagram for product, customer and order entities

ACTIVITY 2 Complete entity relationship diagram ◀

Figure 2.5.5 shows the start of the entity relationship diagram for our QwikFeet case study and shows the relationships between the customer, the order and the product entities. Complete the diagram by adding in the supplier and the credit-card company entities. Show any relationships between the entities.

An answer is shown in Figure 2.5.6. You may be surprised to see that there is a relationship between the credit-card company and the order entities and that it is not between the customer and the credit-card company – after all, it is the customer's credit-card. The key to this is in the scenario. The credit-card company is contacted by QwikFeet asking for payment for the items in the order. So in this situation, the relationship is that the credit-card company provides funds to cover (many) orders. In another database built for another purpose, the relationship between customer and credit-card company may be needed but for this one it is not, since the order rather than the customer is what is transacted.

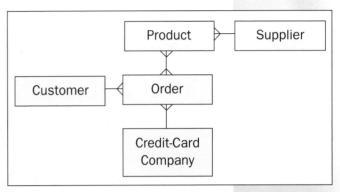

Figure 2.5.6 One possible entity relationship diagram for QwikFeet

Data types

Having sorted out our entities and their relationships it is time to look at the attributes. These are the individual data items we wish to save about our entities. We need to decide not only what attributes we need, but what type of data it will be.

Fundamentally there are three different types of data: text (alphanumeric), number (numeric) and Boolean (although these days sounds, pictures and even animations can be held on a database).

▶ Text

A text or alphanumeric field can contain any of the letters A to Z and a to z, numbers 0 to 9, and any special characters such as ', £, $, (,), &, *, % and ^.

▶ Number

The fundamental advantage of number fields over text fields is that arithmetic operations can be done on them. You can add, subtract, multiply and divide them, as well as find the square root and many other mathematical functions. This field can therefore only contain symbols associated with numbers. Obviously, the numbers 0 to 9 are allowed, but don't forget special characters such as '.' (decimal point) and '−' (minus sign).

Application programming interface (API)

Many database management systems allow us to define a form of application programming interface (API). Effectively this means that we can create data in one application to be accessed in another (in this case a DBMS). This data retains its original format and can be accessed by either application. What this means is best explained by an example. We could create a drawing in a graphics package and hold this as part of the data in our database. Our drawing would be displayed when the record is displayed (for instance in a database form) but we could modify it in the graphics package and the changes would automatically be displayed in the database form.

Two commonly used APIs are OpenDoc and OLE (object linking and embedding). The use of these APIs is outside the Edexcel Unit 2 specification so for the moment it is probably best to stick to text, number and Boolean data types.

Numbers come in all sorts of different formats and most database management systems specify a lot of these as different data types. Fundamentally, a number is a number, but there are a few other options, which we will now look at.

Integer and real numbers

An integer is a whole number, which means you cannot have fractions or decimals if you choose integers as a data type. If you want decimals then there are a number of ways you can ask for them, for instance: 'real', 'decimal', 'single', 'double'. The difference between them, and for that matter any option including the integer, is the way the number is actually stored, which is beyond the scope of this unit. Integer is usually the default largely because, a bit like us, computers find it easier to work with whole numbers. You may see a data type called 'long integer'. This is because with some DBMSs there is a limit to the size of number you can hold as an integer; a long integer therefore allows you to hold larger numbers.

Numeric data types

Integer These are whole numbers (e.g. –200, 0, +20 000). The size of an integer a computer can store depends on how much storage is allocated to it. A byte will store unsigned numbers up to 255. A long (4 byte) integer will store numbers between approximately plus and minus 2 thousand million.

Real A number with decimal places – usually known in computing as a floating-point number (e.g. 0.01, 1/3, 25 678 992.888 76). As a fixed number of bits are used to store an infinite amount of numbers these are inevitably approximations with rounding errors introduced as the number of digits in the number gets longer. A special floating-point algorithm is usually used to deal with rounding errors in a predictable manner. These are useful for fractions and for very large and very small numbers, but should not be used for currency. In simple terms a number defined as 'double (precision)' has twice the storage area of a number defined as 'single (precision)' and is therefore more accurate.

Currency These are fixed-point numbers (e.g. 10.25, £999 999 999 999.999 9, 0.25). Currency can be represented by integers, but can get much larger than even the long-integer data type allows. Furthermore it can have a decimal point to represent the pence (or cents). A special data type is usually used therefore that has the total accuracy of integers but allows very large numbers (in Microsoft Access, for example, this is up to 15 digits before the decimal point) and decimal fractions (accurate up to four digits after the decimal point). The DBMS may also be able to display the number with appropriate currency symbols (£, $, p etc.), although these need not be stored.

Percentage These are a fraction multiplied by 100 (e.g. 30 per cent, 2.5 per cent, 99.99 per cent). Percentages are in fact simply real numbers, but formatted to be displayed as percentages. Thus the number 0.3 will be stored as a conventional floating point number but displayed as 30%.

Date and time formats

Date and time could be stored in a number of ways, including as a special type of numeric data. Microsoft Access currently stores its dates and times as a double-precision floating-point number representing the number of days' difference from 31 December 1899, and has a routine which converts this number to time, day, month and year. The integer part of the date is the number of days and the decimal part represents the fraction of the 24 hours that has elapsed. In this way midday (12:00/24:00) would be 0.5 and 6 p.m. (18:00/24:00) would be 0.75. Therefore midday on 1 January 1900 would be held as 1.5.

▶ Boolean

A Boolean field (sometimes known as a yes/no or true/false field) can contain one of two options. Exactly what these are depend on the DBMS; they correspond to either 'yes' and 'no', or 'true' and 'false'

QwikFeet data

To look at the process of deciding on attributes and data types we will look at the product entity of our QwikFeet database. This is the entity where we are going to store details about the trainers QwikFeet sells. This entity is used in both the order-process and the stock-control system, so we must also bear these in mind.

There are a number of factors we need to think about. We will need to save the make and model of the particular trainer. The customer will also need to know the price at which we sell the trainer. For stock control we will need to know how many we have in stock: QwikFeet hold sizes from 3 to 11 so we need to hold data about how many of each size we have. We do not have to hold the total number of trainers in stock as we can calculate this by adding up how many trainers we have for all the different sizes.

We could however help Dean, the warehouse manager, a little more. Every month Dean orders trainers from the suppliers in batches of 100, but these are ordered a month in advance. He therefore has to know approximately how many he sells in a month. If his stock level at the beginning of the month is less than this, he will have to put in an order else he will not have enough trainers to fulfil customer orders. This value is known in stock control parlance as the 're-order level'. This is the value at which an order is triggered when your stock falls below it. Our final attribute, for the moment, is the buying price, the price which the suppliers will charge us.

Now that we have decided upon what attributes our product entity is going to have, we need to decide which data types they are.

ACTIVITY 3 Identify data types of attributes ◀

Table 2.5.2 shows the attributes of the product entity in tabular form with some of the data types filled in. Copy and complete the table by filling in the other data types with either 'text', 'number' or 'Boolean'. When the data type is number indicate whether you think it is 'integer', 'decimal', 'date/time', 'currency' or 'percentage'.

Product entity	
Attribute	**Data type**
Make	Text
Model	
Selling Price	
Stock Size 3	Number (Integer)
Stock Size 4	
Stock Size 5	
Stock Size 6	
Stock Size 7	
Stock Size 8	
Stock Size 9	
Stock Size 10	
Stock Size 11	
Buying Price	
Re-order Level	

Table 2.5.2 Product entity of QwikFeet database

The primary key

An important concept in a database is the idea of keys. A key is an identifying attribute, which is something which can be used to find a particular entity occurrence or record. Of these, possibly the most important is the **primary key**. The primary key is the attribute (field) which can uniquely identify a particular entity occurrence (record) in an entity (table). This means that if we ask for the record in a particular table whose primary key contains '432', it will return one, and only one, record. These keys are doubly important as they not only identify every record on the database, but are also used to provide the relationships between the entities. Once stored, therefore, the content of a primary key will never change. You will notice that the terminology here is starting to change. This is because we are moving away from the abstract process of design and are starting to talk about physical data.

So let's look at our product fields – are there any which we can use as a primary key? We can forget about the prices and the stock levels as these are going to change quite often. Neither can we use a field as a key if we don't know what it will contain, so we are left with make and model. A particular manufacturer will make a number of different models of trainers and if we stock more than one of them then the make field would not be unique. For example, if we stock two kinds of trainers made by the manufacturer Apollo then the make field for both records would be 'Apollo' and therefore not unique. The model field looks more promising – but can we guarantee that two manufacturers would not use the same name for a style of trainers? It would be unlikely because of trademarking and so on, but we cannot guarantee it.

Actually there is nothing wrong with combining two (or more) fields to form a primary key; in fact, there is a name for this – we call it a **composite key**. So we could form a composite key by combining the make and model, and this will certainly be unique. The other widely used technique is simply to invent another field into which we put a code. Since we are assigning the code and codifying it based on a coherent logic of our own, this is another way we can guarantee the uniqueness of the primary key.

Because composite keys take a lot of typing in when you search a database, we are going to use the latter technique and add a field called stock code. We will then assign a unique stock code to each different type of trainer in stock. We make the data type text, as we will never do an arithmetic operation on this data.

Verification and validation

Computers have a habit of doing exactly what you tell them to do. So if you ask them to do something silly the odds are they will go right ahead and do it. In the same way if you tell them a load of rubbish they will believe you. Not only will they believe you, they will also trot out the same rubbish results every time you put the same rubbish information in. So if you tell them a pair of trainers costs £1.23 instead of £123, that is the value they will use in all their calculations, including calculating how much a customer owes you. This is a concept known as GIGO or 'garbage in, garbage out'.

As you can see, it is of vital importance that the data that goes onto a database is correct and great pains must be taken to make sure that it is. The two major ways of checking the data is correct are known as verification and validation.

Verification in the main is done manually; the data that is input is simply checked against a second source. For instance, one person types in the data and someone else checks what has been typed against the original document.

Validation is done by the computer. Each time data is input it is checked against a set of rules. If it does not comply with these rules then the data is not accepted and an error message is output. There are a number of validation techniques and we shall look at a few now:

- **Length check** The simplest of all the validation techniques, the length check, simply sets a maximum number of characters that can be input into a field. If for instance we decide that the longest name of our trainer manufacturers will be 12 characters, we set the maximum length of our make field to 12 (see Fig. 2.5.7). If we try to put in a name of 13 characters or more, the database will not allow us to do so.

- **Presence check** When you input data there is a possibility that some fields do not have to be filled in. For instance, we may have a field for the customer's mobile phone number, but we may not *require* the person to supply the number. When entering the data this field will therefore sometimes be left blank. Conversely, there are fields that *must* be filled in. On transactional websites these are sometimes marked with asterisks to signify that they are required. A presence check is put on these fields; if there is an attempt to save a record with this field still blank, an error message is printed. Therefore if we wish to set a presence check on the model field we simply set it as required (see Fig. 2.5.8).

- **Range check** A range check will check that a field is between two values. For instance it would be unusual to pay less than £20 for a pair of trainers; in the same way, it would be unlikely to have to pay more than £200. We could therefore set a range check on the selling price field to ensure that what is entered is no less than £20 but is not more than £200 (see Fig. 2.5.9). Look at the demonstration of this.

Figure 2.5.7 Length check set to a maximum of 12 characters

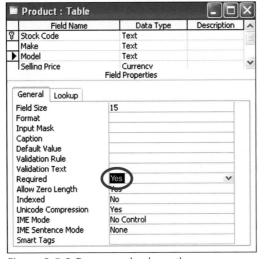

Figure 2.5.8 Presence check on the model field

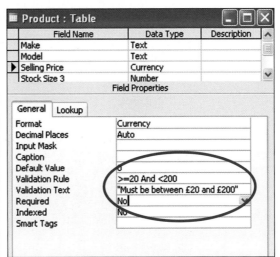

Figure 2.5.9 The range check ensures that price is set to greater than or equal to £20, but less than £200

Figure 2.5.10 This list check ensures that the title given is only one of the specified options

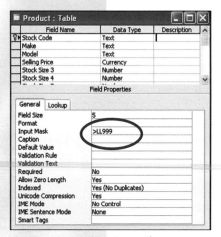

Figure 2.5.11 The picture/format check (or input mask) ensures that the stock code has two upper case letters followed by three numbers

- **List check**   A list check checks that what is entered into a field is one of a list of options. One of the fields we would have in our customer table would be 'title'. The list of options for this would be simply Mr, Mrs, Miss, Ms and Dr. Anything else would produce an error message (see Fig. 2.5.10). Another form of the list check is the table lookup. This means that the data entered into a field must be in a specified field of a specified table.
- **Picture check**   Sometimes known as a format check or an input mask; this form of validation checks that a text field is of a particular format with regards to letters and numbers. For instance let us take our stock code attribute. We are creating this ourselves so we can insist on whatever format we like. We have decided that it should be five characters long and the first two characters must be the first two letters of the manufacturer's name followed by a three figure number (see Fig. 2.5.11). Some database management systems even allow you to force the letters to upper or lower case. The '>' sign in Figure 2.5.11 means that upper-case letters will be stored, no matter whether upper or lower case letters were typed. Now look at the input mask demonstration.

Atomic attributes

Let's turn our attention now to another of our QwikFeet entities, the supplier entity. The first attribute we will have to consider is the supplier's name. One of the things we must note here is that our supplier may not have the same name as the make of trainer, but it should be unique so we could use it as a primary key. What other attributes would we need to have? Obviously we will need the company address so that we can send our orders to them. Maybe we would need a contact name, a telephone number for the contact, and perhaps also a fax number.

Although telephone numbers are numbers it is as well to define telephone numbers as text fields. For example, at no time do you ever perform a mathematical operation on a telephone number, and what happens to the leading zero and the '-' if you store '01555-656443' in a number field? Take care with phone numbers, therefore.

Another field we should take a closer look at is the address field. Let's look at two fairly standard addresses:

23 Farnham Place	The Grange
Camberley	Monkton Terrace
SURREY	Reading
GU51 9PQ	BERKSHIRE
	RD23 6YT

If we were to save the addresses in one field we would probably have to store them something like this:

23 Farnham Place, Camberley, SURREY, GU51 9PQ
The Grange, Monkton Terrace, Reading, BERKSHIRE, RD23 6YT

We have said before that one very powerful reason to use a database is the ability to search for particular data. Imagine a situation where we want to find a list of all our customers in Berkshire. Using the above format we would have to do a complicated scan taking account of the commas to find the county – and even that will not work, as there are two commas before the county in the first address and three in the second.

It is possible to do a substring search, i.e. search for a pattern of letters within a text field (see Chapter 2.6). The problem with this is that it may find records we don't want; for example, people living in Berkshire Close, Wakefield.

In other words, using the above format, we cannot apply the same universal scanning criteria in order to find the piece of information we want.

It is not unusual to want to search for records using parts of an address, and so invariably database designers split up the address attribute into its **atomic attributes**, i.e. its smallest constituent parts. So instead of having one attribute called 'address', we would have five called 'address line 1', 'address line 2', 'town', 'county' and 'postcode'. In this way commas are avoided, since you would simply put the word 'Berkshire' in the 'county' attribute.

The final attribute definition for our supplier entity is shown in Table 2.5.3. The name entity is underlined to signify that this will be the primary key.

Supplier entity	
Attribute	**Data type**
Supplier Name	Text
Address Line 1	Text
Address Line 2	Text
Town	Text
County	Text
Post Code	Text
Contact Last Name	Text
Contact First Name	Text
Contact Title	Text
Contact Phone Number	Text
Fax Number	Text

Table 2.5.3 Supplier entity for QwikFeet. The primary key is underlined

Product entity	
Attribute	**Data type**
Product Code	Text
Make	Text
Model	Text
Selling Price	Number (Currency)
Stock Size 3	Number (Integer)
Stock Size 4	Number (Integer)
Stock Size 5	Number (Integer)
Stock Size 6	Number (Integer)
Stock Size 7	Number (Integer)
Stock Size 8	Number (Integer)
Stock Size 9	Number (Integer)
Stock Size 10	Number (Integer)
Stock Size 11	Number (Integer)
Buying Price	Number (Currency)
Supplier Name*	Text
Re-order Level	Number (Integer)

Table 2.5.4 Product entity for QwikFeet. The asterisk signifies a foreign key

Foreign keys

We have emphasised the importance of relationships in a relational database without actually saying how they are achieved. Fortunately once we establish a relationship, we do not have to worry about it because it is maintained by the database management system and everything happens transparently to the user.

If we go back to Figure 2.5.6 we note that there is a 1:M relationship between supplier and product in that a supplier supplies many products and conversely each product is supplied by only one supplier. To establish a relationship we need to put an extra field into the 'many' end of the relationship (product). This will contain the primary key of the related record in the '1' end of the relationship (supplier). In other words each product record will contain a field containing the primary key of the supplier that supplies that particular product. This new field is called a **foreign key** and is often signified by putting an asterisk against the name (see Table 2.5.4).

To see how this works look at the records shown in Table 2.5.5. The foreign key holds the primary key of the related record so Apollo Footwear Ltd supply QwikFeet with the Delta, the Kite 100 and so on, while Bridge Ltd supply the HyKlass range.

Supplier Name	Address Line 1	Address Line 2	
Apollo Footwear Ltd	Unit 17	March Trading Estate	
Bridge Ltd	Dorking Road		

Stock Code	Make	Model		Supplier Name
AP001	Apollo	Delta		Apollo Footwear Ltd
AP002	Apollo	Kite 100		Apollo Footwear Ltd
AP003	Apollo	Kite 200		Apollo Footwear Ltd
AP004	Apollo	Lite		Apollo Footwear Ltd
AP005	Apollo	Spring 4		Apollo Footwear Ltd
AP006	Apollo	Vulcan		Apollo Footwear Ltd
HY001	HyKlass	Force 2000		Bridge Ltd
HY002	HyKlass	Force 2001		Bridge Ltd
HY004	HyKlass	Force 2002		Bridge Ltd
HY005	HyKlass	Magnum 308		Bridge Ltd
HY006	HyKlass	SuperForce		Bridge Ltd

Table 2.5.5 Supplier and product records. The link between entities is formed by contents of 'supplier name' field

Many to many relationships

One last problem before we move on. The relationship between product and order is many to many. Unfortunately relational database management system software cannot handle many to many relationships as they stand. In which entity would you put the foreign key? What we have to do is create what would be a link record. Table 2.5.4 shows the attributes in our product entity; so far we haven't looked at the order entity.

Activity 4 Identify attributes of the order entity ◀

Create a table similar to Table 2.5.4 to show the attributes of the order entity. Remember to refer to the case study.

A possible answer to the above activity is shown in Table 2.5.6. There are a couple of interesting points worth noting. The primary key for the order entity is a numeric order number. This just happens to be how QwikFeet identify their orders; each is given a unique number one more than the last order processed; actually, a very logical method. Note that the credit-card number has been set as text. The reason for this is that we can set the field length to 16 and ensure that only numbers are entered, by setting a picture check.

To return to our original problem – the many-to-many relationship – we will create a link record which we will call order/product. This will contain, as foreign keys, the primary keys of both the order entity and the product entity, thereby providing a link. Often the two keys are all that appear in a link record, but in this case there is one other attribute. We will need to specify the size of the trainers we wish to buy. We cannot do it in the order as we may be buying more than one size of trainers, so it will have to go in our link record.

What about a primary key? Often you would simply combine the two foreign keys as a composite primary key, but there is the possibility that we would buy more than one pair of the same trainers in the same order. To solve this problem we can combine the order number with a sequence number to form the primary key. The sequence number will simply contain '1' for the first pair of trainers in an order, '2' for the second etc. Table 2.5.7 shows the attributes in our link record.

It is quite difficult to see how this works so Table 2.5.8 shows what is stored in this entity for order number 512. Order number 512 consists of three pairs of trainers. There are two pairs of product code AP002: one pair size 5 and one pair size 6. Also required is a pair of product code HY002, also size 6. To find what these products actually are we would have to look in the product entity.

Order entity	
Attribute	**Data type**
Order Number	Number (Integer)
Date	Number (Date)
Delivery Address Line 1	Text
Delivery Address Line 2	Text
Delivery Town	Text
Delivery County	Text
Delivery Post Code	Text
Credit Card Type*	Text
Credit Card Number	Text

Table 2.5.6 Order entity for QwikFeet

Order/product entity	
Attribute	**Data type**
Order Number*	Number (Integer)
Sequence Number	Number (Integer)
Product Code*	Text
Required Size	Number (Integer)

Table 2.5.7 Order/product entity for QwikFeet

Order Number	Sequence Number	Product Code	Required Size	Quantity
512	1	AP002	5	1
512	2	AP002	6	1
512	3	HY002	6	1

Table 2.5.8 Data stored in order/product entity for order 512

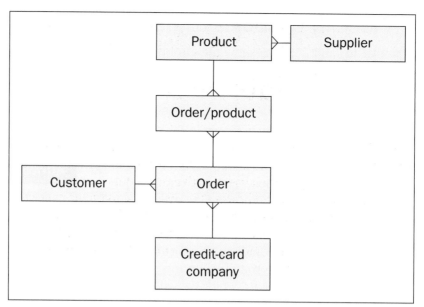

Figure 2.5.12 Using a link record to replace a many-to-many relationship by two one-to-many relationships

We have created a new entity so we will have to redraw our entity relationship diagram. The effect of creating a link record is to replace a many-to-many relationship by two one-to-many relationships (see Fig. 2.5.12).

ACTIVITY 5 Complete QwikFeet database design

You should now be able to complete the design of the QwikFeet database. Create tables similar to Tables 2.5.3, 2.5.5 and 2.5.6 for the customer, order and credit-card company entities.

Conclusion ▶ ▶ ▶

The main reason for having a database is to reduce the duplication of data, and a good structure is vital. If you have a good structure it is easy then to interrogate the database and find the information you want. Creating the right structure is fundamental to a successful database, and it is worth taking the time to do it right.

Building and using a database

Having spent some time designing a database in the previous chapter, in this chapter we are going to build and use it. To do this we need a database management system (DBMS) and of course, our design. At the end of the previous chapter you produced tables showing the attributes and their data types. They should look something like the ones at the end of this chapter. You will notice that we have ignored the credit-card company entity. This is because the data held in this entity is specifically to do with money transfer and we do not really have to look into this in Unit 2.

Building the database

If you think of a database as a series of flat files linked by relationships, each of our entities will form a flat file. The DBMS we are using calls these flat files 'tables' and we shall use this terminology for the rest of this chapter (note that other DBMSs may use different terminology). In the next activity you will build the tables required by your database. To do this you will have to become familiar with the design view of your DBMS. 'Design view' is where you define the structure of your tables; Figure 2.6.1 shows this view of the DBMS we are using. Watch the demonstration of how to set up the supplier table.

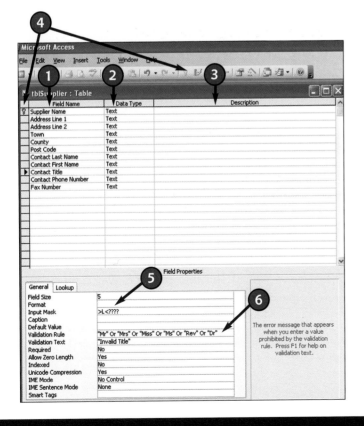

Figure 2.6.1 Design view

1. Field (attribute) names are entered into the column labelled 'Field Name'

2. Data types are entered into the column labelled 'Data Type' (available data types are shown in Figure 2.6.2)

3. The description column is purely documentary. You can enter a comment in here which explains the contents of the field if this is not obvious from the field name. This can be extremely useful to someone who may take over maintenance of the database from you at a later date, as it makes clear your intentions. Anything you put here will appear on the status bar when a field is selected and so it could be used as an online help

4. The primary key is set by selecting the field (or fields) you want as your primary key and clicking on the key icon on the icon bar

5. In this DBMS you set a format check using the input mask property. This one simply forces the first letter you type to upper case

6. This is where you enter other validation rules. This is a list check, ensuring that what is entered is in the list

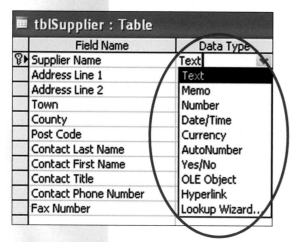

Figure 2.6.2 The encircled list shows the available data types

Naming objects

Within a database you will come across different types of object. In this unit we will show you 'tables' and 'queries', other objects are 'forms' and 'reports'. The DBMS has to be able to recognise each of these objects and therefore each must have a unique name. It is good practice to make these names meaningful so that the objects can be identified and it is not beyond the realms of possibility that you will want to call two objects by the same name. For instance you may have a 'customer' table and a 'customer' form but if you did this the DBMS may become confused. To counteract this problem a convention has been developed and is used by most database designers. When naming objects, designers will put a code at the start of the name. The codes are 'tbl' for a table, 'qry' for a query, 'frm' for a form etc. Therefore the customer table would be 'tblCustomer' and the customer form will be 'frmCustomer'.

ACTIVITY 1 Set up tables

Use your DBMS to set up all the tables required for the QwikFeet database.

Relationships

Figure 2.6.3 Relationships icon

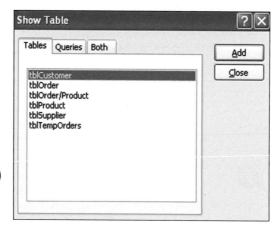

Figure 2.6.4 'Show Table' window

So far all you have done is define a series of flat files. To complete a relational database structure you have to create some relationships. You know what your relationships should look like because you have drawn an entity relationship diagram; you simply need to put this into practice. Watch the demonstration of how to create a relationship.

In the DBMS we are using we assign relationships by clicking on the relationships icon on the icon bar (see Fig. 2.6.3).

Clicking on this the first time brings up the 'Show Table' window. To add the tables to the relationship window simply select each table name and click the 'Add' button (see Fig. 2.6.4). After you have added all tables you require click the 'Close' button.

Once you have 'shown' all your tables you should be presented with a window similar to the one in Figure 2.6.5. You will note that we have rearranged the tables to look similar to the entity relationship diagram. To set a relationship drag the primary key from one table and drop it on the corresponding foreign key in the other table (as indicated in Figure 2.6.5).

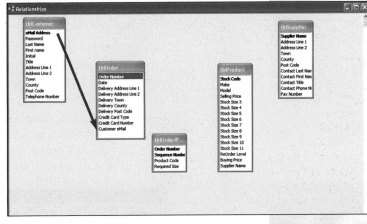

Figure 2.6.5 Setting a relationship

You will be presented with a confirmation window which among other things will ask you if you want to 'Enforce Referential Integrity' (see Fig. 2.6.6). If you were to enforce referential integrity it would mean that the slave record (the one in the table with the foreign key) could not be saved unless there is a master record 'referring' to it. In the example of the customer–order relationship shown in Figure 2.6.5, an order could not be saved unless there is a customer it belongs to. Since it doesn't make sense to have an order without a customer, it

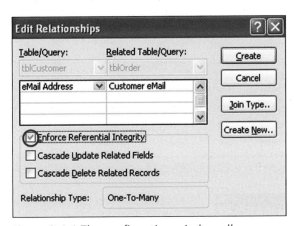

Figure 2.6.6 The confirmation window allows you to specify whether you want to enforce referential integrity

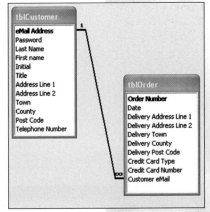

Figure 2.6.7 The created relationship

seems a good idea to set it in this situation. Once you have set referential integrity, click on the 'Create' button and the relationship will be created (see Fig. 2.6.7). You will notice that on the relationship the symbol '∞' appears. This shows the 'many' end of the relationship in the same way as '1' shows the 'one' end.

ACTIVITY 2 Set up the remaining relationships

Create the rest of the relationships, setting referential integrity on all of them. Once you have done this your relationships window should look similar to your entity relationship diagram (see Fig. 2.6.8).

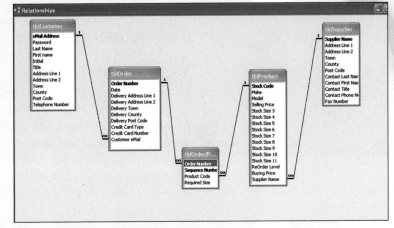

Figure 2.6.8 The complete relationships

Importing data

Having created your database structure you are ready to store some data. The process of inputting data into a database (or any kind of system) is called 'data capture'. The way you choose to do this is called a 'data capture method' and the device used is a 'data capture device'. There are a great many data capture devices these days, ranging from barcode readers to digital cameras, however the most common one is the good old-fashioned keyboard. Through this medium you can either type data directly into the table or you can create a form and use that to input data.

	Stock Code	Make	Model	Selling Price	Stock Size 3	Stock Size 4	Stock Size 5	Stock Size 6	Stock Size 7	Stock Size 8
	AP001	Apollo	Delta	£49.81	23	36	3	23	36	34
	AP002	Apollo	Kite 100	£44.86	42	24	65	43	43	54
	AP003	Apollo	Kite 200	£54.41	25	16	4	43	46	2
	AP004	Apollo	Lite	£44.52	76	63	45	54	34	34
	AP005	Apollo	Spring 4	£68.89	35	25	35	34	63	54
	AP006	Apollo	Vulcan	£55.47	57	63	35	64	3	2
	HY001	Hyklass	Force 2000	£24.73	34	4	57	34	46	46
	HY002	Hyklass	Force 2001	£34.97	27	24	23	7	75	64
	HY004	Hyklass	Force 2002	£41.97	35	53	56	45	34	32
	HY005	Hyklass	Magnum 308	£47.70	25	34	46	23	65	43
	HY006	Hyklass	SuperForce	£52.41	64	64	53	64	34	23
	MN022	Morgan	Hawk	£74.19	24	23	34	34	76	12
	MN023	Morgan	Osprey	£76.56	75	64	65	2	34	45
	MN058	Morgan	Raven	£91.51	13	25	24	54	56	67
	MN077	Morgan	Swallow	£103.71	46	35	35	7	34	34
	SP002	Spike	College	£62.28	8	64	23	45	76	23
	SP003	Spike	Contessa	£67.60	53	24	43	34	45	45
	SP004	Spike	Cussion 20	£86.91	14	64	12	65	34	64
	SP005	Spike	Cussion 30	£98.32	14	23	23	34	53	34
	SP006	Spike	Cussion 40	£110.59	75	56	25	54	45	23
				£0.00	0	0	0	0	0	0

Figure 2.6.9 Data entered into the product table

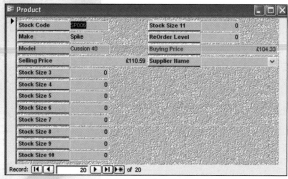

Figure 2.6.10 Form created for the product table using the form wizard

To enter data directly into the table simply select the table you require and 'Open' it. You will be presented with a window similar to Figure 2.6.9. Type the data you want in the spaces under the field names.

Most DBMSs provide a form wizard. This is an easy way of creating forms. You simply select the table or tables you want, start the wizard and answer a series of questions. The DBMS will then create the form for you (see Fig. 2.6.10). Watch the demonstration of how to do this.

The examination board will expect you to be able to create and search tables containing hundreds of records; even with a nice form to help you this would take a long time. The alternative way of getting data into your database is to import it. You can import data into databases from a large number of different data sources, such as other databases, spreadsheets and text files in many different formats. The examination board will supply you with a set of text files, but if you don't like the subject matter chosen by the board your teacher may be able to provide you with some alternative data.

 We have provided a number of text files in the ActiveBook and, assuming your structure matches ours you should be able to import them into your database structure as shown in the demonstration. In the DBMS we are using you have the option when importing data to do so directly into an existing table; or, you can also create a new table. Although in books like this one data often comes in a nice convenient form ready to load into tables, in real life this is very rarely the case. Usually it is only safe to load data straight into a table when the fields match the table; otherwise it is easy to put incorrect data into some of the fields.

Our ActiveBook items have another convenience that doesn't always happen in real life: the fields in the text files are delimited (separated) by commas and the first record in each file contains the field names.

ACTIVITY 3 Assess data files ◀

Investigate the following ActiveBook items:
- Text file of orders
- Text file of customers
- Text file of products
- Text file of suppliers

Which of these do you feel it is safe to import straight into a table? Which do you feel may need an interim step?

Save the four files in your user area.

It should be possible to import the text files of suppliers, customers and products straight into the corresponding tables; however, the file of orders seems to contain data for both the 'tblOrder' and the 'tblOrder/product' tables. You may therefore have to use an intermediate step to get this data into your system.

Before you start importing, however, you will have to think about the order in which you import data. In Activity 2 you set 'referential integrity' on some of your relationships. This means that if you tried to import the 'subordinate' records before you import the 'master', you will not be able to do it. For example, take the relationship between 'tblSupplier' and 'tblProduct'. If you have set referential integrity, then a product record cannot exist in your database unless you have a corresponding supplier record to link it to. In practical terms, if you tried to import the 'tblProduct' table before the 'tblSupplier' table, all the records will be rejected because they violate referential integrity rules. What you need to do therefore is import the supplier table first.

To start the import process, open your database and choose the 'File' menu from the menu bar. Instructions for importing will vary between DBMSs, but the following procedure is common.

From the resulting menu choose 'Get External Data' and 'Import' (see Fig. 2.6.11). You will be presented with a file navigation window labelled 'Import' (see Fig. 2.6.12) which you use to find the file. You will have to change the 'Files of type' field to 'Text Files'. Once you have selected the file (you saved them in Activity 3 into your user area) click on the import button. This will start a wizard.

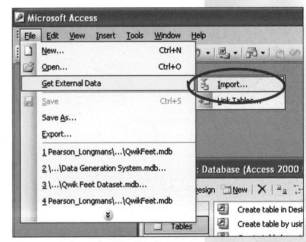

Figure 2.6.11 Starting the import process

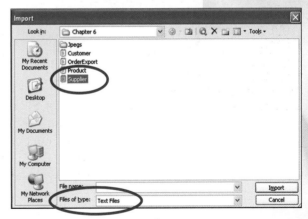

Figure 2.6.12 'Import' window

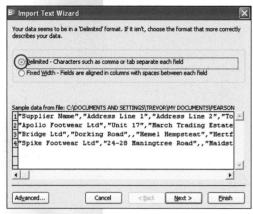

Figure 2.6.13 Specifying the format of the data fields

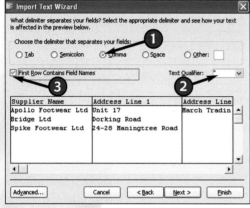

Figure 2.6.14 Separating fields

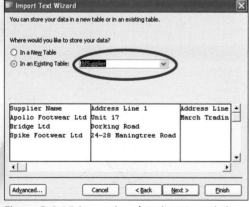

Figure 2.6.15 Importing data into an existing table

- The first stage of the Wizard (see Fig. 2.6.13) is asking how to tell one field from the next. You have two choices. You could make the fields fixed widths. This means that you define how many characters are in each field and that particular field will always be that number of characters. For instance, you might define the 'Product Name' field as 20 characters. If you then put 'Apollo Delta' in it (12 characters) you would have to fill the field up by supplying eight blanks. The alternative is that you delimit the fields with a defined character, in our case a comma. This means that a comma is placed between the end of one field and the beginning of another to tell the process where one field ends and another begins. This is what we use so make sure this option is selected and click on the 'Next' button.

- The next stage of the wizard (see Fig. 2.6.14) asks a little more about your files. First you need to tell it that you are using a comma to delimit the field ❶ . You are also telling it that you are using quote marks (") to show which fields are text fields ❷ . Note: in the text file all the text fields are surrounded by quotes. These quotes will not be copied to the files – it is just a way of telling the import process how to define the fields. You can also tell the wizard at this point that the first row of our text files contains field names ❸ . This can be extremely useful if you are importing to a new table, because if you do not supply field names the import process calls them generically 'field 1', 'field 2' etc, which are not the names you actually want. Ensure that the comma is chosen as a delimiter, quotes are used to qualify text and that the box marked 'First Row Contains Field Names' is checked. Then click the 'Next' button.

- The next stage of the Wizard (see Fig. 2.6.15) is asking you where you want to put your data. As has been mentioned before, there are two options. You can import it into an existing table or you can create a completely new table. In this case you want to import it directly into our 'tblSupplier' table so set the window to reflect this. When you come to import your 'order' data you will want to create a new table. This would be where you would do it. However, for the moment, simply select the 'tblSupplier' table and click on the 'Next' button.

- The final stage of the Wizard simply offers some help options and confirms the name of the file into which you wish to import. Click on the 'Finish' button. Assuming everything is OK with your database structure, the supplier data should be imported correctly.

ACTIVITY 4 Import remaining text files ◀

Import the rest of the text files into your database. You can import the product and customer text files directly into the tables, but the order text file will have to be imported into a new file. You can do this by checking the 'In a New Table' option in Figure 2.6.15. You will be presented with a number of new wizard windows.

Continued on next page

The screen in Figure 2.6.16 allows you to define your fields in more detail; it even allows you not to import some fields. However, we are currently happy with the defaults so just click on the 'Next' button.

The screen in Figure 2.6.17 is asking you to set a primary key. You have three options. You can allow the DBMS to set it for you, in which case it will generate sequential numbers as a primary key. You could nominate one of your fields as a primary key but you do not have a single field which would be unique. As this table will ultimately not form part of your database, as you are only using it to hold data temporarily, you need not set a primary key at all, which is the third option. Select this option and click on the 'Next' button.

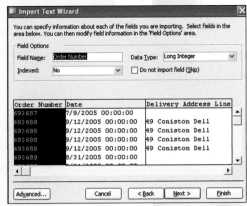

Figure 2.6.16 Importing order data into a new table

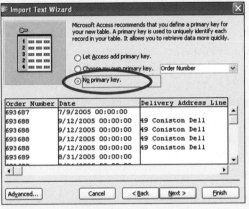

Figure 2.6.17 Setting a primary key

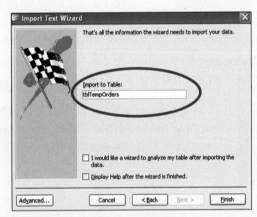

Figure 2.6.18 Naming the table

The screen in Figure 2.6.18 again offers some help options and a chance to name your table. You already have a table called 'tblOrder' so you will have to change the name so call it 'tblTempOrders'. Once you have done this click on the 'Finish' button.

Retrieving the data

You should have now succeeded in loading data into your database. Some of it is not quite in the form you want it but you will deal with this later. Getting data onto a database is all very well but it is not a lot of use if you cannot then retrieve it, preferably displayed in a useful form (see Fig. 2.6.19)

Interrogating a relational database is usually done using SQL. SQL (another acronym) stands for structured query language and is the ANSI (American National Standards Institute) standard language for relational databases. SQL is fairly simple to use as it is based on the idea that most database interrogation can be done through a limited number of instructions such as 'Select', 'Insert', 'Update', 'Delete' and 'Create'. Instructions are known as 'Queries'. Here is an example:

SELECT Product.Make, Product.Model FROM Product WHERE ((Product.[Supplier Name]) = 'Apollo Footwear Ltd');

Figure 2.6.19 "All right then! Can I have the January sales figures *PLEASE?*"

This example would list the make and model of all trainers in the product table where the supplier is Apollo Footwear Ltd. SQL is not particularly difficult to master but it tends to be a little pedantic about its syntax, which can be frustrating. A lot of DBMSs therefore supply a user-friendly interface to help. Although these are not necessarily easier to use, they are less prone to mistakes. The one we will show you is called 'query by example' or, inevitably, QBE for short. Creating queries using QBE is quite straightforward but if you can get the hang of 'real' SQL this approach can be a lot quicker for you in the longer term.

The whole idea of a query is to save you from information overload. If every time you wanted to find a piece of information you had to display and search through all the data on the database it would take you ages. You can therefore develop queries to restrict your view of the database and limit what you have to look through. Queries can do some other clever things, but fundamentally they are there to limit what you see.

Activity 5 Do a manual query ◀

To give you an idea of what we mean, open the 'qryTempOrders' table and find out how many Apollo Delta size 9s were sold in that period. Time how long it takes you. You can do this with a query later on and you can compare the time it takes.

▶ Restricting the fields you see

The first sort of query we will look at is one that restricts the number of fields we see. Imagine that for some reason we wanted a list of our customers' names and telephone numbers. If you open the customer table, the information you want is there, but you have to manipulate the scroll bars to display the name and the telephone number. You would also be displaying the address, which for these purposes is not needed. If you could get rid of the address and anything else you do not presently want, you could probably display the name and telephone numbers at the same time. You could delete the address fields from the table, but this would mean losing data. The alternative, a query, will allow you to see only the fields you want to see without affecting the physical data in the table. For this situation you want a query that will list just the names and telephone numbers.

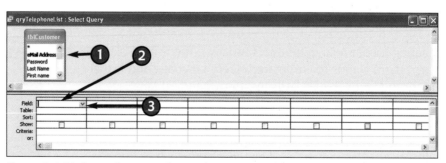

Figure 2.6.20 Query by example window

When you open a new query in design view you are faced with a 'Show Table' window similar to the one when you open relationships. From this you select the table or tables you want (in this case the customer table) and click on 'Add'. Once you have the tables you want in the query you can close the 'Show Table' window. You are then faced with the QBE design window (see Fig. 2.6.20). Creating a query using QBE is then quite simple; you simply copy the fields you want from the table list ❶ into the field section of the query ❷. There are a number of ways you can do this. First you could simply type in the field name. The problem with this is the potential for making mistakes. Alternatively you could point to the field in the table list and double-click. You could also drag the field from the table list into the query. Finally, we could use the drop-down arrow ❸ and select the field from the resulting list.

ACTIVITY 6 Create a query

Create a query called 'qryTelephoneList' (you will be asked to provide a name when we save your query) by adding the customer table to your query and selecting the 'last name', 'first name', 'title' and 'telephone fields', in that order (see Fig. 2.6.21).

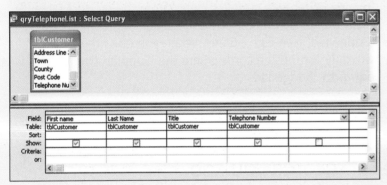

Figure 2.6.21 Create a query

Normally you would view the results of a query by opening it from the database window, but while you are in design view if you click on the icon shown in Figure 2.6.22a you can view the results of your query. You can then return to design view by clicking on the icon shown in Figure 2.6.22b. View the query you created and then return to design view.

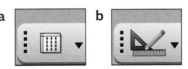

Figure 2.6.22 Icons for switching between data and design view

Your query has done what we set out to do but it could still be improved. Usually, telephone number lists are in alphabetical order. You can sort your queries further by setting the sort parameter in the relevant field (see Fig. 2.6.23) – you can set this as 'Ascending' (A–Z), 'Descending' (Z–A) or 'not sorted'.

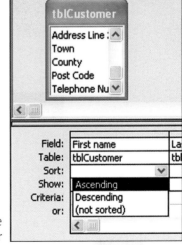

Figure 2.6.23 Sorting the output by alphabetical order

ACTIVITY 7 Sort query results   ◀

Set the sort parameters on 'Last Name' and 'First Name' to 'ascending' and view your results. You should find that it will be sorted on 'Last Name' and that the 'First Name' sort is only effective if the last names are the same. Queries will always be first sorted using the field furthest to the left. If you had wanted to sort on first names, this would have had to appear in the query further to the left than the last name.

Close and save your telephone numbers query.

 Compare what you did in Activities 6 and 7 with the demonstration.

▶ Restricting the records you see

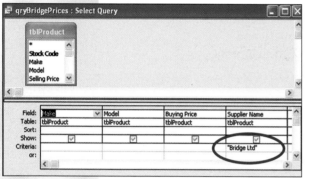

Figure 2.6.24 Restricting the number of records you see

In the same way that you can restrict the fields you see, you can also restrict the number of records you see. You can do this by setting view criteria. Imagine that you wanted to view the cost price of the trainers bought from Bridge Ltd. You would simply create a query selecting the 'make', 'model', 'buying price' and 'supplier name' from the product table. In the 'Criteria' parameter of the 'Supplier Name' field enter 'Bridge Ltd' (see Fig. 2.6.24). When you open this query it will only list those records where the 'Supplier Name' field **is equal to** 'Bridge Ltd'.

ACTIVITY 8 Create a query that restricts the number of records you see   ◀

Create the 'qryBridgePrices' query and check that it works.

You should now have enough knowledge to create the query you did manually in Activity 5. Create the query 'qryApolloDeltaSize9' which lists all the Size 9 Apollo Delta trainers in the tblTempOrders. Time how long it takes you and compare this with how long it took in Activity 5.

The example we have looked at is a very simple criteria; Table 2.6.1 shows a number of other criteria with a description of what they do.

Criteria	Description
>5	List those records where the value in this field is bigger than 5
<100	List those records where the value in this field is less than 100
<=10	List those records where the value of this field is less than or equal to 10

Table 2.6.1: continued on next page

>=10	List those records where the value of this field is greater than or equal to 10
>=5 and <=10	List those records where the value in this field is between 5 and 10
7 or 9	List those records where the value in this field is either 7 or 9
<=#31/12/05# and >= #01/12/05#	List those records where the value of this date field in sometime in December 2005
Like "*" & "Apollo" & "*"	List those records where the letter sequence "Apollo" appears somewhere in this field"

Table 2.6.1 Some search criteria and what they do

▶ Multi-table queries

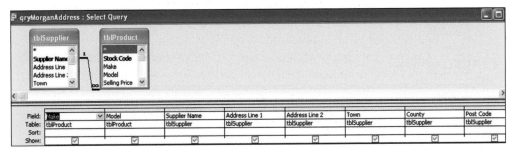

Figure 2.6.25 Query from multiple tables

So far you have used what are known as single table queries, but as long as your relationships are correct, there is nothing to stop you putting as many tables as you like in a query and selecting fields from all of them. Criteria and sorts can be set in exactly the same way. Figure 2.6.25 shows a query that gives the address of the supplier for all Morgan trainers.

ACTIVITY 9 Set up a multi-table query ◀

Create the 'QryMorganAddress' Query and see what it does.

▶ Formulae

Not only can you select fields from more than one table but you can also create fields by calculating them from others. For example, the criterion for ordering new stock of a particular style of trainers is that the total number of those trainers held drops below 250. However, you are storing the number of those trainers in stock by size. To find the total number you have in stock, you will have to add up the trainers you have for each size.

ACTIVITY 10 Create a query involving formulae ◀

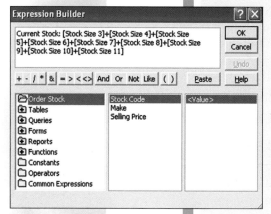

Figure 2.6.26 'Expression Builder' window

Create a query in design view which selects the 'make', 'model' and 'selling price'.

Point to the 'Field' parameter of the next blank field and click the right mouse button. From the resulting menu select 'Build' and the 'Expression Builder' window (Figure 2.6.26) will appear.

Enter the following into the expression window (Note: 'Current Stock' is the name of the new field.)

Current Stock: [Stock Size 3] + [Stock Size 4] + [Stock Size 5] + [Stock Size 6] + [Stock Size 7] + [Stock Size 8] + [Stock Size 9] + [Stock Size 10] + [Stock Size 11]

Close the expression build window by clicking the 'OK' button and enter '<250' into the criteria parameter of the new field.

Save your new query (see Fig. 2.6.27) as 'qryOrderStock' and check out what it does.

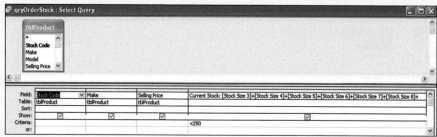

Figure 2.6.27 Query using formulae

 Compare what you did in Activity 10 with the demonstration.

Order and order/product data

If you remember, when you were importing your data you left the job incomplete. You imported the orders as a separate file and you now need to put the data into the tables you have. This will involve two more things you can do with queries – grouping and appending queries. You have two tables to fill, 'tblOrder' and 'tblOrder product'. Because you have set referential integrity, you have to do the 'tblOrder' first.

ACTIVITY 11 Create an append query ◀

Create a new query called 'qryUpdateOrderTable' based on your 'tblTempOrders' table. Select the following fields:

Order Number	Delivery Town	Credit-Card Number
Date	Delivery County	Customer eMail
Delivery Address Line 1	Delivery Post Code	
Delivery Address Line 2	Credit-Card Type	

These are the fields that form the 'tblOrder' table, but if you look at the results of your query you will see that we have more than one record for each order.

Continued on next page

Go back to design view and look for the icon shown in Figure 2.6.28 and click on it.

Figure 2.6.28

This is the 'Totals' icon; once you click it you will see a new line appear in your query design called 'Total'; in this, for every field, you will see the words 'group by'. This is telling the query to group all the records with the same contents in these fields together. These 'group bys' work in a similar way to the sort in that the query will group the records by the field furthest to the left first. As it happens this has done exactly what you want as all the fields for the same order number are the same but theoretically you only need to group by the order number.

Click in the total parameter in the 'date' field and click on the drop-down arrow to list the options you have. This is a very useful function because you can find the total of a group, count how many there are in a group, find the biggest and smallest values and do many other things. However, it's going to be straightforward this time; as all the fields are the same for each order you may as well choose the first in the group, so select 'First' from the list of options.

Do the same for all the other fields except the order number then check and see what your query does.

What you have now should be a list of all your order information for each order, which is exactly what you want on your order file. To get it in there, you have to change your query into an append query. You do this by selecting 'query' from the menu bar and 'append query' from the resulting menu.

A window will appear asking you to choose a table to append to. Use the drop-down arrow to choose the 'tblOrder' table.

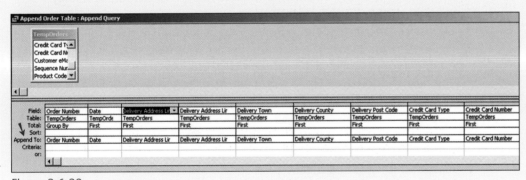

Figure 2.6.29

A new line will appear in your query called 'append to' and you will find some of these parameters filled in. If these are blank then you will have to use the drop-down arrows to select the corresponding fields in the 'tblOrder table' (see Fig. 2.6.29).

An append query needs to write to one of your tables and therefore cannot be run using the view icon in Figure 2.6.22. Close and save your query and open it from the database window. It will then come up with two windows asking you to confirm that you want to update the table and to tell you how many rows you are going to append. If it comes up with a third window it means something has gone wrong and this window is telling you what.

If, however, everything went according to plan your tblOrder table should now contain your order data.

Compare what you did in Activity 11 with the demonstration.

Having got your orders into the database, the tblOrder/Product table can be loaded.

Action queries

Append query   This is an example of what is known as an 'action query' as it performs an action. There are a number of other action queries and here are three examples.

Delete query   When run this will delete all the records selected by the query form the table.

Make table query   This type of query will make a new table based on the data selected by your query.

Update query   This will update a field to a new value in those records selected by the query.

All action queries have in common the fact that once the action is performed it cannot be undone. They should therefore be used with care.

ACTIVITY 12 Append the order/product data ◀

Create a query based on the 'tblTempOrders' table selecting the 'order number', 'sequence number', 'product code' and 'required size' fields.

Change it into an append query selecting the 'tblOrder/Product' table as the 'append to' table.

Run the append query to update the 'tblOrder/Product' table. Check that everything worked all right; if it did delete the 'TempOrders' file.

There are lots of different types of query – the possibilities are almost endless – and we cannot cover everything in this chapter, but we hope we have given you a taste of what you can do.

Reports

There are a number of ways that you can display your data. Most DBMSs provide forms and reports but these will be based on either tables or queries which are the fundamental building blocks of databases. Both tables and queries can be printed out or displayed as they stand but often the result is not easy to read. You have already seen an example of a form produced by a wizard. A similar method can be used to produce a report based on either a table or a query.

As an example let's create a report for our Bridge Prices query.

- In your DBMS select 'Reports' and 'New Report' and in the resulting window choose 'Report Wizard'.
- Choose the required table and query and click on 'OK' (see Fig. 2.6.30).
- In the next window select all the fields for your report by clicking on the double arrow (see Fig. 2.6.31), then click on 'Next'.
- The next window (see Fig. 2.6.32) allows us to group records. This means all records with the same content in a chosen field are grouped together. 'Supplier' is already chosen ❶, but you can also choose 'Make' ❷ and select it by clicking on the selection button ❸. This will mean the make will go into a different section of the report and all records of the same make will be grouped together.
- The next window allows you to sort these records into order, choose an ascending sort on buying price (see Fig. 2.6.33).
- The next window allows you to choose the format of the report. Select 'Stepped' (you can experiment with the other later).
- The next window allows you to choose a style, choose one you like.
- In the next window you can title your report 'Bridge Prices' (see Fig. 2.6.34).
- When you click finish your report will be produced (see Fig. 2.6.35).
- The format can be tidied up by placing the report in Design View and moving things around.

 You can watch a demonstration of this process in the ActiveBook.

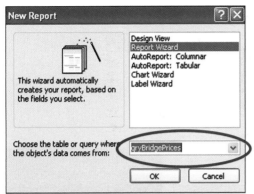

Figure 2.6.30 Select the 'Report Wizard' and the required table

Figure 2.6.31 Click on the double arrow to select all fields for your report

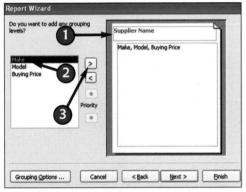

Figure 2.6.32 Grouping records

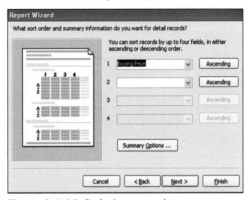

Figure 2.6.33 Ordering records

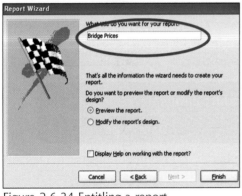

Figure 2.6.34 Entitling a report

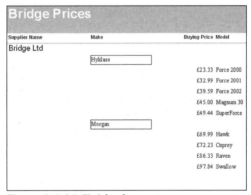

Figure 2.6.35 Finished report

Conclusion ▶ ▶ ▶

A well-structured database is an enormous source of information to an organisation. The ability to use SQL or Query by Example can be a real advantage in management, as it enables you to analyse the data and base your decisions upon it. The better your information the better decisions you will make or, even more importantly, the fewer mistakes you will make.

The database design from Chapter 2.5

Product entity

Attribute	Data type
Product Code	Text
Make	Text
Model	Text
Selling Price	Number (Currency)
Stock Size 3	Number (Integer)
Stock Size 4	Number (Integer)
Stock Size 5	Number (Integer)
Stock Size 6	Number (Integer)
Stock Size 7	Number (Integer)
Stock Size 8	Number (Integer)
Stock Size 9	Number (Integer)
Stock Size 10	Number (Integer)
Stock Size 11	Number (Integer)
Buying Price	Number (Currency)
Supplier Name*	Text
Re-order Level	Number (Integer)

Supplier entity

Attribute	Data type
Supplier Name	Text
Address Line 1	Text
Address Line 2	Text
Town	Text
County	Text
Post Code	Text
Contact Last Name	Text
Contact First Name	Text
Contact Title	Text
Contact Phone Number	Text
Fax Number	Text

Customer entity

Attribute	Data Type
e-mail address	Text
password	Text
Last Name	Text
First Name	Text
Inital	Text
Title	Text
Address Line 1	Text
Address Line 2	Text
Town	Text
County	Text
Post Code	Text
Phone Number	Text

Order entity

Attribute	Data Type
Order Number	Number (Integer)
Date	Number (Date)
Delivery Address Line 1	Text
Delivery Address Line 2	Text
Delivery Town	Text
Delivery County	Text
Delivery Post Code	Text
Credit Card Type*	Text
Credit-Card Number	Text
Customer E-Mail*	Text

Order/Product entity

Attribute	Data Type
Order Number*	Number (Integer)
Sequence Number	Number (Integer)
Product Code*	Text
Required Size	Number (Integer)

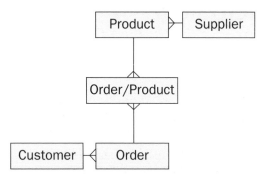

Data and the law

1984 and all that

It is not without a certain irony that the first Data Protection Act in the UK became law in 1984. George Orwell's somewhat jaundiced view of what to him was the future may not have been totally accurate, but elements of it were remarkably prophetic. There may not be hidden cameras spying on us all the time but CCTV cameras seem to be on every street corner. Most of us also wander around with mobile phones in our pockets, oblivious to the fact that it wouldn't be difficult, with the right information, to track our every movement as long as the phone is switched on.

It is a fairly sobering thought that there are an awful lot of organisations that, quite legitimately, hold a great deal of information about us. When you apply for a job or a course at college you fill in an application form which tells the organisation everything from your name and address to your date and place of birth. Similarly when you shop online you supply a lot of personal information, including enough information to take money from your bank account. This information is stored away on a database somewhere and, as you saw in the last chapter, databases are easy to interrogate.

Research into the wallet of one of the authors reveals – apart from a fairly tatty £10 note – two credit cards, one debit card, a cash-point card, two store loyalty cards, membership cards for a golf club and a fitness club, and a driving licence.

All the organisations responsible for these cards hold the author's name, address and date of birth. Most of them, for reasons we will explain later, know his mother's maiden name. What is perhaps surprising though is the other personal information these organisations have access to. Tracking the author's purchases of fuel through the credit cards, use of different ATMs via the cash-point card, his purchases from the two stores using the store cards, and evidence from the DVLA of a little over-exuberance through Sunningdale, could all be combined to produce a fairly accurate picture of the author's movements over the last year. All the credit card and debit card purchases could also give a pretty accurate insight into the author's lifestyle and consumer preferences.

ACTIVITY 1 Who holds information about you? ◄

Try to think of all the organisations and people who hold information about you for perfectly legitimate reasons. What information do they hold? Why do they hold it? What other purposes could it be used for?

You should have had little difficulty in putting together a list of organisations that hold data about you. They range from your doctor to the local video shop. You could probably fill a whole side of A4 and still only have scratched the surface. You may wonder why so many organisations are prepared to spend so much money storing and organising this information. The reason, in the words of

Francis Bacon, is that "Knowledge is power", or from a more cynical point of view, "Information is money". This concept is one of the fundamental principles you will learn about in Unit 3, but for now, let's just look at this from the point of view of a sales organisation on the internet.

The organisation will initially take your details in order to process the transaction. It will need your name and address in order to send you the product, your credit card details so that it can elicit payment, and knowledge of the items you want so that it knows how much to charge you and what to send you. The organisation could decide to hang on to your details so that if you buy from it again you don't need to type them all from scratch. It will also not have escaped its notice that you would be more likely to do so if you don't have to type all of your information in again. If it therefore decides to store your personal information somewhere, this is fairly clear and above board, since processing your current and future transactions with it is the very reason it requires the information.

Every transaction you make with this organisation tells it a little bit more about you. If you buy a particular CD it tells it something about your musical tastes; it can then make recommendations to you, telling you about products it thinks you might like to buy. This directs its marketing in a very specific way, at the sort of people it is likely to be successful with. For instance, if you had bought 'The Best Brass Band Album in the World Ever, Vol.1' it is not a huge leap of imagination to think you may be interested in 'The Best Brass Band Album in the World Ever, Vol.2'.

Figure 2.7.1 Amazon's recommendation page makes recommendations on the basis of previous purchases

The marketing doesn't even necessarily have to make a connection between similar types of music. If the organisation is large enough, it will store the details of a large number of transactions. Consequently if 60 per cent of people who bought 'The Best Brass Band Album in the World Ever, Vol.1' also bought 'Brighouse and Rastrick's Greatest Hits' the organisation could recommend this CD to you, and might expect a reasonable possibility of you purchasing it (see Fig. 2.7.1).

The extent to which this widespread holding of information bothers you will largely depend on your personality; the fact that so much information is held about individuals can make some people feel uncomfortable to say the least. As an individual you have a right to a certain amount of privacy, yet this privacy is being eroded by the amount of personal information that is commonly held by large commercial and government organisations.

ACTIVITY 2 Consider the moral issues of collecting information about individuals

Thanks to advances in forensic science, the police can place someone at a crime scene by comparing their DNA to samples (e.g. a single hair) found at the scene. The problem is that they have to find a suspect to compare the sample against. If there were a national DNA database containing information about the entire population, samples taken from the crime scene could be compared against it to produce a suspect with relative ease. Discuss the moral issues surrounding creating such a database.

The law

▶ Data Protection Act

The focus of Unit 2 is on transactional websites, most of which store personal data in some form or other. As such they have to conform to the rules of the Data Protection Act. The original Data Protection Act, which became law in 1984, was upgraded and extended in 1998. The old law covered computer data; the new one also covers some paper-based records and some CCTV systems.

Under the 1998 law companies which hold personal information such as that gained from a transactional website have to notify the Information Commissioner whose job it is to enforce the Act and promote good practice in the handling of personal information. The Act defines 'personal information' as data about living people who can be identified from that data.

For an organisation to be allowed to process personal information it must meet at least one of the conditions in Schedule 2 to the Act. There are a number of these conditions; if you want to see them all have a look at the complete Act. For the purpose of a transactional website processing could be justified as being "necessary for the performance of a contract to which the data subject is a party".

Organisations which process personal data have to adhere to the eight principals of the Act, as follows.

Personal data must be:

1 processed fairly and lawfully
2 processed only for one or more specified and lawful purpose
3 adequate, relevant and not excessive for the purpose
4 accurate and kept up to date
5 kept for no longer than is necessary for the purpose it is being processed
6 processed in accordance with the rights of the individual
7 protected against accidental loss, destruction, damage or unauthorised and unlawful processing
8 not transferred to countries outside the European Economic Area that do not have adequate protection for personal data.

Should an organisation fail to comply with any of these principals the Information Commissioner has the power to take action against the organisation to force it to comply. The Commissioner may also bring a criminal prosecution against an organisation if he/she is sure an offence under the Act has been committed.

ACTIVITY 3 Find out about data protections ◀

The Data Protection Act 1998 is a complex Act and is worth a much closer study than is possible in this book. The full act is on the HMSO website; an excellent précis of it and advice from the point of view of an organisation can be found on the Business Link website. Study these websites with regard to the transactional website and list the rights consumers have with regard to data held about them.

▶ Distance selling regulations

When you buy an item from a shop you can see what it is that you are buying. You can see what it looks like and make a judgement about its quality. If you keep the receipt, you can even return it if it doesn't live up to expectations, or turns out not to be of 'merchantable quality'. When you buy over the internet, on the other hand, you only see a picture of the item. Regulations for distance selling give the e-consumer certain rights and ensure that the internet retailer abides by certain rules.

The regulations require that the consumer be provided with adequate information prior to the sale, and confirmation of the purchase after the sale. They also provide an after-sales 'cooling off' period, during which time the consumer can return the goods without penalty. The regulations also offer a framework for the cancellation of credit and the return of goods after the cancellation of a sale.

ACTIVITY 4 Investigate distance-selling regulations ◀

The Department of Trade and Industry website publishes full details of these regulations and a factsheet. Read the full regulations and make a list of the responsibilities of the seller and the rights of the buyer.

Data at risk

When you make a purchase over the internet you supply enough information for someone to get money out of your bank account or from your credit-card company. The fact that you supply that information shows a great deal of trust, optimism or possibly even ignorance about the large number of threats this information may be subject to.

Figure 2.7.2 "The zeros are fine but the ones don't half sting!"

One of the fastest growing crimes worldwide is identity theft. Identity theft is where someone wrongfully obtains personal information for the purpose of fraud. If someone has your credit-card number and can support it with the correct name then he or she could be in a position to make purchases or even commit other crimes in your name. There have been many instances of large debts being run up on credit cards simply because the card number together with its matching name were used by an identity thief, with no further checks being done on home address and so forth.

An internet transaction requires that this highly sensitive data be sent from one computer (probably a home one) to another via an unknown number of cables and other computers. More often than not data travels long distances over what are effectively public telephone lines. There are therefore many points at which this data can be intercepted. This is not to mention wireless networks and WiFi (see Fig. 2.7.2), which with their reliance on radio-style transmission may seem even less secure than the ordinary phone line.

Neither is your data necessarily safe once it has been stored by the organisation. Most computer users are aware of the threat of hackers – someone who breaks into a computer to steal, change or destroy data. The Data Protection Act makes the organisation in charge of a transactional website responsible for protecting personal data against these attacks. We will look at a number of methods they can use to do this later on in the chapter. What is often forgotten, however, is the amount of personal information that is held on a home computer. A home computer connected to the internet is under the same level of threat, but is probably a lot less well-protected than the database of a major organisation.

Risk assessment

The first step in securing or protecting data is to understand what threatens your data. This process is known as a risk assessment. In a risk assessment you identify what the risks are and the likely outcomes should the worst happen. Once you understand this you can take steps to minimise the effects.

What sort of threats should you consider? Basically there are two types:

1 Physical threats such as fire, theft, malicious damage and hardware failure.
2 Human error such as input errors or program bugs.

ACTIVITY 5 Assess the risk your coursework is at ◀

Probably the most important data you are responsible for at the moment is your Applied GCE coursework and any other coursework come to that. If you are relying entirely on your school or college to keep it safe for you, then you probably shouldn't. Undertake a risk analysis for your coursework and develop procedures and protection for it. What are the risks? What are the possible worst-case outcomes? In what different ways can you maintain your data integrity?

Hacking and hackers

A transactional website, by its very nature, is extremely vulnerable to the phenomenon known as hacking. Unauthorised access to data held by a transactional website could have significant consequences for the organisation. As well as being in breach of the Data Protection Act, the organisation could suffer serious problems even if the unauthorised access was not meant to be fraudulent. For example, mischievously resetting prices or simply changing the format of the pages could pose serious threats to the organisation's profitability.

The Computer Misuse Act (1990) was passed in order to deal with the growing problem of computer hackers, unlawful information access and misuse in general. Initially hacking wasn't taken too seriously as it was seen as mischievous rather than malicious. Even today, tomfoolery such as guessing a friend's password and seeing what he or she has in his or her files is not uncommon in, for example, schools and colleges. You may be surprised to know that this is a criminal offence punishable by up to six months in prison.

ACTIVITY 6 Find out about the Computer Misuse Act ◀

The Computer Misuse Act covers three levels of offence. Research these levels of offence and the penalties associated with them.

Methods of protection

For the organisation running a transactional website, prosecuting a hacker under the Computer Misuse Act is a little like locking the stable door after the horse has bolted. Although such a prosecution would send a message to others who may wish to dabble in hacking, it is obviously much better to prevent the unauthorised access in the first place, if you can. There are a number of steps you can take to minimise this danger.

▶ Physical Protection

Any organisation which keeps personal data has to protect it from unauthorised access from within the organisation as well as from without. Assume for a moment that all the personal data is held on a single, standalone computer with no connection to any network. To access the data you would have to use that particular computer. Even if there were no password protection or any other protection on that machine the data would be reasonably safe if the computer were locked away in a room that only authorised personnel could enter. On the other hand, if the computer were in the middle of an open-plan office then almost anyone would have the opportunity to access the data.

When you want to use a standalone machine you simply press the 'on' button and the computer will load up the operating system and you are ready to go. Sometimes, if you are very careful, you might have set the system password so that the machine will not boot up unless you supply it; but more often than not no such check is made. Once you are logged on to a standalone machine there is little you cannot do. A standalone machine should therefore be protected physically from unauthorised access.

Of course, by the very nature of a transactional website, a standalone machine is out of the question and this opens up a whole myriad of threats. However, not controlling physical access to your computers simply makes unauthorised access easy.

Remember also that any self-respecting ICT-aware organisation will make backups of its data in case of accidental (or even deliberate) loss or damage. These backups also contain sensitive information and should also be kept under lock and key.

ACTIVITY 7 Research locking equipment

Most locks work in fundamentally the same way physically, but there are numerous ways of opening them, from the standard key through to card locks and the latest biometric locks. These days a simple fingerprint lock (see Fig. 2.7.3) can be bought reasonably cheaply. The Data Protection Act requires that holders of personal data should take reasonable precautions to protect it against accidental loss, destruction, damage or unauthorised and unlawful processing. Research a range of locking equipment, including prices, and decide what would be a reasonable physical protection for the data held by an internet shopping organisation.

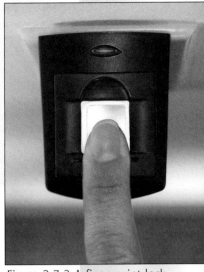

Figure 2.7.3 A fingerprint lock

▶ User names and passwords

By its very nature a transactional website needs to allow remote access, otherwise no transactions could take place. It has to be connected to the internet and therefore locking it in a room will not provide anything other than physical protection. Additional protection is needed to stop potential hackers from being able to access it. The first technique we are going to look at is the user name and password. We tend to come across these so often these days that we take them for granted.

Once you connect your computer to a network you have a large number of people who may be able to look at your computer. In networks within organisations individuals also have the capacity to create files and store them on common drives. Unless you want everyone to have access to all your files you need a way of knowing who owns which files. A user name (or user ID) is a way of identifying yourself to the computer; you supply it when you sign on (see Fig. 2.7.4). Most systems then create, or allow you to create, a user area into which all your files are saved.

In principle these files are 'yours' and no other users can get at them without your password. In practice, one of the main reasons organisations use networks is because they allow you to share files by specifying which other users are allowed to use them. You may give individuals permission only to read your files; or they may be allowed to read them and also to change them. It is up to you to specify what level of permission others have. Note though that there will always be someone who administers the system and therefore needs to be able to access almost everything it contains. There is usually a special user name for this purpose.

User names tend to be static since if you change a user name all the relevant file permissions would also have to change. Computer networks, however, cannot physically differentiate between you and anyone else, so if someone signs on to the network using your user name, the network will assume it is you and give him or her access to everything you have permission to access. This is where passwords come in, giving a layer of protection that a simple user ID does not provide. A password should be a secret code known only to you and the network, thereby corroborating your identity when you sign in.

Figure 2.7.4 Typical log on screen

A transactional website works in much the same way. There is an area of data which contains information about you and only those that need the information to process the transaction should be able to gain access to it. It is likely therefore that this data will be protected by a user name and password. Commonly your email address will be used as a user name as it is unique and has the added advantage that it provides a means of communication with you.

Discussion Attitudes to passwords

Ten comments about passwords:

1 I always use the same password; that way I don't forget it.
2 My password is my favourite footballer's name.
3 My best friend knows my password so that I can leave messages for her in my user area.
4 I keep my password short so that it doesn't take long to type in.
5 I'm always forgetting my password so I have written it in my diary.
6 My password is the same now as it was when I first joined the organisation.
7 I use the word 'password' as my password, no one will ever think of that.
8 I use the first letters of a line of a song for my password then all I have to do is sing it when I sign on.
9 I use a set of six random letters generated by a computer program for my password.
10 Each time the system makes me change my password I immediately change it back to what it was in the first place.

These are real comments made by individuals from a survey about passwords. Discuss the drawbacks of each of the techniques alluded to.

These days people have to remember passwords and PIN numbers for all sorts of things and they are fairly easy to forget. It is in the interests of a transactional website that you should be able to gain access to it, otherwise you will not use it. As part of the registration process, you may therefore be asked either to provide a question about yourself which only you would know the answer to, or you may be asked for information unlikely to be known by a hacker, such as your mother's maiden name. This provides the organisation with a way of identifying you and giving you access, either by giving you a new password or telling you your old one.

▶ Firewalls

Once you connect your machine or network to the internet you become part of a huge network. You can then be 'seen' by anyone else on the internet. Once they know you are there, there is nothing to stop them attempting to access your machine to see what they can find on it.

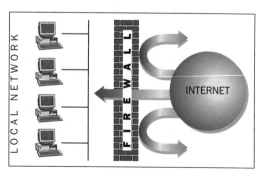

Figure 2.7.5 A firewall 'insulates' a computer to some extent

A firewall is normally a software utility (although there are hardware versions) which sits between your computer (or network) and the internet, monitoring traffic (see Fig. 2.7.5). It operates as a kind of filter; if it doesn't like what it sees it will block access. It is worth remembering that communication with the internet is two-way; a firewall not only monitors incoming packets of information but also outgoing ones as well. It therefore not only stops access to your computer from unknown sources, but will also stop unrecognised software (such as the spyware you may have inadvertently placed on your machine) from transmitting to the internet. For more on spyware, see Chapter 2.4.

▶ Virus protection

The advent of the internet has greatly increased the chances of catching a computer virus. Pre-internet, viruses were passed around on removable media such as floppy disks but now you are more likely to catch one from an email. Common types of viruses are file viruses, boot-sector viruses, email viruses, worms and Trojan horses (see the box in the margin in Chapter 1.1).

Antivirus software works by searching for traces of known viruses; when it finds one it informs the user. It will then repair the infected file, delete it or place it in quarantine where the file cannot infect anything else.

There is a wide variety of virus-checking software on the market and they all depend on being able to identify viruses. To identify them the software has to know about them, yet new viruses are being written all the time. The software, therefore, has to be constantly updated to ensure that any new viruses are detected. When buying antivirus software you may take out a subscription (rather than pay a one-off cost) which will entitle you to regular updates.

▶ Encryption

Data on computers are held in binary code, a series of zeroes and ones. By contrast, the information we require is largely made up of letters and numbers (though it could also be sounds and pictures), for example in a word-processed document or a database. We therefore have to assign a code to a group of these zeroes and ones to represent a letter. This is why preparing data to be stored on computers is referred to as encoding. For instance, the letter 'A' could be represented by 010001 and 'B' could be 010010, and so on. There are a number of standard versions of these codes that computers can work with, the most common of which is ASCII (American Standard Code for Information Interchange). These codes are universally known and accessible, and so if someone could intercept a transmission you make, or interrogate your hard disk, it would be relatively easy to figure out what the binary data is.

This is where encryption can come in, to help you protect your data. Encryption uses a mathematical formula (called an algorithm) to scramble (encrypt) data into what appears to be a meaningless string of letters and numbers. This can then be transmitted; even if it were intercepted it wouldn't make any sense. Hence the data is protected. At the other end a similar algorithm is used to decrypt the data, that is, put it back into its meaningful form. The algorithms are based on a binary number (a series of zeroes and ones) known as a 'key', so even if you knew what the algorithm did you would still have to know the key to decrypt the data. This adds an extra layer of protection.

Common keys are 40-bit and 128-bit. 'Bit' stands for **bi**nary dig**it**, so is either a zero or a one. A 40-bit key would therefore be a series of 40 zeroes and ones. Mathematically there are therefore 2^{40} (1 073 741 824) possible different keys you may need to choose from before you can find the right key and decrypt the intercepted message. A 128-bit key is obviously even more secure, offering you 2^{128} combinations – over 340 000 000 000 000 000 000 000 000 000 000 000 000 different possible keys. These huge numbers therefore make data in transit practically impossible to decrypt.

▶ Secure electronic transactions (SET)

Almost from its inception, the internet was recognised as a powerful potential market place, so long as people could rely on their money transactions being secure and the goods they requested arriving. This did not escape the attention of credit-card companies, or indeed banks. Two of them, Visa and MasterCard, in conjunction with some major computer companies including IBM, decided to develop the secure electronic transaction (SET) protocol. In this situation a protocol is a set of rules by which transactions are governed; the rules of this particular protocol include two encryption methods being applied to transmitted data. SET also includes the use of digital certificates. These are issued by a certification authority (a number of which exist), which confirms that you are actually dealing with the genuine organisation.

When you browse a website you normally do so via an insecure connection, since you are not passing on any sensitive or private information. As soon as you want to undertake a monetary transaction, however, you will be directed to a secure connection and any information you send will be encrypted. You will know you are on a secure connection because one of the icons shown in Figure 2.7.6 will be displayed.

Figure 2.7.6 Secure connection icons

If you double click on this icon you can have a look at the details of the digital certificate of the company you are dealing with (see Fig. 2.7.7). When you supply your credit-card number to a secure site, only an encrypted form of the number is passed through the site – it is decrypted when sent with details of your purchase to the credit-card company.

Conclusion ▶ ▶ ▶

It is vitally important that the customers of a transactional website have confidence that their data will be protected. If they do not have this confidence, they simply will not use the site. Informed e-consumers should be aware:
* of what steps are taken to protect their personal details
* that legislation such as the Data Protection Act and the Distance Selling Regulations are there to protect them
* what rights and expectations they can have because of these Acts.

To build confidence, informed e-consumers should be further aware of what measures are taken to protect their data – passwords, encryption, SET, virus protection and firewalls – and know what measure of protection each of these provides. They should know what these measures can do to protect their personal data and more importantly what they cannot do. To a certain extent, personal responsibility for one's own data must also come into play at all times.

Figure 2.7.7 You can see a company's digital certificate by double-clicking on the secure connection icon

Tackling the Unit 2 assessment

For the Unit 2 assessment you are required to submit an **eportfolio** containing three major pieces of evidence:

1 The results of your investigation into a commercial transactional website
2 Screenshots and output from a database you have created, along with recommendations based on an identification and interpretation of trends within the data
3 An evaluation of your performance and the performance of your database.

Item 1 is the investigation into a real transactional website. Item 2 is proof that you designed and implemented a database and used it to analyse a data set that was given to you, along with recommendations you make based on the analysis. Item 3 is largely about how well your database works and how it could be improved.

Part 1 Investigate a transactional website

This involves two equally important steps: investigation of a real transactional website and the creation of the electronic document that will provide the evidence of the investigation.

Step 1: Investigation

You are asked to provide three separate pieces of evidence:

a A **description** of the design of a commercial transactional website plus an in-depth **evaluation** of key features of the design. (**2a**)
b **Detailed diagrams** illustrating the chain of events leading up to and triggered by an online purchase of a product and the associated information flow, giving a **clear picture of back office processes**. (**2b**)
c A **description** and **analysis** of the potential threats to customer data and the measures taken to protect it. (**2c**)

▶ Choosing a website

In order to conduct a successful investigation into a commercial transactional website it is imperative that you choose a suitable website to investigate. First and foremost, it must be a commercial website that conducts transactions. 'Transaction' can have several different meanings, but in this context it essentially refers to an exchange of funds for goods or services.

The website should ideally be one you can register on as a customer in order that you are able to experience the full range of what the website can offer from initial entry to the site through to aftersales service. Alternatively if this is not possible you should choose one that you can see a full demonstration of how it works. The demonstration may be a tool in the website, or it may be a demonstration by a teacher, friend or relative.

You must choose a website that has all the features required in the specification. For example, it must:

- have a range of goods on offer
- provide product information
- capture and use customer information
- use different methods to engage, retain and entice customers
- allow payment transactions to be carried out.

Most commercial transactional websites will do all of these as a matter of course. However, a single-page website offering just one good or service for sale is unlikely to have sufficient depth to make it worthwhile studying. On the other hand, if you select a website you regard as perfect, remember that in evaluating it you will have to recommend means of improving it. Most of the commercial websites featured in Chapters 2.2 to 2.4 have been selected as suitable to illustrate the points required by the coursework, and thus should form a good basis for you to start considering which website to investigate.

▶ Breaking down the requirements

2a is in two parts.

A **description** of:

1. its structure and navigation
2. the type and range of goods on offer
3. the product information provided
4. types of transactions that can be carried out
5. payment methods available
6. methods used to capture customer information
7. four different techniques employed to engage, retain and/or entice customers.

and an **evaluation** of:

1. the effectiveness of methods used to capture customer information
2. two of the techniques employed to engage, retain and/or entice customers
3. the effectiveness of the site as a whole and the 'customer experience' it provides.

Note the difference in meaning between 'description' and 'evaluation'. The first descriptive part is purely investigative. You should study your chosen website in some depth using the material in Chapters 2.2 to 2.4 as a guide. You should look at the menus and links, and follow these to get a feel for the structure and navigation of the site. You should write a description and ideally draw a diagram illustrating how the site designers have made a logical layout for the site (if indeed, you regard the design and navigation as logical).

The first five points listed in the description section above are essentially factual and should all be answered with a description of what you find, along with examples in the form of screenshots (or possibly partial screenshots) to illustrate your findings.

The final two points of the section are partly deduced and partly subjective. First, the methods used to capture customer information will include:

- analysis of purchase histories and sales information
- loyalty schemes
- surveys
- competitions
- cookies
- spyware.

For methods used to engage, retain and entice, it will be obvious if the site runs loyalty or reward schemes, surveys or competitions. You will be able to tell if it uses cookies, either because it greets customers by their name or user ID before logging in, or by direct analysis of your cookies folder (see Chapter 2.4 for an how to do this). The extent to which the site analyses purchase histories and sales information will not be totally apparent unless you have access to inside information. Nevertheless, to some extent it can be inferred from the types of information asked for at checkout and from the correspondence it has with its customers.

The second part of **2a** requires that you do three evaluations. First you should evaluate the effectiveness of methods used to capture customer information; then you should evaluate two of the techniques employed to engage, retain and/or entice customers, and finally you should evaluate the effectiveness of the site as a whole and the 'customer experience' it provides. As stated in Chapter 1.8, an evaluation will consider how well the purpose is met overall by considering:

- the purpose itself
- the strengths of the site
- the weaknesses of the site
- finally, possible alternatives and improvements.

There may be a tendency to create too subjective an evaluation. For example, it is relatively easy to state: "I think that the competition on the site meets its purpose as it does collect comprehensive customer information in a way that is engaging to the customer". The more 'hard' or objective data you can introduce to strengthen your case, the better your evaluation will be. First you could list the actual data collected. You could describe the competition, state how you feel it attempts to be engaging and whether it succeeds in this or not. You could try to identify people who might find it engaging and those who might not, and why. You could comment on placement, emphasis, multimedia, 'wow' factor etc. Really hard data from the site, such as data on how many people actually entered the competition, will almost certainly be impossible to find. Yet simple test, questionnaire or survey data would be relatively easy to collect. How many of your friends or relatives as a percentage did or would give their details and enter the competition if they clicked on the page? This would be better than your opinion alone and it would add some weight to your evaluation.

2b requires a set of **detailed diagrams** illustrating the chain of events leading up to and triggered by an online purchase of a product and the associated information flow, giving a **clear picture of back office processes** including:

- maintenance of the virtual shopping basket
- identification and authentication routines
- payment processing
- stock control
- despatch and delivery.

Unless you are given access to an actual commercial transactional website you will not know *exactly* what happens at each stage of operation of the website, but a careful reading of Chapter 2.3 alongside your chosen website will give you a sufficient idea of what is happening during each process. Your diagrammatic analysis should fit the facts for the website and be detailed enough to give a clear picture of the back office processes involved. It does not need to be a 100 per cent correct explanation of the actual process in each case.

The Edexcel specification for **2b** states that "Students should use **flowcharts** and **information flow diagrams** to depict relevant back office processes." Chapter 2.3 gives a detailed account of how to produce these diagrams. You can choose the exact mix of information flow diagrams and flowcharts to best suit the site you have chosen to investigate, but to give sufficient breadth and sufficient depth it is best to use the diagrams in combination.

2c requires a **description** and **analysis** of the potential threats to customer data and the measures taken to protect it, including:
- potential threats to customer data collected by organisations via their websites
- protective measures employed by organisations
- examples of relevant legislation.

To gain higher marks in this section you will have to analyse the threats to data, and balance them against the legislation and the protection measures you have described, to come up with an assessment of the risk. Most of the information you will need for this section is in Chapter 2.7. The most relevant legislation currently is the Data Protection Act, the Computer Misuse Act, and the distance selling regulations. Your analysis should be submitted in the form of a report using one of the examination board's recommended formats.

Step 2: The creation of the documents for your eportfolio

You can decide on the formats in which you present this evidence for your portfolio, although these must be from the standard formats specified by Edexcel. The most obvious one would be portable document format (PDF) as this can be created simply from any number of software packages; then the document can be read in its original format whatever system the assessor is using to view the portfolio.

The simplest method of producing the results of your investigation in this first part of the coursework is to create the report in a word processing program. A good word processor will allow you to write your findings, edit them and save them effectively. Crucially, it will allow you to combine information from different sources – such as written information, diagrams and screenshots – in an attractive and interesting manner. When your document is complete you will be able to proof read your work and in addition to checking its accuracy use the program's built-in tools such as the grammar- and spell-checkers.

To take screenshots of your website it is best to have your favourite graphics package open, press 'ALT' and 'Prt Sc' to capture the screen to the clipboard, and then paste the contents of the clipboard into the graphics package. Although you can also paste immediately into your word processing application, this gives less flexibility for later editing and amendments, and has other storage implications.

You will not always need the whole screenshot to illustrate the point you wish to make, in which case you can use the crop tools from the graphics package to crop the image prior to saving. You should save your screenshot as a JPEG image at the lowest image quality that is acceptable for what you require. This is likely to be around 30 to 50 per cent of the original resolution, which constitutes a great saving in storage space (see Chapter 1.7 for more details on graphics file formats). The screenshot can then be inserted into your report at the desired location.

The information flow (document flow and or data flow variants) and flowchart diagrams should ideally be drawn using specialist drawing tools such as Visio, SmartDraw or OpenOffice Draw, or one of the many other packages with smart linking and resizing. A CASE tool such as Select SSADM is also an excellent package to use for this task. If unavoidable it is possible to create the diagrams in general packages such as Word or Publisher using the drawing toolbar, or in bitmap packages such as Paint, but resizing and moving becomes very problematic and the time taken to produce the diagrams will increase a great deal, and the quality suffers. The output of these applications can be imported into your word processed report, usually using the clipboard, or at least by exporting a JPEG version of the file which can then be inserted into the report.

Once the final report is complete and checked for accuracy it should be converted to PDF using one of the many converters available. The main tool used by industry is Adobe Acrobat. Using this you simply print the document to PDF. A number of alternative PDF creation tools, some of which are free (sometimes paid for by banner advertising), use this same method (see Figure 2.8.1). When the PDF printer has been chosen click 'OK' and you will be prompted to name the file for saving. Figure 2.8.2 shows this and Figure 2.8.3 shows the results of saving the file in this way.

This is by far the easiest method of creating PDF files, but it is also possible to upload files to a converter on a network or on the internet. These may be free services or the provider may charge. All such converters work with all reasonably straightforward files, although very complex files may not be rendered perfectly by all PDF creators, so it is important to check the results very carefully once the file has been created. Generally the PDF document is a read-only document that is perfect for viewing by a third party; you should still keep a copy or copies of your word-processed report in a safe place as it is in an editable format. Then if the final PDF file is not correct you can still edit the original report and then re-render it into PDF, i.e. you cannot normally work directly on the PDF file.

Once you have proof read your work for a final time and checked that there are no errors or omissions, the file is ready for adding to your eportfolio.

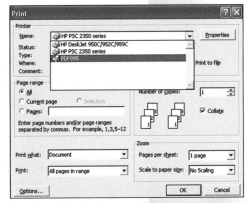

Figure 2.8.1 Printing to PDF

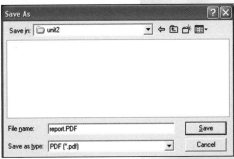

Figure 2.8.2 Save as PDF

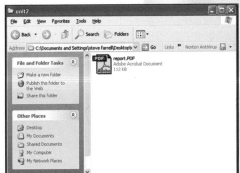

Figure 2.8.3 The saved PDF file

Part 2 The design, creation and use of a relational database

The second piece of evidence you need to create is a set of annotated screenshots and output from a database you have created, along with recommendations based on the identification and interpretation of trends you find within the data.

Step 1: The database

For this section the examination board will supply you with a dataset. That is a set of data based around a scenario. You do not have to use this dataset and scenario; your centre could supply one instead if they wish. The dataset should be a substantial size and will, almost certainly, be provided as one file (probably delimited text). Inherent in this dataset will be a database structure which will, at a minimum, contain one one-to-many relationship. This dataset will provide the basis for your database work in this unit and will be supplied in plenty of time to prepare your answers.

You will be expected to create a database, use it to analyse the data, and identify a trend suggested by the data. The methods you can use are identified in Chapters 2.5 and 2.6. This section is about providing the evidence required by your portfolio; as such, it is wise to create a word-processed document of evidence as you work.

The first thing you will need to do is to study the dataset and deduce the structure. There will be at least one one-to-many relationship. The fields contained in the entity on the 'one' side of the relationship can be identified by groups of attributes containing exactly the same data for a number of records. This may be a name and address, or something similar. In your evidence document draw an entity relationship diagram (remember – as in your entire report – to label the diagram with a brief explanation of what it is).

Entity: Customer

Attribute	Data type	Description	Validation
Customer ID	Number	Customer primary key	Unique identifier
Customer Last Name	Text	Contains surname of customer	Presence check
Customer First Name	Text	Contains customer first name	
Address Line 1	Text	Contains first line of address	
Town	Text		
County	Text		
Post Code	Text	Contains the post code	Picture check >LL9AL9LL
etc.			

Table 2.8.1 Table for database relationships

Having decided on your database structure you will need to decide what attributes go with which entity and the data types of these attributes. At this point you should decide on any validation rules you think you should apply. You can document all this in the form of tables (see Table 2.8.1). Do not forget to include any foreign keys that may be necessary.

Next you will need to create your tables using your database design. A screen dump of each table in design view and an explanation will supply most of the evidence you will need. Major validation evidence should also be included.

Create any relationships and provide a screenshot of your relationships window.

Importing the data should be done in two stages. First import the dataset as a new table and load the data into the two tables using 'Summation' and 'Append queries', as shown in Chapter 2.6.

The document of evidence is to make things easier for the people who mark your portfolio. This will usually be your teacher and perhaps an examination board moderator. These people are only human and may miss something if it is hard to find. If you make things easy to spot you can be confident you will get the marks.

The next thing you will need to do with your database is to interrogate the data and identify a trend. Remember that a trend normally happens over a period of time, so you will probably need to look at the data with relation to time periods. The sort of thing you are looking for is something like "The sales of Apollo Delta trainers are falling off at a rate of about 10 per cent a month." You will not be told what the trend is – indeed, there may be more than one possibility. You will have to investigate the data and see what occurs to you. You need to do this using queries (QBE or SQL). It is a good idea here to keep a log of what you do and the queries you use, as the results of one action may suggest something else and you do not want to waste time going over ground you have already covered.

Once you have identified your trend you will need to explain how you found it and make a recommendation based on the data. We suggest you use a separate document (from the evidence of your database build) to present your trend and recommendation. Include the design of the query which shows the trend; if you can import this data into a spreadsheet and create a chart this would also be good to show. Your recommendation should be supported by evidence from the database and concern a future action. A suitable recommendation would be "I would recommend that QwikFeet Ltd stop selling the Apollo Delta trainer in 2006 as current trends predict that less than 25 would be sold in that year. As we cannot order stock in batches of less than 100 we would have to store 75 unsold trainers".

The final aspect of this section (Assessment Evidence e) is the evaluation. Evaluation is a tricky skill to learn. You need to make evaluative comments about your database and your own performance. An evaluative comment indicates 'how well' something performs its functions; to make such a comment you need to state clearly what the function (or functions) of the database is (or are). No database is perfect; there is always room for improvement and to achieve higher marks you will need to suggest possible improvements. Finally, you will have to collect feedback from others on your database and you should take this into account in your evaluation.

Step 2: Creating the files for the eportfolio

You should have at this stage four files to include in your eportfolio:

1 The collection of evidence compiled while creating your database
2 The database itself
3 The recommendation and supporting documentation (identifying a trend)
4 The evaluation

Apart from the database itself all these can be included as PDF files. At the time of writing, the examination board does not require the database itself but evidence that it has been created. You will need to show the designs of all your tables and queries as well as the data. You must also show evidence of any relationships and validation rules you create.

There may be a limit to the size of your eportfolio so you will have to make a judgement about what you include.

Figure 2.8.4 "I would strongly advise you to hand in your work by the deadline Simpkins"

Unit 3

The Knowledge Worker

The Collected thoughts of
S Farrell
&
T Heathcote

The End

Figure 3.1.1 Putting pen to paper

Legend has it that a venerable old maths teacher was once heard to say (to anyone who would listen), "Life is an undignified lurch from one problem to the next". A somewhat jaundiced view of the world, no doubt, but maybe not that far from the truth. Your typical human being faces a continuous series of problems from the minute she or he gets up to the time she or he falls asleep. Most 'problems' are small though, and therefore do not seem to be 'real' problems. For instance, "Shall I have corn flakes or toast for breakfast?" is one such problem. In an average day, we are presented with thousands of these problems and we solve them using the most powerful computer in the world – the human mind. This particular computer is a truly wonderful thing – it can receive data as inputs from many parts of the body, process this data and convert it into actions at speeds that would make the microchip engineers at Intel weep with frustration. This unit is about just this process – solving problems by making decisions about inputs – something that human beings do almost every waking minute of every day at an almost unbelievable rate.

For example, take the plight of the authors of this book.

On a grey Saturday afternoon, one of them is sitting for minutes on end, staring at a blank word processing document. He is trying to think how to introduce this unit. This is not an unusual situation for an author – getting the first word down on the page can often be a problem. The scenario demonstrates the first part of the problem-solving process – you need to *decide what the problem is*. However, one should not look at problems too literally – taking them at face value can defeat the object of the problem-solving process. If the problem merely is 'getting the first word down on the page', the solution is easy – just type a random word and then you are away. This will not do, however, since typing the word "Aardvark" is unlikely to start an avalanche of ideas on the subject of "The Knowledge Worker". It stands to reason, therefore, that merely getting the first word on the page is not the problem. The real problem is first to identify the problem itself. In our case, the problem is encapsulated in a little phrase we saw earlier in this paragraph, "… how to introduce this unit". Identifying the *real* problem is an oft-overlooked stage in the problem-solving process. A surprising amount of time and money in business is spent solving problems that never really existed, while the real problem remains unsolved. In the end then, a quick analysis of the author's situation shows that the problem is not 'getting the first word on the page' but, rather, a complete lack of inspiration as regards how to introduce this unit.

The next stage in our problem-solving exercise is collecting information. Information comes in numerous shapes and forms and is collected in many different ways. Our first task is to decide what sources of information are available to us, then decide on the reliability of these sources. We could ask other authors how they manage to overcome their initial 'writer's block'. There are problems with this, however, in that firstly we might not be able to get hold of these authors in the time frame required – we have a deadline to work towards. Most problem-solving exercises work to deadlines; it follows that, often, the decision about what information to use is based on what can be collected within that time frame. Let us say we do get hold of other authors, who advise us – how reliable is the information they supply? What works for one author may not work for another. We may also be in competition with other authors, and it may not be in their interests to solve our problems for us.

Perhaps we are better off relying on our own experience. We collect information as a matter of course, every day of our lives, initially by trial and error, until such time as all this information becomes what we call 'knowledge'. For example, if you put your hand in a flame, it hurts. You do not actually have to put your hand in a flame to find this out, you already have this knowledge. Whether you have this knowledge because you have experienced the situation or because you have been told (taught) it, the knowledge is still there and is still the same. In our case, the vast experiences and extensive learning of the author tells us that writer's block can usually be solved by breaking off and doing something completely different for a while.

There is a lot to this information-gathering process and we will look at it in greater detail in later chapters. The outcome of the information gathering will initially suggest possible courses of action, and what the outcomes of those actions may be. In the case of our writer's block, the author has a number of alternatives for breaking off from work, but pressure from the publishers will rule out anything the slightest bit time-consuming. The best option, then, is probably to make a cup of tea or coffee. This will cause a break in the process; the intake of caffeine may even stimulate a few dormant brain cells.

The coffee-making procedure seems simple enough, but it is not without its challenges. The path to the kitchen is through the dining room. Blocking this path are two sets of golf clubs, left out after a morning's round with the co-author, in which a lot of brainstorming and planning for the book usefully took place. So, other than our writer's block, we now have a second problem. This is not an unusual situation in problem-solving – the times when the process does not identify at least one other problem are rare. Such sub-problems need to be solved in exactly the same way as the primary concern. Firstly, we collect information relevant to the problem. Our sophisticated ocular input devices (usually called 'eyes') tell us that there is actually a path to the kitchen, but only if you squeeze yourself between the golf bags and the dining table. At the same time, our *knowledge* tells us that there is room for two sets of golf clubs in the cupboard under the stairs. Our knowledge also tells us that, at some point, the dining room will be invaded by what sounds like a large number of hungry children (but is really only three) thereby putting the health of the golf clubs, and perhaps also the children, at risk.

Our two courses of action are therefore as follows:
- to squeeze around the golf bags, or
- to put them away, thereby clearing a definitive path through to the kitchen.

The first option may be the easiest, but carries some risk of tripping over the clubs. The second option may well delay the coffee, but it will save time when future cups of coffee are needed. In addition, it will be safer for the golf clubs and have the added advantage of not upsetting other members of the household. Clearly then, putting the clubs away – a sub-task that takes seconds – is probably the best option.

Figure 3.1.2 Problem solving isn't just about finding the right information

Displacement activities

So the author decides to put the golf clubs away and then makes the coffee, but not before also tackling a few dirty dishes he suddenly notices by the sink. This shows another aspect of the problem that one should be careful of – the ability to get distracted from the initial task. Often this distraction may be unnecessary, and a drain on one of our most valuable resources: time. On other occasions, though, the 'distraction' may even become the priority, and rightly so – when you are in a swamp, surrounded by alligators, it is sometimes difficult to remember that your initial objective was merely to drain the swamp, you now have other priorities!

Every so often, it is therefore necessary to remind ourselves what our original problem was. In this particular case, it was a blank document. We analysed the data available to us as regards possible solutions to the problem, and made a decision about what to do based on that data. We undertook those actions. The final thing we now need to do is to evaluate the outcome. Since the best part of this introductory chapter appears now to have been written, the initial problem was clearly solved. There have also been some supplementary benefits, in that the dining room is now clear of golf clubs, the kids are happily scoffing their tea there, and the author's wife is in a better mood.

Conclusion

One of the things about decision making is that the better your knowledge of the situation the better your decisions are likely to be. If you want to make good decisions, you need a lot of knowledge. In business a lot of managers say "nothing can beat experience", and they are doubtless right – because with experience comes knowledge. However, knowledge can also be created from data, and in this information age, a large amount of data is available to us from a wide variety of sources. As a knowledge worker your task is to turn this data into knowledge and use this knowledge – along with your experience – to solve problems.

3.2 Understanding the problem

Introduction

In this unit you will hear a lot about 'problem-solving' and 'decision-making'. Neither of these terms fully describes accurately what we are trying to achieve. We are looking at the use of information to inform management. A 'problem' implies that something is wrong and needs fixing. In many cases nothing is actually 'wrong', rather, we are looking at ways we can make things better. The word 'decision' is also a little restrictive as it seems to suggest a selection from a series of concrete options – either this clear-cut choice or that clear-cut choice. This is rarely the case as most decisions are compromises between several conflicting factors, each of which needs to be weighed up.

As we are looking at using knowledge in a business environment perhaps one of the clearest examples of such multifaceted compromises are the factors involved in manufacturing and selling a single product. Imagine you are selling footballs to the general public – how much will you charge for your footballs? Obviously the cheaper your footballs are, the more you will sell. At £100 a football you will sell few, if any. If you were to sell them for £1 you would sell a lot more – so many more, in fact, that if your customers were to kick their balls into their neighbours' greenhouses, they might simply buy another ball from you, rather than face their neighbour's wrath.

But there are many other factors that affect the decision regarding which football to buy. For example, consider advertising – how will this affect sales? What if FIFA were to choose your football as the official football of the next World Cup? Also, how much is it going to cost to make your footballs? Generally there are two kinds of costs: variable costs and fixed costs. Variable costs are costs which are linked to the number of footballs you produce, such as the cost of raw materials. The more footballs you make, the more leather you use. Fixed costs, however, do not vary. The rent you pay for your factory will be the same whether you make five footballs a day or 500 000.

This may sound straightforward but things are not quite as simple as they initially seem. A fixed cost may be a one-off set-up cost, such as buying a machine, or it could be a periodic cost, such as renting the factory space. You may have a limited factory capacity – producing 500 000 footballs may require moving to a bigger factory. This move may then require you to take out a loan, which in turn will involve repayments with interest. Seemingly simple situations have a habit of getting very complicated very quickly and it is often easy to lose sight of what our original objective was. Fundamentally, the point of setting up our football-making factory is to make money – doubtless the more money, the better.

Identifying the problem

Accepting that the word 'problem' is not always appropriate, the first thing to do in this process is to identify what the 'problem' is. Fortunately this is not that difficult as usually the problem will come to you. Identifying the 'problem' helps management to make decisions. The function of any manager is to undertake the tasks assigned to her or him, utilising the resources available. These resources can be people, equipment or money. The tasks assigned are those delegated by senior management. If, however, you are at the top of the tree, your task is basically to maximise profits. Resources are assigned, often as a result of negotiation between the manager and other individuals who manage those resources. Most management decisions come down to money in one way or another – a manager can manage resources in any way she likes, within reason, as long as the budget for those resources is adhered to. For example, whilst a manager has a budget for departmental salaries, another for capital equipment, and another for consumables, his ability to move money between these budgets is usually limited.

What is important is to identify exactly what you need to achieve, and what constraints you are under. Imagine, for example, you are the sales manager for a large machinery manufacturer. Your boss tells you that the fuel expenses of your salesmen are too high, and that you must reduce them. Your task seems fairly simple, so imagine you tell your salesmen not to make trips of more than 50 miles. This will almost certainly reduce your fuel costs – but has it actually solved the 'problem'?

The answer is clearly 'no'. The face-to-face, personal touch is important when it comes to selling certain types of goods – such relationships often define whether a customer buys from you or from someone else. So, not allowing your salesmen to visit all their customers will probably have a disastrous effect on sales. When your boss calls you in to explain this drop in sales, your retort – "Ah! but I have reduced the salesmen's fuel costs by 30 per cent!" – is probably not going to compensate for the lost sales, which are the 'bigger picture'.

The initial specification of the problem, therefore, leaves a lot to be desired. For a start, you have no idea what a successful solution would be. Would a 2 per cent reduction be all right, or is 5 per cent or 10 per cent needed? What you think constitutes success is actually not important – you need to find out how your boss defines 'success' in this instance.

You also need to know what constraints you are working under. Unless you can identify totally pointless journeys that could be curtailed, it is likely that the business, currently done face-to-face, will have to be done in another way – for example, by phone. This will increase the phone bill, so what sort of an increase is acceptable? You would be saving at one end and spending at the other.

It doesn't take much thought to notice that there appears to be a link between sales and fuel expenses – would a reduction in sales be acceptable? We can assume not. So one constraint for our challenge is that sales should not drop. We also need to realise that, if there is a link between fuel costs and sales, an increase in sales would likely have been partly the result of more customer visits and therefore greater fuel costs – quite the opposite of the task we have been set. As one of the primary functions of a sales force is to increase sales it is pointless to turn away customers' invitations to visit them on the basis that you will not make your fuel cost reduction target!

In reality, then, it seems more likely that a good manager would have set your target as some kind of sales/expense *ratio*, rather than a straight reduction of the overall fuel bill. We would therefore be wise to go back to our boss to 'redefine' our problem and also to renegotiate our constraints. It is also better that we negotiate from a position of, if not strength, then knowledge. Before we start negotiating therefore, let's find out as much as possible about the situation.

Understanding the problem

When you start to investigate an apparently simple business situation it is often surprising how quickly it gets complicated. Our intention, remember, is to model the situation and to use this model to predict what will happen under different sets of circumstances, thereby deciding on a plan of action. Predictions, by their nature, are not fool-proof and different models will demonstrate a different level of accuracy. Nevertheless it stands to reason that the more factors you take into account when you build your model, the more accurate it is likely to be.

Most business situations involve a large number of factors that each plays its part. It is often difficult to think of them all, especially on your own. Even more difficult is ensuring that you take all of these factors into account when analysing a 'problem'. The solution is to write them down as you think of them.

An extremely useful technique for documenting your problem is the **spider diagram**. This technique is used in many fields, so it is unlikely that you haven't come across it before. At its simplest you write your problem in the centre of a page and write all the factors that affect it around it, connected by lines. You can then look at each of these factors and add other lines describing the things that affect them (see Fig. 3.2.1). Remembering that our objective, in thinking of all these factors, is to build a more accurate model, we will suggest a slight variation on the standard spider diagram.

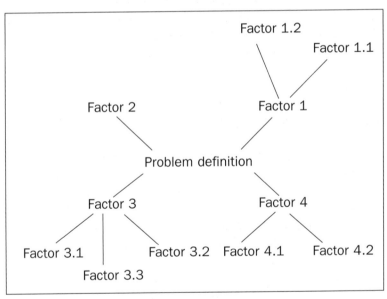

Figure 3.2.1 Example of a spider diagram

▶ A model spider diagram

The main difference between our new diagram and the standard spider diagram is that, as you think of each factor, you are required to make a judgement on how much control you have over it. If you have full control over that item then you <u>underline it</u>. If you exert no control over it then you put a box around it.

If you have full control over an item it will, most likely, be an input into your model, one of the things that you will be able to vary to see the effects. If an item has a box around it then you cannot control it – but if it is important to your model you will have to find some way of predicting it. For example,

Figure 3.2.2 Spider diagram – stage 1

something like the VAT rate would be pretty constant, and could be treated that way. An algorithm, however, would have to be found to predict seasonal changes in sales patterns.

If an item ends up neither boxed nor underlined, it is probably because it is a mixture of things you can control and things you have no control over. It will need to be broken down until you have identified the bits you control.

Let's take the examples of the football manufacturer and the large machine manufacturer previously mentioned. Like almost any manufacturer, their main 'problem' will always be to maximise profits.

To find out what your profits are you simply take your costs away from your revenue, so the first two items to put on our diagram are these (see Fig. 3.2.2). We do not have complete control over either of these, but we do set the price of our product and we do set the salaries of our employees. Both revenue and costs, therefore, need to be broken down further.

Let us start by looking at the revenue. Assuming for a moment that we manufacture a single item, our revenue will simply be the price we sell the item at, multiplied by the number we sell. We exercise total control over our selling price (see Fig. 3.2.3), we can set it at what we like. But what about the number that we sell? We can have some effect on this, not least by setting the price at a marketable rate. In the end, though, we need people to want to buy our product and we cannot control the customers' final decision on this. We will therefore need to break this down a little further and see where it takes us.

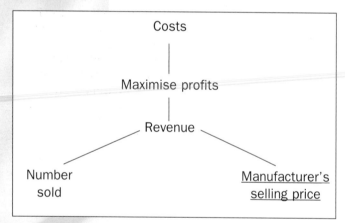

Figure 3.2.3 Spider diagram – stage 2

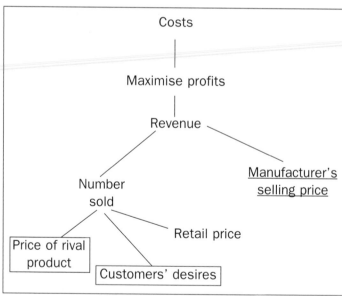

Figure 3.2.4 Spider diagram – stage 3

What affects the number of items we sell? Well a large part of this is the retail price, not the price that we, the manufacturer, sell it on to the retailers, but what the retailers sell it for. We therefore do not fully control this. What else can affect the number we sell? One thing would be the selling price of rival products – something that we have no control over at all – so let's put a box around it. The other thing that we need to put in our diagram is the desire of customers for our product. We have little control over their final decision whether to buy or not, so we need to put a box around it (see Fig. 3.2.4).

We still need to look at the retail price. Which factors do we control and which do we not? In the end this is clearly quite simple – the only thing we truly control is the manufacturer's selling price. We need to add in the revenue the retailer wants to gain from the sale of an item (retailer's mark-up) and how much the government wants (VAT and other taxes), neither of which we control (see Fig. 3.2.5).

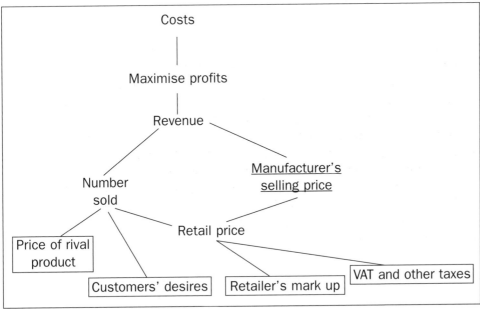

Figure 3.2.5 Spider diagram – stage 4

ACTIVITY 1 ◀

Expand the diagram in Figure 3.2.5 by breaking down the Costs in a similar way to how Revenue is broken down.

Marketing and the decision to buy

You might argue that marketing strategies and advertising can affect customers' potential desire for the product, and you could well be right. The effects of these things are notoriously difficult to predict, though. Marketing departments have their own models for predicting the effect of their strategies, yet these are not always accurate. In the end a successful strategy involves affecting the choice of a large number of people. As an example, take the advent of the 'visible designer label'. Some labels are 'cool', some are not, and this has a huge effect on sales. The real problem is that you cannot really know whether a label will be 'cool' until you release it. For this reason, in our model we consider that the *final* decision by a potential customer to actually buy a product is really their decision alone, so we put a box around it.

A problem – the QwikFeet warehouse

Although business is mainly about making money, not all business problems are finance related, so in this unit we are going to look at a problem that isn't directly finance related. In Unit 2 you were introduced to QwikFeet Trainers PLC, an Internet retailer specialising in the supply of sports training shoes to the general public. Throughout this unit we are going to look at an ongoing problem which faces Dean Rabette, the Warehouse Manager at QwikFeet. Dean is a key man at the company as he is in charge of most of the practical aspects of the QwikFeet operation.

When a customer buys a pair of trainers over the web, after the finance arrangements have been dealt with, the type of trainer and the delivery address are displayed on a computer in the warehouse. One of Dean's warehouse staff will print off the order and visit the warehouse to find trainers of the right size.

Assuming the member of staff finds the required trainers there, they will be placed in a standard plastic delivery envelope. An address label is printed from the computer and placed on the envelope. The envelope is put in a bin to be collected by the courier service that evening and the order is marked on the computer as 'dispatched'. The trainers should then be delivered within three days of the original order.

If the required trainers in the right size are not in the warehouse then the warehouse staff member will make an emergency order direct to the manufacturer/supplier. An emergency order can take up to four days to process; this means the customer would not get their trainers for seven days. There is a heavy premium for these sorts of orders, so QwikFeet makes very little profit on trainers ordered in this way.

Dean is in charge of orders from the suppliers, so the situation we will try to help him with is to create an ordering strategy that reduces emergency orders to a minimum and preferably eliminates them. He makes his order monthly, and (except for emergency orders) trainers are ordered in batches of 100. The orders are submitted on the 15th of each month for delivery on the 1st day of the next month.

The trainer suppliers like to have some idea of which trainers to make and when, so they offer a discount to retailers who give them a clearer idea of their requirements. In December of each year Dean tries to work out what his requirements are for the next year and he sends these to the suppliers. Each month that he is within 5 per cent of his estimate he is given a 10 per cent discount by the supplier.

Currently the warehouse has room for a maximum of 4000 sets of trainers. Overall sales are increasing and at some point it will be necessary to increase the warehouse capacity. This will obviously increase QwikFeet's costs; consequently, the senior management would like Dean to cope as long as possible with the current capacity.

Dean's 'problem' is therefore two-fold. He needs to know each month how many batches of trainers to order to ensure he has the correct trainers to satisfy next month's orders. He needs also to be able to predict, within 5 per cent, what trainers he will be ordering throughout the next year.

Fortunately the two facets of the problem are very closely connected; we can therefore look at both. First we look at how many of a particular trainer to order each month, to ensure we have enough for the demand next month. This would have to be repeated for each trainer type. In order to predict the year's orders we would have to repeat the process for each month. For brevity in our spider diagram we are going to call the trainers being studied 'Trainer A'.

Dean's problem will be:
- To ensure there are enough pairs of Trainer A in the warehouse to cover next month's sales.

The first factor that will affect this is:
- The number of Trainer A sold next month.

Other factors would then be:
- The number of Trainer A in the warehouse at the beginning of the month
- The number of Trainer A ordered for next month
- The space available in the warehouse.

Let's have a look at each of these to see how much control Dean has.

Clearly Dean has absolutely no control over the number of trainers sold next month, so we can safely put a box around this factor.

Less easy to ascertain is the second factor. The number of trainers in the warehouse at the beginning of the month will depend on the number of trainers present in the warehouse at the beginning of the previous month, the number of trainers ordered in the previous month, and the number of trainers sold in the previous month. The challenge here is in overcoming a never-ending 'dependency loop', because the previous month's starting number depends on the starting number in the month previous to that, and so on. To overcome this problem we have to accept and decide that there must be a starting point. In the case of Dean's model, we choose 31 December of the previous year. At this point there would be a set number of trainers in the warehouse, but in terms of Dean's model he has no control over how many that would be (it depends partly on sales), so we can put a box around it.

Now to the third factor. The temptation might be to say that we have total control over the number of trainers we order, but this is not in fact the case. We have control over *the number of batches we order* but the *number in a batch* is defined by our suppliers. So this will have to be split into a factor we can control and one we cannot.

The final factor – space available in the warehouse – is again split into *the capacity of the warehouse* and *the total number of trainers in the warehouse*. We know the capacity of the warehouse to be 4000 trainers so this seems fixed; at the same time, we know that senior management are aware that more space could eventually be needed, so we could see this as an input variable in Dean's model. Using the same arguments for the *Total number of trainers in the warehouse* as we did for the *number of Trainer A in the warehouse*, we complete the diagram as per Fig. 3.2.6.

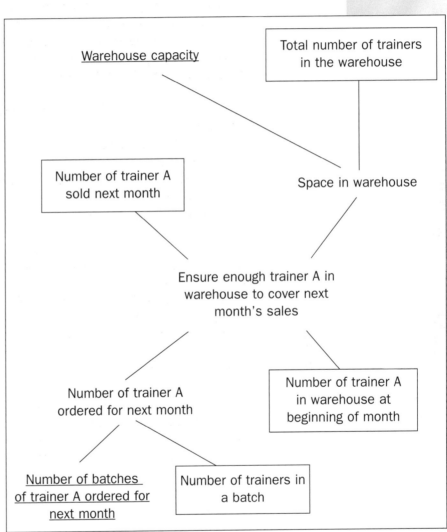

Figure 3.2.6 Spider diagram – stage 5

Discussion

Calthorpe Game Balls PLC was established in 1992 and specialised in making cheap football and rugby balls using a new process involving plastic-coated leather. In 1992 the balls retailed for about £2 each; currently they sell for about £5. Neil Laughlin joined the company as a machine operator in 1994 and was promoted to production manager in 2002. Neil had been aware that the company had been struggling in recent years and was also aware that in 2004 the company made an overall loss. The senior management took a number of measures to try to improve the situation, but when the 2005 profit and loss figures came out they showed no improvement. Ever since, Neil had been expecting some major action, and indeed it came in the form of a visit from the finance director, Jill Soer.

Jill showed Neil the chart in Fig. 3.2.7. The chart, Jill claimed, demonstrated a steady increase in revenue since 1992 but also that overall company costs had been rising at a quicker level – to such an extent that in the last two years, they had exceeded revenue. Obviously this situation couldn't be allowed to continue. Jill further pointed out that the biggest cost increase was in salaries, other company costs being stable over the intervening years. The senior management had discussed the situation and had decided, as a matter of urgency, to reduce staff; they were therefore asking Neil to reduce the number of production workers by four over the next year. Turnover of staff at the factory was not high and it was expected that only two of the reductions would be through natural wastage. At least two production workers would therefore have to be made redundant incurring such costs as that involved.

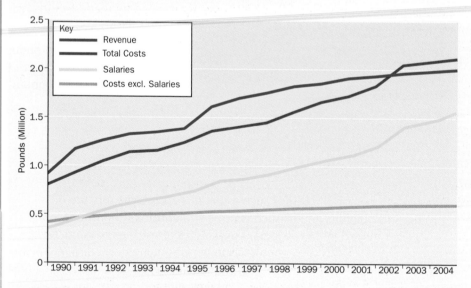

Figure 3.2.7 Calthorpe Game Balls PLC – costs and revenue

Natural wastage Natural wastage is the term used to describe workers retiring or simply leaving an organisation for another job.

Having listened to Jill's arguments, Neil was not convinced that the senior management's reading of the situation was correct. He felt that the solution they proposed was unlikely to have a beneficial effect on the situation. Jill gave Neil a week to sort out his arguments; he would present his plan to the board at the meeting in a week's time.

Neil felt that the first thing he needed was more information as the chart only showed an overview of the situation. A couple of days searching produced the raw figures given in the ActiveBook. Using these figures discuss Neil's situation with regard to the following questions:

1 What is the problem from the company's point of view?
2 What is the problem from Neil's point of view?
3 Is Jill's reading of the situation correct?
4 Is the plan of action Jill proposes likely to be successful?
5 Apart from a reduction in the wage bill what other effects could Jill's plan of action have?
6 What other courses of action could be taken?
7 What are the likely effects of these courses of action?

Conclusion ▶ ▶ ▶

Although the situation at Calthorpe Game Balls PLC is pure fiction and one would hope that no manufacturing company would make the decisions required to bring this situation about, it does bring up a number of interesting points.

The first point is about information itself. We state numerous times in this section that the better the information, the better the decisions you make. Information, however, can be a double-edged sword and can sometimes be presented in such a way as to show a situation quite different to that which actually exists. If you put your mind to it, presenting information in a certain way and utilising seemingly innocuous omissions, figures can be made to show a significantly different picture. There is a famous quote, often attributed to Mark Twain, although he in turn was quoting Benjamin Disraeli, which says that "There are three kinds of lies: lies, damned lies and statistics".

The chart shown to Neil by Jill shows exactly what Jill says it does and as such the plan of action proposed appears logical. It is only when you look more closely at the figures that a number of other issues become apparent. We will look at this further in Chapter 3.3 when we study information sources.

The second point concerns the fact that in most situations you are dealing with people. If figures are adept at showing one thing while meaning another, human beings are even more skilful at this kind of presentational sleight-of-hand. The average person (if there is such a thing) is a complex mixture of needs, desires and opinions and as such is not a straightforward proposition. Often, in a decision making process, the personal desires of the person making the decision are as big a factor as any statistical figures being quoted. Questions such as 'Which of these options is likely to give me the best chance of a promotion' are never spoken but are often involved in the final choice of actions. This phenomenon is known as the 'hidden agenda' and it seems reasonable to admit that we all have them to some extent or other.

Let us look at the Calthorpe situation from Neil's point of view. He has worked for the company for a long time, entirely within the production area. Many of the production workers will be friends of his so, naturally, he will not be happy about making them redundant. He may also view a reduction in the number of people working for him as a threat to his 'empire'. He would be unlikely to agree to the redundancies without a fight even if the figures showed unequivocally that his department is overstaffed. You could also question Jill's motives in presenting the information in the way she did, when it is obvious from the figures that the chart only shows part of the picture.

The third point that should be considered is that costs and revenue are not the only factors in business decision-making, nor should they be. The nice thing about costs and revenue is that they are measurable, or at least they appear to be. It is always easier to make decisions based on things that can be measured definitively, because then you can see if your decision is successful. It is much harder to take into account things that are not measurable as you are unsure of what their effect will be. For instance, what would be the effect on the remaining workforce if two of their number were made redundant? Would productivity go down because of a lowering of morale? Or perhaps it would increase if the remaining workers were 'frightened' into working harder?

The final point is that situations can be inclined to force you to take a particular course of action. 'Your profits are being squeezed – therefore you **must** reduce costs.' On the other hand the ability to 'think outside the box' and come up with an innovative solution to a situation is a very useful attribute to have in business, yet strangely, is often undervalued.

Figure 3.2.8 "I see you've forgotten to pay the electricity bill again"

Collecting information

Introduction – information and information sources

If we look back at the spider diagrams we produced in Chapter 3.2 all the extreme factors (the ones nearest the edge) are either underlined (factors we have control over) or boxed (factors we have no control over). As all these factors affect our model they will all have to be taken into account. The underlined items are our input variables, which we can adjust, to see the effect of different combinations; but for the time being we do not have to worry too much about them.

Our main problem lies with the boxed items as we have no control over them at all. Our model needs to take these factors into account so somehow or other we are going to have to come up with a value for these. These factors may well have had a value in the past and if this is the value we want there is no problem, we simply find out what it was. In modelling, however, more often than not we require knowledge of what the value will be in the future, and this is obviously a little trickier. If the factor is constant, such as the distance as the crow flies between the London Eye and the Eiffel Tower, again there is no problem because it will be exactly the same distance in the future as it was in the past. All we have to do is find out the value. Meanwhile, other factors can be considered *almost* constant. For example, the rate of VAT has been much the same for a number of years; it would seem reasonably safe to assume it will be the same for the near future.

A major concern for our model is when a factor is changing fairly continuously and unpredictably, for example the exchange rate between the Euro (€) and Sterling (£). Imagine that your company exports a good or service to the Euro-zone on the continental mainland. The price of your goods is clearly affected by how many Euros the continental buyer needs to exchange to pay you in pounds. This rate varies by the minute according to the vagaries of the international money market; a small shift one way or the other can have significant effects on a company's profits. To take this kind of input into account we have to look at the situation historically, and somehow come up with an algorithm to try and predict what the value would be in the future, when we want it.

Whatever prediction we make for these values they need to be to be based on something concrete, we cannot just pull a value out of the air. The more we know about a factor the more accurate our prediction is likely to be. What we need, then, is **information**.

Data, information and knowledge

Before we actually move on to methods of gaining this information we first need to understand what, in computer terms, we mean by the term 'information' and also what we mean by the related terms 'data' and 'knowledge'.

Figure 3.3.1 "Isaac, come in and do your homework, you'll never learn anything sitting under that tree all day"

The world of Information and Communication Technology is littered with terms formed using the word data, for example, database and data processing. All computer systems process data so it is here that we will start our definitions. Data are words, facts, figures, transactions, sounds or pictures **encoded** in such a way that they can be stored on a computer. The computer will then **process** this data and output it as information. The idea of processing is important in this operation – the process takes what is essentially a meaningless set of figures, and organises them into a form that will be output in such a way as to be of use to the user of the system. This output is **information**. An important concept in all this is the concept of usefulness. What is output from whatever system you create must be perceived by whoever is using the output to be of use or potentially be of use. If this is not the case, then the whole operation is pointless and the output is not information – because it is not informing anyone about anything.

When you can take this information and use it to achieve a result then it becomes **knowledge**. As an example think of a doctor who can take a set of symptoms, relate them to a particular complaint and decide upon a course of treatment. An enlightening quote about this from the Internet is attributed to Ken Davenport of the Northeast Iowa Regional Library System, in a letter printed in the May 1, 2002 edition of *Library Journal* (vol. 127, no. 8, p. 10). He says "Data are not information. Information is data endowed with relevance and purpose. Knowledge is information endowed with application. Wisdom is knowledge endowed with age and experience".

Data sources

So that we can process data and turn it into information, we need to get our data from somewhere. Where we get our data from is naturally called a **data source**. There is an assumption, throughout this unit, that we are processing this data on behalf of some kind of organisation. If our data source is within the organisation it is known as an internal data source, so you are collecting **internal data**; if it isn't it is an external data source and it is called **external data**. If the data is collected directly for the purpose we are using it for then it is known as **direct**, sometimes **primary**, data. Most Management Information Systems, however, rely on the fact that data collected for one reason can be extremely useful for a number of other operations. When used in this way it is known as **indirect** or **secondary** data. Finally in this paragraph of further definitions, the process of encoding data for storage on a computer is known as **data capture** and the way we do this is called the **data-capture method**.

Database

The first data source we are going to look at is the database. We have looked a little bit at databases in Unit 2. A database is basically a large amount of data stored on a computer. This data is managed, organised and processed by a Database Management System (DBMS). Generally the data is not held in the right form for it to be easily accessed by humans and their own processing system (the brain); the use of SQL or Query by Example (see Unit 2) is necessary to allow us to extract information from databases.

Most organisations of a reasonable size have a database of some kind or another. The corporate database can contain a huge amount of information, if you know where and how to look for it. A large company database can contain information about its employees, its customers and its suppliers. It can contain information about salaries, length of service, sales, costs and even company cars. The vast majority of company problems can be solved using information from its own database, as long as that database has been set up properly. For example, a properly organised corporate database concerning previous sales and financial records is clearly a source of financial and sales information, and can therefore be used extensively in sales forecasting.

Databases are usually an internal data source; but it is clear that data can be put to so many uses that it has a value, possibly for other organisations too – in which case it may even have a monetary value. This value depends a great deal on the quality of the data: is it accurate, is it up to date, and is it useful in the context we wish to use it? Anything that has a value to someone can become a business opportunity; as a consequence there is an increasing trade in the information databases provide. Of course, if you are going to sell information you have to be careful not to fall foul of the Data Protection Act (see Chapter 2.7). Yet overall, bearing in mind that there is a cost involved in keeping data accurate – spending time and money on collecting it, and storing it in a meaningful way – if there is a value to that data (because it provides information), selling it can be a profitable business.

Surveys as sources

In many professional and business situations, you may actually be faced with a fundamental data challenge: that the information you need to solve a particular problem simply does not exist, so you have to collect it. One example of this would be trying to find out what the potential sales of a new chocolate bar are. It is possible that you may have come across this form of market research already: a number of interviewers work the high street, armed with a large supply of the chocolate bar and an equally large supply of survey forms. They stop passers-by, give them a chocolate bar to try, ask them if they would buy it, and if so, how much they would pay for it. This is a well known and fairly simple method of data collection – but beware, it is not quite as straight-forward as it seems. For your results to be useful, you have to be aware of what effects the way you go about the survey may have on the data you collect.

Figure 3.3.2 Typical high street survey

▶ Methodology

The first issue you have to decide upon is the sample size. Whenever you do a survey you will have defined a group of people you are trying to gauge the reaction of. This could be 'All people currently living in the UK', 'Residents of Reading', 'Students over the age of 25', or even 'Everybody in the world'. Let us call this target group your '**population**'. Ideally, for totally accurate results, you would ask your questions to every member of your population. Obviously, if your population is large, you cannot do this. In this situation you ask a percentage of the population, which is known as a **sample**.

The size of your sample relative to the population is very important to the usefulness of the data you collect. The sample must be large enough to be representative of your total population, but not too large. The problem with making it too large is simply that the survey will take too long and cost too much. There are a lot of different methods and systems for calculating a representative sample size; it is worth a few minutes searching the Internet to find out more about this. You will find lots of different methods, including the offer of courses in calculating sample size; it is a complex, mathematical business.

The next challenge you face in conducting surveys is that the people you choose to approach must be representative of your whole population. Let's start here by talking about our chocolate bar. Our population, assuming our intention is to launch this bar in Britain, is actually the whole of the UK. We may decide that a sample size of 100 000 will be representative of this. Yet there are a significant number of people in the UK who don't even like the taste of chocolate. A large part of the population, at any one time, will also be on a diet, and will frown on the idea of eating chocolate. There are even a significant number of people who are allergic to chocolate, or have some other medical situation in which chocolate is banned. All of these people not only would not buy your chocolate bar, but would not want to or be able to take part in your survey. In other words, they are present in your population but are not available for your sample, as they would not take part if asked. Your survey of 100 000 chocolate-eating people, therefore, would predict higher potential sales than would actually ever be the case.

When you are launching a product, you usually have some sort of idea of the type of person you are aiming it at. The theory is that particular products appeal to particular types of people. Marketing organisations (and many other statisticians) tend to use a system of classification called the **socio-economic group**. In this system, people are classified by their occupation and targeted for specific marketing accordingly. Traditionally these groups are as in Table 3.3.1.

Group	Members
A	Top management and professionals
B	Middle management
C1	Clerical workers
C2	Skilled manual workers
D	Semi-skilled workers
E	Manual workers

Table 3.3.1 Socio-economic groups

The targeting of these groups can be shown using the example of newspapers. *The Times* and *The Independent* are aimed at Groups A and B, whereas *The Sun* and *The Star* are aimed at groups C, D and E. The content and the language are adjusted for the groups the papers are intended for.

Recently the government has found this grouping a little restrictive, possibly even unrepresentative of the current UK population. The new groupings are listed in Table 3.3.2.

The National Statistics socio-economic classification analytic classes	
1	Higher managerial and professional occupations
1.1	Large employers and higher managerial occupations
1.2	Higher professional occupations
2	Lower managerial and professional occupations
3	Intermediate occupations
4	Small employers and own account workers
5	Lower supervisory and technical occupations
6	Semi-routine occupations
7	Routine occupations
8	Never worked and long-term unemployed

Table 3.3.2 Socio-economic groups – new classification
Source: Office for National Statistics

The reason we are looking at socio-economic groups is that, to be representative, the proportions of each group in your sample must be the same as in your population. Otherwise, once again, your results will be skewed. If, therefore, you conduct your survey at an expensive golf club you must be aware that you will not come across many people from socio-economic groups D and E. In the same way, your sample must contain the same age profile as your population. Marketing strategies need to target age ranges – there is little point surveying Zimmer-frame use within the confines of a primary school, for instance.

Note also that the factors we have taken into consideration in this section on methodology are not exhaustive. The survey designer could continue to take into account more and more factors (e.g. geographical spread of population) in an attempt to achieve greater accuracy. At some point, however, you reach the stage where this increase in accuracy is not worth the effort involved. Your survey will need to be completed within a time limit. So long as the survey size is reasonable compared to the size of the population as a whole, and other factors such as age and socio-economic group are taken into account, your survey will usually be a fairly accurate predictor of the potential behaviour of the whole population. For example, when predicting the results of national elections, most polling organisations survey around 1500 people, whilst the eligible voting population of the UK runs into tens of millions.

Sensors as sources

Data can be captured directly from the environment using devices known as sensors. The purpose of a sensor is to convert a physical stimulus into an electronic signal which a computer can turn into a numerical value. All sorts of things can be sensed these days, including temperature, light intensity, sound level, rotation, position, humidity, pH, dissolved oxygen, heart rate, breathing, wind speed, motion, to name just a few. This method of data capture is known

Figure 3.3.3 Formula 1 racing car telemetry

as 'data logging'; you may well have come across it in science lessons. The sensors will sense at regular intervals the current value of the thing they are measuring. This data is then stored on a computer.

Another word you may have come across is the word 'telemetry', which means 'to automatically measure and transmit data from a remote source'. This source could be anything from a jet aeroplane on a test flight over the middle of the Atlantic to a dolphin whose vital signs are being studied in the Indian Ocean. A very well-known example of telemetry is that of the Formula 1 racing car (see Fig. 3.3.3). The modern Formula 1 car can have over 200 sensors supplying information to the team pit, such as engine temperature, wind resistance, tyre wear and petrol consumption (see the Formula 1 website). Over 150 000 measurements of one kind or another are made and stored every second. This data allows the technicians and mechanics to monitor the state of the car while it is in a race. More importantly from our point of view, they can use this data to create models which will help them decide on a pit stop strategy, or perhaps what maximum revs to set to ensure the engine will last a whole race. In other words, these models can help attempt to predict the future.

The internet as a source

You will have learned a lot about the internet in previous units; here we are looking at it in the role of a data source. There are an incredibly large number of statistics and facts available on the world wide web. You have already come across a couple of these, such as the CIA World Factbook (see the website of the US Government's Central Intelligence Agency) and the UK government statistics website (see the National Statistics website). Getting your data from the Internet has some advantages in that the data is already encoded for computers, i.e. it is already captured. But you may have to manipulate it to get it into the form you want.

The Internet as a statistical source has strengths as well as weaknesses. Anyone with a minimal amount of computing ability can create a web page. Although this means that you will almost certainly find data relevant to your problem, there is no guaranteeing it will be accurate, up to date, or even true. You will have to make a judgement about the quality of your data source before you consider using it. You can probably have a reasonable amount of confidence in CIA's Factbook and the UK government's statistics site, but you may not be so confident about 'Bill Smith's web site of interesting statistics'. You will need to be able to tell when the statistics were last updated so that you can see how current they are, how they were gathered, and by whom.

The printed word as a source

In these days of the world wide web, it is often all too easy to forget about the printed word as a source of data. In choosing this route you do face the problem of capturing the data. Nevertheless, books, newspapers, professional journals and government publications can be fascinating sources of information. Many organisations, including the government, publish information in hardcopy form. The advantage of this format is in not having to wade through masses of useless information to get to the bit you want – you can simply use the traditional contents page and index to guide you (see Fig. 3.3.4).

Figure 3.3.4 Traditional sources of information found in a library

Prediction techniques

We are collecting this data to predict what the value of something is at some time in the future or under a certain combination of conditions. We are going to base our prediction either on past values, or values under different sets of conditions. There are a number of techniques that we can use and we will look at some of these now.

▶ Extrapolating a sample

Apart from constant or virtually constant values, such as VAT, this technique is probably the easiest form of predicting with some accuracy. For instance, if X people from your sample would buy your product, then to predict the number who would buy your product from the total population you divide X by the number of people in your sample and multiply the result by the number of people in your population.

For example, a car franchise might like to be able to predict what the sales of a new car will be over the next three years. The car is aimed at the family market and the area covered by the franchise contains 200 000 families. The franchise asks 1000 families if they would buy the car in the next three years; 10 say that they would.

The sample size is therefore 1000 out of a population of 200 000. The number from your sample that would buy your product is 10.

The prediction for the sales over the next three years would be:

$$\frac{10}{1000} \times 200\,000 = 2000$$

This is not the most difficult of mathematics. As we said before, however, we may need to take into account the socio-economic profile of our sample, including the age range perhaps. This is why these marketing surveys don't just ask you whether you would buy a product but ask you all sorts of other questions such as 'Do you own your own house?' and 'What is your occupation?'. These background questions are there to establish the profile of the sample so that the results can be adjusted to fit the proposed population. The technique used to compensate is to take the results for each group separately and add up the results.

ACTIVITY 1 Calculate survey positive results ◀

Open this model which takes the grouped results and produces an overall value. Don't worry about the DIV/0 error message to start with – it is there simply because there is no data in the spreadsheet. It will disappear once you put some in.

Imagine a supermarket chain is trying to find out whether a new product is going to sell. One Saturday afternoon they position a number of employees in the car parks of five of their biggest stores to ask their customers what they think. They ask 10 000 people if they would buy the product and 500 say 'Yes'.

Research has shown that the supermarket caters for approximately 1 000 000 customers. If we don't make any adjustments for sub-populations that may not

Continued on next page

buy the product, you would expect $500 \div 10\,000 \times 1\,000\,000 = 50\,000$ people to buy it.

Previous surveys, however, have analysed the socio-economic distribution of their clientele and established the following figures.

Socio-economic group	A	B	C1	C2	D	E	Total
Number in population	3000	7000	155 000	155 000	310 000	370 000	1 000 000

Analysis was done on the survey and the following information was found.

Socio-economic group	A	B	C1	C2	D	E	Total
Number in sample	102	232	1305	3001	2928	2432	10 000
Positive responses in sample	81	152	155	32	44	36	500

1 Enter these values into the model and see what the predicted sales are using the model.
2 What would be the problem with using our original estimate of sales (50 000)?
3 What kind of product would produce these results?

▶ Best case/worst case scenarios

You would use the 'best case/worse case' prediction technique when the information you have collected varies strictly between two values. You will be finding out what will happen if the lowest value occurs all the time, and what will happen if the highest value occurs all the time. The assumption, then, is that the actual value occurs somewhere in between.

One area where this has been used commercially is with endowment mortgages. With a normal mortgage a bank lends you an amount of money to be repaid over a number of years. Your repayments are based on paying this money back over this period of time. For example, if you borrow £200 000 over a period of 25 years and the initial interest rate is 3 per cent per annum (per year), then in the first year you will have to pay back one twenty-fifth of the capital (£200 000 ÷ 25 = £8000), plus the interest accrued over the year (£200 000 × 0.03 = 6000). In this way you will pay off the full £200 000, plus interest, at the end of the 25 years. The total value to be paid in the first year would be £14 000. This would be split into 12 monthly payments of about £1667. Obviously if you actually do repay this way, the amount you owe will reduce each year, and because of that so will the amount of interest you are charged. In reality what the bank will do is try to flatten out your monthly repayments so that they are more consistent (using complicated formulae which we will not delve into here).

Figure 3.3.5 Endowment mortgages were a popular method of house purchase

An endowment mortgage is, however, slightly different. In this type of mortgage you do not pay back any of the capital value (the original £200 000 you borrowed) during the term of the mortgage, but simply pay back the interest accrued each year on the capital you owe. Meanwhile, an additional amount is invested on your behalf in property, the stock market and so on, so as to pay off the whole of the original £200 000 in one swoop at the end of the 25 years. This additional amount is calculated using a worst-case scenario based on the predicted performance of the funds you invest in. The theory is that the amount invested on your behalf will be enough to pay off the loan after 25 years. In the best-case scenario, you would even have some money left over to keep for yourself. In reality, endowment mortgages are often seen as a less attractive way of repaying a mortgage these days, precisely because many of those started in the 1990s appear not to be on target to achieve even the worst-case scenario and pay off the full capital value of the mortgage.

ACTIVITY 2 Calculate endowment mortgage repayments

Open this model that will calculate repayments and investment value in an endowment mortgage. To see how it works follow these instructions:

1   Imagine that a borrower wants to borrow £200 000; you simply enter 200 000 into cell B2.

2   Let us say, for the moment, that their bank is charging 4 per cent interest on loans. Enter 4 per cent (0.04) into cell B5 and replicate it across to cell Z5.

3   The bank estimates that at present investments are appreciating at a rate of between 4 per cent and 7 per cent. As we have no information to the contrary we will assume that this range of return on our investment – from the worst-case to the best-case scenarios – will continue over 25 years. Enter 4 per cent (0.04) into cell B9 and replicate it across to cell Z9. Enter 7 per cent (0.07) into cell B10 and replicate it across to Z10.

4   What we have to do now is to find an annual investment value that, on our worst-case scenario, will net us £200 000 by the end of 25 years. In effect, we need to put the smallest value we can into Cell B3 that will cause cell Z7 to show a figure over £200 000. To help you, cell Z7 will turn red if the accrued value is less than the amount borrowed (B2). Experiment with values until you find the smallest value (to the nearest penny) that will cause Z7 to be over £200 000.

5   Now imagine that at first, everything goes to plan, and in the first year the investment increased by 5.6 per cent. Enter 5.6 per cent (0.056) into cell B11. Look at cell Z7 and you will see that even if the worst-case scenario were to actually happen for the remaining 24 years, we are starting to make a bit of a profit.

6   For the next three years the investment still grows between our estimates, although tending towards the worst case, with values of 5.2 per cent, 4.6 per cent and 4.2 per cent. Enter these values into cells C11–E11. We are still within our range so our worst-case scenario is still showing a bit of a profit.

Continued on next page

7 In Year 5, however, we have a little problem because our investment only grows by 3.9 per cent. Enter 3.9 per cent into cell F11. This is not necessarily a problem in the long-term but it does mean that we have to adjust our worst-case scenario for the following year, as it is now varying between 3.9 per cent and 7 per cent. Change the value of G9 to 3.9 per cent and replicate it across to cell Z9. The first little warning sign now appears. Our worst-case scenario now gives us a shortfall of about £2000. But we may still feel no need to panic, as the stock market will probably recover and give us growth nearer our best-case scenario.

8 During the next three years things get worse though, and the growth for these years is 3.5 per cent, 3.2 per cent and 3.15 per cent respectively. Enter these values and adjust the worst-case scenario for the following year to 3.15 per cent. Our worst-case scenario is now starting to look serious. Even the profit we make from our best-case scenario is starting to show a significant fall.

9 The next five years show a slight recovery but not yet back into our original range. Enter 3.3 per cent, 3.35 per cent, 3.47 per cent, 3.5 per cent and 3.8 per cent into the next 5 years' 'stock market actual'.

10 The next year our investment increases by 4.1 per cent and we breathe a sigh of relief, maybe we'll be OK. But this upturn flatters to deceive and the next five years are 3.7 per cent, 3.65 per cent, 3.55 per cent, 3.4 per cent and 3.2 per cent. Enter these values into 'stock market actual'.

11 The stock market then starts to recover and the next three years shows 3.5 per cent, 3.8 per cent and 4.05 per cent growth. Enter these values.

12 This recovery is too late for us though, since even if next year's growth is 4.6 per cent we find that when we enter it, even our best-case scenario is going to make a loss.

13 Even if we have a miracle now and the next year's growth is 7.5 per cent, it is too late and we make a loss of the best part of £1000. Enter 7.5 per cent into Y11. The value shown is the final value as it is worked out on the final year's growth.

14 Try a few different values in the model and check out the formulae to see if you can figure out how they work.

15 Use the model to decide whether it is better to have high growth at the beginning or the end of the mortgage period.

16 Try to think of another real-life situation where the best-case and worst-case scenarios need adjusting regularly over time.

You can also use the above model to see what happens to repayments as the interest rate goes up and down.

▶ Trends

The last prediction technique is probably the most common: predicting trends, which is based upon trying to continue a trend. Here we are attempting to find the next value in a series. Mathematically speaking, we are trying to define a function based on previous values and then use it to predict the next value. You will be pleased to know that at this level you are unlikely to come across anything other than a linear function (i.e. a straight-line graph).

Let us start with the simplest situation: where we have two occurrences of something and we have to predict a third. What we do is base our prediction on the assumption that if there is a rise or fall between the first and second value, there will be an identical rise or fall between the second value and the third. This is quite a big assumption to make, however. When you only have two values there isn't really much evidence to say whether this assumption is valid or not. It is therefore wise to find as many values as you can. If you only have two values, let's call them V1 and V2, then the third value V3 is calculated by adding to V2 the value of V2–V1, or: V3 = 2V2–V1.

It is preferable, of course, to have several values and if we do have these spreadsheets offer us the 'TREND' function to find the next value. The formula of this is simply =TREND(Array of known y-values, Array of known x-values, Cell of x-value you want to predict). Figure 3.3.6 is an example that finds the thirteenth value in a series. Row 1 contains the number in the sequence and row 2 contains the values. The formula in cell M2 will calculate the thirteenth value. Watch the demonstration of this function.

G11			ƒx									
	A	B	C	D	E	F	G	H	I	J	K	L	M
1	1	2	3	4	5	6	7	8	9	10	11	12	13
2	6	9	13	14	17	19	23	27	30	35	36	40	=TREND(A2:L2,A1:L1,M1)
3													

Figure 3.3.6 Finding the thirteenth value in a series

Conclusion ▶ ▶ ▶

Having looked at a number of ways to predict a value, in the next chapter we can have a shot at creating a model.

Introduction

In the previous chapters we have collected information and assessed its quality with respect to accuracy. It is now time to analyse it with respect to its content. To do this by hand would be laborious to say the least. It is possible to plot a number of graphs and work out trends from them, but it will be much more efficient to create a computer model.

A model is a representation of a real-life situation. For example, a model car is designed to look like a smaller version of the real thing. Our models are computer models however, and will be designed to represent the situations in which we wish to make our decisions. Unlike the model car, our models will not look like the real thing but will be an abstract representation of the situation using mathematical formulae. As soon as the word 'formulae' is mentioned most will realise that we will be building our models using a spreadsheet application.

The mention of mathematics may also cause some consternation. There is no way we can avoid this, though, as spreadsheet models are mathematical by nature. Fortunately most of the maths required is reasonably easy. Not so fortunately, the formulae required by a model depend on the circumstances the model is trying to describe, and there is no way we could cover every possible combination in this book.

Arguably the best way to understand the process of modelling is to build one and use it, so for the rest of this chapter we will try to set up and use a model to help Dean Rabette of QwikFeet. At this stage it is worthwhile reminding ourselves what his problem is.

The scenario

QwikFeet is an online supplier of trainers. They buy trainers from a number of suppliers at one price and sell them over the internet to the general public at a higher price. A customer can sign on, browse details of the trainers available, and buy them by supplying their credit-card details. If the required trainer type and size are in the warehouse they are dispatched to the customer. If QwikFeet do not have the correct type and size in the warehouse, the trainer has to be emergency ordered from the suppliers. Emergency orders are costly, though, as the price charged by the supplier is higher.

Dean Rabette is in charge of the warehouse at QwikFeet. He is responsible for ordering all trainers from the supplier. One of his main objectives is to reduce the emergency orders to a minimum. He orders trainers in the middle of the month for delivery at the beginning of the next month. This means that he has to try to estimate what trainers would be sold between the time he makes the order, and the end of the following month when the next order is delivered. The more informed this estimate is, the more likely it is to be correct. This is why Dean is going to use a model. To add to Dean's equation, his suppliers offer a discount if he can predict a year's sales within 5 per cent (5%). At the beginning of the year therefore, he will have to come up with a prediction for the whole year's sales.

There are two other factors that Dean will have to take into account when he creates his model. Firstly, apart from emergency orders, trainers are supplied in batches of 100 pairs. Secondly, the warehouse has a capacity of 4000 pairs of trainers maximum at any one time.

Dean's model will have to be based on some form of data. In Chapter 3.3 we looked at possible data sources; probably the best source of data for this situation is an internal one. Dean has available to him the sales figures for 2003 and 2004, and he is going to use these figures, initially, to predict the orders for 2005. It is likely that these sales figures would have originally been held in a corporate database, so Dean will have to import them into his spreadsheet. It is possible to import from a database into a spreadsheet, but in our case the figures have been imported into text files which you can find in the ActiveBook. The first activity in this section, therefore, is to create a spreadsheet containing this data for Dean's benefit.

ACTIVITY 1 Start the model ◀

1 Open a new spreadsheet.
2 Import the 2003 figures from the ActiveBook into the first worksheet of your spreadsheet. Start the import into cell $A$6. The text file is delimited by a comma (,) and contains all the row and column headers you need.
3 Rename this worksheet '2003 figures'.
4 Import the 2004 figures from the ActiveBook into the second worksheet of your spreadsheet. Start the import into cell $A$6. The text file is delimited by a comma (,) and contains all the row and column headers you need.
5 Rename this worksheet '2004 figures'.
6 Into both spreadsheets, copy the QwikFeet Logo from the ActiveBook and put in appropriate headings as shown in Fig. 3.4.1.

QWIK FEET
Sales Figures 2003

Make	Model	January	February	March	April	May	June	July	August	September	October	November	December
Apollo	Delta	199	154	153	179	161	176	166	181	168	155	198	169
Apollo	Kite 100	24	16	33	19	28	37	32	24	29	44	26	22
Apollo	Kite 200	32	14	35	30	28	27	32	33	32	30	42	28
Apollo	Lite	25	21	24	27	32	25	22	25	35	34	39	25
Apollo	Spring 4	28	19	36	32	27	22	32	26	30	25	34	22
Apollo	Vulcan	109	82	67	93	83	75	77	77	87	90	78	88
Hyklass	Force 2000	42	18	32	26	34	25	30	36	36	34	33	28
Hyklass	Force 2001	28	21	22	19	29	26	32	28	29	29	25	28
Hyklass	Force 2002	41	24	24	31	26	23	15	31	24	22	25	28
Hyklass	Magnum 308	33	25	25	34	27	25	25	33	30	24	27	26
Hyklass	SuperForce	30	28	19	41	22	32	28	34	24	31	32	19
Morgan	Hawk	165	146	124	155	139	127	113	155	108	168	154	137
Morgan	Osprey	28	22	27	29	35	34	23	22	32	27	32	28
Morgan	Raven	32	25	26	25	33	20	36	26	29	27	35	28
Morgan	Swallow	33	32	25	29	31	29	23	30	27	33	37	21
Spike	College	59	56	50	59	55	59	41	63	46	50	60	43
Spike	Contessa	42	29	20	36	35	29	27	34	27	37	28	31
Spike	Cussion 20	33	19	25	22	30	26	19	35	24	28	31	27
Spike	Cussion 30	138	114	109	113	111	117	87	125	121	114	116	98
Spike	Cussion 40	198	157	149	185	157	128	137	176	166	182	186	132

2003 Figures / 2004 Figures /

Figure 3.4.1 Example of 2003 sales figures worksheet

When we copy formulae into different cells using the fill handle this is known as replicating. The cell addresses in the formula will change relative to the cell being copied. Imagine that cell O6 contains =B6+C6. If this formula is replicated down cell O7 will contain the formula =B7+C7. If the formula is replicated across Cell P6 will contain the formula = C6+D6. This is known as **relative** addressing.

There are, however occasions when you may not want this to happen. Imagine that when we replicate our formula we want the value C6 to remain the same. We simply put the dollar ($) character in front of both the column letter and the row number. Cell O6 will therefore contain =B6+$C$6. When replicated down cell O7 will now contain =B7+$C$6 and when replicated across cell P6 will contain =C6+$C$6. This is called **absolute** addressing.

We can now, of course, start to be clever and anchor only part of the address. Let's imagine cell O6 contains = B6+$C6. Here we have anchored only the column and the row is left to adjust. Replicating down O7 will now contain =B7+$C7 whereas if we replicate across P6 will contain =C6+$C6.

Obviously you can anchor the row and change the column too.

SPREADSHEET TECHNIQUE 1

Import comma delimited text data

1 From the Data Menu choose 'Import external data' and from the resulting menu select 'Import data'.

2 In the 'Select data' source window change the 'Files of type' field to show 'Text files' and search for the required file (see Fig. 3.4.2). Once you have selected the correct file click on the 'Open' button.

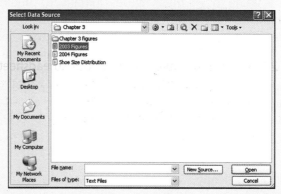

Figure 3.4.2 Select data source window

3 A wizard will start. In the first window of the wizard ensure that the 'Delimited' radio button is selected and click on the 'Next' button.

4 In the next window of the wizard ensure that the comma (,) is selected as a delimiter and click on the 'Finish' button (see Fig. 3.4.3).

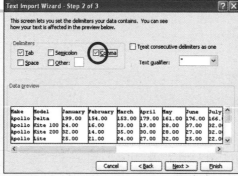

Figure 3.4.3 Setting a comma (,) as a delimiter

Figure 3.4.4 Ensuring the data starts in cell A6

5 The next window will ask you where you want to start importing. Choose the cell you require and click on the 'OK' button (see Fig. 3.4.4).

 Now watch the demonstration of this technique.

SPREADSHEET TECHNIQUE 2

Rename a worksheet

1 Point to the sheet tab for the sheet whose name you wish to change (see Fig. 3.4.5) and click the right button.
2 From the resulting menu choose rename.
3 The name on the sheet tab will change to reverse view and you will be able to type in the new name.

Now watch the demonstration of this technique.

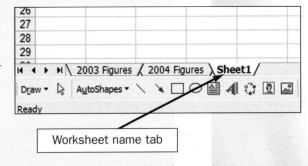

Worksheet name tab

Figure 3.4.5 Worksheet tab

We now have the 2003 and 2004 sales figures in our spreadsheet and our objective is to use these to predict 2005 sales figures. We will, therefore, need somewhere to store our 2005 figures. Probably the neatest way to do this is to create a new worksheet which we will call 'Predicted 2005 figures' and make it the same format as the 2003 and 2004 sales figures.

ACTIVITY 2 Prepare the predicted sales worksheet

1 Open your Spreadsheet.
2 Copy Cells A1:N26 of either 2003 figures or 2004 figures.
3 Select a new spreadsheet and paste starting from cell A1.
4 Change the heading to read 'Predicted 2005 sales'.
5 Clear all data and formulae out of cells C7:N26 (see Fig. 3.4.6).

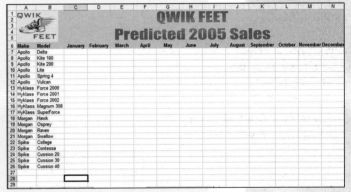

Figure 3.4.6 Predicted 2005 sales worksheet

Predicting trends

When we try to predict what a future value will be based on previous figures, we try to find the trend and assume that the next set of figures will follow the same trend.

To follow a trend we have to calculate the next number in a series and for this we need a mathematical equation. Some of the more sophisticated models use complex polynomial equations, but to calculate trends using these you would need more points of reference. With only two points of reference, our 2003 and 2004 figures, we can only assume a linear trend. The mathematicians amongst us will know that the formula of a linear equation is $y = mx + c$, where m is the gradient of the graph and c is the value of x when $y = 0$.

A number of spreadsheets provide functions which will predict the next value in a series based on such a linear equation (Microsoft Excel has the TREND function), but as we have only two previous values we do not need to use this feature.

The January figures for the Apollo Delta and the Apollo Kite 100 are shown in Figure 3.4.7; also shown is the difference between them. We can see that QwikFeet sold 161 more pairs of Apollo Delta trainers in 2004 than in 2003. A linear trend would mean that we will sell 161 more pairs of Apollo Delta Trainers in 2005 than we did in 2004. Therefore, to get a predicted 2005 value, we add the difference between the sales for the two years 2003 and 2004 to the 2004 sales figure.

Trainer	Jan 2003 sales	Jan 2004 sales	Difference
Apollo Delta	199	360	161
Apollo Kite 100	24	56	32

Figure 3.4.7 Trend for Apollo Delta and Apollo Kite 100 trainers

The formula to predict the January 2005 sales for the Apollo Delta would therefore be:

= '2004 figures'!C7 + ('2004 figures'!C7 - '2003 figures'!C7)
or in simpler form:
= 2*'2004 figures'!C7 - '2003 figures'!C7

This formula applies to the January sales of the Apollo Delta trainer but similar formulae are needed for all other months and all other trainers. The only things that will differ are the cell values we use. To apply the same formula to all the other months, therefore, we can replicate (copy) it into all the other cells.

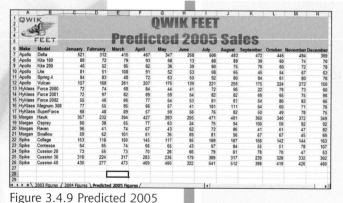

Click here and drag horizontally (vertically).

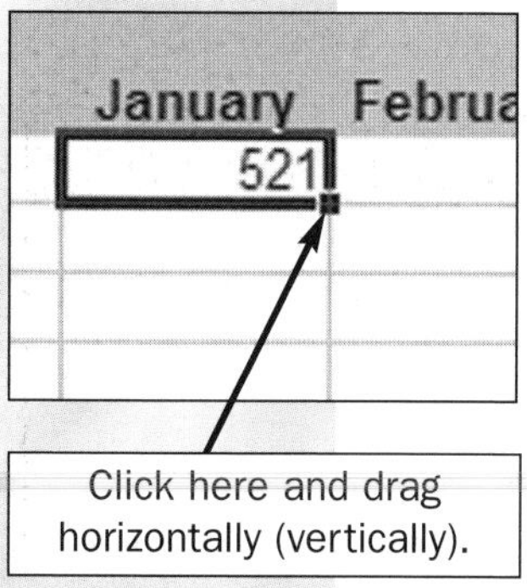

Figure 3.4.8 Select the small square at the bottom right hand corner of the cell to replicate

Figure 3.4.9 Predicted 2005 sales figures

ACTIVITY 3 Predict 2005 sales

1 Enter the formula to calculate the January sales of the Apollo Delta trainer into cell C7 of your 'Predicted 2005 sales'.
2 Replicate this formula to calculate the values for February to December.
3 Replicate again to calculate the values for all other trainers.

SPREADSHEET TECHNIQUE 3
Replicating

1 Point to the small square (this is known as a fill handle) at the bottom right of the cell you wish to replicate (see Fig. 3.4.8).
2 Drag horizontally (or vertically) to select all the cells up to N7.
3 The formula will be copied to all the selected cells; the cell addresses in the formula will be automatically adjusted accordingly.

Now watch the demonstration of this technique.

You will now have predicted the sales of each make of trainer for each month (see Fig. 3.4.9).

The Knowledge Worker

A data capture worksheet

Having predicted our likely sales we need to create a form through which we can input our monthly orders. This is going to be our main data entry worksheet as these are the values Dean has control over. Remember we buy from our suppliers in batches of 100 pairs of trainers, so using this form we need to input the number of batches of each trainer we wish to order each month. As the form is going to be of the input type, we ought to put some **validation** on it to ensure we cannot enter invalid data. For example, we know that we cannot order fractions of batches, therefore the input value must be an integer. We also cannot order a negative number of batches, so our minimum value must be zero. Likewise, the warehouse can only hold 4000 pairs of trainers so the maximum number of batches we can order would be 4000 divided by 100 (40).

The consequences of inputting a wrong value into the ordering system could be disastrous. At best we could be without certain trainers; at worst we could overflow the warehouse. We need to put a value in for each trainer type in each month, so the format of this sheet can be similar to all the others.

> **Validation** Validation in this context is where input data is checked by the computer to ensure that it conforms to certain rules. For instance, a numerical value may have to be within a certain range, or a text value may have to be a variant on certain configuration of letters and numbers (e.g. 'always three letters followed by three numbers'). Data is validated to reduce human errors in inputting.

ACTIVITY 4 Create the data capture worksheet

1 Create a new worksheet called 'Data capture', you may have to insert a new worksheet.
2 Copy cells A1 to N26 of one of your other worksheets and paste them into your 'Data capture' worksheet, starting at cell A1.
3 Change the title to 'Order input form' and delete any values in cells C7 to N26 (see Fig. 3.4.10).
4 Set the value of cells C7 to N26 to zero.
5 Set validation rules for cells C7 to N26 to limit the input to a whole number between 0 and 40 (the maximum number of batches we can order). Validation rules and other cell formats can be replicated in the same way as formulae.
6 Set a suitable error message to appear if invalid data is submitted into one of these cells.
7 Set a help message to appear telling the user what is to be input into these cells when the cell is selected.

Figure 3.4.10 The order input form will be our main data capture worksheet

SPREADSHEET TECHNIQUE 4

Create a new worksheet

1 From the menu bar choose 'Insert'.
2 From the resulting window choose 'Worksheet'.
3 You will be transferred to a new sheet called 'Sheet*n*' (where *n* is a number).

Now watch the demonstration of this technique.

SPREADSHEET TECHNIQUE 5
Set a validation rule (range check), input message and error alert

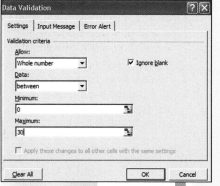

Figure 3.4.11 Validation setting window

1 On the menu bar click on 'Data' and from the resulting menu click on 'Validation'.
2 The 'Data validation' dialog window will appear showing the validation criteria 'Allow any value'.
3 Using the drop down arrow on the 'Allow' field, choose the type of number you require e.g. 'Whole number'.
4 Ensure the 'Data' field says 'between'.
5 Set the minimum value and maximum values (see Fig. 3.4.11).
6 Click on the input message tab.
7 Enter a suitable title and message in the appropriate fields (see Fig. 3.4.12).
8 Click on the Error alert tab.
9 Enter a suitable message (see Fig. 3.4.13).

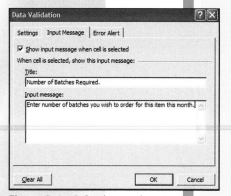

Figure 3.4.12 Setting an input message

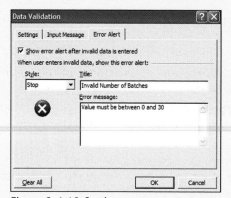

Figure 3.4.13 Setting an error message

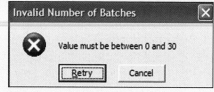

Figure 3.4.14 Example of an error message

Figure 3.4.14 will appear if an invalid value is entered in this cell.

Now watch the demonstration of this technique.

Warehouse contents

Let us recap what we have done so far. We have imported the sales data for 2003 and 2004 into two worksheets in our spreadsheet. We have then created a third worksheet of a similar format, which we have used to calculate some predicted 2005 figures. We have also created an input form which we can use to input combinations of orders. We now have to make our model show the effects these combinations of orders will have on the contents of the warehouse. We want this model to help us to select a combination of orders that will keep emergency orders to a minimum while at the same time ensuring that we do not overfill the warehouse.

Our next form, therefore, will be our main output screen. There will be a number of things on it, but to start with it must show which trainers are in the warehouse at any one time, so that we can keep continuous track of the number of each type of trainer in the warehouse.

ACTIVITY 5 Create the warehouse contents worksheet

1 Create a new worksheet called 'Warehouse contents'.
2 Copy cells A1 to N26 from one of your other worksheets and paste them to your 'Data capture' worksheet starting at cell A1.
3 Change the title to 'Warehouse contents' and delete any values in cells C7 to N26 (see Fig. 3.4.15).

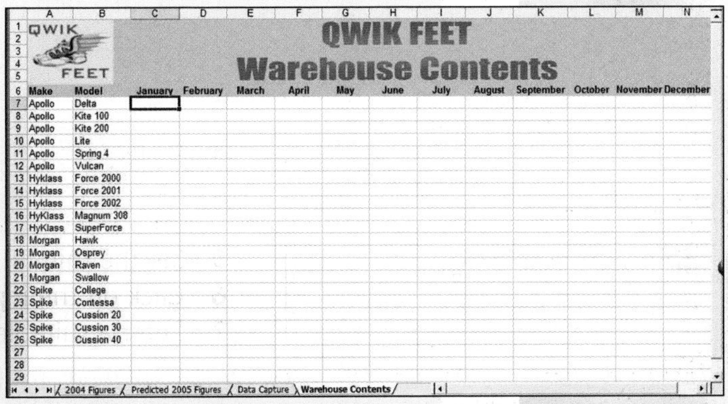

Figure 3.4.15 Warehouse contents worksheet

At this point it must be remembered that the trainers we order in January will not be delivered until 1st February. The contents of the warehouse in January are therefore whatever we have in stock at the end of December of the previous year, plus whatever we ordered that same December. We have to start somewhere so we will make the January values input values. We will therefore have to calculate the January values manually to start us off, and these figures will need to be validated.

February values are a little more complicated and are calculated as follows. The number of Apollo Delta trainers in the warehouse in February is the number that was in there at the beginning of January (C7) minus the number sold in January ('Predicted 2005 figures'!C7) plus the number ordered in the middle of January ('Data capture'!C7*100). In terms of a formula cell, D7 should contain the following:

=C7-'Predicted 2005 figures'!C7 + ('Data capture'!C7*100)

Notice that we multiply the value on the 'Data capture' worksheet by 100. This is because we buy trainers in batches of 100 pairs.

We should notice at this stage that if the number we sell in any particular month is more than the number remaining at the end of the previous month added to the number we ordered in the previous month, then the result of this formula is going to be negative. Obviously the idea of storing a negative number of pairs of trainers is physically absurd, yet this value does at least show that in this situation, we will likely have to make a number of emergency orders, as our sales will be bigger than our stock.

Clearly this is exactly what we are trying to avoid, and if this is likely to occur, we want to see it immediately – we don't want to have to search for negative values. So we need to highlight these values in some way. We can do this by using a technique called 'conditional formatting': we can make the format of a cell containing a negative number a different colour to one containing a positive number.

ACTIVITY 6 Display the warehouse contents

1. In your 'Warehouse contents' worksheet set the whole of the January sales figures to zero.
2. In these cells set validation to check for whole numbers between 0 and 4000, with suitable input and error messages.
3. Enter the formula = C7-'Predicted 2005 figures'!C7+('Data capture'!C7*100) into cell D7.
4. Set 'Conditional formatting' to make the background of the cell red if it contains a negative number.
5. Replicate the cell through the range D7:N26.

SPREADSHEET TECHNIQUE 6

Set conditional formatting

1. On the menu bar select 'Format' and from the resulting menu choose 'Conditional formatting'.
2. In the Conditional Format window (see Fig. 3.4.16):
   a. Set the first cell to 'Cell value is'.
   b. Set the second cell to a condition e.g. 'less than'.
   c. Set the third cell to a value e.g. '0'.
   d. Click the format button and choose a format.

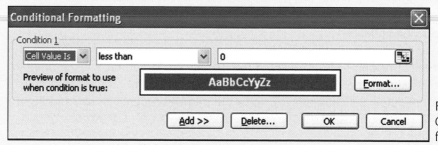

Figure 3.4.16 Conditional formatting

Now watch the demonstration of this technique.

Total warehouse contents

The other thing we need to know is the maximum number of trainers in the warehouse at any one time, so that we never exceed the 4000 trainer-pairs limit. This is a fairly simple process, as all we have to do is to calculate the total for each month.

ACTIVITY 7 Calculate totals

1. Enter 'Trainers in warehouse' in Cell A27 and make it bold.
2. Merge cells A27 and B27.
3. Into Cell C27 enter a formula to add cells C7 to C26 (=SUM(C7:C26)).
4. Set conditional formatting to show a green background if the value exceeds 4000.
5. Replicate this formula across to Cell N27.

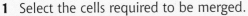

SPREADSHEET TECHNIQUE 7

Merge two cells

1 Select the cells required to be merged.
2 On the menu bar, select format, and from the resulting menu select cells.
3 In the 'Format cells' window click on the 'Alignment' Tab and check the 'merge cells' option (see Fig. 3.4.17).

Now watch the demonstration of this technique.

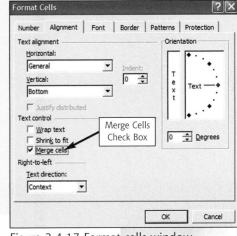

Figure 3.4.17 Format cells window

▶ Shoe sizes

The issue of shoe sizes is a difficult one. Our model will give us some idea of what the sales will be of each type of trainer, but it does not give us any idea of what sizes these will be. If we were to take into account trainer sizes our model would become exceedingly complicated. To keep things simple we will make the assumption that distribution of sizes bought by customers, and therefore the sizes we need to order, is pretty consistent no matter which type of trainer we choose. Although it is not necessarily part of the model it would be nice to know what the distribution of sizes is; then we can calculate the number of each size in a batch of 100. We therefore need information about the sizes of shoe that customers buy. The ActiveBook contains the distribution of shoe sizes sold between January 2003 and December 2004.

ACTIVITY 8 Investigate shoe size distribution ◀

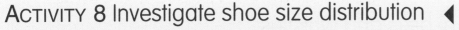

1 Create a new worksheet called 'Shoe distribution'.
2 Import the data into the spreadsheet starting at cell A1.

If you have successfully imported the data you will have two columns, one labelled 'size' and the other labelled 'number of sales'. It would also be helpful if we knew the total number of trainers we had sold during the period.

3 Enter 'Total' into cell A11 and a formula to add up cells B2:B10 in cell B11.

Our spreadsheet is now telling us, for example, that out of every 36 950 pairs of trainers sold about 907 would be size 3. This is useful information but we also need to know how many size 3 pairs we need to order in a batch of 100. To find this mathematically we need to divide the number by the total number of trainers sold, and then multiply this by 100. You could try this if you like, the formula for cell C2 is below, but you will probably end up with a real number – suggesting a fraction of a pair:

=B2/B11*100

As we cannot order 0.454668 of a pair of trainers this is obviously not what is required. We need to round this number to the nearest whole number. We do this using the 'ROUND' function. Our new equation is below:

=ROUND(B2/B11*100,0)

Continued on next page

There is still one minor adjustment to make before our formula is complete. If we were to replicate this formula down for the rest of the sizes the formula in cell C3 would be:

=ROUND(B3/B12*100,0)

This is not what we want because there is no value in cell B12 and this will cause an error. Although we want the first cell in the formula to change, we will always be dividing by the value in cell B11, so we do not want this to change when we replicate. We do this by putting '$' in front of the Column letter and row number, as below:

=ROUND (B2/$B$11*100,0)

This is called 'absolute addressing'.
   4 Put the formula in Cell C2 and replicate it down to cell C10.
   5 Enter 'Number per 100' in cell C1.

The results in this column give us some idea of how many of each size to order in each batch of 100 pairs. We still have a small problem, though. If you put a formula in cell C11 to add up the column you will see what the problem is. The column adds up to 101, suggesting we need to order more than 100 pairs, which according to our model we cannot. This error is caused by what are called 'rounding errors'. In the end the problem isn't a huge one, we just need to implement a procedure to get round it. One way to do this is to think: *As we don't sell that many more size 11 pairs than we do size 3 pairs, I will simply order two size 11 pairs instead of three.*

▶ Final bells and whistles

Our model is, to all intents and purposes, complete. We could, however, spend a little time smartening it up. We could colour some of the cells or we could add graphics to make it look more interesting. Good sense would make us remember that we are using colour to identify problems visually – such as there being too many trainers in the warehouse or running out of a particular trainer – so the model is fine as it is.

Whenever we create a viable system, we must also bear in mind that the biggest threat to its stability is the user. Often, systems you create will eventually be used by others, some of whom may not be as computer literate as yourself. In this situation you must take some steps to protect your formulae. Your application should allow you to protect worksheets so that you can only change cells if you unprotect them by supplying a password. There are several worksheets in your model which have no input cells, at all so we could start by protecting these worksheets. The forms in question are '2003 figures', '2004 figures', 'Predicted 2005 figures' and 'Shoe size distribution'.

If we were to do this we would be left with two sheets that are still unprotected, the 'data capture' sheet and the 'Warehouse Contents' sheet. On each of these forms we need to allow inputs. We can still protect these sheets, but before we do so we have to unlock all those cells we want to allow our users to enter data into.

ACTIVITY 9 Protect the model ◀

1 Protect the '2003 figures', '2004 figures', 'Predicted 2005 figures' and 'Shoe size distribution' worksheets.
2 Unlock Cells C7:N26 on the 'Data capture' worksheet.
3 Protect the 'Data capture' worksheet.
4 Unlock Cells C7:C26 on the 'Warehouse contents' worksheet.
5 Protect the 'Warehouse contents' worksheet.

SPREADSHEET TECHNIQUE 8 ◀

Protect/unprotect a worksheet and unlock cells

Protecting a worksheet

1 Select the worksheet you wish to protect.
2 On the menu bar select 'Tools' and from the resulting menu select 'Protection'
3 Another menu will pop up; select protect sheet.
4 You will be asked for a password in a window. The window will also give you a selection of checkboxes, allowing you to specify what the user can do without supplying a password. Leave these selections at default; just supply a password.
5 You will then be asked to confirm your password; when you have done so your worksheet will be protected.

Unprotecting a worksheet

1 Select the worksheet you wish to unprotect.
2 On the menu bar select 'Tools' and from the resulting menu select 'Protection'
3 Another menu will pop up; select unprotect sheet.

Unlocking cells

1 Select the cells you wish to unlock.
2 On the menu bar select 'Format' and from the resulting menu select 'Cells'
3 The Format cells window will appear; choose the 'Protection' tab
4 Uncheck the 'Locked' check box.

Now watch the demonstration of these techniques.

Conclusion ▶ ▶ ▶

We now have a model that we can use to help us solve our problem. How we go about using this is covered in the next chapter. Before we move on, however, it is always worth going back to our original problem to check that we are still heading in the right direction. Are we?

Figure 3.4.18 "For goodness' sake Frankenstein, I said create me a DATA model"

Using and refining the model

Preparing the model

Having built the model we are now almost in a position to use it to inform our decisions. Many models have more than one purpose and will therefore have variables in them; they will also have to be set up by entering the constants to start with. So when you use a model you need to have a plan about what you are going to vary and what is going to remain constant. When you have decided on this you can enter the constants and start investigating the situation. A complicated model can have a large number of variables, but varying all of them in a particular session can be counter-productive. You are more likely to want to see how alterations to each individual variable affect the whole.

In order to make our model we have to remind ourselves of what our objective is. It is quite easy to lose sight of your original intention, wasting time investigating things that do not matter. In that case let us remind ourselves of the problem facing Dean Rabette at QwikFeet. What we are trying to do is to create an ordering strategy for trainers. The following constraints apply:

- The total number of trainers in the warehouse should not exceed 4000 pairs.
- Trainers are ordered in batches of 100 pairs.
- Trainers are ordered on the 15th of each month and are not delivered until the 1st of the next month.

Let us look at our model first and see what we need to know prior to using our model. Our model has six worksheets, named as follows:

- 2003 figures
- 2004 figures
- Predicted 2005 figures
- Data capture
- Warehouse contents
- Shoe size distribution

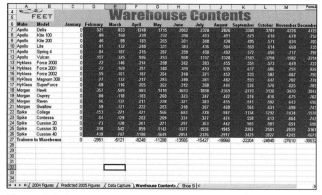

Figure 3.5.1

The '2003 Figures' and the '2004 Figures' worksheets contain data from which we predict 2005. The data has been entered so there are no further inputs on these worksheets. 'Predicted 2005 figures' contains only calculated values and no inputs. 'Shoe size distribution' also contains no inputs, which leaves us with 'Data capture' and 'Warehouse contents'. We will therefore be using the 'Data capture' worksheet to experiment with the various options; but before we do that we will have to set up the 'Warehouse contents' worksheet with the January data.

At present our model shows that there are no trainers in the warehouse in January (see Fig. 3.5.1). If we order trainers in January they don't actually get delivered until February. Consequently if we want to have trainers available in January they must be delivered the previous December. Therefore it stands to reason that there are already trainers in the warehouse in January and these must be entered.

ACTIVITY 1 Enter initial data ◀

The following data is a count of the trainers in the warehouse on 31 December 2004. Enter it into your model.

Make	Model	Number left at end of December 2004
Apollo	Delta	523
Apollo	Kite 100	89
Apollo	Kite 200	51
Apollo	Lite	82
Apollo	Spring 4	86
Apollo	Vulcan	158
HyKlass	Force 2000	75
HyKlass	Force 2001	74
HyKlass	Force 2002	56
HyKlass	Magnum 308	79
HyKlass	SuperForce	70
Morgan	Hawk	360
Morgan	Osprey	81
Morgan	Raven	102
Morgan	Swallow	61
Spike	College	161
Spike	Contessa	70
Spike	Cussion 20	77
Spike	Cussion 30	320
Spike	Cussion 40	433

Planning a strategy

We can now use our model by entering values into the 'Data capture' cells.

Using our model involves us entering values into the 240 blank cells in the 'Data capture' worksheet: even accepting that the only values we can enter are in the range 0 to 5, that makes 1440 different possibilities! Furthermore, when you take into account the different combinations of these values, you are talking about an astronomical number of different options. You couldn't possibly test them all; you simply wouldn't have the time.

Entering random values and noting the results would also not work as you need to recognise a trend. You need to have a strategy which you are going to use to investigate a model. If you have a large number of variables and you change too many at once, you will have no idea which changes brought about the result. Some changes may have had a positive effect while others a negative one. It is best if you can keep as much constant as you can on each inspection.

When you are interrogating models you are answering what we call "What if? ..." questions. For instance, you may have a model which predicts sales and you may be wondering "**What** would happen to my sales **if** I were to raise my selling price by 10p an item?". Here you are simply altering one variable, and it is therefore this one variable that has caused the effect. If you ask, however, "**What** would happen to my sales **if** I were to raise my selling price by 10p **and** reduce my advertising budget by 5 per cent?". You would not be sure which of the factors was dominant in the results.

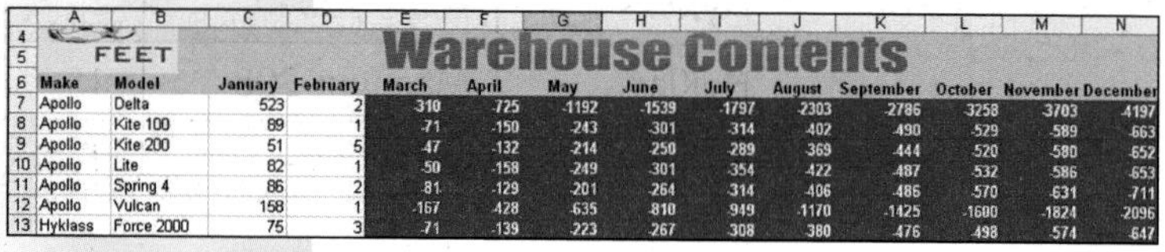

Figure 3.5.2

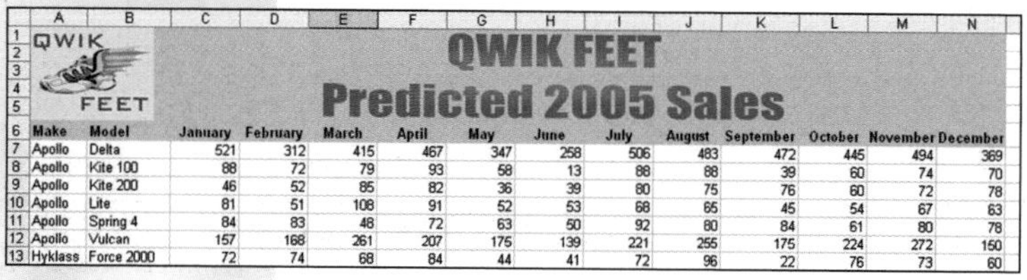

Figure 3.5.3

Different models need different strategies and unfortunately there are no hard and fast rules for developing strategies. You must, however, be clear about what you want to find out and also what the result of each interrogation will mean.

Going back to our warehouse model, it is probably logical to look at January first, then move on to February, March and so on. But even now we must be sure what our model is showing us. Look at Figure 3.5.2, especially the row containing the figures for the 'Apollo Delta'. Under January it says we have 523 pairs of these trainers. What we must be aware of is that this means we have 523 pairs of these trainers at the **beginning** of the month. If we look along a column we find that in February, at the moment, we only have two pairs of trainers. Once again this is at the **beginning** of the month. Moving on to March we have −310 trainers. Obviously this is rubbish – we cannot possibly have a negative number of trainers. So what does it mean?

To answer this we have to look at the predicted February sales for the Apollo Delta in the 'Predicted 2005 sales' worksheet (see Fig. 3.5.3). In February it is predicted that we will sell 312 pairs of Apollo Delta trainers, so if we have two pairs in the warehouse and we sell 312 we do of course end up with the −310 figure. So what is it telling us? In effect, it is telling us that in February we had an opportunity to sell 310 pairs of trainers that we didn't have in the warehouse. In this situation QwikFeet would invoke the emergency ordering system which costs them a lot of money. The extra cost for 310 emergency pairs would be quite significant, so we really ought to think about ordering some. For the trainers to be there in February we have to order them in January.

If we are starting with January's order, our objective would be to make an order in January that will be delivered in February and cause the figures at the beginning of March to be positive. In the case of the Apollo Delta, the colour of cell E7 would then turn from red to white.

ACTIVITY 2 Using the model ◀

Enter values in Column C of the 'Data capture' form, which will make the whole of the March column in the 'Warehouse contents' worksheet positive. Keep experimenting until you are sure these values are as small as possible.

Our values are in the table on the right.

Calculating the number we need to order is actually quite easy when you consider that each batch ordered is 100 pairs. If the number left in March is −310, we would need 400 to make this positive, so we will need to order four batches. In this case it has given us no problems at all. Our order plus the trainers we already have in the warehouse will coincide. Let's see what happens with the February order.

ACTIVITY 3 Using the model continued ◀

Enter the smallest order figures for February that will ensure positive values for April in the 'Warehouse contents'.

The values we decided on produced the 'Warehouse contents' shown in Figure 3.5.4.

The fact that the 'Trainers in warehouse' total has turned green is significant – it means that we would overflow the warehouse. The warehouse has a capacity of 4000 yet we want to put 4387 pairs of trainers in it. Obviously we can not do this so we will have to reduce our order. However, if we reduce the order it is inevitable that we are going to get some potential emergency order situations – the trick is to make sure these are as few and far between as possible. We have to reduce the number of trainers in the warehouse by 387; as we order in batches of 100 we need to reduce the order by 400.

Apollo	Delta	4
Apollo	Kite 100	1
Apollo	Kite 200	1
Apollo	Lite	1
Apollo	Spring 4	1
Apollo	Vulcan	2
HyKlass	Force 2000	1
HyKlass	Force 2001	1
HyKlass	Force 2002	1
HyKlass	Magnum 308	1
HyKlass	SuperForce	1
Morgan	Hawk	3
Morgan	Osprey	1
Morgan	Raven	1
Morgan	Swallow	1
Spike	College	2
Spike	Contessa	1
Spike	Cussion 20	1
Spike	Cussion 30	3
Spike	Cussion 40	3

ACTIVITY 4 Interrogate the model ◀

Can you think of a strategy for interrogating our model to find out how to reduce the February order by 400, whilst also ensuring that potential emergency order situations are kept to a minimum?

Discuss this with your fellow students and write out what the final strategy would be.

Figure 3.5.4

Make	Model	January	February	March	April	May	June	July	August	September	October	November	December
Apollo	Delta	523	402	490	75	392	-739	-997	-1503	-1886	-2458	-2903	-3397
Apollo	Kite 100	89	101	129	50	-43	-101	-114	-202	-290	-329	-389	-463
Apollo	Kite 200	51	105	153	68	-14	-50	-89	-169	-244	-320	-380	-452
Apollo	Lite	82	101	150	42	-49	-101	-154	-222	-287	-332	-386	-453
Apollo	Spring 4	86	102	119	71	1	-64	-114	-206	-286	-370	-431	-511
Apollo	Vulcan	158	201	333	72	-135	-310	-449	-670	-925	-1100	-1324	-1596
Hyklass	Force 2000	75	103	129	61	-23	-67	-108	-180	-276	-298	-374	-447
Hyklass	Force 2001	74	102	105	23	-66	-125	-179	-261	-343	-412	-477	-552
Hyklass	Force 2002	56	101	155	69	-8	-62	-115	-196	-277	-331	-411	-494
Hyklass	Magnum 308	79	102	147	62	-4	-61	-102	-203	-314	-368	-428	-499
HyKlass	SuperForce	70	102	154	65	8	-42	-98	-174	-256	-306	-355	-433
Morgan	Hawk	360	303	471	77	-350	-633	-838	-1309	-1710	-2070	-2410	-2782
Morgan	Osprey	81	101	163	98	21	-42	-66	-141	-235	-335	-394	-486
Morgan	Raven	102	106	165	91	24	-19	-81	-153	-239	-280	-341	-388
Morgan	Swallow	61	102	140	39	-22	-57	-126	-207	-303	-370	-437	-492
Spike	College	161	208	190	40	-105	-222	-317	-486	-673	-873	-973	-1117
Spike	Contessa	70	106	141	67	1	-64	-107	-204	-289	-343	-394	-421
Spike	Cussion 20	77	104	149	76	6	-20	-86	-165	-226	-394	-374	-421
Spike	Cussion 30	320	302	378	61	-222	-457	-636	-1025	-1342	-1581	-1909	-2241
Spike	Cussion 40	433	303	526	53	-416	-821	-1143	-1684	-2196	-2594	-3012	-3438
Trainers in Warehouse		3008	3157	4387	1260	-1790	-4057	-5919	-9360	-12696	-15332	-18102	-21124

The strategy we came up with was as follows. We reduced the order for each trainer by one batch. This would give us Figure 3.5.5 which shows a complete set of red figures for April. These red figures show the number of potential emergency order situations for each trainer in March, if 100 pairs less were ordered in February. All we have to do is look for the four numbers with the smallest magnitude. The order for these trainers will remain as they are, and we will restore all the other orders to what they were before (one more batch). This should ensure the minimum number of potential emergency ordering situations.

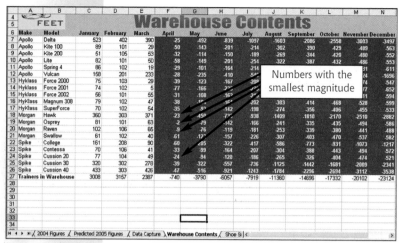

Figure 3.5.5

Make	Model	January	February	March	April	May	June	July	August	September	October	November	December
Apollo	Delta	523	402	490	75	-392	-739	-997	-1503	-1986	2458	-2903	-3397
Apollo	Kite 100	89	101	129	50	-43	-101	-114	-202	-290	-329	-389	-463
Apollo	Kite 200	51	105	153	68	-14	-50	-89	-169	-244	-320	-380	-452
Apollo	Lite	82	101	150	42	-49	-101	-154	-222	-287	-332	-386	-453
Apollo	Spring 4	86	102	119	71	-1	-64	-114	-206	-286	-370	-431	-511
Apollo	Vulcan	158	201	333	72	-135	-310	-449	-670	-925	-1100	-1324	-1596
Hyklass	Force 2000	75	103	129	61	-23	-67	-108	-180	-276	-298	-374	-447
Hyklass	Force 2001	74	102	105	23	-66	-125	-179	-261	-343	-412	-477	-552
Hyklass	Force 2002	56	101	155	69	-8	-62	-115	-196	-277	-331	-411	-494
Hyklass	Magnum 308	79	102	147	62	-4	-61	-102	-203	-314	-368	-428	-499
Hyklass	SuperForce	70	102	154	65	8	-42	-98	-174	-256	-306	-355	-433
Morgan	Hawk	360	303	371	-23	-450	-733	-938	-1409	-1810	-2170	-2510	-2882
Morgan	Osprey	81	101	63	-2	-79	-142	-166	-241	-335	-435	-494	-586
Morgan	Raven	102	106	65	-9	-76	-119	-181	-253	-339	-380	-441	-488
Morgan	Swallow	61	102	140	39	-22	-57	-126	-207	-303	-370	-437	-482
Spike	College	161	208	190	40	-105	-222	-317	-486	-673	-831	-973	-1117
Spike	Contessa	70	106	141	67	1	-64	-107	-204	-288	-343	-394	-472
Spike	Cussion 20	77	104	49	-24	-94	-120	-186	-265	-326	-404	-474	-521
Spike	Cussion 30	320	302	378	61	-222	-457	-636	-1025	-1342	-1581	-1909	-2241
Spike	Cussion 40	433	303	526	53	-416	-821	-1143	-1684	-2196	-2594	-3012	-3438
Trainers in Warehouse		3008	3157	3987	860	-2190	-4457	-6319	-9760	-13096	-15732	-18502	-21524

Figure 3.5.6

Our final February order values were as follows:

Apollo	Delta	4
Apollo	Kite 100	1
Apollo	Kite 200	1
Apollo	Lite	1
Apollo	Spring 4	1
Apollo	Vulcan	3
HyKlass	Force 2000	1
HyKlass	Force 2001	1
HyKlass	Force 2002	1
HyKlass	Magnum 308	1
HyKlass	SuperForce	1
Morgan	Hawk	3
Morgan	Osprey	0
Morgan	Raven	0
Morgan	Swallow	1
Spike	College	1
Spike	Contessa	1
Spike	Cussion 20	0
Spike	Cussion 30	3
Spike	Cussion 40	5

You may be wondering why we have used the word 'potential' when referring to the emergency ordering situation. If you think about it, the first orders in any month will almost certainly be filled, as the stock will be there – it is only the later orders that will be a problem. If we run out within seven days of the end of the month then there would be no point in invoking an emergency order as the new order will arrive just as quickly, and any delay for our customers would be minimal.

The 'Warehouse contents' worksheet now looks something like Figure 3.5.6. Interestingly, the May values for the HyKlass Superforce and the Spike Contessa are positive, which means we do not have to order any in March.

ACTIVITY 5 Minimise potential emergency ordering

Use the model to create an order for March which minimises potential emergency ordering situations in April. Remember that you don't have to order either the HyKlass Superforce or the Spike Contessa.

In doing Activity 5 did you notice a weakness in our model? When we entered the figures for March the red values indicating the potential emergency ordering situations for February disappeared. We now have no record of the number of these situations. This is because the indication of these was at the beginning of the next month and our new order is added at the beginning of that month. More on this later; in the meantime we can continue with our strategy.

ACTIVITY 6 Create orders ◀

Complete your model by creating orders for April to October.

Figure 3.5.7 shows the orders up to October, but it is a little difficult to know where to go from here, as we have found another weakness with our model.

ACTIVITY 7 Order predicting problems ◀

Discuss the problems involved in predicting orders for November and December. Does the model show us what we need to know in order to predict these orders? If not, what else do we need?

Make	Model	January	February	March	April	May	June	July	August	September	October	November	December
Apollo	Delta	4	4	4	4	2	5	5	5	5	4	0	0
Apollo	Kite 100	1	1	1	1	0	0	1	1	1	0	0	0
Apollo	Kite 200	1	1	1	0	0	1	1	1	0	1	0	0
Apollo	Lite	1	1	1	1	0	1	0	1	0	1	0	0
Apollo	Spring 4	1	1	0	1	1	0	1	1	1	1	0	0
Apollo	Vulcan	2	3	2	2	1	2	3	1	3	2	0	0
Hyklass	Force 2000	1	1	1	0	1	0	1	0	1	1	0	0
Hyklass	Force 2001	1	1	1	1	0	1	1	1	1	0	0	0
Hyklass	Force 2002	1	1	1	0	1	0	1	1	1	0	0	0
Hyklass	Magnum 308	1	1	0	1	1	0	1	1	1	0	0	0
Hyklass	SuperForce	1	1	0	1	0	1	1	1	0	1	0	0
Morgan	Hawk	3	3	5	3	2	5	3	4	4	3	0	0
Morgan	Osprey	1	0	1	1	0	1	1	1	0	1	0	0
Morgan	Raven	1	0	1	1	0	1	0	1	0	1	0	0
Morgan	Swallow	1	1	2	0	1	0	1	2	1	2	0	0
Spike	College	2	1	2	1	1	0	1	2	1	0	0	0
Spike	Contessa	1	1	0	1	1	0	1	1	1	0	1	0
Spike	Cussion 20	1	0	1	1	0	1	1	1	0	1	0	0
Spike	Cussion 30	3	3	3	2	2	4	3	2	4	3	0	0
Spike	Cussion 40	3	5	5	4	3	5	5	4	5	4	0	0

Figure 3.5.7

Refining the model

It is worthwhile just quickly recapping what, ideally, Dean Rabette wants the model to do. Firstly, he wants it to help him decide what to order each month. We are on our way to achieving this, but really we want a year's figures so as to give our suppliers a good idea of what we want, thereby putting ourselves in a position to claim the 10 per cent discount. We have made some progress but in our initial investigations we have found a few problems with our model which we are about to look into.

1 If an order is filled by the emergency ordering system the model still acts as if a set of trainers have been taken from the warehouse.

2 Once the next month's order has been put in, there is no way of identifying the number of potential emergency order situations.

3 The figures we use to help us decide our monthly order are two months ahead, so we cannot tell what to order from November onwards.

Before we start you will need to make a copy of your model as it is at the moment, since we are going to make some changes to it, including deleting all the values we have just put in.

Taking into account emergency ordered items

At the moment our model can show negative figures for the number of pairs of trainers in the warehouse, but this is obviously nonsense. In addition, these impossible values will have an effect on the total number of trainers in the warehouse. To see what we mean, look at the warehouse contents worksheet. If you look at the value for February you can see that the total is actually well within our limit of 4000. However, if you count up the number of real trainer pairs in the warehouse, it comes to 4900. This value is compensated for by the negative values. Clearly this is a situation we cannot afford to have in our model, as it may invalidate our answers.

As we were making our way through the orders using our model, we identified – at the end of each month – a number of orders that would potentially have to be ordered by the emergency ordering system. We also know that it was possible we may not have actually put in these orders, if we were close enough to the end of the month. We now need to change our mind a little on this and assume that they are all dealt with by emergency orders. In this way the smallest number of a particular type of trainer we can have in our warehouse is zero (0). We must change our model to reflect this.

The first thing we need to do is to initialise our spreadsheet so that we can start to work on it.

ACTIVITY 8 Refine the model ◀

1 Reset all the order values on the 'Data capture' worksheet to zero.
2 Reset the initial January values of the 'Warehouse content' worksheet to zero.
3 Turn off the protection on the 'Warehouse content' worksheet.

Now we need to look at the formulae in the 'Warehouse content' spreadsheet. Let us start by looking at the contents of cell D7, currently it contains the following formula:

=C7-'Predicted 2005 figures'!C7+('Data capture'!C7*100)

We only want it to store this value if it is over zero, otherwise we want it to contain zero. I am going to use a simple 'if' function to do this.

If you have never used an 'if' function before the format is as follows:

=if(*condition, value if condition is true, value if condition is false*)

The condition we wish to test is whether C7-'Predicted 2005 figures'!C7+('Data capture'!C7*100) is greater than zero. If the condition is true then we want the cell to contain the value C7-'Predicted 2005 figures'!C7+('Data capture'!C7*100). If the condition is not true we want the cell to contain zero.

The formula therefore should look like this:

=if(C7-'Predicted 2005 figures'!C7+('Data capture'!C7*100)>0,C7-'Predicted 2005 figures'!C7+('Data capture'!C7*100),0)

ACTIVITY 9 Further refinements ◀

1 Enter the formula into cell D7 and replicate it to all the other February 'Warehouse content cells'. Replicate the February cells to March, April, and May, etc.
2 Re-enter the original January values.

Our problem now is that we have no way of telling how much to order in January, as the value for March will be zero until we order enough in January to make it positive. Before we made the change we could tell how big the order had to be by the size of the negative value in March. It will also be difficult to decide how to change the order when the normal order would overfill the warehouse, as our strategy used the magnitude of the negative values. If we create a worksheet that holds the values at the end of the month we can kill two birds with one stone – not only solving this problem, but also using it to calculate the total number of potential emergency order situations. In fact we can make it a lot easier for ourselves if we were to store not the number of pairs of trainers in the warehouse at the end of the month, but the number of potential emergency order situations we would have under these conditions.

What we need is a new worksheet.

ACTIVITY 10 Create the potential emergency orders worksheet ◀

1 Create a new worksheet called 'Potential emergency orders', and position it after the 'Warehouse contents' worksheet.
2 Enter the normal headings and the make and models of the trainers as shown in Figure 3.5.8.

As we are calculating values at the end of the month we need to start in January, so our first formula will be in Cell C7 of our new sheet. To calculate the number of trainers in the warehouse at the end of the month, we simply take the number we predict we will sell from the number in the warehouse at the beginning of the month. As we want to display the number of potential emergency orders we need to negate it, or conversely, take the number of trainers in the warehouse at the beginning of the month from the prediction of the number of trainers sold. Once again we only really need to see the value if it is greater than zero so we need to create another 'if' statement.

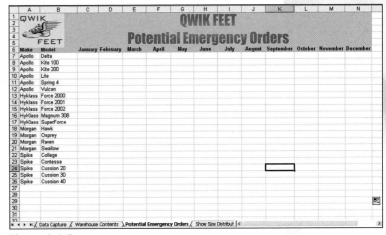

Figure 3.5.8

=IF('Predicted 2005 figures'!C7-'Warehouse contents'!C7>0,'Predicted 2005 figures'!C7-'Warehouse contents'!C7,0)

ACTIVITY 11 Display potential emergency orders

Enter the formula into Cell C7 of the new worksheet and replicate it across all trainers and all months.

The other thing we need to be aware of is that we will need to decide upon what to order in December, so we will need an extra column in the new worksheet to show the values for next January. This of course gives us a little bit of a problem – since we do not have predicted values of sales for January. So we will need a new column in our 'Predicted 2005 figures' worksheet. Although the formula in this would be similar to those in the others, instead of using the '2003 figures' and the '2004 figures' to find the 'Predicted 2005 figures', we will use the '2004 figures' and the 'Predicted 2005 figures' to predict what, in effect, the 2006 figures are.

The formula we used to calculate January's (2005) sales for the Apollo Delta was as follows:

    =2*'2004 figures'!C7-'2003 figures'!C7

The one we will need for 2006 therefore is:

    =3*'2004 figures'!C7-2*'2003 figures'!C7

A bit of maths ...

A little bit of mathematics is unavoidable in spreadsheets and the particular brand of mathematics we use is algebra. To some people algebra is a breeze whilst to others it is a complete mystery. Love it or hate it, the only way to explain how the above formula was derived is to resort to algebra. Let's look back at what we know.

When working out the 2005 January figures for the Apollo Delta we simply assumed that the increase for 2005 would be the same as for 2004. The increase in sales for 2004 is the difference between the 2004 figures and the 2003 figures. In spreadsheet terms that is:

    ='2004 figures'!C7-'2003 figures'!C7

To calculate the 2005 figures we therefore need to add this difference to the 2004 figures.

    ='2004 figures'!C7-'2003 figures'!C7+'2004 figures'!C7

Reducing this we get:

    =2*'2004 figures'!C7-'2003 figures'!C7
    which is the formula we have put in 'Predicted 2005 figures'!C7.

Extending this, it stands to reason that if the difference is the same for 2006, the 2006 figures would be the difference plus the 2005 figures:

    ='2004 figures'!C7-'2003 figures'!C7+'Predicted 2005 figures'!C7

We must of course remember that the 'Predicted 2005 figures' are themselves calculated and are:

=2*'2004 figures'!C7-'2003 figures'!C7

So substituting this value for the 2005 figures we get:

='2004 figures'!C7-'2003 figures'!C7+2*'2004 figures'!C7-'2003 Figures'!C7

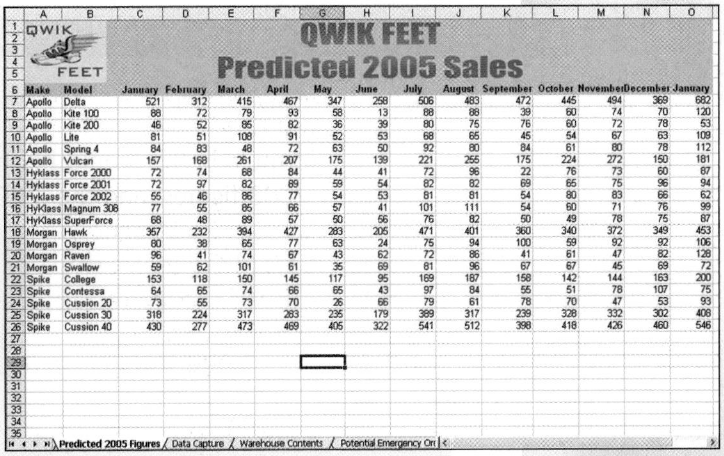

which reduces to:

=3*'2004 figures'!C7-2*'2003 figures'!C7

ACTIVITY 12 Predict values for January 2006

1 Unprotect the 'Predicted 2005 figures' worksheet.
2 Create a new column headed January.
3 Enter the above formula in the Apollo Delta row.
4 Replicate it down for all trainers (see Fig. 3.5.9).
5 Re-protect the 'Predicted 2005 figures' worksheet.

QWIK FEET
Predicted 2005 Sales

Make	Model	January	February	March	April	May	June	July	August	September	October	November	December	January
Apollo	Delta	521	312	415	467	347	258	506	483	472	445	494	369	682
Apollo	Kite 100	88	72	79	93	58	13	88	88	39	60	74	70	120
Apollo	Kite 200	46	52	85	82	36	39	80	75	76	60	72	78	53
Apollo	Lite	81	51	108	91	52	53	68	65	45	54	67	63	109
Apollo	Spring 4	84	83	48	72	63	50	92	80	84	61	80	78	112
Apollo	Vulcan	157	168	261	207	175	139	221	255	175	224	272	150	181
Hyklass	Force 2000	72	74	68	84	44	41	72	96	22	76	73	60	87
Hyklass	Force 2001	72	97	82	89	59	54	82	82	69	65	75	96	94
Hyklass	Force 2002	55	46	86	77	54	53	81	81	54	80	83	66	62
HyKlass	Magnum 308	77	55	85	66	57	41	101	111	54	60	71	76	99
HyKlass	SuperForce	68	48	89	57	50	56	76	82	50	49	78	75	87
Morgan	Hawk	357	232	394	427	283	205	471	401	360	340	372	349	453
Morgan	Osprey	80	38	65	77	63	24	75	94	100	59	92	92	106
Morgan	Raven	96	41	74	67	43	62	72	86	41	61	47	82	128
Morgan	Swallow	59	62	101	61	35	69	81	96	67	67	45	69	72
Spike	College	153	118	150	145	117	95	169	187	158	142	144	163	200
Spike	Contessa	64	65	74	66	65	43	97	84	55	51	78	107	75
Spike	Cussion 20	73	55	73	70	26	66	79	61	78	70	47	53	93
Spike	Cussion 30	318	224	317	283	235	179	389	317	239	328	332	302	408
Spike	Cussion 40	430	277	473	469	405	322	541	512	398	418	426	460	546

Predicted 2005 Figures / Data Capture / Warehouse Contents / Potential Emergency Orc

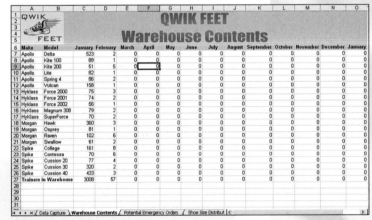

Figure 3.5.9

Because the new worksheet needs the contents of the warehouse at the beginning of January we will have to have a January column in our 'Warehouse contents' worksheet. However, the formulae of these columns is going to be of the same form as the rest of the worksheet, as is the new column of our new 'Potential emergency orders' worksheet, so we can simply replicate the formulae across.

QWIK FEET
Warehouse Contents

Make	Model	January	February	March	April	May	June	July	August	September	October	November	December	January
Apollo	Delta	523	2	0	0	0	0	0	0	0	0	0	0	0
Apollo	Kite 100	89	1	0	0	0	0	0	0	0	0	0	0	0
Apollo	Kite 200	51	5	0	0	0	0	0	0	0	0	0	0	0
Apollo	Lite	82	1	0	0	0	0	0	0	0	0	0	0	0
Apollo	Spring 4	86	2	0	0	0	0	0	0	0	0	0	0	0
Apollo	Vulcan	158	1	0	0	0	0	0	0	0	0	0	0	0
Hyklass	Force 2000	75	3	0	0	0	0	0	0	0	0	0	0	0
Hyklass	Force 2001	74	2	0	0	0	0	0	0	0	0	0	0	0
Hyklass	Force 2002	56	1	0	0	0	0	0	0	0	0	0	0	0
HyKlass	Magnum 308	79	2	0	0	0	0	0	0	0	0	0	0	0
HyKlass	SuperForce	70	2	0	0	0	0	0	0	0	0	0	0	0
Morgan	Hawk	360	3	0	0	0	0	0	0	0	0	0	0	0
Morgan	Osprey	81	1	0	0	0	0	0	0	0	0	0	0	0
Morgan	Raven	102	6	0	0	0	0	0	0	0	0	0	0	0
Morgan	Swallow	61	2	0	0	0	0	0	0	0	0	0	0	0
Spike	College	161	8	0	0	0	0	0	0	0	0	0	0	0
Spike	Contessa	70	6	0	0	0	0	0	0	0	0	0	0	0
Spike	Cussion 20	77	4	0	0	0	0	0	0	0	0	0	0	0
Spike	Cussion 30	320	2	0	0	0	0	0	0	0	0	0	0	0
Spike	Cussion 40	433	3	0	0	0	0	0	0	0	0	0	0	0
Trainers in Warehouse		3008	57	0	0	0	0	0	0	0	0	0	0	0

Data Capture / Warehouse Contents / Potential Emergency Orders / Shoe Size Distribut

Figure 3.5.10

ACTIVITY 13 Complete the warehouse contents worksheet

1 Create a January column for the 'Warehouse contents' worksheet and replicate the formulae from the 'December' column (see Fig. 3.5.10).
2 Create a January column for the 'Potential emergency orders' worksheet and replicate the formulae from the 'December' column.
3 Set 'Conditional formatting' on the 'Potential emergency orders' worksheet to change the background to red if the value of the cell is greater than zero (see Fig. 3.5.11).
4 Re-protect the 'Warehouse contents' worksheet – you will have to unlock the cells in the first January column again so that you can enter initial values.

QWIK FEET
Potential Emergency Orders

Make	Model	January	February	March	April	May	June	July	August	September	October	November	December	January
Apollo	Delta	0	310	415	467	347	258	506	483	472	445	494	369	682
Apollo	Kite 100	0	71	79	93	58	13	88	88	39	60	74	70	120
Apollo	Kite 200	0	47	85	82	36	39	80	75	76	60	72	78	53
Apollo	Lite	0	50	108	91	52	53	68	65	45	54	67	63	109
Apollo	Spring 4	0	81	48	72	63	50	92	80	84	61	80	78	112
Apollo	Vulcan	0	167	261	207	175	139	221	255	175	224	272	150	181
Hyklass	Force 2000	0	71	83	84	44	41	72	96	22	76	73	60	87
Hyklass	Force 2001	0	96	82	89	59	54	82	82	69	65	75	96	94
Hyklass	Force 2002	0	45	86	77	54	53	81	81	54	80	83	66	62
HyKlass	Magnum 308	0	65	85	66	57	41	101	111	54	60	71	76	99
HyKlass	SuperForce	0	48	89	57	50	56	76	82	50	49	78	75	87
Morgan	Hawk	0	229	394	427	283	205	471	401	360	340	372	349	453
Morgan	Osprey	0	37	65	77	63	24	75	94	100	59	92	92	106
Morgan	Raven	0	36	74	67	43	62	72	86	41	61	47	82	128
Morgan	Swallow	0	60	101	61	35	69	81	96	67	67	45	69	72
Spike	College	0	110	150	145	117	95	169	187	158	142	144	163	200
Spike	Contessa	0	59	74	66	65	43	97	84	55	51	78	107	75
Spike	Cussion 20	0	61	73	70	26	66	79	61	78	70	47	53	93
Spike	Cussion 30	0	222	317	283	235	179	389	317	239	328	332	302	408
Spike	Cussion 40	0	274	473	469	405	322	541	512	398	418	426	460	546

Data Capture / Warehouse Contents / Potential Emergency Orders / Shoe Size Distribut

Figure 3.5.11

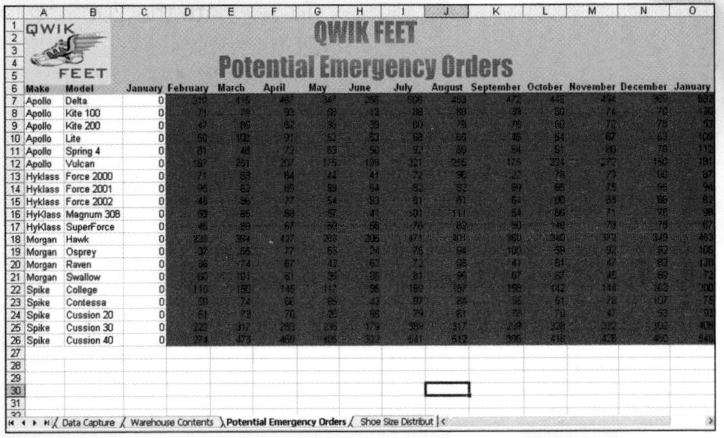

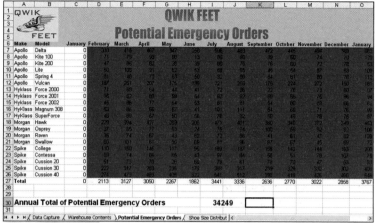

Figure 3.5.12

Before we start to use our refined spreadsheet there are a few other little formulae we need to put in our new worksheet. Firstly, we need to add up all the potential emergency orders for each month. This is not a difficult operation, we simply need a sum function at the bottom of each column. The second change is equally easy – we have to total the number of potential emergency orders for the year. It is worth noting, however, that the annual total does not include the January 2006 values.

ACTIVITY 14 Final refinements

1 Enter formulae to calculate monthly totals of potential emergency orders.
2 Enter a formula to calculate the annual total of potential emergency orders (see Fig. 3.5.12).
3 Protect the 'Potential emergency orders' spreadsheet.

We can now use this refined model to investigate the situation of Dean Rabette. We can use the same strategies as we used before but the technique will be slightly different. We can no longer look two months ahead in the 'Warehouse contents' worksheet as these values are now normally zero. We also cannot use the same technique to decide which option is likely to produce the least potential emergency order situations. The new technique is as follows:

1 Enter the number of trainers in the warehouse for January (these are the same as last time and are entered straight into the 'Warehouse contents' for each trainer type.
2 Start with January (2005).
3 For each trainer check the potential emergency orders for the next month. If the value is zero no trainers need to be ordered.
4 If the value is not zero then enter the smallest number into the corresponding cell on the 'Data capture' worksheet that will change the potential emergency orders to zero.
5 When all trainers have been checked look at the total trainers in the warehouse for that month. If the value of this total is less than 4000 the order is good.
6 If the total is more than 4000, reduce the order by one batch of those trainers that will cause the lowest number of emergency orders. Repeat this until the total in the warehouse is less than or equal to 4000.
7 Move on to the next month.

ACTIVITY 15 Using the refined model

Using the new refined model create an ordering strategy for the year 2005.

Conclusion ▶ ▶ ▶

There are only a few differences between the results we got with our unrefined model and the new refined model, but these could yet have been important. The results show that, on a few occasions, a batch of trainers does not need to be ordered until a month later. Our model has succeeded in giving Dean an idea of his orders for the whole of the year. What is interesting, however, is that the predicted potential emergency orders for January 2006 is greater than the whole of 2005. This seems to indicate that maybe the size of the warehouse will become critical in 2006. Maybe this is an area we can investigate?

Figure 3.5.13 "Hey Deano – Where do you want these trainers then?"

Presenting your results

Introduction

Figure 3.6.1 Example of a presentation

In the previous chapters you have created a model for Dean Rabette which was designed to help him do his own job. He has complete control over the operation so he does not need to persuade anyone to do as he suggests. This is not normally the case, though – normally you will have to present your findings to someone and you may even have to persuade him or her to follow your suggested actions. This will often be your management, or it may even be potential customers for whatever product you are supporting.

Part of the examination will require you to present your findings, which is probably your most important consideration at the moment. You are likely to have two options:

- you may be required to present your findings in a presentation, or
- you may be asked for a report.

In the real world, there is an outside chance you may be asked to present your findings in a newsletter or a leaflet, for instance if you are reporting to a nature conservation group on the effect urbanisation is having on the population of the badger. But more often than not, you will probably be required to do both a report and a presentation. The reason for this is that you can put more detail in the report, but your management will want the salient facts pointed out to them directly. In the case of the examination, it would be unlikely that you would be required to do both. Whichever medium is required of you, there will be marks allocated relevant to that medium. For instance, in a presentation you may get marks for a consistent background or the use of slide transitions. In a report you may get some marks for a table of contents or a consistent style. The majority of marks will be for the content, of course. This means that if the examination asks for a presentation and you produce a report you will probably only lose a few marks.

What is certain is that it is difficult to include the detail required for this section in the slides of a presentation alone. You will hear a lot about fitness-for-purpose in this chapter and a set of slides with too much detail may well be considered not fit-for-purpose. Remember that when you give a presentation the slides you produce are there to accompany and enforce what you say. If you are asked for a presentation you will be expected to produce detailed notes about what would be said while these slides were showing. It is in these notes that you will be able to provide the depth of analysis required.

A report, on the other hand, is not just for reading – it is also to be referred to as well. It is therefore important that the important points are easily found: so the use of headings, tables of contents and indexes is encouraged.

Awareness of audience and fitness for purpose

In both cases mentioned above, the examination board will be looking for evidence of:

- awareness of audience, and
- fitness for purpose.

We will now look at what each of these means, and consequently how they are judged, before we move on to discuss the contents of the report or presentation.

▶ Awareness of audience

The idea behind awareness of audience is that the report or presentation is suitable for the people it intends to inform. This is obviously a fairly subjective concept, as what one person considers suitable may differ from what another person considers suitable. What aspects of a report or a presentation are 'audience sensitive', for example? To give you an idea, do the following activity.

ACTIVITY 1 Study differences in presentation

The BBC's website caters for a wide range of people. At the time of writing there were areas on business, entertainment, sport, gardening and a children's area, amongst many others. Each of these areas has significantly different presentational styles depending on the 'type' of people it is aimed at. Possibly the biggest contrast is between the business section (see Fig. 3.6.2) and the children's section (see Fig. 3.6.3). Study these two areas and make a list of things that are different. For each difference, describe with the use of an example how they are slanted towards their particular audience.

You may like to repeat the exercise where the differences are more subtle, say, between the Radio 4 and the Radio 1 areas.

Figure 3.6.2 Business section of the BBC website

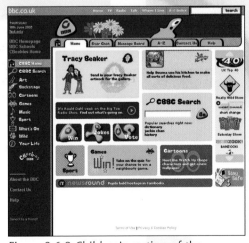

Figure 3.6.3 Children's section of the BBC website

In the first part of the activity you may have identified the following.

Language

The language in the children's section is on the whole simpler, using common words. The general feel is that the site is talking to someone it knows, with whom it is on first-name terms. There is a tendency to use modern idiomatic words.

The language in the business area is more formal and many more technical terms are used. It is as if it is talking to someone it has met for the first time, and is therefore treated as an acquaintance rather than a friend.

Font and size

The font in the business section is traditional, even ordinary, and the same font is consistent throughout the area. The font size only varies for headings and headlines and although coloured letters are used they are few and far between, and are coloured simply (e.g. red or blue) for emphasis.

In the children's section a wide variety of visual devices are used. The fonts vary and although traditional ones are used in places, there are all sorts of other exciting fonts on display. The sizes vary, too, as do the colours, and there is a more exciting use of shades and backgrounds.

Pictures and layouts

Pictures in the business section tend to be either photographs or charts, and are mainly static. They are relevant to the topic being discussed and often have a caption. Apart from the pictures and the occasional heading, the page is made up of a white background with black writing.

The children's area makes much greater use of colour, sometimes showing many different background colours on the same page. There is very little plain white background. Although there are a number of photographs there are a lot of cartoons and also a number of animations.

▶ Fitness for purpose

It is clear from the evidence above that each area of the BBC website is definitely aimed at a distinct type of person. The difference between the children's section and the business section is quite marked, but there are major differences also between the business section and the sports section, for example. This is interesting as there are a number of individuals who would fall into both groups. When thinking about the audience you not only have to consider the individuals you also have to consider the context within which you are working.

This latter point is an example of fitness for purpose. Imagine the case of Richard Sharpe a successful City financial consultant and Arsenal supporter. In his role as a financial consultant he wears a sober three-piece pin-striped suit, Italian made black shoes, carries a leather briefcase and accesses the business pages of the BBC website. He talks about stocks and bonds and limited liability options and probably has business lunches at Langan's restaurant. As an Arsenal supporter, however, he wears a replica football shirt with the number 10 on the back, denim jeans and a red woolly hat. He talks about Thierry Henry and the off-side trap, and lunches on a pint of beer and a meat pie of questionable origin. Richard Sharpe the Arsenal supporter accesses the sports pages of the BBC website. The contents, layout and presentation of a report on the performance of a particular share portfolio will be different to the Arsenal – Spurs match report as the two documents have different purposes. Although they both inform, the report is to help Richard make decisions whereas a big objective of the match report is to entertain. Depending on which of Richard's personas is active he will have different expectations of the documents. The portfolio report should be presented in such a way that Richard should have confidence in the information contained. Too much colour or a fancy font would make the report seem

Figures 3.6.4 Richard Sharpe – Arsenal supporter

Figure 3.6.5 Richard Sharpe – City financial consultant

frivolous and flowery language would seem out of place. The purpose of the match report, however, is to entertain and in this situation Richard would be disappointed if the report did not contain the occasional eulogy over the way "Henry gracefully slid past the lunging tackles of the Spurs central defenders and calmly lifted the ball over the despairing dive of the goalkeeper".

It is important, when you make a presentation, that you think not only about who your audience are but also about why they are there.

This unit is about using information and communication technology (ICT) to help with the decision making process within the *business* environment. Largely, therefore, we are looking at a fairly specific audience and context: presenting an idea to a group of business managers. The object of the exercise will be to persuade them to go along with whatever idea you are presenting. To do that, you have to persuade them that you know what you are talking about, that you have good ideas, and that you have the ability to carry them through. In other words, you need them to take you seriously. In a situation like this you are presenting yourself, as much as your ideas. Your presentation or report must show that you are professional, thorough, knowledgeable, responsible and innovative.

Every situation is different but there follows a few suggestions which as a bottom line are worth following. For example, it is possible to use humour in these situations but it is always a risk and you have to be sure of your ground. The following are guidelines rather than rules; one of the real skills of presentation is knowing if, when, and how to break these rules.

▶ Presentations

The first point to understand about presentations is that you do not necessarily have to use presentation software. These days one would probably expect the use of a computer and a projector, but there may be occasions when these are not available, in which case there is nothing wrong with using an overhead projector and acetate sheets. However, we will most likely be in a situation where we are viewed as knowledgeable in ICT and as such a reluctance to use a computer might be viewed suspiciously. Nonetheless, there have been effective presentations created using word processors and desk-top publishers, not to mention multimedia and web-design software.

Whatever you use you need to keep it simple. Don't overfill your slides; make sure they are easy to read and are relevant to what you want to say. Your chat should expand on the slides, rather than the other way round.

Style

There are a number of applications designed specifically for presentations and if you have one available it would seem a pity not to use it. The modern versions of these powerful programmes can do some amazing things, but it is very easy to overuse them. Let us look at a few of the common features and decide how best to use each.

Background and foreground

Most presentation applications provide a number of background features. Probably the simplest is the plain background colour. You can pick a single colour for your slide; alternatively, you can choose a pattern or a texture (see Fig. 3.6.6); you can insert a picture; you can use some pre-set themes. Your company may even have its own pre-set theme – if it hasn't, you could decide to make one (see Fig. 3.6.7). The demonstration shows how to do this.

You need to use a clear colour for your writing so that your audience can read it. The more complicated your background is, the more difficult it will be to find a colour for your font that will contrast with the background. Plain backgrounds or ones with few colours are best; meanwhile, the font should be simple and large enough for your audience to read it. Most people prefer to look at dark writing on a light background, though an alternative is to use the opposite – light writing on a dark background. Note also that bright colours are difficult to look at for any length of time. Probably the most impressive background is a bespoke company template; most companies have one, but if one is not available they are easy enough to make.

Whatever background and font you choose to use, make sure you use these consistently throughout the presentation. Your audience will be visually lost if you change the overall theme mid-way through.

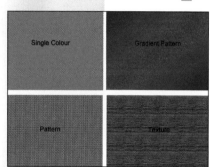

Figure 3.6.6 Examples of standard backgrounds

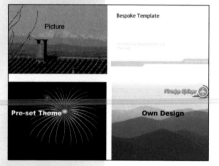

Figure 3.6.7 Examples of bespoke backgrounds

Pictures, diagrams and charts

A picture paints a thousand words, so they say, and certainly in a presentation this can be so. Charts and graphs can often communicate a situation or trend much more effectively and quickly than any number of words. In a presentation you have to limit your use of words. Lengthy descriptions in the middle of a presentation are unlikely to be read. If you want your audience to know what something will look like, use a drawing or a photograph. Don't add pictures just for the sake of it, however, especially simplistic cartoons or irrelevant clip art.

Animations and slide transitions

A lot of computerised presentation applications come with the ability to animate your objects within a slide, and have interesting options for passing from one slide to another. Both of these can add to the professionalism of your presentation.

For example, having your bullet points appear one at a time is a useful presentation technique, since it stops your audience reading ahead and consequently not listening to what you have to say on a particular point. Having each of these points slide up from the bottom or side of the screen can add another dynamic dimension to your presentation. But choose your animations carefully and don't overdo it: it can be off-putting if a presentation keeps stopping so that a slow or over-elaborate animation can be completed, for example.

Slide transitions can also be effective and add to your presentations but again, simple is best – your presentation needs to flow and your audience will not want to wait too long for the next slide to appear.

Automatic transitions and animations

Note that there is often a facility to set the slide transitions and the appearance of your objects on a timer. In a normal presentation this should be avoided because you need to keep control of the presentation and adjust the speed to the needs of your audience. However, this facility could be useful if you want to put a presentation onto a CD or floppy disk, for your audience to view without you being there. You can even add voice recordings to these.

Word-processed reports

If you are asked to present your findings in a report it will be expected that the report be word-processed. There are probably not as many ways to go wrong with a report as there is with a presentation, simply because you do not have as many options. As with the presentation though, simplest is usually best.

Choice of font

On modern computers we have a very large range of fonts to choose from, some of them quite exotic. When choosing a font it should be appropriate for its purpose. Generally, this means that it shouldn't be too fancy, since its main purpose is to be very readable. Some companies even have a preferred 'house' font and if this is the case with your organisation, you should probably use it.

'Sans serif' fonts such as Helvetica or Arial are popular these days for their simplicity and modernity. (A serif is a small line added to the basic form of a letter, as a form of embellishment. Sans serif means 'without serif' or 'without embellishments'.) But there is also a theory which suggests that people find the serif type fonts – such as Times New Roman, Palatino – easier to read over long periods. The little 'tails' help to distinguish between the letters, and provide very subtle guidelines for the eye as it moves across the page. Ease of reading is of course the key, and the problem with the more exotic fonts is that it is occasionally like trying to interpret someone's handwriting, it takes just that little bit more effort. You want people to read your report fully and with interest, so you need to make it as straightforward for them as possible.

Colour is also an issue, especially coloured writing. Black on white provides the best contrast and there are several practical reasons why this should be the choice for your report. Most paper found around offices is white; any other colour tends to mean printers and copiers have to be especially loaded and will also be more expensive. Most reports need to be photocopied. Not only are colour copiers rarer, it costs significantly more to copy a colour report than a black and white one. A black and white copier can also find it difficult to distinguish certain colours. Most reports will end up being copied in black and white – so, even if you present your original in colour, choose them carefully so that they can be distinguished when copied in black and white.

Pictures, tables and charts

Pictures, tables and charts are extremely important in a report for two reasons. Firstly, as mentioned earlier, a picture or chart can often display the same information as a page of writing, but can do so more instantaneously and succinctly. A picture can also break up a report and make it less imposing. If you are to persuade your audience that your report should be acted on, you need it to be read; the first page is important in deciding if a report will be read or not. Imagine you are in the position of your audience and you are faced with two reports to read. The first page of one is an unbroken sea of writing, while the first page of the second is nicely laid out with a chart, a diagram and a relevant picture. Human nature will make you look on the second report with more sympathy.

With pictures, tables and charts colour can be very powerful, especially in charts. But remember these colours may also have to be distinguished on a black and white copy made with a photocopier.

What is also important, however, is that the pictures, tables, and charts are relevant. It is likely, in this case, that the tables and charts may be taken from your model and it is worth taking a few minutes to show a couple of things you can do with a spreadsheet to help you.

ACTIVITY 2 Calculate sub-totals

It is often nice, in a list of data, to have sub-totals and grand totals. It is often these bottom line figures your audience is interested in. It is easy enough to insert a line in the relevant place and add a formula totalling up the range you wish. As shown in the demonstration, spreadsheet packages, these days, often come with a sub-totals function which does all the hard work for you.

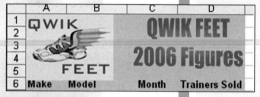

Figure 3.6.8

1 Open a spreadsheet package and rename the first worksheet '2006 figures'.
2 Create the usual QwikFeet heading with title '2006 figures' and column headings 'Make', 'Model', 'Month' and 'Trainers sold' (see Fig. 3.6.8).
3 Import the file from the ActiveBook starting at cell A7 (it is a text file, comma delimited with no headings).
4 Select rows 6 to 246.
5 Select the 'Subtotals' option from the 'Data menu'.
6 Click on 'OK' button when the window shown in Figure 3.6.9 appears to indicate that the headings are in the first line of the selection.

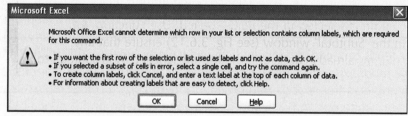

Figure 3.6.9

7 In the 'Subtotal' window (see Fig. 3.6.10) ensure that the 'Make' column is selected in the field labelled 'At each change in' **1**.
8 In the 'Subtotal' window (see Fig. 3.6.10) ensure that the 'Sum' column is selected in the field labelled 'Use function' **2**.

Continued on next page

9   In the 'Subtotal' window (see Fig. 3.6.10) ensure that any columns already checked in the list box labelled 'Add subtotal to' are unchecked and the 'Trainers sold' column is checked ❸.

10 In the 'Subtotal' window (see Fig. 3.6.10) click 'OK'.

You should find that each time the 'Make' changes an extra line has been inserted showing the total 'Trainers sold' (see Fig. 3.6.11).

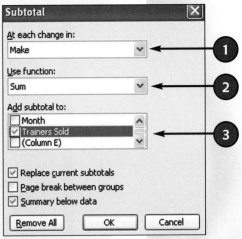
Figure 3.6.10

·	75	Apollo	Vulcan	September	239
·	76	Apollo	Vulcan	October	252
·	77	Apollo	Vulcan	November	217
·	78	Apollo	Vulcan	December	222
−	79	**Apollo Total**			12048
·	80	Hyklass	Force 2000	January	65
·	81	Hyklass	Force 2000	February	69

Figure 3.6.11

ACTIVITY 3 Create nested sub-totals

Often, such as in the case of Activity 2 there is a necessity to create sub-totals within sub-totals or nested sub-totals as they are called. For instance we may wish to know the total 2005 figures for each model of trainer as well for each make. When we create nested totals we start with the 'outside' totals; in this case the 'Make'. We have already done this so we can start from where we left off in Activity 2 (you can also watch a demonstration of this technique).

1 Open the spreadsheet created in Activity 2.
2 Select rows 6 to 251 (new extent of worksheet).
3 Select the 'Subtotals' option from the 'Data menu'.
4 Click on 'OK' button when the window shown in Figure 3.6.9 appears to indicate that the headings are in the first line of the selection.
5 In the 'Subtotal' window (see Fig. 3.6.12) ensure that the 'Model' column is selected in the field labelled 'At each change in' ❶.
6 In the 'Subtotal' window (see Fig. 3.6.12) ensure that the 'Sum' column is selected in the field labelled 'Use Function' ❷.
7 In the 'Subtotal' window (see Fig. 3.6.12) ensure that any columns already checked in the list box labelled 'Add subtotal to' are unchecked and the 'Trainers sold' column is checked ❸.
8 In the 'Subtotal' window (see Fig. 3.6.12) ensure that the 'Replace current subtotals' is unchecked ❹.
9 In the 'Subtotal' window (see Fig. 3.6.12) click 'OK'.

Subtotals have now been added for both 'Make' and 'Model' (see Fig. 3.6.13).

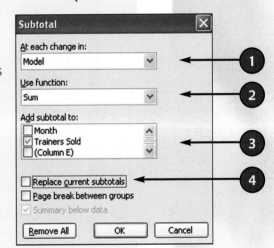
Figure 3.6.12

67	Apollo	Spring 4	September	79
68	Apollo	Spring 4	October	93
69	Apollo	Spring 4	November	84
70	Apollo	Spring 4	December	76
71		**Spring 4 Total**		926
72	Apollo	Vulcan	January	227
73	Apollo	Vulcan	February	191
74	Apollo	Vulcan	March	256
75	Apollo	Vulcan	April	238
76	Apollo	Vulcan	May	222
77	Apollo	Vulcan	June	211
78	Apollo	Vulcan	July	242
79	Apollo	Vulcan	August	244
80	Apollo	Vulcan	September	239
81	Apollo	Vulcan	October	252
82	Apollo	Vulcan	November	217
83	Apollo	Vulcan	December	222
84		**Vulcan Total**		2761
85	**Apollo Total**			12048
86	Hyklass	Force 2000	January	65
87	Hyklass	Force 2000	February	69
88	Hyklass	Force 2000	March	87

Figure 3.6.13

ACTIVITY 4 Apply a filter ◀

You've probably noticed that our datasheet is getting a touch long. If we want to see details about sales of 'Spike' trainers we have to scroll all the way down. The demonstration shows how we can make it easy for ourselves by applying a filter.

1 Open the worksheet created in Activity 3.
2 Select cells A6 to B272 (the 'Make' and 'Model' columns).
3 From the 'Data' menu choose 'Filter' and from the resulting menu choose 'Autofilter'.

Drop-down arrows should appear at the top of both columns (see Fig. 3.6.14).

4 Click on the drop-down arrow next to the 'Make' header and choose 'Spike' from the list of options (see Fig. 3.6.15).

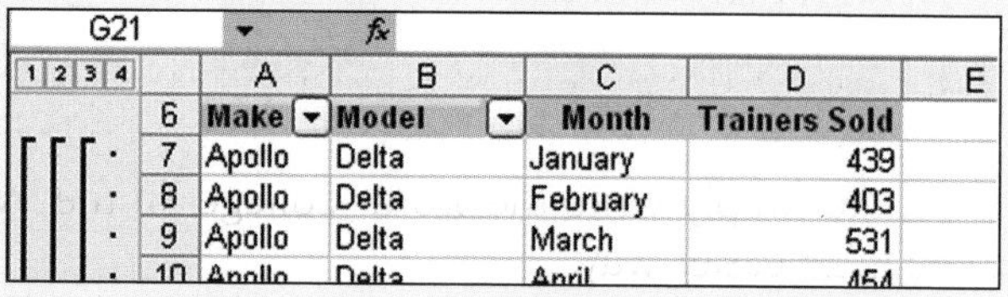

Figure 3.6.14

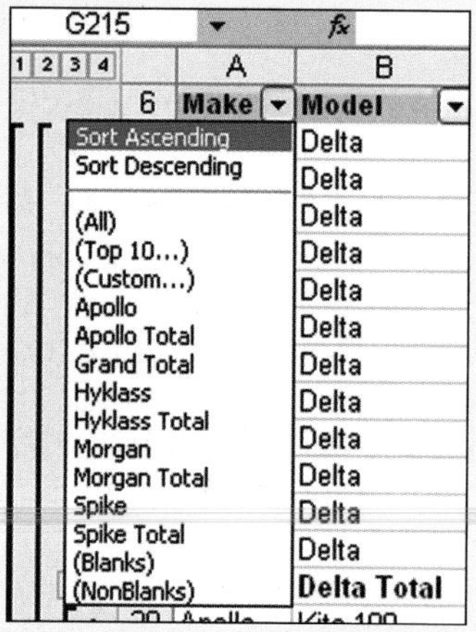

Notice that although only 'Spike' details are now shown the row numbers correspond to how they were before. The other data has not been deleted, just hidden as you will see if you choose the 'All' option. Obviously you can choose any of the other options or further refine the filter by choosing an option from the 'Model' list.

Figure 3.6.15

An area of spreadsheet can be inserted into a report simply by selecting the area you want, 'copying' it from the spreadsheet and 'pasting' in your report, as shown in the demonstration. It will probably appear in the report as a table.

ACTIVITY 5 Generate a chart from a spreadsheet ◀

Producing a chart from a spreadsheet is something most of you will have done many times. There are numerous different types of charts and a large number of options. There is no way we could cover all of them in this book but this activity will create a bar chart showing the monthly sales for all the 'Spike' trainers. This is also shown in the demonstration.

1 Open the spreadsheet you created in Activity 4 and select 'Spike' using the 'Make' filter and 'All' using the 'Model' filter.
2 Select cells D205 to D216
3 Click on the 'Chart icon' (see Fig 3.6.16).

Figure 3.6.16

Continued on next page

The first window of the chart wizard allows us to pick a type of chart.

4 We require a simple bar chart which is the default so click on 'Next'.

The second window of the chart wizard simply defines the data range which is for the 'College' model but there is a tab labelled 'Series' which we can use to set up the chart to show other models as well.

5 Click on the 'Series tab' (see Fig. 3.6.17)

At the moment the name of our current series is 'Series 1'. It would be much better if it said 'College' as that is what we are showing. We could simply write the word 'College' in the 'Name' field ❶ but there is an easier way.

6 Click on the 'Name' field in the wizard window and then click on cell B205 in the worksheet.

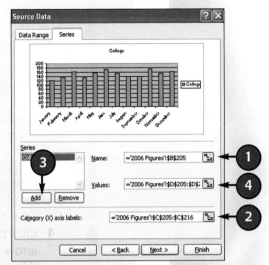

Figure 3.6.17

This will put the cell address into the 'Name' field but as the cell contains the word 'College' that is what the series will be named. The labels on the X-axis also leave a lot to be desired we want them to be the months of the year. Again we can type 'January; February; ...', etc. but again there is an easier way.

7 Click on the 'Category (X) axis labels' field ❷ in the wizard window and then select cells C205 to C216 in the worksheet.

Again these cells contain the values we want and they will be written on the X-axis. Unfortunately we still have only the 'College' series so we need to add some more. We do this by clicking on the 'Add' button ❸.

8 Click on the 'Add' button in the wizard window. A new series called 'Series 2' will be created.

9 With 'Series 2' selected click on the 'Name' field and then click on cell B218 in the worksheet.

10 Click in the 'Values' field ❹, ensure anything in there is deleted and then select cells D218 to D229 in the worksheet.

You will now have inserted a series for the 'Contessa' model. All that remains is to repeat the process for the other models.

11 Repeat steps 8, 9 and 10 for the 'Cussion 20' model (Name = B231, Values = D231:D242)

12 Repeat steps 8, 9 and 10 for the 'Cussion 30' model (Name = B244, Values = D244:D255)

13 Repeat steps 8, 9 and 10 for the 'Cussion 40' model (Name = B257, Values = D257:D268)

14 Click on the 'Next' button.

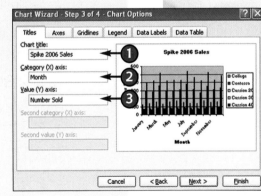

Figure 3.6.18

The next window allows us to put some labels on our chart (see Fig. 3.6.18).

15 Enter 'Spike 2006 Sales' into the 'Chart title' field ❶.

16 Enter 'Month' into the 'Category (X) axis' field ❷.

17 Enter 'Number sold' into the 'Category (Y) axis' field ❸.

18 Click on Next.

Continued on next page

The next window is asking you how you want the chart saved.

19 Check the 'As new sheet' option and enter 'Spike sales 2006' into the name field (see Fig. 3.6.19).

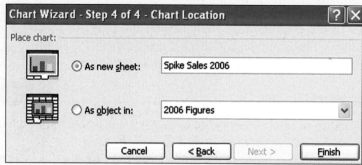

Figure 3.6.19

 The 'Microsoft Excel' spreadsheet in the ActiveBook was created by these activities.

Headings and styles

As with most ICT, reports need to be planned (even designed) before you start to write them. Not only do you need to decide upon fonts and sizes, you need to be aware of the structural levels of your report. The report will need a title. A good report will be broken into sections, perhaps chapters, and each section will have a heading. There will probably be sub-sections and even sub-sub-sections that also need their own headings. The styles of these headings (e.g. bold, underlined, italic, slightly bigger font, etc.) should be decided upon before the report is started and should be consistent throughout.

Use the 'Header' and 'Footer' options so that the title of the report and your name appear on every page. You will also need page numbers on every page.

If you are presenting a report you will need to refer to parts of it and you will therefore need the ability to say things like "If you look at the projected sales chart on page 16 ...". It is a touch difficult to do this if you do not have page numbers.

It is unlikely that, for this unit, you will be required to write a report big enough to need a table of contents, largely because the report will be written under examination conditions. Be aware that other units or reports in the workplace may require a table of contents so that the reader can find their way around.

Contents of the presentation or report

The awareness of your audience and the fitness for purpose of your report is very important as it says a lot about you. It tells your audience whether you are a person to be taken seriously or not. However, the biggest factor in the decision about whether your proposals are to be backed or not are the contents of the report. Because the contents of the report will vary depending on the context, there are no hard and fast rules as to what to include. We can nevertheless create a template of sections and describe the sorts of things that will go into them. Creating a presentation is slightly different from creating a report; headings and sections are not as well-defined as in a report. Nonetheless a template of sections will provide your presentation with an order that will be fundamentally the same as a report. We will now look at each of these possible sections in turn, starting with your 'Introduction'.

▶ Introduction

The first thing we need to establish is what we are doing and why we are doing it. The why may be that your boss has asked you to achieve something or perhaps you have a difficulty performing the function you are assigned. Whatever the case, it needs to be stated. This will establish criteria against which the success of your recommendations can be judged. Many situations are too wide-ranging to look at holistically and it could be that, for the time being, you are only looking at a small area of your task. If this is the case you will need to establish the boundaries of your investigation so that the audience do not expect a complete solution to the whole situation. But you must nevertheless explain how you expect the area you are looking at will affect the entire situation.

You will need to explain what is happening currently: how the current system works and what it achieves. If you can, you should try at this point to evaluate how well or how badly the current system works. This will help you when you come to evaluate the improvements suggested by your recommendations.

▶ Options

When you make decisions you are choosing between at least two options and this will be what you are asking your audience to do. They will, therefore, need to know what the options are. In most cases one option will always be to leave things as they are. You will also have a recommendation to make which would be a second option. It is advisable to have at least one more option to discuss. This third option will tell your audience that you have thought about the problem very carefully and have not just jumped to the first conclusion you thought of. It will also give your audience a choice because as is often said in business "Doing nothing is not an option".

All these options need to be described in detail. Your audience must know exactly what they are choosing between.

Figure 3.6.20 Doing nothing is not an option!

▶ Methods, sources and assumptions

The purpose of this section is to build up confidence in your recommendation and to do this you need to make your audience aware of the method you used to come to the conclusions you did. What was your technique for carrying out your investigation?

They will also need to know the sources of your information, i.e. the data upon which your recommendation is based. They will need to be reassured of the data's reliability, accuracy, currency, and fitness for purpose.

They will not need a description about how your model works but will need to know what it does and what it shows.

Finally they will also need to know what assumptions you have made in coming to your conclusions. If you are predicting something you will always make some assumptions. For example in a business situation, you may assume sales will continue to rise in the same way as in the past, or that demand for the product will not change, and will instead be static. These assumptions need to be listed and some idea of the likelihood of them being correct would also be useful.

▶ Recommendation and justification

This is probably the most important area of the report or presentation as this is the area that will decide whether your proposal will be accepted or not.

Making the recommendation is easy, justifying it is not. Having said that it must be perfectly clear to your audience exactly what it is you are recommending. Never be afraid to state what you feel is obvious. Somewhere in this section, preferably at the beginning you need to start a sentence with the words "I (We) recommend that …".

How exactly you justify your decision depends largely on what you have found out in your investigations, but there are a limited number of grounds that a decision can be justified upon and we can look at a few of those.

The first and most obvious ground is financial. In fact, in business, you could be justified in saying that it is the only ground – in some way, your recommendation will contribute to the overall financial success of the company. Whatever area we are looking at there will almost certainly be a connection to the financial situation in the effect these areas will have on revenue.

Any new system or method will have a set-up cost. This is the amount of money needed to create the environment for the new system to run. This will not just mean the equipment needed – there are a number of other factors you need to take into account. You may need to train employees to use the new system or you may need fewer people under the new system, in which case redundancy payments will need to be taken into account. There may be installation costs for the new system and perhaps a new area to house it will be necessary. Continuing with the current situation would not involve these costs, so they will have to be justified against projected savings in using, or the extra revenue created by, the new system.

The cost may be justified against future savings in the running costs (the costs it takes to run the system). This will include such things as the cost of power, administration costs, maintenance costs and the salaries of the operators. There will be running costs for the old method too and for there to be any chance of justification financially, the new system must either be cheaper to run than the old system or enable expansion in some way to increase revenue. Assuming the costs of the new system are less than that of the old your audience will need to know how long it will take before the set-up costs are covered by the savings or alternatively, how soon the extra revenue will pay for the new system.

Although cost isn't the only criteria, most other justifications have a financial element. Your proposal could be justified under an increase in efficiency. It could allow a function to be done quicker or with fewer mistakes. On its own this would be unlikely to sway your audience unless there were no set up costs.

Ordinarily it would be expected that this be linked either with an increase in revenue or a reduction in costs (such as overall payroll).

A further justification would be enhancing the company image. A new method of doing something may be more efficient and will therefore increase customer satisfaction.

Perhaps the only justifications which do not have some financial element are if you have reached the limits of capacity in an old system that must therefore be updated, or you are responding to some new legislation. In either of these you will still need to show that your proposal will be the most cost-effective and/or productive to implement, as compared to alternatives.

Finally, you must be aware that you are working with human beings and there will almost certainly be a hidden agenda. Try to think of what the changes will mean, in personal terms, to your audience. This should tell you which of your arguments are most likely to persuade.

Conclusion ▶ ▶ ▶

There is an old adage when giving a presentation or writing a report which goes something like "Tell them what you are going to tell them, tell them and then tell them what you told them".

In the conclusion you must re-state your recommendation and support this with your most powerful arguments. Managers are busy people and will often read the conclusion first. This must be focused enough and interesting enough to make them want to read the rest of the report.

Figure 3.6.21 "Very persuasive argument Simpkins"

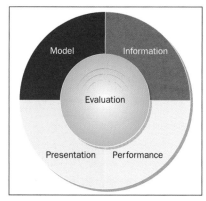

Figure 3.7.1 Performance evaluation

Evaluation

The final and, in many ways, the most difficult topic in this unit is that of evaluation. Part of the examination will almost certainly contain an evaluation section. You will be asked to evaluate the model you have used and its effectiveness. You will need to evaluate the information your model provides and the data you used. You will need to evaluate your presentation or report. You may even be asked to evaluate your performance as an ICT user (see Fig. 3.7.1), which is possibly even more challenging. Evaluation is a very wide-ranging and complex skill. There are university courses in evaluation; people write books on different approaches to evaluation; others develop evaluation systems. There is even a British evaluation society – the UK Evaluation Society. It is not expected that you will need to study evaluation techniques to this level; rather, you will simply comment upon how well something has performed.

Having said this, the examiners will be expecting a little more than a brief comment saying, "I think it worked fairly well". To give you an idea of the level expected of you, you need to know why it is necessary to evaluate your work. Here is an explanation.

Most of the exercises you have done have been one-off exercises based on a scenario given to you. Although each of these models is loosely based on a business situation, it is not real life. Once you have found the answers to the questions you will probably never use the model again.

In real life however, the same issues have a habit of re-emerging regularly, often annually. What tends to change over time is the base data. This will mean that you may have to go through the same exercise again, using the same model but with different data. Therefore if you evaluate your model, your work and even your performance, you will know where to improve it next time. Effectively, you are evaluating to inform improvement. Each year, as your model and your performance improves, the information you get out of it should become more accurate and consequently more useful.

▶ How you defined the problem

To comment on the performance of something the first thing you have to establish is what it is supposed to do. We defined the function we are trying to perform right at the beginning of the process (in the 'understanding the problem' section); the ultimate evaluation is, of course, how well the function has addressed this problem at the end. Has the problem been solved entirely, partially or not at all? It would be unusual if the process had been perfect and no improvements could be made. Even if your problem has been solved, you should still be looking for a better solution, perhaps a cheaper solution or a quicker one.

The first part of your evaluation must be, therefore, *to define the problem again (and the specific area you are looking at) so that you can then evaluate against it*. It can also be useful to restate any objectives or targets you set yourself, especially if they are quantifiable. If your target is a 5 per cent saving in petrol costs and you achieve a 4.8 per cent saving, it is fairly easy to quantify how well you have done.

▶ How you collected information

Having defined our problem and thinking back through the process, we collected information and will have to evaluate this information with regard to accuracy and fitness for purpose. We know that the more accurate our information is, the more likely we are to make good decisions. So we must ask ourselves, *how accurate is the data*?

This is often not an easy question to answer but we can get pointers by asking such questions as:

- How reliable is the data source: do we trust it to provide accurate information, is it a recognised source for this kind of information?
- How old is the data (the older it is the less accurate it is likely to be)?
- How volatile is the data: how quickly does it change?

Having asked ourselves these questions we need to ask, *is there a more accurate source of data*? It may be that although our data source isn't perfect it is the best available.

Having looked at the accuracy of the data we now need to know if it is the right data to use. Obviously, primary data or data collected specifically for our purpose is normally the best kind to use. It is sometimes not viable to do this, however, and you may have to adapt data collected for other reasons. The more you have to process this data to get it into a useful form, the less fit for purpose it will be.

▶ How you created the model

A similar approach can be used to evaluate the model you have created. It is, however, quite difficult to make an absolute evaluation as the model tends to be a prediction of the future and you will not really know how successful it is until a specified time has passed. In a real life situation you can wait for the time to pass then look at the model retrospectively. This can be very informative because you will know what did actually happen; this should make it easy to identify weaknesses in your model. Unfortunately, in the examination you will not have that luxury; you will have to make your judgements without the clearest evidence to back it up. The best thing to do is to think of as many ways as you can to improve the model; that will give you a good idea of how good it is.

The 'fitness for purpose' evaluation is really quite straightforward. Does your model give you the information you need to make your decision? Would your decision have been easier if you had more information or different information?

Finally you could make a comment on how easy your model is to use. In real life people move from job to job and someone else could end up using your model. Would he or she find it easy to use and understand? Could it be improved by adding help tips and labels?

Remember that there is really no such thing as the perfect model, for the simple reason that life is unpredictable. For example, the National Meteorological Office has been evaluating and improving its forecasting models for years, but even with the most advanced modelling technology it can still be caught out by the unexpected.

How you presented your solution

Figure 3.7.2 "Now then Captain, as part of your evaluation you need to explain whether you feel there was a better alternative solution to a broken ice cube machine?"

When you are evaluating this section you are definitely evaluating your own performance, as the presentation or report is your work from start to finish. Do the slides in your presentation look professional, not too crowded or busy? Is your report well laid out with informative headings and sub-headings? Most importantly, do they say what you want them to say? Is there anything you could have said which would have made your argument weightier? Although it may seem like you are doing the examiners' job for them by saying what is wrong with your work, it does allow them to give you some credit for things you may not have had time to do.

Assessment

The assessment for this unit is a practical problem-solving task undertaken in examination conditions. You will be expected, in the two hours of the examination, to go through many of the stages we have discussed in previous chapters of this unit. It is possible that a practical examination using computers is new to you. It may also be new to your school or college. Bearing this in mind, the remainder of this chapter is given over to advice and tips on how to approach the examination. Then, if you want to find out what works best for you personally, have a go at the examples in Chapter 3.8.

What you can expect

The examination paper will give you a scenario which you will need to investigate. You will probably be provided with a spreadsheet model which will be of use to you during your investigations. It is unlikely that you will be expected to create a new model from scratch, as you will probably not have the time to do that. If you do have to provide a model from scratch, it would be a simple one. There may be something wrong with the model or it may be incomplete, either way it is likely to need some work before it will properly perform the function you need it to do. In addition to the examination paper and the model, there may be word-processed documents and text documents. The word-processed documents will be one of two types:

- They might provide you with some information vital to your model, for instance, a letter from HM Revenue & Customs telling you the current income tax rates.
- Alternatively, they may provide you with tips and help, and will be in the guise of a memo from a colleague or a predecessor.

The text files will be the data you will have to import into your model.

Part of the scenario and the model will be made available to you prior to the examination. You will be allowed to investigate the model to see how it works. You will not, however have access to the data files and you will be given a clean copy of the model on the day of the exam.

Figure 3.7.3 Typical examination situation

▶ Approaching the task

As this is a practical examination there will always be a temptation to start work on the computers as soon as possible. A lot of time can be wasted just looking through files to see what they are. You will be working to a tight deadline: two hours is not a long time to achieve all that you are supposed to and you will not have time to waste. Having said that, normal examination techniques apply, and the first thing you should do is to read the paper thoroughly, all the way through. As you are doing so you can check that you have the files required and that you can open them. If anything is missing you must tell the invigilator of the exam immediately.

In the examination you will be asked to do some or all of the following tasks:

1 Create a summary of the situation, identifying the problem you need to solve.
2 Analyse some data sources with respect to helping you solve your problem.
3 Test and possibly correct the spreadsheet model; you may need to provide your own test data.
4 Load data into your model.
5 Use your model to answer some 'what if' questions or check out the results of some pre-defined options.
6 Refine the model to take into account factors which were not in the original model.
7 Produce graphical representations of your results.
8 Write a report or create a presentation presenting your findings.
9 Evaluate your work.

It may sound like an obvious thing to say but the key to success in this examination is to do what the question paper asks you to do. As we have said before, time will be tight, so you will not have time to put in macro buttons to move between sheets or to format the worksheets in striking colours. In general you will get marks for completing what you are asked to do. The only exception to this is that you may get presentation marks for the final presentation of your results. You could simply mention in your evaluation that the model could be improved by the use of background colours, and you may get marks for that comment. Other than that it is more important that the model works.

Throughout the examination you will be asked to save various documents with specific names. It is important that you use these names so that the examiner can easily see which stage of the examination a piece of work comes from. In addition you will need to make sure that you save your work at regular intervals; by now you will have learnt that the one thing computers can often be relied on to do is to crash. When you are doing this make sure you do not overwrite any of the assessment files. You need to have a routine to ensure you do not do this. Each time you are asked to save something with a specific name, save it again immediately with 'Temp' added to the name. For example, if you are asked to save your model as 'Model_1', as soon as you have done so, save it again as 'Model_1Temp'. Do not worry that you have more files than necessary; the examiner will ignore those with 'Temp' added . Do not delete these temp files, it wastes time and there is always a possibility you will want to go back and change something.

A common exam technique is not to start at the beginning, but rather answer the questions in your own preferred order, starting with the one you are most confident about. You will not be able to do this with this examination, as the latter activities depend to some extent on the previous activities. Remember that you are undertaking a problem-solving exercise which requires the various stages to be done in order. What you can do, however, is to keep a couple of documents open to make notes for your presentation and evaluation as you go along. The advantage of this is that when you get to these activities, you will have the basis of what you want to say jotted down in note form. You also have the added advantage that if you run out of time, the examiner may be able to give you some marks for your notes.

Conclusion ▶ ▶ ▶

This practical computing exam is probably a situation that will be unfamiliar to you, so a practice under exam conditions is almost a must. When you approach the tasks work steadily and don't rush, because that is when mistakes occur. Most of all, as it says in the *Hitchhiker's Guide to the Galaxy* – "**DON'T PANIC!**".

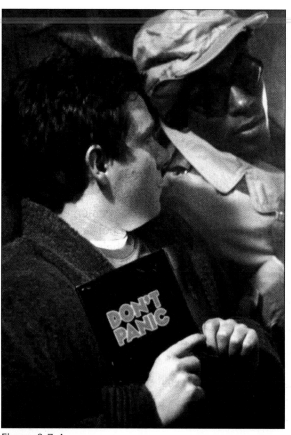

Figure 3.7.4

Practice assessments

Introduction

The purpose of this chapter is to show you the sorts of questions you could expect in an exam. We have tried to create papers as close to the format of the actual examination as possible. The first set of questions is about the QwikFeet scenario and is based on the model you created and refined in Chapters 3.3 and 3.4. The other two sets are entirely self-contained questions and will follow closely the format of Unit 3 examination. As mentioned in the previous chapter, this form of examination may well be new to you; if it is, we would advise you strongly to try at least one of these sets under examination conditions.

Example assessment 1 – QwikFeet warehouse space

The problem

Dean Rabette is the warehouse manager for QwikFeet. QwikFeet is an online retailer of trainers (the footwear). Their customers sign on to the QwikFeet website, where they can browse photographs of the various trainers and order them online. When an order is made, it is the responsibility of Dean's department to get the trainers from the warehouse and send them by courier to the delivery address, if the trainers are in stock. In this scenario delivery is within three days. If, however, the trainers are not in stock, Dean's department has to 'emergency order' them from the manufacturer. This not only extends the delivery time, but also cuts QwikFeet's profit margin for those trainers, as the manufacturer charges more for emergency orders. Currently QwikFeet sell trainers at 6 per cent more than they buy them for, but on an emergency order the profit margin is reduced to 1 per cent. (These figures do not take into account the 10 per cent discount QwikFeet get for keeping their orders within 5 per cent of their prediction.)

Dean has created a model which helps him predict orders for the year. This model, amongst other things, predicts the approximate number of emergency orders which would have to be made. Dean's predicted figures have identified that by January 2006, the level of emergency orders may start to increase. He feels that a possible solution may be to increase warehouse space. QwikFeet currently rent two warehouse units which have space for 4000 pairs of trainers (2000 in each warehouse). These units cost QwikFeet £450 a month each. Further identical units could be rented at the same price. Dean has been asked to investigate the possibility of renting some more space and present to his management his thoughts on the best time to do this, how much space to rent, and how this can be justified financially. To help him do this Dean has his current model, which helps him work out what trainers to order.

He has also started work on a model (see the ActiveBook) to help him decide when is the best time to start renting new warehouse space. Finally, there are price lists (also in the ActiveBook) from each of the suppliers.

Due to pressure of work, Dean has had to stop work on his model but has asked you (as a member of his department) to take over the task and present the results to his management.

ACTIVITY 1 Information you have available

Currently you have available your working spreadsheet from the exercise in Chapters 3.3 and 3.4.
- Rename this file QwikFeet 2005.
- Make a copy of this file and call it QwikFeet 2006 V1.

(1 mark)

ACTIVITY 2 Understand the problem

You should look at all the information available and make sure that you understand what the problem is.
- Using word processing software, create a summary of the current situation, the information currently available, and what additional information you need to make a decision.
- Save your summary as INTRO. You will need to include this in your final presentation.

(10 marks)

ACTIVITY 3 Collect the data

You will need to modify your QwikFeet 2006 V1 spreadsheet and use it to collect data for your Storage Space Requirement spreadsheet.
- Modify the QwikFeet 2006 V1 spreadsheet to show figures for 2006 instead of 2005 by changing the formulae in the predicted figures worksheet and any relevant labels.
- Enter suitable figures into the Warehouse Content worksheet for January 2006. (Hint: look at the same worksheet in the 2005 model.)
- Enter values into the Order Input Form to minimise emergency orders.

(5 marks)

Explaining the new model

The first page of the new model is called 'Input Sheet' and is where the values for emergency orders you have just worked out in Activity 3 will be entered. **Do not enter them yet as you will need to make modifications to the new**

model first. The next worksheet is called 'Prices'. Once the prices the manufacturers charge are entered, various other bits of information are worked out. **Again do not enter the prices yet**. The third sheet (when complete) will work out your potential profit loss (Potential Loss) depending on which month you start renting the new space. Notice the drop down box (see Fig. 3.8.1) allows you to choose this month. The fourth sheet is a Lookup table which is used in some of the formulae to work out a month number given the name of the month. The final page, Results, is simply somewhere where you can store the amount of profit loss for each situation, i.e. how much profit is lost if we start renting the new warehouse in January, February ... December, never.

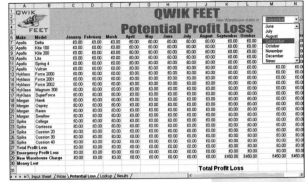

Figure 3.8.1 Example of drop down box

ACTIVITY 4 Test the new model ◀

- Using the Price Lists, enter the manufacturer's prices into the new model.
- There are a number of errors in the new model; using suitable test data find and correct these errors.
- In the Potential Loss worksheet a suitable formula will have to be entered in the Money Lost row.
- A suitable formula will need to be entered into cell M31 to calculate the Total Profit Loss.
- Save your model as QwikFeet Warehouse model V1.

(9 marks)

ACTIVITY 5 Using the spreadsheet model ◀

You are now ready to enter the potential emergency orders into your new model.
- Import the data from the old model into the new one (important – there may be a reason to re-use this model next time the warehouse starts to fill up).
- Use the model to work out the money lost if the new warehousing is available in January, February, March, April, May, June, July, August, September, October, November, December, and if the new warehousing isn't available at all.
- Enter these values into the Results worksheet.
- Create a suitable chart or graph to present your findings.
- Save the model as QwikFeet Warehouse model V2.

(24 marks)

ACTIVITY 6 Recommendations ◀

You should now have enough knowledge about the situation to make a decision. Look carefully at all the information available including the results of using the model and decide on the best course of action.

Create a presentation for your management recommending a course of action. You should include:

Continued on next page

- a summary of the current situation
- the alternatives you considered
- other factors you considered
- the decision you came to
- justification of your decision including graphical and textual information in support of your recommendations.

(26 marks)

ACTIVITY 7 Evaluation ◀

Write an evaluation of your solution. This should include:
- How well has the model done what it set out to do? Has it helped you to decide on a course of action?
- How could things be changed to predict warehousing needs over a longer period?
- Are there any weaknesses in the data? If so, what are they, and what effect are they likely to have?
- How would the models need to be adjusted if a new line of trainers were to be sold?

(15 marks)

(Total for paper: 90 marks)

Example assessment 2 – Jensen Racing pit stops

The worksheets in the model provided with this exercise are password protected. There should be no need to change any protected cells but should you require to do so the password is 'pearson'.

The problem

Mark Bayfield is the team manager of the Jensen Racing Company's motor racing team. The team runs two cars in the Micro Endurance Class, a series of races for single seater racing cars with engines of no more than 1600 cc.

The series consists of 16 races which take place over 16 weekends in the period March to September. Each race takes place at a different venue over a distance of about 150 miles. The exact distance varies because the race has to be run over a whole number of laps and the lap distance at each venue varies. During the course of the race a car can make as many pit stops as it likes to replace old tyres and take on board extra fuel. The fuel tanks are not big enough to load enough fuel to complete the race, so teams have to make at least one pit stop. At the same time, no team has ever made more than four pit stops.

The team has available four different types of tyres known as A, B, C and D. Each type is made of a slightly different compound. Tyre A tends to be softer which means it will grip the track better, which in turn leads to faster lap times. Unfortunately Tyre A will 'go off' quicker, that is, after a while the tyre will lose its grip and the lap times will increase. Tyre D is the hardest compound and as such the grip is not as good as Tyre A; consequently the lap times are not quite so good initially, but Tyre D will outlast Tyre A and the lap times will be more consistent. Tyres B and C are medium compounds with properties between those of the other two tyres.

As team manager, one of Mark's duties is, in consultation with the drivers and mechanics, to decide on a pit-stop strategy. He has started work on a model (see the ActiveBook) to help him, but has been unable to complete it. He has employed you as his IT assistant. The first job he has given you is to sort out the pit stop strategy for the race at Brookfield Park race track in two weeks' time. You will present the strategy to the team.

He has given you two internal memos. The first is from Alan Stevens (see the ActiveBook), the cars designer and aerodynamicist. Alan is a mathematics graduate so Mark is inclined to use him for other things as well, in this case, fuel consumption calculations. The second is from Helen Staines (see the ActiveBook), who is the supervisor of the pit crew. She has been putting the crew through their paces at Brookfield Park and has written to give her opinion of how long a pit stop would take.

Mark has also given you a text file (see the ActiveBook) which shows the lap times of each tyre. Each list shows the lap time after a number of laps.

You need to use these documents to complete the model and make your recommendations.

ACTIVITY 1 Understand the problem ◄

You should look at all the information available and make sure that you understand what the problem is.
- Using word processing software, create a summary of the current situation and identify Mark's problem. Describe what you need to do and the information currently available. Describe also any additional information you may need to help make your decision.
- Save your summary as INTRO. You will need to include this in your final presentation.

(12 marks)

ACTIVITY 2 Analyse the data ◄

You have a number of data sources (Memos and Text File) which you will need to use in your data model. For each source:
- Identify the data source and evaluate its reliability.
- Describe any assumptions you are making or any items of information which are missing.
- Describe how the information will be used to help solve the problem.

(20 marks)

ACTIVITY 3 Test the model

Using the information from the two memos:
- Enter suitable formulae in column B of the Fuel Consumption worksheet to calculate the fuel required to complete the number of laps in column A.
- Enter suitable formulae in column C of the Fuel Consumption worksheet to calculate the time penalty for carrying the amount of fuel in Column B.
- Enter values for the 'Pit Lane Delay' and the 'Fuel Rate' in the results page.
- Import the Lap Times Data into the Lap Times Worksheet (start at cell A9)
- Save your model as 'Jensen Racing model V1'.

(10 marks)

ACTIVITY 4 Using the spreadsheet model

Use the model to decide upon a pit stop strategy. You will need to investigate one, two, three and four pits stops and for each:
- Enter suitable lap numbers to stop on.
- Decide upon a Tyre type and enter it in the Yellow results area.
- Enter the estimated total time for the race in the Yellow results area.
- Create a suitable chart or graph to present your findings.
- Save the model as 'Jensen Racing model V1'.

(24 marks)

ACTIVITY 5 Recommendations

You should now have enough knowledge about the situation to make a recommendation. Look carefully at all the information available, including the results of using the model, and decide on the best pit-stop strategy.

Create a presentation for the team describing your recommended strategy. You should include:
- a description of what you did and the information you used
- the alternatives you considered
- other factors you considered
- the decision you came to
- justification of your decision including graphical and textual information in support of your recommendations

(21 marks)

ACTIVITY 6 Evaluation

Write an evaluation of your solution. This should include:
- How well has the model done what it set out to do? Has it helped you to decide on a course of action?
- What would need to be changed to make the model work for a different track?

Continued on next page

- Are there any weaknesses in the data? If so, what are they, and what effect are they likely to have?
- How would the model have to be changed if a new tyre compound were introduced?

(15 marks)

(Total for paper: 90 marks)

Example assessment 3 – ShipSafe transport routes

The worksheets in the model provided with this exercise are password protected. There should be no need to change any protected cells but should you require to do so the password is 'pearson'.

Introduction

This example differs slightly from the others. Both the QwikFeet and the Jensen Racing problems concentrated largely on some reasonably complex models. The model for this exercise is a little less complex, although in fairness some of the formulae take a little understanding. One formula involves a nested VLOOKUP, which is a VLOOKUP within another VLOOKUP. Fortunately, it is not necessary to create or modify this formula, so testing the model itself is fairly easy. As such, this section will get fewer marks than in the other examples. For this example there is a range of data sources; you will be required to analyse these data sources and comment on the reliability and accuracy of each. In one case you will need to choose which source to use.

The problem

ShipSafe is a secure delivery agency which transports valuable cargoes in armoured vans across the south of England. One of its major customers is Shines Ltd, a jeweller with outlets in many major towns in the south of England. Sean Davies is a driver for ShipSafe. Over the years he has done the 'Shines route' many times and has become their preferred driver; he now does that route all the time. The route has been the same for many years. He calls at the Shines depot in Reading and picks up secure boxes for all the shops. These boxes contain replacement items for stock the shops have sold, thereby keeping the shops well stocked. He then drives to shops at Bracknell, Farnborough, Aldershot, Farnham, Woking, Slough, Staines, Maidenhead, Leatherhead, Andover, and Winchester, in that order, to drop off the boxes. At each shop he picks up an empty secure box which was used to deliver yesterday's replacement stock. These empty secure boxes are delivered to the depot at Reading when all the shops have been visited.

Recently, Sean has discovered that some of the boxes he delivers to the shops are empty and consequently that part of the journey is wasted. If a shop has a day when it doesn't sell anything there is no need to replenish stock. Sean believes that if he were to know which sites did not need a visit, he could adjust his route and save some money in fuel costs.

As a keen computer user, Sean has created a model (see the ActiveBook). The model is designed to help him work out the best route, but he is unsure how to proceed. He is particularly unsure where to get the mileage data. He has asked you to take over the idea, make it work, and help him with a presentation to ShipSafe and Shine management.

ACTIVITY 1 Understand the problem ◀

You should look at all the information available and make sure that you understand what the problem is.
- Using word processing software, create a summary of the current situation and identify Sean's problem. Describe what you need to do and the information you will need.
- Save your summary as INTRO. You will need to include this in your final presentation.

(8 marks)

ACTIVITY 2 Data sources 1 (travelling distances) ◀

Sean's model requires the distances between all the towns to be known. There are three text files containing this information. The format of each source is in the form of a matrix showing the distance in miles between the various towns. You will notice that each of these sources has slightly different values. You will notice too that the distance between each town and itself is 99 999 miles. This is simply a given high value and needs to be so, or the model will not work.

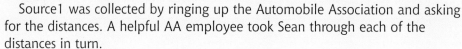

Source1 was collected by ringing up the Automobile Association and asking for the distances. A helpful AA employee took Sean through each of the distances in turn.

Source2 was collected from the 2001 Michelin Road Atlas Sean had in the van for when he was asked to drive on unfamiliar routes.

Source3 was taken from an online atlas, a free source of directions and maps on the internet.

Using word processing software, write an analysis of the three information sources. This should include:
- A comparison between the three sources with regard to their likely accuracy and suitability for purpose.
- A recommendation of which source to use, with supporting arguments.
- A suggestion for alternative data sources which may be either more accurate or more suitable for purpose, and describing the method of data collection.
- Save this as DATA SOURCES 1. You will need to include this in your final presentation.

(16 marks)

ACTIVITY 3 Data sources 2 (travelling distances) ◀

If you examine the Results worksheet of Sean's model, you will see that two further items of data are needed. Firstly, it is necessary to enter a value for the fuel consumption of the van in miles/litre. Sean signed on to the van manufacturer's website and found two figures. The site said that for urban driving, the fuel consumption is 4.13 miles per litre and for motorway driving 6.43 miles per litre. Sean feels he does about half urban and half motorway driving, so suggests you take an average for the overall consumption. He has also found out that the price of diesel fuel at the garage he uses is 82p a litre.

- Add to your analysis of the data sources (DATA SOURCES 1) an evaluation of these data sources. This should include:
  - A discussion on the likely accuracy of the data sources, and those factors which may lead to inaccuracies.
  - A suggestion of how more accurate data could be collected.
- Resave this as DATA SOURCES 1. You will need to include this in your final presentation.

(6 marks)

ACTIVITY 4 Test the model ◀

Using the information above:
- Enter suitable formulae in cells D15, D17 and D19 of the Results worksheet.
- Enter values for the 'Miles/Litre' and the 'Fuel Cost/Litre' in Cells D16 and D18 of the Results worksheet.
- Enter suitable test data into the Distances worksheet of your model.
- Save your model as ShipSafe Model V1.

(8 marks)

ACTIVITY 5 Enter data ◀

- Import your choice of data into the Distances worksheet of the model, you will need to start the import at cell B3.
- Experiment with the model and develop a strategy to decide upon a route. (Hint: if, in the 'Choose Route' worksheet you put an 'N' to the left of all the shops you don't want to visit and all the shops you have already visited including Reading, the nearest town to where you are will be highlighted in red.)
- In a new word-processed document describe the strategy you will use to decide in which order the shops should be visited.

(10 marks)

ACTIVITY 6 Using the spreadsheet model

As an example, Sean has studied last week's deliveries and has found the following information.

Day	Empty secure boxes delivered to:
Monday	Woking
Tuesday	Aldershot; Bracknell; Winchester
Wednesday	Leatherhead; Winchester; Andover; Slough
Thursday	Farnborough; Maidenhead
Friday	Aldershot; Farnham; Staines; Andover

- Using your strategy to work out suitable routes for each day, use the model to work out potential savings for each day. Note that you will have to work out the distance travelled on the normal (old) route to fill in cell D22 of the Results worksheet. Store your results in row 23 of the Results worksheet.
- Create a suitable chart to illustrate your findings.

(18 marks)

ACTIVITY 7 Recommendations

You should now have enough knowledge about the situation to make a decision. Look carefully at all the information available, including the results of using the model, and decide upon what sort of savings could be made.

Create a presentation for the managements of ShipSafe and Shines. You should include:

- A description of what you did and the information you used.
- The alternatives you considered.
- Other factors you considered.
- The sorts of savings which could be made.

(14 marks)

ACTIVITY 8 Evaluation

Write an evaluation of your solution. This should include:

- How well has the model done what it set out to do? Do you think the managements will back your plan?
- Have you investigated enough situations? If not, how would you suggest Sean should proceed to investigate further?
- Are there any weaknesses in the data? If so, what are they and what effect are they likely to have?

(10 marks)
(Total for paper: 90 marks)

Index

AAC format 109
absolute addressing 256, 264
accessibility 53, 55–6
  changes in access 44
  e-books 68
  homeless internet use 51–2
  telecoms 41–2
  websites 161, 168–70
  see also digital divide
accounts, online 147
acquirers 155
action queries 208
Adobe e-books 63–5
adware 174–5
age factors 53–5, 56
AIFF format 109
algorithms 236
Amazon checkout 153–4
ambulance services 23
analysis 113–14, 224, 254–65, 301
animations 107–8, 282–3
API *see* application programming interface
append queries 206–8
application programming interface (API) 185
archiving online 19
assessments 110–16, 221–8, 294–306
assets 82–3, 94
assumptions 289–90
atomic attributes 190–1
ATRAC format 109
attributes 181, 183, 187, 190–1, 193–4
audiences 74–6, 279–83
authentication online 146–7
authorisation of payments 154–5
automated assessments 15
automatic slide transitions 283
automation effects 24
AVI format 107
awareness of audience 279–83

B2B *see* business-to-business
B2C *see* business-to-consumer
back-office databases 179–94
  see also databases
background font 282
bandwidths 75, 89
banking 13, 24, 31–3
BBSs *see* bulletin board systems
BECTA *see* British Educational Communication and Technology Association
best case/worst case predictions 250–2
bits 220
blogs 2–5, 7–8
bookmarks 100–1
books 17, 62–73, 134–5, 248
Boolean data 187
brand image 128
British Educational Communication and Technology Association (BECTA) 58

broadband 52–3, 60, 125
broadcasting 45
browser support 75
BT (British Telecommunications) 22, 59
bulletin board systems (BBSs) 9–11
business 19, 27, 124–37
  see also e-commerce
business-to-business (B2B) 123
business-to-consumer (B2C) 123
buying decisions 237
buying online 32, 145–7, 153–5

CALL *see* Community Access to Lifelong Learning
call centres 25
Calthorpe Game Balls PLC 240–2
Cambodia 44–5
cameras 102–5
cantennae 47
capturing information 170–2
  see also data capture method
cascading style sheets (CSS) 4, 62, 67–8, 83, 86–92, 169
CASE *see* Computer Aided Software Engineering
cells
  merging 263
  unlocking 265
charities 119, 121
Charney, Howard S. 126
charts 282–8
chat 6–8, 127–8
checkout online 153–4
children's e-books 71, 72
chip and PIN 155
choice 32, 135
civil rights 34–6
class 51–2
Cleartype 64
'clicks-and-mortar' businesses 128–31, 135
clients, email 5
CNC *see* computer numerical control
collaboration online 126
collecting information 230–1, 243–53, 293, 298
comma delimited text data 256
commercial organisations 118, 128–31
communication 26–7
communities online 9–11
Community Access to Lifelong Learning (CALL) 58
community websites 128
competitions 165–6
compiled HTML e-books 63, 66–7
compressing images 102
Computer Aided Software Engineering (CASE) 141
Computer Misuse Act 215–16
computer numerical control (CNC) 24

Computers within Reach initiative 58
computing students 52
conditional formatting 262
conferences online 9–11
confirmation of orders 154–5
consumer base growth 124–5
content management systems 2
convenience 32, 135
cookies 147, 172–5
copyright 102
costs 236–7, 240, 242, 290–1
coursework risk assessment 215
crime/crime prevention 33–4
cropping images 102
CSS *see* cascading style sheets
currency data 186
customer entity data 210
customer services 166–70
customers 146–50, 155, 160–78

DakNet case study 44–5
data 243–4
  assessing files 199–200
  importing 198–201, 256
  law 211–20
  practice assessments 298, 305
  QwikFeet model 267, 298
  retrieving 201–6
  risk 214–15
  types 185–7
  verification/validation 188–90
  see also information
data capture method 244, 259–60
data flows *see* information flow diagrams
data logging 247–8
data processing 244
Data Protection Act 213
data sources 244–8, 301, 304–5
data stores 138, 139
database management system (DBMS) 181
databases 179–80, 244–5
  back-office 179–94
  building 195–6, 226–8
  content management systems 2
  designing 179–94, 226–8
  importing data 198–201
  information use 212
  internet searches 99
  order/product data 206–8
  police service 34
  primary key 188, 191
  relationships 183–4, 192–4, 196–7
  reports 208–9
  retrieving data 201–6
  shopping basket processes 151
  transactional websites 181–3
  using 195–210, 226–8
date formats 186–7
DBMS *see* database management system

Acknowledgements

We are most grateful to the following companies for permission to reproduce their
website material:

About: www.about.com; Accessify: www.accessify.com;
Amazon: www.amazon.com; Apple/itunes: www.apple.com;
ATOC Ltd: www.livedepartureboards.co.uk;
BAA Ltd: www.baa.co.uk; BBC: www.bbc.co.uk/weather;
The British Library: www.bl.uk,The British Heart Foundation: www.bhf.org.uk;
Black and Decker Ltd: www.blackanddecker.co.uk;
Boots: www.boots.com; CD Wow:www.cdwow.com;
Central Intelligence Agency: www.cia.gov; Community Wireless: www.wlan.org.uk; Consumer
Link: http://uk.consumerlink.com;
Dewey Browse:www.deweybrowse.org; Disobey:www.disobey.com;
Dell: www.dell.co.uk; Elly Thompson: www.ellythompson.co.uk;
E Book Mall: www.e-bookmall.com; E. Books Cube: www.ebooks3.com;
Evans Cycles: www.evanscycles.com; Evisu: www.evisu.com;
First Direct: www.firstdirect.com; GamePlay: www.gameplay.co.uk;
Game: www.game.net; Google: www.blogger.com. & www.google.com;
Hertfordshire County Council: www.hertsdirect.org;
IEEE Spectrum Online: www.spectrum.ieee.org;
Internet World Stats: www.internetworldstats.com;
Interflora: www.interflora.co.uk; Jhai Foundation: www.jhai.org;
Life Long Learning: www.lluk.org.uk; Max Design: http://css.maxdesign.com.au; Microsoft
Encarta: www.microsoft.com; Music Room: www.musicroom.com;
Nectar: www.nectar.com; NetGrocer: www.netgrocer.com; Next: www.next.co.uk;
NHS Direct: www.nhsdirect.nhs.uk; No21D: www.no2id.net;
Odeon Cinema: www.odeon.co.uk; O'Reilly Network: www.oreillynet.com;
Office of Public Sector Information: www.jobcentreplus.gov.uk;
Open Directory: www.dmoz.org; Penguin: www.penguin.co.uk;
Planet Monk: www.planetmonk.com; Private Lessons Channel: www.privatelessons.net;
Project Gutenberg: www.gutenberg.org; Prospects: www.prospects.ac.uk; Rosetta Project:
www.editec.net; Sainsburys: www.sainsburystoyou.com; Stockport Council:
www.stockport.gov.uk; Strathclyde Police: www.strathclyde.police.uk;
Tale Wins: www.talewins.com; Teen Arrive Alive: www.teenarrivealive.com;
Teoma: www.teoma.co.uk; Tesco: www.tesco.com; Unleashing the Killer App: www.killer-
apps.com; University of Virginia Library: http://etext.lib.virginia.edu;
Vauxhall Motors Ltd: www.vauxhall.co.uk; Virgin Wines: www.virginwines.com;
Web Fetch: www.webfetch.com; We Read:www.weread.org;
Web Aim: www.webaim.org; World Bank: www.worldbank.org; World summit:
www.wsisgeneva2003.org; Xdrive: www.xdrive.com; Zone Alarm: www.zonealarm.com.

Photo acknowledgements:
ActionPlus p248(t); Alamy/E.Maynard p23,A.Segre p31(t), Education Photos p29,
N.Nicholson p45(t), S. Sarkis p45(b), A.Caminada p58, M.Boulton p129(b),
R.Chapple/Thinkstock RF p217(t), StockAbcd p248(b), Robert Harding World Imagery p250,
J.Morgan p295; Corbis RF (unit openers), J.Shaw/Reuters p39,
Getty Images/J.Franco p20, I. Mukherjee p42, M.Powell p131(t);
Panos Pictures/D.Sansoni p10, S. Torfinn p25, Caroline Penn p38, J.L. Dugast p48; Pearson
Education p16, 94, 103, T.Clifford 21; Photodisc Sports & Recreation p105(tl); Ronald Grant
Archive p296; Sainsbury's p31(b), S.Rafferty p60; Zefa/D.Mendelsohn p131(b);
Cover images © Jim Craigmyle / Corbis and © Ted Horowitz / Corbis.

Every effort has been made to trace the copyright holders and we apologise
in advance for any unintentional omissions. We would be pleased to insert
the appropriate acknowledgement in any subsequent edition of this publication.